T0347403

RESEARCH IN DEVELOPMENTAL
AND COMPARATIVE PSYCHOLOGY
VOL. 1

BEHAVIORAL
DEVELOPMENT

GARLAND REFERENCE LIBRARY
OF SOCIAL SCIENCE
VOL. 677

RESEARCH IN DEVELOPMENTAL AND COMPARATIVE PSYCHOLOGY

GARY GREENBERG
ETHEL TOBACH
Series Editors

BEHAVIORAL DEVELOPMENT
*Concepts of Approach/Withdrawal and
Integrative Levels*
edited by Kathryn E. Hood, Gary
Greenberg, and Ethel Tobach

BEHAVIORAL DEVELOPMENT

Concepts of Approach/Withdrawal and Integrative Levels

edited by

Kathryn E. Hood
Gary Greenberg
Ethel Tobach

GARLAND PUBLISHING, Inc.
New York & London / 1995

Library of Congress Cataloging-in-Publication Data

Behavioral development : concepts of approach/
withdrawal and integrative levels / edited by
Kathryn E. Hood, Gary Greenberg, and Ethel Tobach.
    p.   cm. — (Research in developmental and
comparative psychology ; vol. 1)
    Papers originally presented at the fifth T. C.
Schneirla Conference at Pennsylvania State University,
Nov. 1989.
    Includes bibliographical references.
    ISBN 0-8153-1709-3 (alk. paper)
    1. Developmental psychology—Congresses.
2. Psychology, Comparative—Congresses.   3. Developmental psychobiology—Congresses.   4. Psycho-
physiology—Congresses.   I. Hood, Kathryn E.   II.
Greenberg, Gary.   III. Tobach, Ethel.   IV. 5th T. C.
Schneirla Conference.   V. Series.
BF712. 5.B44 1995   94-24356
155—dc20   CIP

Contents

Series Editors' Preface

Research in Developmental and Comparative Psychology is a scholarly series of works dedicated to honor the contributions of T. C. Schneirla. A consistent critic of anthropomorphism, Schneirla questioned vitalistic approaches that stressed only similarities in human and animal behavior. He stressed the concept of integrative levels as an alternative approach that clarifies the continuities and discontinuities in the evolution of behavior. Most significant was the emphasis he placed on the study of developmental processes as alternatives to the formulations of heredity and environment as contradictory explanations of the evolution of behavior. Schneirla's criticism of ethology, based on the integrative levels concept, stands today as a valuable basis for criticism of sociobiology. Schneirla's opposition to biological reductionism influenced research on the relationship between psychology and physiology. His approach/withdrawal theory, first formulated some 30 years ago, continues to form the basis of research and theory in the areas of behavioral development and emotional behavior.

Although he died in 1968, Schneirla is still recognized as one of the foremost theoreticians in comparative psychology, and the rebirth of interest in comparative psychology is evident in the work of many of his students and colleagues. The T. C. Schneirla Research Board convenes biennially to bring together the best writers on issues in comparative psychology. These sessions are co-sponsored by Wichita State University, The American Museum of Natural History, New York and the Graduate Center of the City University of New York. The session on which this book is based was supported by the Center for the Study of Child and Adolescent Development at the Pennsylvania State

University, Wichita State University and by The American Museum of Natural History.

Gary Greenberg
Ethel Tobach

Introduction

This volume represents the substantive content of the Fifth T. C. Schneirla Conference, held at Pennsylvania State University in November of 1989, under the sponsorship of the T. C. Schneirla Research Fund, the Center for the Study of Child and Adolescent Development, headed by Richard Lerner and David Palermo, and the College of Health and Human Development, headed by Dean Anne Petersen, with special support from Paul Cornwell, Department of Psychology. As in the previous conferences (Greenberg & Tobach, 1984, 1987, 1988, 1990, 1992), The Wichita State University, The American Museum of Natural History, and the City University of New York Graduate School co-sponsored the proceedings.

Participants included invited speakers from the USA and abroad as well as faculty and graduate students from the Departments of Human Development and Family Studies, Psychology, and from the College of Agriculture at Penn State, The University of North Carolina, New York University, and the Soviet Union. Presenters were asked to evaluate the usefulness of T. C. Schneirla's approach/withdrawal concept for understanding behavioral development as they study it. Several "Young Scholars" were awarded travel stipends to attend the conference: David Eastzer, Alexander Skolnick, and Alison Nash. We were honored at the conference by the presence of Leone Schneirla. Robert and Beverley Cairns, who participated in the conference, drove to Penn State with Mrs. Schneirla. This volume is dedicated to her memory in appreciation and in special remembrance of her interest in the continued impact of her husband's work. She was a gentle and encouraging member of the T. C. Schneirla Research Foundation Board.

The principles that underlie the approach/withdrawal concept are these: 1) the significance of the intensity of the adequate stimulus; 2) the process of development; 3) the concept of integrative levels. The following chapters address these principles in different ways.

A historical review and analysis by Greenberg sets the context for considering approach/withdrawal (A/W) theory. In tracing the references Schneirla himself cited in his various approach/withdrawal papers, Greenberg delineates a possible developmental sequence of the A/W concept. Schneirla read and reflected ideas from, among many others, Wundt, Darwin, Jennings, Pillsbury, and his own teacher, J. F. Shepard. He then developed these ideas on the basis of his experimental studies into the theoretical position which guides thinking and research in comparative and developmental psychology today.

Contemporary theoretical issues are considered in the chapter by Hood, drawing links between A/W theory, traditional dialectical theory, and new ideas from nonlinear dynamical systems theory. The structure of approach and withdrawal processes is placed into the dialectical formulation developed by Hegel. Hegelian dialectical theory is proposed as an appropriate model for the study of development because it explicitly portrays the emergence of new forms over time. The dialectical process that results in the emergence of novel forms is a boundary process, one that shares important features with boundary processes under investigation in fractal theory, an area of contemporary significance in nonlinear dynamics. Applications of these approaches to the understanding of aggressive behavior are explored.

Contributions by Topoff and Rosenblatt add critical insights to the theoretical presentations. Topoff, Schneirla's last doctoral student, discusses the important features of A/W theory and shows how they stand in opposition to the instinct ideas of the classical ethologists. Schneirla intended the A/W concept to serve as a comparative framework for relating evolutionary processes to behavioral development. Schneirla's application of these ideas to the understanding of behavior in ants demonstrates his use of both laboratory and field research for confirming the validity of theoretical notions.

Two points are raised by Rosenblatt: how to assess stimulus intensity in a non-circular manner, and how to understand dyadic behavioral patterns as A/W processes. Rosenblatt notes the asymmetry of A and W processes: in the approach system, behavior can be continuously guided by external stimuli, while in the W system, external stimuli interrupt ongoing A-processes and shape behavior only intermittently if at all. He further notes that in humans, A/W processes become internalized attitudes and attentional processes that often are laden with significant emotional content in life-long integrative processes.

The chapters that follow are focused on developmental change, and on behavioral processes in relation to the A/W concept. The behavioral development of birds, rodents and humans are considered as A/W processes at multiple levels of analysis. A crucial aspect of A/W theory is its dependence on the idea of levels of integration. The molecular aspects of the organism are fused with the molar; the pieces are part of the whole and of necessity influence it. Thus Schneirla found it important to seek a full understanding of biochemical and physiological processes involved in behavioral events. This aspect of his thinking forms the framework for this section of the book.

The sea hare *Aplysia* provides the simple nervous system that is subjected to analysis in the chapter by Walters. By functional analyses of the neuronal structures that subserve meaningful behaviors in this organism, Walters demonstrates that aspects of A/W interactions occur at the neural system level, where independent and parallel neural codes exist for stimulus intensity and stimulus quality. This level of analysis may contribute to the synthetic understanding of higher-level processes in other organisms as well.

In a multilevel analysis, Calamandrei and Alleva discuss two opposing physiological processes in rodent behavioral development, the inhibitory cholinergic neurotransmitter system, and its antagonistic system, the adrenergic arousal system. Both systems are involved in behavioral changes at weaning. The cholinergic system is subject to regulation by the neurotrophic factor, nerve growth factor. NGF reacts within minutes to psychosocial stress, indicating a possible pathway by which behavior might alter neurological development. In addition, NGF

alters responses to novelty (neophobia), suggesting a link to
A/W processes in young rodents.

In discussing his research on brain areas involved in learning by chicks, Rose addresses the significance of the "levels" aspect of the A/W concept. At what level is it proper to study memory? While eschewing the neurological reductionism made popular in the 1950s and 1960s, Rose shows that it is nevertheless important to examine events at a molecular level and at a neural systems level for a fuller understanding of behavioral phenomena at the molar level.

A/W processes in socialization are discussed in the next three papers. Social behavior is analyzed in relation to hormonal and neural levels; the emergence over time (seconds, minutes, and weeks) of coordinated dyadic forms; the consolidation of A/W tendencies in social relationships with familiar and novel social partners; and the implications of these processes for interpretations of evolutionary theory.

Rosenblatt reviews the emergence of maternal behavior, its sensory and hormonal basis, and developmental changes in rodent maternal response. The theoretical approach and its application employs an "A/W biphasic processes" concept rather than a threshold concept: behavioral components of A and W processes are held to be simultaneously and independently altered, each by specific elements of the stimulus situation. The interaction of the two separate processes results in the initiation and maintenance of observed behaviors; for example, approach behaviors appear at once when released from opposition by withdrawal responses. This model of dynamic equilibrium is used to explain the emergence of maternal behavior in virgin female rats, as withdrawal responses to pup odors abate after several days of exposure to pups. Each component of maternal behavior (retrieving, nest-building) has stimulus-specific A/W links, which are altered by endogenous changes in circulating estrogen. The dynamic model integrates A/W theory with richly elaborated empirical findings to explain a set of social behaviors of clear evolutionary significance.

Aggressive behavior is the social form that is taken to three levels of analysis in the review by Gariépy. The genetic-ontogenetic analysis of aggressive behavior supports the proposition that a developmental shift (neoteny) results from selective breeding for high or low aggressiveness in mice: the "genetic" change is actually an ontogenetic change. The behavioral analysis shows that selection on the basis of aggression operates by shifting the threshold for an opposing behavioral system: "freezing," or tonic immobility is discussed as a component of a generalized inhibition system that is developmentally labile and sensitive to experience effects as well as to selective breeding. The neural analysis identifies two dopaminergic brain systems involved in these genetic behavioral patterns. Interestingly, one area (nucleus accumbens) is developmentally stable; the other (caudate nucleus) is developmentally labile, and also is functionally altered by social experience. Implications of these relationships are explored and Gariépy formulates a specific proposal: that social behavior functions as an active coordinating force at the interface of two domains; external conditions of social stimulation, and internal self-regulation of stimulus intensity. By this proposal, behavior serves as the integrative origin of novel biobehavioral adaptations.

The development of social relationships, attachments to peers and others, is discussed by Nash in light of contemporary revisions of evolutionary theory and current research findings on children's social abilities. Deficiencies in Bowlby's attachment model, which was derived from classical ethology, are reviewed and attachment theory is extended to include social relationships with individuals other than the mother. Contemporary comparative research supporting the extended model is presented. For example, children may show more interest toward novel strangers than to familiar moms. The emergence of higher-level social relationships from A/W tendencies includes the interest of children in conflict itself, not just in a contested toy or object.

The discussion of individual differences draws on Schneirla's assertion that some individuals may come to manifest predominant approach tendencies while others manifest predominant withdrawal tendencies. In his chapter on A/W concepts as central to the analysis of individual differences in personality, Windle puts in place a historical context for the use of opposing concepts in understanding individual differences, and carefully discriminates among the different uses of A/W-like ideas in different theoretical treatments, including an account of theories about brain areas as opposed activation and inhibition systems. The derivation of one contemporary measure, the Dimensions of Temperament Scale, follows directly from Schneirla's account of A/W processes as central to behavioral development. A higher level construct is proposed: a "goodness of fit" model, in which individual characteristics are viewed in relation to a specific context. For example, a "difficult" child whose behavior is predominantly influenced by withdrawal might be negatively evaluated by teachers in an American school system. However, under conditions of famine, children with "difficult" temperamental styles have a better survival rate than their more docile peers. By proposing outcomes based on goodness of fit, the explanatory power of the model is substantially increased.

Individual differences in temperament, physiology, and social behavior in human infants are viewed as self-regulation processes in the chapter by Stifter. She presents these as adaptations based on A/W processes, especially discussing the infants' use of withdrawal processes to support approach. By using withdrawal (gaze aversion) to reduce a too-high level of stimulation, infants can self-regulate to extend the duration of social encounters. Stifter's chapter integrates multiple approaches to the study of emotion (vagal tone, coding of facial expression, behavioral responses to stress or novelty, and bidirectional analyses of dyadic interaction sequences) to portray the pattern of developmental change in response to novelty from approach behaviors (typical of young infants) to a transitional phase in which both approach and withdrawal are components of the response to novelty (age 7-9 months) and the appearance in older infants of a response to novelty consisting mostly of withdrawal behaviors. The dynamic structure of interactions between sympathetic and parasympathetic branches of the autonomic nervous system is posed as key to understanding temperament.

In the last section, the continuing discussion of the concept of integrative levels is carried forward in chapters by Tobach and by Lerner, with commentaries by L. Vroman and G. Vroman. Tobach notes that it is the analytic question posed for investigation that defines the level, methods, instrumentation, and organism most appropriate to the task. In addition, she proposes an explicit recognition of how integrative levels can guide an understanding of change, by distinguishing the concept of levels from the quality of complexity. Changes in complexity are changes in level, but the concept of complexity fails to capture the "processural relationship" among levels, as they are historically related in development and evolution. Change follows from inherent contradictions within and between levels, and the process of resolving or transcending contradictions produces new forms.

Two formulations of the concept of levels refine the concept from the vantage of a biophysicist, L.Vroman, and a medical anthropologist, G. S. Vroman. Despite these two different epistemological bases, the characterizations of levels are stikingly similar.

Lerner issues a call for the integration of research and practice in the study of human development, not only to fulfill the mission of service, but also to realize the goals of science. He proposes that only through intervention research can scientists evaluate the adequacy of their conceptual framework for human development. For example, because humans are paedomorphic and reach highest levels of functioning late in life, the A/W concept may provide an appropriate focus throughout much of the life span, as changing meaning systems link diverse persons to diverse contexts. Citing examples of areas for application (the "fluctuant state" of adolescent romance; sudden shifts in the meaning of food among anorexic and bulimic adolescents), he emphasizes the importance of putting diversity at the center of the analysis. By understanding gender, ethnic and cultural patterns, and by using multidisciplinary, multivariate longitudinal research designs, scientists may shift the core analytical framework from a personological to a person-context relational one. Lerner's proposal exemplifies Schneirla's recommendation that important intercultural comparisons among humans can best be achieved by the multivariate longitudinal study of "discrete populations representing different strata within a general cultural framework." (Schneirla, 1959)

To close, we refer to a volume that followed from a confer-ence at the American Museum of Natural History, a conference dedicated to Schneirla's work. In the introduction to that volume, the editors propose that: "It seems clear that some future conference on behavioral development could profit by a session devoted exclusively to Schneirla's formulation of the biphasic processes underlying A/W and their implications for development." (Tobach, Aronson, & Shaw, 1971, p. xviii) That proposal is addressed here and this volume aims to realize Daniel Lehrman's suggestion that:

> In addition to (or instead of) serving a function like that of an engineer, the scientist can also serve a function like that of an artist, or a painter or poet—that is, he sees things in a way that no one has seen them before, and he finds a way to describe what he has seen so that other people can see it in the same way. This function is that of widening and enriching the content of human consciousness, and of increasing the depth of contact that human beings, scientists and nonscientists as well, can have with the world around them. This function of arousing and satis-fying a sense of wonder and curiosity about the riches of the natural world, and of strengthening the civilized human being's weakened feeling of being part of the world around him, is a function served by . . . the work of T. C. Schneirla and the scientists influenced by him. (Lehrman, 1971, p. 471)

Kathryn E. Hood
Gary Greenberg
Ethel Tobach

REFERENCES

Greenberg, G., & Tobach, E. (Eds.). (1984). *Behavioral Evolution and Integrative Levels*, (Vol. 1). Hillsdale, NJ: Erlbaum.

———. (1987). *Cognition, Language, and Consciousness: Integrative Levels*. (Vol. 2). Hillsdale, NJ: Erlbaum.

————. (1988). *Evolution of Social Behavior and Integrative Levels*. (Vol. 3). Hillsdale, NJ: Erlbaum.

————. (1990). *Theories of the Evolution of Knowing*. (Vol. 4). Hillsdale, NJ: Erlbaum.

————. (1992). *Levels of Social Behavior: Evolutionary and Genetic Aspects*. Award winning papers from the third T. C. Schneirla Conference. The T. C. Schneirla Research Fund, Wichita.

Lehrman, D. S. (1971). Behavioral science, engineering, and poetry. In E. Tobach, L. R. Aronson, & E. Shaw (Eds.), *The Biopsychology of Development*. NY: Academic Press.

Schneirla, T. C. (1959). Comments on Dr. Cattell's paper. In M. R. Jones (Ed.), *Nebraska Symposium Motivation* (Vol.VII). Lincoln, Nebraska: University of Nebraska Press.

Tobach, E., Aronson, L. R., & Shaw, E. (Eds.) (1971). *The Biopsychology of Development*. New York: Academic Press.

SECTION I

The Concept of Approach/Withdrawal as Fundamental to the Analysis of Behavioral Development

CHAPTER 1

The Historical Development of the Approach/Withdrawal Concept

Gary Greenberg

The fifth T. C. Schneirla conference on which this volume was based was planned to acknowledge the significance of his Approach/Withdrawal (A/W) concept, his most important contribution to comparative psychology. This is the distillation and expression of a set of general organizing principles that attempt to explain behavior in terms of biphasic processes based on stimulative characteristics and effects. The usefulness of the concept is demonstrated by its successful application to a broad range of behaviors in many species (McGuire & Turkewitz, 1979; Schneirla, 1965; Turkewitz, Gardner & Lewkowicz, 1984). The A/W concept has important implications for the general understanding of behavioral development (Turkewitz, 1987).

Other papers in this volume address the applicability of the A/W concept and have traced its development since Schneirla's death in 1968. The focus in this paper is on its possible genesis. Although the first full version of the A/W concept appeared in 1959 (Schneirla, 1959), Schneirla had introduced discussion of it in his earliest works. He first presented his ideas in a unified form in a paper delivered at the 1939 American Psychological Association meeting, but this was published only as an abstract without references (Schneirla, 1939). In all of the presentations of A/W, Schneirla acknowledged that he "stood on the shoulders of giants" by identifying many of those who especially influenced his thinking.

Theodore C. Schneirla began his graduate work at the University of Michigan in 1925 under the direction of John F. Shepard, who taught a course in comparative psychology there. The illustrated notebook Schneirla kept in Shepard's course served as the outline for the book he wrote with his close friend Norman Maier, the now-classic *Principles of animal psychology* (1935). At Michigan Schneirla came in contact with H. S. Jennings and Walter Pillsbury. Jennings, who was at Michigan between 1903 and 1906, apparently did much of the work for his own important book, *The behavior of lower organisms* (1906), at Michigan. Pillsbury came to Michigan in 1897 after graduating from Cornell, where he studied under Titchener (Murchison, 1932). He established, and later directed, the psychology laboratory at Michigan. One of Pillsbury's important intellectual characteristics was his eclecticism, reflected in the diversity of his writings. Among his students were Shepard, Schneirla, and Clark L. Hull. Schneirla stayed at Michigan among this group of people until the summer of 1927 when he went to the University of Oklahoma to begin his work with ants. Later that fall he moved to New York University where he remained until 1930 when a fellowship allowed him to transfer to Lashley's laboratory in Chicago.

The influence of this intellectual climate on Schneirla is reflected in the book he wrote with Maier. He tells us in footnotes to the 1959 and 1965 A/W papers that this book contains the essentials of the A/W concept. While this is indeed true, this idea was not presented in a unified fashion until much later.

In their discussion of A/W, McGuire & Turkewitz (1979) show it to be comprised of three basic statements or principles: The Approach/Withdrawal Intensity Hypothesis; The Levels Concept; and The Maturation-Experience Principle. I found this organization to be useful and so employed it in tracing the thinking that led Schneirla to his final formulation of these ideas. What follows is an analysis of the ideas and sources that Schneirla used in developing the three premises of the A/W concept.

The first of these principles is the A/W Intensity Hypothesis, which states that the "intensity of stimulation basically determines the direction of reaction with respect to the source. . . . [F]or all organisms in early ontogenetic stage, low intensities of stimulation tend to evoke approach reactions, high intensities withdrawal reactions with respect to the source" (Schneirla, 1959/72, p. 299). All three written versions of A/W theory begin with a statement of this binary character of organismic response. The 1939 abstract begins, "Various theoretical systems in psychology have been built upon a priori acceptance of a negative-positive differentiation in behavior" (p. 295). The 1959 paper starts with the statement that, "The aspect of *towardness* or *awayness* is common in animal behavior" (p. 297). And, the final version (1965) begins: "In the evolution of behavior, operations which appropriately increase or decrease distance between organisms and stimulus sources must have been crucial for the survival of all animal types" (p. 344). Schneirla meant this as a universal principle (e.g., "I submit that approach and withdrawal are the only empirical objective terms applicable to *all* motivated behavior in *all* animals" (1959/72, p. 298, italics in the original). While his references reveal that this dual property of behavior had been acknowledged as early as Wundt and Titchener, and that its evolutionary survival value and implications for individual behavior was recognized by Jennings, Schneirla was the first to incorporate this line of thought into a coherent explanation of behavioral origins.

Schneirla was drawn to evolutionary thought from his beginnings, and accordingly many Darwinian ideas found their way into his writing. For example, the discussion (Schneirla, 1959/72, p. 328) of A/W mechanisms in infant facial expressions invokes Darwin's (1873) concept of "antithesis": "The muscles involved in smiling and grimacing stand in an opposition to each other; different stimulus intensities evoke each of these responses . . . low-intensity shocks to cheek or mastoid regions . . . [produced] a mechanical 'smile'. . . with higher intensities, a different grimace involving facial musculature more widely." It may be that Schneirla was influenced by the related ideas of Wundt, Holt and Sherrington on this matter, although he clearly developed them in his own manner.

Wundt (1892) had raised the matter of stimulus intensity in his extended treatment of reflexes saying that in general the intensity of reflexive movements were dependent on the intensity of the impinging stimuli: The weakest stimuli do not excite reflex movements; moderate intensities elicit moderate movements such as those of a single limb; still higher stimulus intensities involve still more reflexive movements; and, the highest intensities induce movements of the entire organism. I encountered several versions of this notion in preparing this manuscript.

Wundt (1907) later proposed that stimulus intensity evoked the qualitative dimensions of pleasantness and unpleasantness.

> At first a pleasurable feeling arises with weak sensations and increases with the increasing intensity of the sensations to a maximum, then the feeling sinks to zero at a certain medium sensational intensity, and finally, when this intensity increases still more, the feeling becomes unpleasurable and increases until the sensational maximum is reached (p. 89).

This is an early expression of the general idea of "optimal stimulation," a concept introduced by Lueba (1955) whom Schneirla (1959) credited for providing him with important guidance.

While Titchener (1910) did not accept all that Wundt said, he appears to have agreed with him that stimulus intensity was an important factor in feelings, sensations and behavior. One of Titchener's students was Walter Pillsbury, who studied as an undergraduate with still another of Wundt's students, H. K. Wolf (Pillsbury, 1930). It is clear, then, that Pillsbury (with whom Schneirla would later study) was quite familiar with their thinking on these issues. An important work by Pillsbury was *Fundamentals of psychology* (1916). Citing Jennings' (who was among the most significant influences on Schneirla) description of amoeba behavior, Pillsbury said that the amoeba sends out a pseudopod in response to stimulus contact depending on the intensity of that stimulus. When stimulated gently the amoeba will not respond; moderate intensities elicit pseudopod extension; if the stimulation is stronger the amoeba will move away from it. This is true of the protozoan's responses to light, heat, motion, gravitation, and chemicals.

Some researchers, however, denied that this intensity-behavior relationship held for all stimulus modalities.

Titchener, for example, thought that the chemical sense did not respond in this way. Years later this same argument formed the basis of Pfaffman's (1961) criticism of A/W. Schneirla (1959) criticized Jennings' ability to find conditions under which amoeba will *approach* higher simulus intensities, pointing out that Jennings' experiments did not falsify the intensity-withdrawal hypothesis but rather, revealed something about the cleverness of the investigator.

In another section of his book, Pillsbury's (1916) description of the relationship of stimulus intensity to reflexive behavior of "spinal dogs" mirrors what Wundt (1892) had said earlier and what Sherrington (1906) would say later about it. Pillsbury pointed out animals display dichotomous response tendencies, referring to them as responses which indicate either something of benefit or of injury to the organism, of unopposed and of opposed action, although Schneirla used the terms approach and withdrawal differently.

John Shepard, a student of Pillsbury's, was steeped in the theories of Jennings. Shepard stayed on at Michigan after graduating in 1906, and in 1909 taught the first ever comparative psychology course there (Demarest, 1987) in which Schneirla was enrolled. In one of his few written works, Shepard (1906) reported that the results of sensory stimulation differed as a function of stimulus intensity: mild, pleasurable stimulation had a constricting (sympathetic) effect on heart rate and other physiological processes and stronger stimulation had a dilating (parasympathetic) effect. This formulation is strikingly similar to Schneirla's statement (1965) that "the stimuli adequate for eliciting A-processes [approach] are those exciting neural input effects which are quantitatively low, regular, and limited in their ranges of magnitude. Stimuli adequate for W-processes [withdrawal] are those exciting neural input effects which are quantitatively high, irregular, and of variable, extensive ranges"(p. 45).

Several sources cited by Schneirla appear to have provided him with views about the physiological foundations of A/W Theory. These include a book by Fulton (1926) who explained that bodily contractions and reflexes involve both excitatory and inhibitory neural processes, a positive and a negative way of responding (i.e., approaching and withdrawing), the more intense the stimulus, the greater is the neural effect and thus the greater is the withdrawal response—noxious stimuli are of greater intensity than beneficial (positive) ones.

A paper by Holt (1931) contains a related reference to spreading neural excitation with increasing stimulus intensity and subsequently with the organism's withdrawal from the stimulus. He wrote:

> Every organism *at first* responds positively towards (i.e., so as to get more of) *any* stimulus. If, however, the stimulation is, or becomes, very intense, the transmitted excitation "spreads" (Sherrington, 1906, pp. 150–2) [a reference also cited by Schneirla, 1939, 1959] in the central nervous system, overflowing into diverse and random motor channels, and the young organism is thrown into a state of more or less general and incoordinated activity; it wriggles, writhes, howls, and so on. In fact any muscles may become involved; and if the stimulation becomes strong enough, general motor spasms will ensue. But some of these energetic though random movements may carry the organism out of range of the stimulus. Then the stimulation ceases, and so will the organism's movements. . . . [V]ery strong stimuli are in general the harmful ones; their 'intensity,' as Sherrington (1906, p. 228) has said, 'constituting their harmfulness' (p. 94–95).

While many of the earlier sources I have cited may have provided Schneirla with thoughts about the binary nature of behavior, it was a 1953 paper by Kempf that shaped his development of this line of thought. Kempf discussed two response types, *acquisitive* (positive, stimulus-seeking) and *avoidant* (negative, moving away) in a holistic, anti-reductionistic (levels) perspective, referring to self-organization, the bidirectionality of organismic-environment interactions, and the significance of environmental factors, even in hereditary matters. These ideas are at the very heart of Schneirla's thinking, particularly with respect to this first principle of the A/W Theory.

The second major statement of the A/W Theory is not so much a formal postulate as it is a recognition of the significance of the concept of integrative levels in understanding behavioral capacities (Aronson, 1984). The increasing influence of levels thinking resulted in a symposium on the concept at the University of Chicago in 1941 (Redfield, 1942). Papers presented there included Hyman's "The transition from the unicellular to the multicellular individual," Gerard's treatment of "Higher levels of integration," Jennings' "The transition from the individual to the social level," Carpenter's "Societies of monkeys and apes," and several others. The monograph which resulted from the symposium was the definitive word on levels in 1942. The reference citation to this monograph in Schneirla's 1953 levels paper says, "Especially articles by Jennings, Alee, Carpenter" (Schneirla, 1953/1972, p. 253).

Schneirla's intellectual development took place in a climate rich in this mode of thought, which his writing reflects. Indeed, several of his papers are devoted to discussing the utility of the levels concept in psychology, culminating in this unique use of the idea:

> through evolution, higher psychological levels have arisen in which through ontogeny [Approach and Withdrawal processes and] mechanisms can produce new and qualitatively advanced types of adjustment to environmental conditions. Insects are superior to protozoans, and mammals to insects, in that ontogeny progressively frees processes of individual motivation from the basic formula of prepotent stimulative-intensity relationships (1959/72, p. 300).

In one formulation of this view Schneirla identified five such psychological levels as follows:

> I believe that a strong case can be made for differentiating the following levels in capacity to modify behavior:
>
> 1. fluctuant changes, through peripheral effects (e.g., protozoans);
>
> 2. sensory integration, habituation, based on central trace effects (e.g., flatworms);
>
> 3. contiguity-type conditioned responses (worms);
>
> 4. selective learning (different in insects; mammals);
>
> 5. insight, reasoning (higher mammals) (1959/72, p. 302).

Though he later changed the terminology associated with these levels (Greenberg, 1989; Tobach & Schneirla, 1968) the capacities attributed to them remained essentially the same. As Aronson (1984) pointed out in his contribution to the first Schneirla conference, these levels provide an important replacement for the traditional but often criticized evolutionary scale: "lower" organisms operating at the lowest behavioral levels and "higher" organisms at the higher levels. Nervous system complexity follows these taxonomic and behavioral trends and increasing nervous system complexity allows for increased behavioral plasticity. Thus, from protozoan to primate, nervous system complexity increases and behavioral plasticity becomes increasingly likely. Neural complexity provides for the emergence of new ways of interacting with the environment.

The levels concept requires several levels of analytical knowledge for the most complete understanding (Feibleman, 1954). It does not surprise us, then, that Schneirla was well versed in physiology. Indeed, both the 1959 and 1965 A/W papers contain detailed discussions of the physiological mechanisms and processes underlying approach and withdrawal behavioral adjustments. Schneirla's reference lists for those two papers include Shepard (1906) on organic changes and feelings; Fulton (1926) on muscular activity and reflexes; Kuntz (1929); Sherrington (1906); Goldstein (1939); Gellhorn (1943) on the autonomic nervous system; and many other such works.

It is not inconceivable that Shepard could have pointed Schneirla in the direction of the levels concept given such writings as: "Whether in terms of peripherally or centrally aroused stimuli, there is some difference in organization which gives the ant, the rat and cat, and the person different types of control of behavior" (1914, p. 58). Schneirla later wrote on differences in psychological capacities among these organisms (Schneirla, 1962; Schneirla & Rosenblatt, 1961).

Another significant reference cited by Schneirla was a paper by Pick (1954) who contributed the following as a potential source of ideas: "As we proceed along the phylogenetic scale it is the nervous system which attains increasing importance in the development of new adjustment mechanisms, apparently because of its plasticity, versatility, and faculty of integrating peripheral function" (p. 301).

The third and final component of the A/W Theory is the Maturation-Experience Principle which links behavioral capacity to developmental achievement rather than to biologically determined events and processes. Schneirla was an ardent, though constructive, critic of vitalistic thinking, particularly as exemplified by instinct theory. In this instance his constructive approach resulted in the development of an alternative to instinct theory, of which A/W theory is only one component. The serious disagreement between these positions resulted in an intellectual battle in the 1950s and 1960s. Schneirla's position was spelled out in many of his papers, perhaps most clearly in the "Interrelations between the 'innate' and the 'acquired' in instinctive behavior" (1956/72).

Schneirla's conception of behavioral development is essentially an epigenetic one: Behavior is not something an organism is born with, but rather something it develops. Organisms which function at the different behavioral levels (see above) are characterized by different behavioral potentials (Kuo, 1967). The biological uniqueness of a species dictates that it interact differently with its environment than other species. Behavior arises as a result of this interaction. As the organism changes (i.e., matures) its development is directed along one pathway or another. Changing maturational possibilities, then, changes the organism's final behavioral repertoire. "This formulation corresponds to a fundamental concept of modern embryology according to which organism and development medium are inseparably related [i.e., fused]" (Schneirla, 1965, p. 352). It would appear that Carmichael's 1927 reference to "psychological epigeneiss" is the first use of that terminology for the position Schneirla came to advocate.

The concepts of *maturation* ("the contributions of tissue growth and differentiation and their functional trace effects at all stages") and *experience* ("the contributions of stimulation from the developmental medium and of related trace effects") are central to this line of thought (Schneirla, 1965, p. 352).

An important intellectual question during Schneirla's time as a student was concerned with the relative contributions of maturation and experience (practice) to instincts. Indeed, by the time Schneirla went to study with him, his teacher John Shepard and his colleague F. S. Breed had already published observations on the roles of maturation and practice in the development of the pecking behavior of the newly hatched chicken (Shepard & Breed, 1913). Shepard's position, that the behavior was essentially improved by maturation and not by practice, was unique. Indeed, later Bird (1925) would say, "To my knowledge one experiment only [i.e., Shepard and Breed's] supplies the basis for the contention that maturation rather than practice is effective in producing greater accuracy of response" (p. 68). Bird's own observations led him to side with Shepard and Breed: "A part of the increase [in accuracy] is attributed to general physiological development, which occurs during the first few days of post-natal life, irrespective of practice in pecking" (p. 90).

The situation surrounding this controversy is best summed up (and resolved) by the following pair of quotations, the first from Bird (1933) and the second from Kuo (1932):

> Precisely what bodily factors are subsumed under maturation is not possible to say, in spite of the impatience exhibited by psychologists who feel obliged to take a stand in this matter. The data of this study suggest that as yet unknown factors, operating within the chicks, affect the complex pattern called feeding. . . . Nor can we indicate what aspects of the chick environment enter into the bodily development responsible for improvements in accuracy of pecking (Bird, 1933, p. 364).

> Enough facts have been presented to demonstrate that changes in gross anatomy and environment are important factors in determining embryonic behavior in birds. . . . One has only to observe a chick embryo for several days to be reasonably convinced that external . . . stimuli play a very important part in determining embryonic behavior and that embryonic activities are rarely *spontaneous* (Kuo, 1932, p. 265).

Schneirla, of course, was familiar with these arguments and his writings reveal which side he favored.

There were several who were engaged in work on embryonic development in this period. All acknowledged their debt to the pioneering work of Coghill, while at the same time taking the opportunity to offer their criticisms of various of his conclusions. Certainly both Kuo and Allan Fromme were in that tradition. Fromme's (1941) observations of frog embryos identified important antecedents of later behavior which are practiced before hatching, in the embryo stage. Such work seemed to indicate that there were important experiential precursors to behaviors that had otherwise been attributed to instinct. What happened to an organism even in its embryonic stages influenced what it did after birth. At that time few could imagine attributing any significance to behavior happening to an embryo, much less imagine how to observe it. Gottlieb (1971) has referred to this difficult process as the search for nonobvious experiential precursors of behavior. Thus it is clear from Kuo's (1932, 1967) work that the newly hatched chick's pecking behavior has an experiential history and can be attributed to that history rather than to some biologically determined set of factors. Similar analyses hold for all behaviors of all organisms in Schneirla's A/W theory.

I have attempted in this review to trace the lines of thought that led Schneirla to the development of his theoretical thinking most clearly stated in the three principles making up his Approach/Withdrawal concept. It seemed necessary, as well, to provide a thorough discussion of those principles for, while his theoretical position was still incomplete at the time of his death in 1968, many researchers have been influenced by his ideas, which they have extended and modified. This has certainly been true of Gilbert Gottlieb, Gerald Turkewitz and Richard Lerner. Today Lerner is among the few developmental psychologists working within a systematic theoretical framework. Indeed, the most modern version of Schneirla's arguments have been made by Lerner (1984, 1992) in an epigenetic position he labels "developmental contextualism." The fruitfulness of Lerner's approach attests to the viability and significance of Schneirla's ideas, which form the basis of much of his thinking.

REFERENCES

Aronson, L. R. (1984). Levels of integration and organization. In G. Greenberg and E. Tobach (Eds.), *Behavioral evolution and integrative levels*. Hillsdale, NJ: Erlbaum.

Bird, C. (1925). The relative importance of maturation and habit in the development of an instinct. *Pedagogical Seminary and Journal of Genetic Psychology, 32,* 68–91.

————.(1933). Maturation and practice: Their effects upon the feeding reactions of chicks. *Journal of Comparative and Physiological Psychology, 16,* 343–366.

Carmichael, L. (1927). A further study of the development of behavior in vertebrates experimentally removed from the influence of external stimulation. *Psychological Review, 34,* 34–47.

Darwin, C. (1873). *The expression of the emotions in man and animals.* New York: Appleton.

Demarest, J. (1987) Two comparative psychologies. In E. Tobach (Ed.), *Historical perspectives and the international status of comparative psychology.* Hillsdale, NJ: Erlbaum.

Feibleman, J. K. (1954). Theory of integrative levels. *British Journal for the Philosophy of Science, 5,* 59–66.

Fromme, A. (1941). An experimental study of the factors of maturation and practice in the development of the embryo of the frog, *Rana pipiens. Genetic Psychology Monographs, 24,* 219–256.

Fulton, J. F. (1926), *Muscular contraction and the reflex control of movement.* Baltimore: Williams and Wilkins.

Greenberg, G. (1989). Levels of social behavior. In G. Greenberg and E. Tobach (Eds.), *Evolution of social behavior and integrative levels.* Hillsdale, NJ: Erlbaum.

Gellhorn, E. (1943). *Autonomic regulations.* New York: Interscience.

Goldstein, K. (1939). *The organism.* New York: American.

Gottlieb, G. (1971). *Development of species identification in birds.* Chicago: University of Chicago Press.

Holt, F. B. (1931). *Animal drives and the learning process.* New York: Holt.

Jennings, H. S. (1906). *The behavior of lower organisms.* New York: Columbia University Press.

Kempf, E. J. (1953). Neuroses as conditioned, conflicting, holistic, attitudinal, acquisitive-avoidant reactions. *Annals of the New York Academy of Sciences, 56*, 307–329.

Kuntz, A. (1929). *The autonomic nervous system.* Philadelphia: Lea and Febiger.

Kuo, Z.-Y. (1932). Ontogeny of embryonic behavior in Aves III. The structure and environmental factors in embryonic behavior. *Journal of Comparative Psychology, 13*, 245–272.

———.(1967). *The dynamics of behavior development.* New York: Random House.

Lerner, R. M. (1984). *On the nature of human plasticity.* Cambridge: Cambridge University Press.

Lerner, R. (1992). *Final solutions: Biology, prejudice and genocide.* University Park, PA: Pennsylvania State University Press.

Lueba, C. (1955). Toward some integration of learning theories: The concept of optimal stimulation. *Psychological Reports, 1*, 27–33.

Maier, N. R. F., and Schneirla, T. C. (1935). *Principles of animal psychology.* New York: McGraw-Hill.

McGuire, I., and Turkewitz, G. (1979). Approach-Withdrawal Theory and the study of infant development. In M. Bottner (Ed.), *Cognition, growth, and development: Essays in memory of Herbert G. Birch.* New York: Brunner/Mazel.

Murchison, C. (1932). *The Psychological Register.* Worcester, MA: Clark University.

Pfaffman, C. (1961). The sensory and motivating properties of taste. In R. R. Jones (Ed.), *Current theory and research on motivation, Vol. 9.* Lincoln: University of Nebraska Press, 71–110.

Pick, J. (1954). The evolution of homeostasis. *Proceedings of the American Philosophical Society, 98*, 298–313.

Pillsbury, W. B. (1916). *Fundamentals of Psychology.* New York: Macmillan.

Pillsbury, W. B. (1930). Walter B. Pillsbury. In C. Murchison (Ed.), *A history of psychology in autobiography, Volume 2.* New York: Russell and Russell.

Redfield, R. (1942). *Levels of integration in biological and social systems.* Lancaster: Cattell Press.

Schneirla, T. C. (1939). A theoretical consideration of the basis for approach-withdrawal adjustments in behavior. *Psychological Bulletin, 37*, 501–502.

———. (1953). The concept of levels in the study of social phenomena. I. M. Sherif and C. Sherif (Eds.), *Groups in Harmony and Tension.* New York: Harper, 54–75. Reprinted in L. R. Aronson, E. Tobach, D. S. Lehrman, and J. S. Rosenblatt (Eds.). *Selected Writings of T. C. Schneirla.* San Francisco: Freeman, 1972, 238–253.

———. (1956). Interrelationships of the "innate" and the "acquired" in instinctive behavior. In P. Grasse (Ed.), *L'Instinct dans le Comportement des Animaux et de l'Homme.* Paris: Masson, 387–452. Reprinted in L. R. Aronson, E. Tobach, D. S. Lehrman, and J. S. Rosenblatt (Eds.), *Selected Writings of T. C. Schneirla.* San Francisco: Freeman, 1972, 131–188.

———. (1959). An evolutionary and developmental theory of biphasic processes underlying approach and withdrawal. In M. R. Jones (Ed.), *Nebraska Symposium on Motivation, Vol. 7.* Lincoln: University of Nebraska, 1–42. Reprinted in L. R. Aronson, E. Tobach, D. S. Lehrman, and J. S. Rosenblatt (Eds.), *Selected Writings of T. C. Schneirla.* San Francisco: Freeman, 1972, 295–339.

———. (1962). Psycholigical comparison of insect and mammal. *Psychologische Beitrage*, 6, 509—520.

———. (1965). Aspects of stimulation and organization in approach-withdrawal processes underlying vertebrate behavioral development. In D. S. Lehrman, R. A. Hinde, and E. Shaw (Eds.), *Advances in the Study of Behavior, Vol. 1.* New York: Academic Press, 1–74. Reprinted in L. R. Aronson, E. Tobach, D. S. Lehrman, and J. S. Rosenblatt (Eds.), *Selected Writings of T. C. Schneirla.* San Francisco: Freeman, 1972, 344–412.

Schneirla, T. C. and Rosenblatt, J. S. (1961). Behavioral organization and genesis of the social band in insects and mammals. *American Journal of Orthopsychiatry*, 31, 223–253.

Shepard, J. F. (1906). Organic changes and feeling. *American Journal of Psychology*, 17, 522–584.

Shepard, J. F. (1914). Types of learning in animals and man. *Psychological Bulletin*, 11, 58.

Shepard, J. F., and Breed, F. S. (1913). Maturation and use in the development of an instinct. *Journal of Animal Behavior*, 3, 274–285.

Sherrington, C. S. (1906). *The Integrative Action of the Nervous System.* New Haven: Yale University Press.

Titchener, E. B. (1910). *A Textbook of Psychology.* New York: Macmillan.

Tobach, E., and Schneirla, T. C. (1968). The biopsychology of social behavior of animals. In R. E. Cooke (Ed.) *The biologic basis of pediatric practice.* New York: McGraw-Hill. Reprinted in L. R. Aronson, E. Tobach, D. S. Lehrman, and J. S. Rosenblatt (Eds.), *Selected Writings of T. C. Schneirla.* 1972, 505–535.

Turkewitz, G. (1987). Psychobiology and developmental psychology. The influence of T. C. Schneirla on human developmental psychology. *Developmental Psychobiology, 20,* 369–375.

Turkewitz, G., Gardner, I., and Lewkowicz, C. J. (1984). In G. Greenberg and E. Tobach (Eds.), *Behavioral Evolution and Integrative Levels.* Hillsdale, NJ: Erlbaum.

Wundt, W. (1892). *Lectures on Human and Animal Psychology.* (Trans. by J. E. Creighton and E. B. Titchener). New York: Macmillan, 1894.

Wundt, W. (1907). *Outlines of Psychology.* New York: Stechert.

CHAPTER 2

Dialectical and Dynamical Systems of Approach and Withdrawal
Is Fighting a Fractal Form?

Kathryn E. Hood

"Where humanists despair, dialecticians lick their chops."
Rappoport, 1986

At the second Schneirla conference in New York City in November 1985, during discussion about nature and nurture and how they "coalesce," the middle ground in the concept all at once gave way in my mind. Beyond the imagined clarity of the two extremes—nature and nurture—lies the challenge: to represent a middle ground of nature-nurture interactions as something other than a littered field of unwieldly contingencies, willy-nilly particulars, and domain-specific ephemerae. A conception of interaction as a murky mixture, blend, or composite cannot be the dynamic developmental model that we seek. This chapter presents a new and more powerful conception of interaction that may lift that crucial concept out of the muddle. What remains when the middle ground falls away is a related pair of concepts that define each other by their opposition (like "inner" and "outer" do)—and a boundary between them. That boundary opens the way for the appearance of new forms, in a dialectical structure. To characterize such a boundary is the chief aim of this article.

The synthesis proposed here draws from psychology, philosophy, and mathematics. The result is a speculative conceptual integration of Schneirla's fundamental theory of development, Hegel's dialectical theory of becoming, and fractal theory, the recently discovered systematic of novelty. Rather than building a critique, these discussions proceed from a provisional acceptance of the assumptions of each theory. The intent is to assess the complementarity of each view with the others, and what each adds. As an alternative to reductionist/positivist theories of science, the proposed integration of these relatively unexplored domains may open some new ways of thinking about origins of novel behavioral forms in development.

Schneirla's theory of behavioral development posits two fundamental processes, approach and withdrawal, as responses to events in the world. These two fundamental tendencies are elaborated during development to become complex behavioral forms. Schneirla's theory will be considered in relation to Hegel's philosophy of the dialectic of nature. Hegel's view is not familiar to many scientists schooled in British analytical philosophy. Hegel constructs an account of nature and knowledge about nature from assumptions about *becoming* as the fundamental process in a spontaneously active, novelty-producing world. The third theory, dynamical systems theory, is an experimental method used to mathematically model nonlinear complex systems, often with surprising results. By the inclusion of dynamical systems and fractal theory in this discussion, the opposed behavioral tendencies of approach and withdrawal are drawn as a dialectical unity with a fractal boundary, one which contains infinitely regressive levels of fractal forms. Fractal forms are unique geometrical shapes resulting from dynamical systems in physical phenomena, such as fluid mechanics, and from empirical investigations of local probability functions in some mathematical domains derived from iterative, self-recursive equations. Because fractal theory represents spontaneously generated forms as boundary events, the present discussion aims to configure fractal theory in relation to dialectical transformations at the boundary between opposed pairs, approach and withdrawal, in the process of *becoming* or behavioral development.

Potential applications of these concepts to the study of aggressive behavior will be proposed to begin to assess the usefulness of this conjunction of ideas.

Schneirla's Approach/Withdrawal Theory

T. C. Schneirla's theory of behavioral development proposes that species-typical and adaptive behaviors are the result of two fundamentally opposed tendencies in all organisms. By Schneirla's (1939, 1959, 1965) biphasic approach/withdrawal theory (A/W theory), young organisms tend to approach a source of low-intensity stimulation, and tend to withdraw from a source of high-intensity stimulation. The opposition of the two simple tendencies, approach and withdrawal, and their interactions and elaborations are sufficient to account for the appearance during development of complex species-typical behavioral forms and for the variety of individual behavioral adaptations. Schneirla proposed that these A/W processes link individual development with organismic evolutionary change.

> Inevitably, in both evolution and ontogenesis, these functional conditions are related to the fact that low-intensity stimulative changes are likely to be followed by beneficial results, high-intensity stimulative changes by noxious results. My biphasic A/W theory is grounded on the universality of this state of affairs in the relationship of every species to its characteristic habitat. Selection pressure would favor a corresponding approach-withdrawal dichotomy, and would promote its stabilization in the genotype through genetic assimilation. This fundamental fact has affected the evolution of all mechanisms underlying adaptive behavior. . . . This is a wholistic theory designed for studying *all* adaptive patterns of behavior attainable in a species under the conditions of individual development. (Schneirla, 1965, p. 348 in 1972, emphasis in original)

The interaction of the two elements of the process, the approach response (to low-intensity stimulation) and the withdrawal response (to high-intensity stimulation) is effective in modulating stimulus intensity. Approach to the source of stimulation increases the intensity of stimulation received by the organism. The opponent function, withdrawal, serves to distance an organism from the source of stimulation and thereby to reduce intensity. In a world of constantly varying stimulation, organisms will physically move themselves about in order to equilibrate the intensity of stimulation, and thus to accrue favorable outcomes and to avoid harm.

Developmental Integration of Approach and Withdrawal

Of the two fundamental elements of behavioral development, approach and withdrawal, the tendency to approach stimulation is developmentally prior and primary. In early development, approach behaviors occur from self-stimulation, for example, by the heartbeat. The elaboration of approach behaviors, their increased efficiency and organization form the basis for the development of all species-typical behaviors (Schneirla, 1965).

To indicate how it is that these opposed tendencies give rise to forms of behavior, Schneirla embeds them in a matrix of developmental change. For example, an infant's approach to the warmth provided by a mother may be a first step in the eventual development of complex social behavior. The processes are not obvious ones. "These important functions, which cannot be considered innate in the traditional sense, are the product of a complex process of changes in embryonic and postnatal development which, with the species-normal genotype under species-standard ontogenetic conditions, seems inevitable" (Schneirla, 1965). In embryonic or early development, there already exists a graded approach to low-intensity stimulation. Through contiguity learning, specific kinds of environmental events are "canalized" by sensory receptors (also the result of natural selection) and these specific events gradually gain control of approach behaviors.

W-processes appear later in development, from emotional states (or "tensional changes") in response to relatively intense stimulation. They are first organized in opposition to and inhibitory of undifferentiated A-processes, and later in opposition to patterned A-processes. As development proceeds, different organ systems are integrated into the A/W system. Early in development, the "somatic and visceral components of A/W processes are dominant, with the interactions of the autonomic [nervous system] divisions developing slowly" (Schneirla, 1965).

Initially, tactile-proprioceptive stimulation directs patterns of motor behavior. After birth, other sensory stimuli can arouse patterns of motor behavior. In later development, environmental stimuli are mediated by the CNS and autonomic nervous systems, with the parasympathetic system activated in A-responses, and the sympathetic system activated in W-responses (see the discussion by Stifter, this volume). W-processes also become patterned, and they are organized in more complex relationships to A-processes. Paradoxically, in later development, W-processes may energize, rather than oppose, A-processes. Schneirla's account of that transition is only briefly sketched (Schneirla, 1965, Figure 30 and p. 383–4, but see Stifter, this volume, for an example).

The development of species-typical social behaviors involves the integration of approach behaviors in relation to conspecifics. Because social settings are a given for many species, ". . . processes of socialization and formation of the social bond begin at birth, if not earlier," based on processes of mutual sensory stimulation by both parent and offspring (Schneirla & Rosenblatt, 1963). Schneirla (1959) notes that for complex social behaviors like parenting, the developmental process must include perceptual learning through social experience. "It is plain that in the normal situation, the sequence of changes in the mutual approach-withdrawal relationships of parent and young cannot be mainly the result of critical periods synchronized to inevitable processes of physiological maturation. Instead, these behavioral changes must represent a progression of stimulative-response relationships in which maturational influences must be complexly related to influences of experience and of mutual behavioral effects" (1965, p. 398 in 1972).

Approach/Withdrawal Integration vs. the Fixed Ethogram

With the elaboration of A/W theory, a developmental account of species-typical behavioral forms is proposed as an alternative to the fixed-trait, fixed-perceptual-filter models of ethology. In his discussion for the *Nebraska Symposium* volume, Schneirla (1959) notes that efficient approach and withdrawal responses are the central components of adaptive behavior, such as choosing an environmental niche, or responding to another organism. Schneirla cites as an example the finding that a toad will approach to flick a tongue at a small moving object (relatively less intense stimulation) as though to consume prey. A larger moving object (more intense stimulation) elicits more intense approach, a lunge, as though to aggress against a conspecific. A still larger moving object (very intense stimulation) causes the toad to withdraw or retreat, as though to evade a predator. The proposal is that an enemy is recognized by its size and brusque movements, rather than by any specific qualitative features that are somehow innately recognized by prey.

The analysis is furthered in *Advances in the Study of Behavior* (Schneirla, 1965), where Schneirla presents a series of experiments to illustrate these points. Ethologists Lorenz and Tinbergen found that young goslings showed species-typical "escape responses" to models of predators, hawks, which were passed overhead, but not to models of geese. The ethological interpretation was that this was evidence for an innate perceptual schema for recognizing danger, a species-specific "sign stimulus" (in this case, a hawk shape) eliciting genetically programmed recognition and fear responses. By classical ethological theory, the young animal's response is to a certain quality of stimulus objects, such as a red spot (gulls peck at a red spot on the parent's beak) or a receding visual array (chicks and kittens back away from a visual cliff), or a hawk shape.

However, Schneirla presents a series of experiments from other laboratories that supports a reinterpretation of these findings. The proposition of A/W theory is that, for goslings, it is the sudden increase in stimulus intensity produced by the blunt-shaped leading edge of the hawk model that is the cause of withdrawal. By contrast, the shape of the long-necked, slender goose model does not produce a sudden increase in stimulus intensity, and does not produce a W-response. This interpretation is supported by the finding that the gosling's fear response is not limited to a specific stimulus (a hawk-shaped stimulus) but can be evoked by any large swooping object, such as a stuffed duck or a black disk or a tea table. Schneirla proposed that the hawk-shape effect results not from an innate perceptual schema in goslings for detecting hawks, but rather from a "sudden massive increase in retinal stimulation" produced by any large or swooping object. In similar arguments, Schneirla (1965) notes that the response of naive animals to a visual cliff actually results from motion parallax, rather than an innate schema of distance perception. Why is a location causing motion parallax avoided? Because motion parallax constitutes rapid and intense changes in stimulation, it arouses the W-response, an organized motor response to any kind of intense stimulation.

By the developmental analysis, it is a process of integrated approach and withdrawal which develops rather than an ethogram. The developmental integration of approach and withdrawal is common to all species and situations.

A Threshold Model of Approach/Withdrawal

Schneirla proposed his theory as one designed for studying all adaptive patterns of behavior (1965). Figure 1, a schematic representation of the theory, highlights two aspects of the process.

First, it is important to note that two different kinds of domains are represented, one that is dimensional and one that is not. The domain of the approach response is a graded domain in which approach is linked to changes in the level of stimulation, so that low levels of stimulation evoke low levels of approach behavior, and higher levels of stimulation evoke higher levels of approach behavior. However, the withdrawal response to stimulation that is too intense, over threshold, is not a graded response and is represented here as an all-or-none response. W-processes lack the tonic support that maintains the A-system, so that W-processes are phasic or episodic responses to too-intense stimulation, responses that interrupt ongoing A-processes. (Schneirla, 1965, p. 384; also see 1959, p. 318, 321, 330 in 1972). The domain of withdrawal is, in this sense, a nondimensional domain. Schneirla refers to the threshold model: "This conception envisages negative-positive responses as fundamentally attributable to the differential arousal of excitation-reaction systems which function as though they possessed distinctively different activation thresholds."

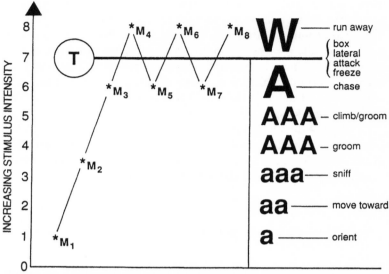

Figure 1. From moment to moment (M_1 to M_2 to M_3, etc.), perceived stimulus intensity (left vertical axis) produces A, approach behavior or W, withdrawal behavior (if the stimulus intensity exceeds level "7" in the hypothetical schema). Increasing stimulus intensity produces increasingly strong and directed approach behaviors, but beyond the threshold (circled "T"), too-intense stimulation produces withdrawal, an all-or-none response. As the withdrawal response increases distance from the source of stimulation and reduces stimulus intensity, approach behaviors may reappear. By this model, organisms will seek the maximum level of stimulation below threshold, titrating stimulation by approach and withdrawal behaviors. The sequence M_4-M_5-M_6-M_7-M_8 illustrates how the threshold may capture behavior. The switching of A and W at threshold opens the possibility of new behavioral forms arising (here: highly stereotypic forms of mice: box, lateral display, attack, freeze). See the discussion below: "Fractal boundaries as models for behavioral development." Alternatively, this threshold might be represented as a cusp catastrophe.

The second point concerns the structure of A/W activity. A unique process occurs at the threshold point, the point of transformation of approach into its opposite, withdrawal. This point would seem to capture the behavior. By this account, animals would approach ever more strongly as the source of stimulation became more proximal and more intense, until at threshold the intensity passes into the range evoking withdrawal. As the animal withdraws from the source, the stimulus intensity is reduced, and returns to the range evoking strong approach behaviors. This sequence, recurring, would imply that behavior oscillates around the threshold of A and W (unless W-processes propel the animal beyond the range of stimulation sufficient for A-processes). The threshold captures behavior. In a social setting, it is at this threshold or point of social contact that new forms of social behavior will emerge, such as grooming, mating, and aggressive behavior in species-typical forms.

Figure 1 represents typical patterns of moment-to-moment changes in mouse social behavior in the schematic sequence M_1 to M_8 (moment 1 to moment 8, like Guthrie's [1935] moments). After initial approach with sniffing and chasing behaviors (moment 1 to moment 3), the intensity of stimulation becomes too intense, and the W-response, running away, occurs. From a distance, stimulation is reduced sufficiently to arouse intense approach, chasing (in moment 5), and the cycle repeats to moment 8. Tighter oscillations around the threshold would produce species-specific stereotyped social behaviors characteristic of mouse aggressive behavior (box, lateral display, attack) or of blocked retreat (freeze). Other representations of A/W processes are based in changes over hours or days. It is such a difference in temporal scaling that results in the different depiction of A/W processes, for example, by Rosenblatt (this volume) or by Miller (in Gray, 1987, p. 144–145).

An important source of complexity in the analysis of social behavior derives from the fact that at any moment the source of stimulation may itself move. Social partners each may be mobile, so that each can alter the intensity of the social stimulation that they present to others and that they receive from others by moving closer or further away from others. The sequential process of social interaction might be thought of as more or less predictable cycles of mutual approach and withdrawal that titrate stimulation for each individual.

It remains to formulate an account of behavioral responsiveness to stimulation, considering the psychophysical abilities of each species and of individuals in a broad conception of A and W as fundamental elements of development. The developmental analysis could be applied to extend investigations of A/W-like processes at one age (for example, Bengtsson, 1983; Blanchard, Blanchard, and Hori, 1989; Taylor, 1979; Van der Poel, Mos, Kruk & Olivier, 1984). One systematic perspective that includes developmental parameters has been provided for the study of aggressive behavior in mice (Cairns, Gariépy, & Hood, 1990). How can an A/W analysis add to that perspective? Does it make a plausible account of behavior, or suggest new questions, new experiments?

A/W Processes in the Initiation of Aggressive Behavior

In a coordinated series of studies by Robert Cairns and his associates, several levels of analysis are presented in the study of aggressive development: the interactive process that leads to the first attack, the cumulative effects over time of individuals' social experiences, and effects over generations on behavior and physiology of individuals selectively bred for differences in aggressive behavior. The results of these studies here are placed into the theoretical context provided by Schneirla in his considerations of social organization, aggressive behavior, and approach/withdrawal processes in behavioral development.

Behaviors that appear after the neonatal period, such as eating, drinking, following (imprinting), courtship, solicitation and sexual behavior, aggressive behavior, maternal behavior, and dispersal also must develop from A/W tendencies, by this theory. Schneirla's original conception of orientation was focused on very young organisms. However, he also noted that differential A and W responses to stimuli of varying intensity "may be basic to the differentiation of patterns such as feeding, mating, and flight . . ." (Schneirla, 1959). Aggressive and sexual behaviors become important later in development, after sexual maturation has occurred; responsiveness to conspecific aggressive and sexual behavior is also developmentally timed, and dependent on sexual maturation. For this discussion, we might consider the organism's first exposure after puberty, after hormonal and maturational/neural sensitivities have attained adult condition, as the time for "early experience" and the consolidation of stimulus intensity and approach/withdrawal tendencies as elements in a behavioral system such as aggressive behavior.

Aggressive behavior derives from Schneirla's "organic set" of withdrawal responses. In his 1959 article, Schneirla included aggression as a withdrawal response to intense stimulation (Figures 23 and 24). He proposed that the study of social organization must begin with an account of the forces that draw animals together into a group, and that ". . . trophallactic relationships in the early life of individuals in the social group may be postulated as furnishing group-approach tendencies opposing aggression. Withdrawal tendencies may serve underlying dominance relationships. Aggression-dominance adjustments arise through conflict and friction among group members, as in sharp competition over limited food or space; hence, they have to do with "social distance" rather than with group unity directly (Schneirla, 1953, p. 251 in 1972).

Can the interplay of approach and withdrawal be observed in social and aggressive interactions in mice? Yes, and much more. In addition to approach and withdrawal, several complex species-specific forms predictably emerge during social interaction. From several studies by Cairns and associates (summarized in Cairns, 1973; also see Cairns, Hood & Midlam, 1985), we know that socially naive males (adults reared in social isolation) show a highly stereotyped series of behavioral forms during their first encounter, in response to specific kinds of stimulation provided by an adult conspecific. In a sequence of mutual exploration and dyadic escalation, the naive animal may, at once or after some time, approach, sniff, then freeze, groom, climb on, then bite the partner's rump, or attack with full-blown wrestles and tumbles. If strongly counterattacked, the naive subject may show the species-typical upright-defensive boxing posture, orienting to the partner. After an attack sequence and then a rest, the naive subject may approach the partner with another species-typical behavioral form, the lateral display, or sideways feint. Alternatively, the subject may avoid the partner, run away, jump or freeze. These fighting forms are substantially similar in young, old, female, male, naive and experienced mice. Where and how do they arise in isolation-reared males? If we are not satisfied just to call them "innate," then we might ask: How do behavioral forms arise from elementary A/W processes?

The complete answer surely will not be simple, but first steps to a full developmental/interactional account have been achieved. In Cairns and Scholtz's (1973) experimental analysis of dyadic control in the escalation to first attack, a demonstration of the interactive sequencing that leads to full attack is made clear. Fighting is not "released" by an odor or by any single feature of the social partner. Rather, the escalation from exploration (sniff) to attack requires dyadic participation, with both partners responding instantaneously to the social behaviors and increasing social stimulation from the other. Behaviors of arousal and orientation may channel specific features of fighting sequences; for example, an attacked animal may use anticipatory defensive movements to deflect an approach into the form of sideways feint (lateral display) rather than attack. When this interactive dance is interrupted by muting the behavior of one of the partners (as Cairns and Scholtz did using a sedative drug), then the dyadic escalation sequence is interrupted, and fighting does not occur. It takes two to tango, or to tangle. Fighting is not a solitary form.

Learning Shifts the Threshold between A and W

By Schneirla's account, the threshold between A and W is not a fixed limit, but rather a relationship that changes in relation to the current environment and in relation to past experience. Contiguity or S-R learning provides animals with cues about the predictable contents of their environments, enabling animals to mobilize A or W-responses to anticipate, seek or avoid events. A-processes are themselves reinforcing and self-reinforcing, leading to contiguity learning about stimuli in the environment. W-processes produce avoidance of environmental stimuli, and selective learning about the environment through negative reinforcement: that is, removal of an aversive stimulus (Schneirla,

1965). Changes in response to the same stimulus over time present a model of habituation and learning. With repeated exposure to the same stimulus, A-processes may wane. Similarly, W-processes may be attenuated by repeated exposure to stimulation so that A-processes are activated rather than W-processes–habituation (Schneirla, 1965, p. 389–91 in 1972). By this account, in habituation, the A/W threshold has been raised, relative to objective stimulus intensity (but see Hailman, 1970).

With accumulated learning, "perceptual meanings often modify, occlude, or reverse the earlier effects of stimulus intensity" (Schneirla, 1959). In the succession of interactions, an animal's previous response shapes subsequent behavior, with "qualitatively new processes of selective learning developing through the situation-altering effect of action" (Schneirla, 1959). By this account, the organism's behavioral adaptation to stimulation by habituation, sensitization, and selective learning can be described as an ongoing interplay of A and W tendencies, and changes in the threshold between them.

In a later discussion, Tobach and Schneirla (1968) proposed an A/W analysis over levels of integration that includes both approach and withdrawal as elements of aggressive behavior. "Attack on the biosocial level is an intense approach response; on the psychosocial level it is an integration of both approach and withdrawal. The withdrawal in this instance is complexly elaborated on the psychosocial level as it derives from anticipation of future events based on past experience, which may be defined as fear." (On this point, see Figure 1 and discussion below, in "Dialectical Approaches to the Study of Behavior.")

Learning Shifts the Threshold for Aggressive Behavior

The profound alteration of social behavior by repeated tests over the life-span exemplifies learning-produced changes in response to stimulus events.

In the following figure from Cairns, MacCombie, & Hood (1983), the developmental course of aggressive behavior by isolation-reared male mice is depicted, with the first behavioral test occurring at different developmental periods, followed by

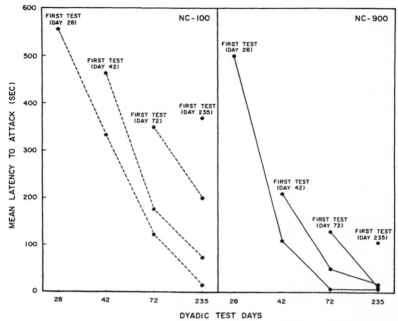

Figure 2. Latency to first attack in mice repeatedly tested beginning at age twenty-eight, forty-two, or seventy-two days. At age 235 days, the three longitudinal groups are compared to littermates tested for the first time at that age. (NC-100 = low-aggressive line; NC-900 = high-aggressive line). Cairns, MacCombie, & Hood (1983). © The American Psychological Association. Reprinted with permission.

repeated tests. Two kinds of mice are represented, those selectively bred for high aggressiveness (NC-900) and those bred for low aggressiveness (NC-100). Most interesting for this discussion are the dramatic changes in latency to attack between the first and second test, regardless of age. This difference is the result of a very brief (ten minute) social encounter that often does not involve aggressive behavior—mere exposure to the test situation is sufficient to hasten the appearance of aggressive behavior in subsequent tests. By one possible interpretation using an A/W analysis, this change might be described as a change in A/W balance; after the first test experience, sensitization to social stimulation may lower the A/W threshold, which is the boundary between A and W where aggressive behavior occurs, by this model (Fig. 1). If duration of exposure to social stimulation is considered to be a measure of accumulated stimulus intensity, then over repeated tests the A/W threshold becomes lower and aggressive behavior arising at the A/W threshold results from less stimulation (shorter duration of exposure to stimulation) than in early tests. Latency to first attack is reduced over repeated tests.

Other interpretations are possible (see below). The effects of social learning also depend on the developmental stage and the prior experience of the subject (Cairns, Hood, & Midlam, 1985). For animals that are too young, isolation housing does not enhance aggressiveness. Moreover, changes in the subject's behavior after social experience will evoke altered responses in the social partner in subsequent encounters (Cairns, Hood, & Midlam, 1985).

The opposite process occurs in animals housed together and continually exposed to social stimulation. Animals habituated to social stimulation are less reactive and are slower to attack a novel conspecific (Hood & Cairns, 1989), perhaps as a function of higher A/W thresholds produced by continuous social stimulation.

Individual Differences in A/W Processes

Schneirla noted the prevalence of individual differences in these behavioral domains. "Presumably, the relationships of A-processes to W-processes attain varying patterns of central control through development, depending upon species abilities, individual tensional levels, and other conditions. The limitations of generalizing in these matters are shown not only by comparisons of vertebrate classes and of precocial and altricial types within classes, but also of individuals within a species, in their patterns of A/W development" (Schneirla, 1965, p. 393 in 1972).

"Because this theory views behavioral development as a progression of patterned changes resulting from the roles of the 'maturation' and 'experience' variables functioning intimately together in fused complexes, both structural and behavioral phenotypes would be expected to arise according to circumstances . . . Depending upon individual conditions, such phenotypes might diverge toward the dominance of either A-processes or of W-processes over behavior" (Schneirla, 1965, p. 400 in 1972). "Individual conditions" here would include all experiences of the organism, its current state of excitability, its developmental history, and relevant external conditions. Any of these factors might alter the A/W threshold, so that some individuals might approach stimuli of higher intensities which for other individuals produce withdrawal.

Natural selection or selective breeding, as "genetic assimilation," may induce alterations over generations in individuals' characteristic receptor, neurotransmitter and hormone response parameters, factors that influence A/W balance. In particular, there is the possibility of some extreme individuals of "abnormally high tension" showing predominant W-tendencies (Schneirla, 1965). Individual differences may arise from differences in "characteristics of receptor and other structural-functional specializations . . . These individual situation-canalizing factors also are of course results of natural selection" (Schneirla, 1965). Schneirla particularly notes that in "individuals of abnormally high tension," W-processes may gain a continuous tonic support (1965, p. 384 in 1972), so that withdrawal behaviors would characterize some types of individuals.

Selective Breeding Shifts the Threshold for Aggressive Behavior

One significant aspect of Cairns' program of research has been the implementation of selective breeding for differential aggressive behavior (for a review, see Cairns, Gariépy, & Hood, 1990; on females, see Hood & Cairns, 1988; Hood, 1988, 1992). As a method of analyzing sources of individual differences in behavior, and to delineate the processes involved in organism-environment interaction effects, selective breeding procedures were carried out for twenty-five generations. As a result, the behavioral phenotype shifted rapidly within a few generations. In the chapter by Gariépy (this volume), the progression of behavioral changes produced by selective breeding in this series of studies is presented. Briefly, the change produced is in the low-aggressive line. In that line, males are less likely to approach, slower to attack (see NC-100 in Figure 2 above) and more likely to flee, freeze, kick, or show a startle reaction in response to social stimulation (see Gariépy, this volume).

Can we think of these experimentally produced individual differences as differences in A/W thresholds? The application here is inevitably more complex. Because low-aggressive line males show a distinctive pattern of behaviors oriented toward reducing stimulation—they flee or freeze when first approached by a conspecific—we might postulate that they are "individuals of abnormally high tension" for whom *any* social stimulation evokes W-responses. Only after a relatively long period of social exposure (minutes rather than seconds) do the low-aggressive line males habituate sufficiently to enter the realm of the hypothesized A/W threshold, where instead of W-responses, other behaviors such as attacks become possible.

Alternatively, we might postulate that high-aggressive line males are "individuals of abnormally high tension" because they rapidly attack, and attack behaviors will function to reduce stimulation if the social partner then flees. If we consider attack as a W-response (as Schneirla initially did), then both lines respond with W-responses, ones of different quality (see the discussion by Gariépy in this volume).

Other lines of evidence can help to clarify these possible interpretations. Neurotransmitter and peripheral hormone levels have been characterized in the selectively bred lines, for dopamine (Gariépy, this volume; Lewis, Gariépy, Gendreau, Nichols & Mailman, 1994), and for GABA (Weerts, Miller, Hood, & Miczek, 1992). These findings from both dopamine and GABA support an interpretation of the high-aggressive line as strongly aroused, relative to the low-aggressive line. For example, the low line, but not the high line, shows elevated levels of endogenous GABA inhibitory activity. If GABA system activity is experimentally elevated in the high-aggressive line by administration of the anxiolytic agent benzodiazepine, then the level of aggressive behavior by those animals is significantly reduced, and prosocial behavior is increased. This result suggests that animals in the high aggressive line may be *more* anxious or fearful than the low-aggressive line, a somewhat surprising interpretation.

This interpretation is supported by the results of cortico-sterone assays after social stress: twenty minutes after the initiation of social contact, high-aggressive line males show a significant increase in corticosterone, relative to low-aggressive and control line males (Hood & Jones, in preparation). These findings are shown in Figure 3, in which circulating levels of the stress-related hormone corticosterone are represented for males after no social stress ("undisturbed") and for males assayed twenty minutes after the start of a ten-minute social encounter. Parallel assays of testosterone show no reliable pattern of difference among the lines.

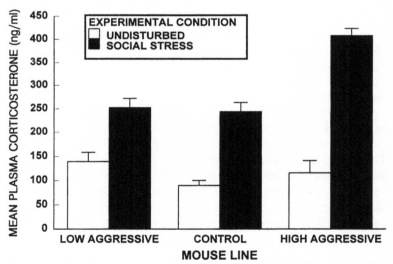

Figure 3. Circulating corticosterone in mice selectively bred for low levels of aggressive behavior, high levels of aggressive behavior, and an unselected control line. Samples were taken twenty minutes after the start of a dyadic behavioral test, for the "social stress" groups.

By these convergent findings from assays of dopamine, GABA, and corticosterone, high-aggressive line males are more aroused, possibly more fearful (if we interpret the endogenous GABA activity of low-aggressive line males as anxiolytic), and, of course, more aggressive, than the low-aggressive line males. Hormone-behavior correlations show that corticosterone, *not* testosterone, distinguishes high and low-aggressive individuals. Within the low-aggressive line, corticosterone is positively related to freezing behavior, as expected from research by other investigators. However, considering the lines together, corticosterone is positively correlated with attack frequency and negatively correlated with attack latency, and shows the opposite relationship to freezing behavior. Testosterone levels are not correlated with differences among the lines in aggressive behavior (Hood and Jones, in preparation).

Summary

This discussion demonstrates the range of possible interpretations of A/W theory in relation to some experimental findings, as well as the degree to which the theory is yet incompletely specified in relation to specific social behaviors, and some possible directions for progress in the analysis. The interpretation of aggressive behaviors as A- or W-responses or as A/W boundary events raises problematic issues, for example, in interpreting the effects of stimulus events consisting of behavior by other animals, in characterizing subjects' internal motivational states and in understanding the relationship between neurotransmitter or hormonal states, motivational or emotional states, and behavior. At present these relationships are provocatively ambiguous. However, the potential usefulness of this effort may follow from a reconsideration of the role of fear vs. appetitive motivation in the instigation of aggressive behavior. For example, if children fight because of fear, not just from anger, or perhaps from a dynamic interaction of both states, then a specific and different course of therapeutic intervention would be recommended to fit the new motivational analysis.

The present discussion originated in a tangle of nature-nurture issues. Empirical studies with these animals have been explicitly designed to assess nature-nurture, or genotype-environment, or—more accurately—organism-experience interactions over the life span. To directly determine the extent of plasticity in the genotype by challenging the stability of differences produced after selective breeding (as recommended by Kuo, 1976), animals from each selectively bred line have been tested in a variety of conditions and in life-span longitudinal series (Cairns, MacCombie & Hood, 1983; Hood & Cairns, 1989). The results of these manipulations underscore the significance of Kuo's recommendation: by varying social rearing and testing conditions, selective breeding effects may be obscured or eliminated. The phenotype produced by selective breeding holds true only within the exact conditions of the selective breeding procedure itself. If the experiential field of the organism is altered, the phenotype responds with dramatic and rapid adaptation in patterns that are not limited by its particular selective breeding history. These findings exemplify Schneirla's (1966) assertion that with regard to "genetic" and "environmental" factors, the "condition of related but disjunctive entities is improbable . . . [Rather,] at all stages, the maturational and experiential processes, and the trace effects of these processes, are inseparably coalesced." (For discussion, see Johnston, 1987; Lehrman, 1970.)

The question remains of why the forms and sequencing of aggressive behavior are similar in animals that fight immediately, and in animals that fight reluctantly or only after an attack by the partner. Females show the same forms as males, in maternal aggression and in virgin females (Hood & Cairns, 1988; Hood, 1988, 1992). How is it that these animals are doing what looks like the "same" thing? How are these most durable and reliable forms produced? Can approach-withdrawal theory help us answer these questions? To continue, the question will be reframed in the context of another theory, the theory of the dialectic.

Dialectical Approaches to the Study of Behavior

Social behavior in its full expression challenges our most advanced theoretical conceptions. Sameroff (1982) noted that "theories at the level of complexity of clockworks and thermostats are used to explain the phenomena of social systems. Although theorizing at any level is better than nothing, a level of theorizing appropriate to the level of complexity will be a necessity." To extend theory from mechanics to dynamics, the concept of development can be taken as primary for understanding social systems. Here we will extend this speculative account to consider dialectical relationships in social development. In an early prediction, the dialectical theorist Engels (1880/1940) proposed that "the organic process of development, both of the individual and of the species, by differentiation, [will be] the most striking test of rational dialectics."

Schneirla's developmental theory of A/W processes proposes a relationship between approach and withdrawal that is here construed as a dialectical relationship. Schneirla (1965) defines approach and withdrawal as "antagonistic and reciprocal." Tobach (1970) further notes that ". . . euphoria and dysphoria are continuously changing into each other as they are contiguous on the [tensional adjustment or emotion] continuum." She proposes a dynamic nonlinear relationship between qualities. For example, positive feedback produced by a quantitative change (such as a repetition of social behavior) might cause an "explosion," like fighting behavior, or an "implosion," like freezing behavior. On the psychosocial level, then, A and W may be seen as components of a dialectic, organized in an opposition that energizes behavior and provides a possible source for new forms of behavior. Other theorists have posited opposed factors as basic to behavior (recently, Archer, 1976; Miller, reviewed in Gray, 1987; Solomon, 1980). It is Schneirla's proposal of a *developmental* analysis of opposed factors that distinguishes his theory.

In particular, Tobach and Schneirla (1968) characterize aggressive behavior as a boundary event. "The apparent paradoxical character of aggression as both approach and withdrawal . . . (is an) example of a mesolevel. It is the hallmark of the levels concept that each level contains within itself the possibility of change to a preceding or a successive level. Where both tendencies are strongly in evidence a mesolevel is formed." (On the concept of levels, see Tobach, this volume.)

To explore the implications of a dialectical-developmental conception, the fundamental principles of dialectical theory are presented, based on Hegel's ontological analysis in his early work, *Science of Logic* (1812; 1969). In particular, this question will be raised: Where do complex forms of behavior come from, and *how* do these forms arise from simple behavioral taxes like A and W? What is it that happens in the process of activation or antagonism of dialectical polarity—approach and withdrawal—that creates complexity, like the elaborate forms of species-typical behavior?

Dialectical Theory vs. Reductionism

Early theorists of the organism, including J. S. Haldane, J. B. S. Haldane, Needham, and Novikoff, have proposed a conception of the organism as a dynamic, spontaneously active integrated whole (see Greenberg, this volume). This conception contrasts sharply with the assumption of reductionist scientists in the positivist tradition. By the reductionist view, the organism is best understood when it is reduced to its simplest parts, such as (for sociobiology) its genes. The organism is conceived as an assembly of specific fixed parts working together like a machine, reactive when acted upon by an external stimulus. Behavioral processes are seen as epiphenomena of physical structures, and every ability or behavior is assumed to have a physical mechanism; an organ, a structure, or a concrete representation (for example, an engram located in the brain). According to this model, it is by understanding the parts that we can deduce the behavior of the organism. The reductionist model is a deductive linear model based on group differences in selected outcome variables. It is not a developmental model. Biologists, in particular, "represent today the stronghold of reductionism and antitheory" (Sameroff, 1982). In addition, Sameroff notes that ". . . positivism was antithetical to a discipline that took as its subject matter, development (i.e. the manner in which facts and their interrelations change over time)." (For a discussion, see Allen, 1987; Lerner, 1986, 1992.)

By contrast, dialectical theory is an open systems theory. The organism functions like a flame or a river; it remains although materials pass through it. The conception of an organism as a complexly organized whole with embedded interactive parts adds the properties of multiple relationships to each of the parts. The parts of the whole are defined by their relationships to each other, not by some quality that each has independently. Furthermore, these relationships are not themselves fixed or static. The philosopher of science Kosok (1976) views dialectical theory as a meta-theory that requires specific domain-related subtheories for its application. Dialectical logic "addresses itself not to the primary data of a particular science as such, but to the developed or quasi-developed theoretical structures *of* the sciences." As Sartre (1960) noted: "[H]ow the dialectic process can bring about the unity of dispersive profusion and integration must be discovered empirically *in each instance.*"

The use of dialectical relations as a basis for understanding reality, rather than as a method of dialogue, originates from the German philosopher Georg Wilhelm Frederich Hegel. This discussion draws only from his *Science of Logic* (1812; 1969), in which he presents a view of natural phenomena as resulting from the activity of opposed entities maintained in tension, one with the other. Later works by Hegel and by other theorists used this conception to understand social organization: Marx, Engels, Sartre, de Beauvoir, and others. Dialectical theory and methods were the focus of lively discussion in the 1970s in the USA and Britain, for example, in the journal *Human Development* (especially in 1975 and 1976) under the leadership of Riegel (1976), Rychlak (1976) and Meacham (1977); also see Datan and Reese (1977) and Sameroff (1983). Compared to reductionist or mechanical models of behavioral development, dialectical models seemed timely and promising.

The present discussion aims to build on that work, rather than to critique it (although that also would be useful: see Baltes and Cornelius, 1977; Heshka, 1986), in order to explore the possible significance of dialectical theory for developmental theory. This task involves simultaneously negotiating Hegel's dense prose and also opening a capacious intellectual space for the radical imagination to obtain perspective on Hegel's proposal. To begin, it will be useful to comment on two prevalent misconceptions. Hegel's ontology is not simple idealism, and it is not teleological. The end of the developmental or historial process does not act to shape the process. Elucidating these points exceeds the scope of this chapter: to suspend disbelief will suffice (or see Flay, 1984).

In various passages of Hegel's discussions this proposal is put forth: that reality is relational, and the relations are fluid ones. Change is fundamental. The pattern of these relations gives the world both material and functional continuity. These patterns constitute both evolution and individual development. After reading Lamarck's 1809 work, *Philosophie zoologique*, Hegel proclaimed the relevance of dialectics to science: "that which is dialectical therefore constitutes the moving spirit of scientific progress." (Hegel, 1830/1970; the *Encyclopedia*: Section 81 of Remarks). Decades later, Engels (1880/1940) proposed that dialectical relationships exist in the world, as well as in our thinking about the world: "To me there could be no question of building the laws of dialectics of nature, but of discovering them in it and evolving them from it."

More recently, Levins and Lewontin (1985) have presented dialectical theory as a challenge to the reductionist program in biology. Interestingly, in the process of formulating their book, *The Dialectical Biologist*, they "set about to write a chapter on dialectics—only to discover that in twenty-five years of collaboration we had never discussed our views systematically!" Those views represent a conception of development that turns reductionism inside out: Process is prior to structure and structure is but the transitory appearance of process. They are reciprocally determined. Activity or change is the basic state of nature, arising from inner contradiction at every level. It is from this activity that new forms emerge. "For us, contradiction is not only epistemic and political, but ontological in the broadest sense. Contradictions between forces are everywhere in nature, not only in human social institutions" (Levins & Lewontin, 1985).

Three principles of the dialectical process put forward by Levins and Lewontin (1985) are paraphrased here:

I. Self-negation or internal contradictions consist of tension or energy that produces dynamic change. Stability in form or function results from a process of internal self-regulation, so that equilibrium is a dynamic balance, a form of motion, in which change is always potential.

II. Interpenetration of entities (for example, organism and environment) occurs at the boundary of two domains, so that small changes in one domain can produce large effects in the other.

III. Integrative levels of entities are distinct in terms of complexity, qualitative differences and integrated interactions at boundaries. Changes arising from lower levels may appear unpredictable when viewed from higher levels of complexity.

Dialectical Change as Reflection and Transformation

To characterize the change process itself and how it operates to produce novel forms is important for the potential application of dialectical theory to developmental science. In dialectical theory, change results from a process of reflection within a dialectical relationship. It is the tension or contradiction between the two elements and their reflection of each other in the dialectic that creates a new entity at the next higher level of ontology.

> More precisely, when the difference of reality is taken into account, it develops from differences into opposition, and from this into contradiction, so that in the end, the sum total of all realities simply becomes absolute contradiction within itself. Ordinary—but not speculative—thinking, which abhors contradiction, as nature abhors a vacuum, rejects this conclusion; for in considering contradiction, it stops short at the one-sided *resolution* of it into *nothing*, and fails to recognize the positive side of contradiction where it becomes *absolute activity* and absolute ground . . . Now the thing, the subject, the Notion, is just this negative unity itself; it is inherently self-contradictory, but it is no less the *contradiction resolved*: it is the *ground* that contains and supports its determinations (Hegel, 1812/1969, p. 442).

The concept Hegel used to describe the process of dialectical activity or change is "sublation"; the technical term in German is *Aufhebung* or *aufheben*, to be *aufgehoben*. The word has a double meaning: to reverse or cancel (as in mathematical re-

duction of fractions), to balance one thing with the other—and
also to lift up, to keep or preserve, to be "utterly absorbed" (from
the Muret-Sanders Dictionary and elsewhere). The process of
sublation is one by which two entities defined in a relationship
of opposition are lifted up and transformed by being represented
in that relationship at a higher level of reflection or complexity.
In a dialectical process the oppositions are not just abolished but
are preserved by "transformative transcendence" in new synthe-
ses as unities in opposition (see Flay, 1984 for a discussion).

The elegant discussion by Kosok (1976; also see 1984), who
also constructs his account from the *Science of Logic*, most usefully delineates the activities of negation, reflection, and levels of
complexity. He characterized the dialectical process as a
"continual cyclic feedback relation that spirals, as the process returns to the same element on a higher level, a new level. In transcendence . . . each opposed element is canceled and yet preserved as a negative element while being raised to a higher or
richer level, in which it is joined with its opposite in a state of
transition without contradiction." Moreover, "dialectical logic is
a type of temporal logic involving a memory system in which the
negation of an element preserves the negated element as *that
from which* the negation appeared." The negation "retains the
previous state as a perspective of orientation" or as a reference
base for the next higher level of complexity. This reflection creates a "mutual 'boundary' state of mutual implication as possibilities." The process of reflection is infinite, and never resolved
as a completed product. Determinacy at each level requires a
higher level of analysis and reflection to reveal the opposition of
the relevant contraries. When an account of a natural phenomenon contains contradictions, those serve as "indicators of
the need to expand the context of a universe of discourse; an expansion of 'the given terms'." Moreover, this system is "open to
empirical validation within a historically developing consciousness" (Kosok, 1976). Such a dynamic ontological organization
would seem to poise organisms to spring into change,
developmental transformation, and behavioral elaboration.

Dialectical Relations and Relations of Relations

One formulation of Hegel's ontological account of the nature of relations between things, and how they operate to maintain reality is presented in Figure 4, based on his *Science of Logic*. Three levels of relationships are proposed by Hegel.

I. Positing Reflection: "Reflectedness into Self"

This first level of Hegel's account obliquely addresses the classical question: "Why is there something rather than nothing?" Hegel takes it as given from immediate perception that entities exist (for a discussion, see Flay, 1984). Hegel asserts that an entity exists as a process of relationship between figure and ground: an entity exists in opposition to the indeterminate domain of nonexistence, nothingness, or nonbeing. The relationship of opposition consists of a state of tension or contradiction within the entity as a result of its inner reflection-and-negation of the outer domain of nonbeing. By reflecting the domain of nonbeing, an entity includes within itself a reflection of nonbeing. That opposition maintains the entity as an existent bounded thing against the context of nonexistence. Hegel calls this level of ontology "the one of the thing." In Figure 4, the entity "e" exists because it is "Not-that," or (e = not [not e]), and that reflection-and-negation of "not-e" is represented inside the entity e. This relationship of tension is maintained in infinitesimal moments, or infinitely small units of reflection. (It may be useful here to imagine activity at the level of fundamental particles of matter, conceived as constantly winking back and forth between matter and antimatter—being and nonbeing—in infinitesimal moments.) This level of ontology can be thought of as "simple" being.

II. External Reflection: "Repelling of Reflection from Itself"

In the second level of relationships, Hegel addresses the issue of concrete existents: "Why is there this thing and not some other thing?" At this level, an entity is in relationship with another entity, so that each entity is distinguished as not being that

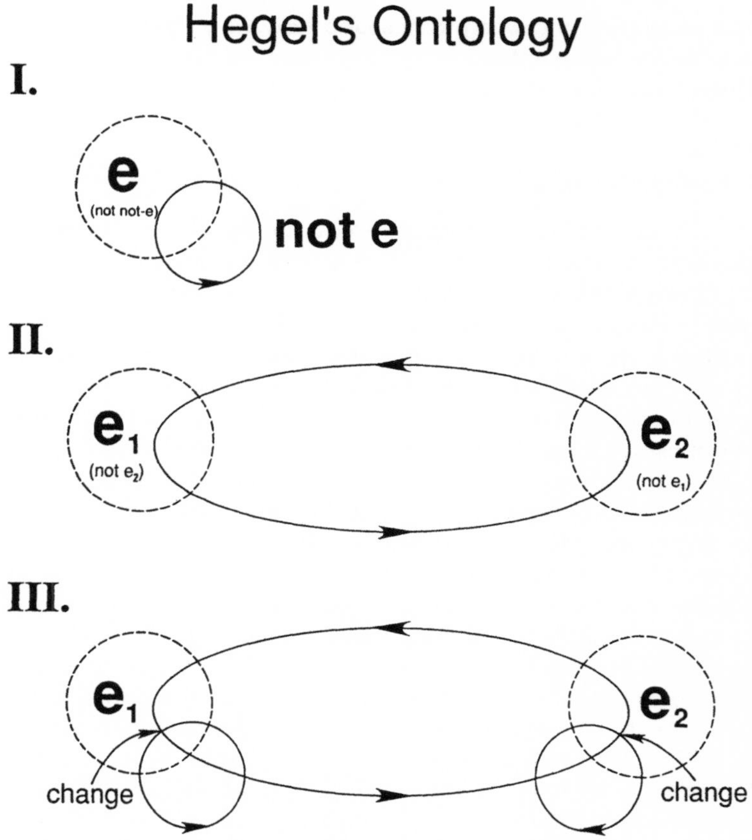

Hegel's Ontology

I.

II.

III.

Figure 4. Hegel's ontology is represented at three levels.

I. *Simple being.* An existent entity e in a context of nonexistence. This can be imagined as a one-dimensional point, or as a bounded entity, one which contains within itself the reflection of its negation, (not e). The relationship of reflection and negation is represented by a circle (with an arrow on it). The union of contraries e and -e generates activity, imaginable as winking, or phasic motion to and fro, in and out, between two states. This motion maintains the entity and generates the next level.

(continued next page)

other entity, as being a different entity from the other. Entity "A" exists (as "A") because it is "not entity B" or, in Figure 4, (e_1 = not e_2) and that reflection-and-negation is represented within each entity. This level of ontology is inherently relational, and Hegel asserts that the property of relatedness becomes "self-sub-sistent itself" as the determinate quality of a particular thing. "The difference of things has sublated itself" to create a new form, that of quality (Hegel, 1812/1969 p. 491). The second ontological level of relationship provides specificity and quality to an entity that distinguishes it from everything else that exists that is not that entity. However, it is not an essential quality inherent in that entity, but rather a process of negation-and-reflection that produces specificity and quality. It is that entity in relation to another entity, and their internal mutual reflection of each other, their providing a context for each other, that provides each with a specific identity. Again, the relationship is one of negation (each is not the other) and reflection. In reflecting and

---

(continued from previous page)

II. *Relational being.* Two entities, each a union of e and not-e, are in rela-tion to each other as e_1 and e_2. The entity e_1 contains a reflection and negation of e_2 as "not-me" and gains concrete identity in the process. The parallel operation occurs for e_2. In relational being, the shape formed by the relationship of reflection between the two entities re-quires two dimensions to exist. The relationships of the two entities here are represented in the form of an ellipse; there are two reflections here, not one.

III. *Becoming.* Movement in time occurs because of the relationship be-tween simple being and relational being. That relationship is indicated here as the points of intersection between the circles representing Level I and the ellipse representing Level II processes of negation and reflec-tion. The points of intersection are marked by arrows labeled "change." As a result of the tension generated by the union of two relationships within each entity: simple being (e and not-e) and relative being (e_1 and not-e_2, within e_1, and the parallel union of simple and relative being within e_2), these shapes may spin or cycle like alternating current. The movement of spinning or cycling creates three dimensions. In three-dimensional space, entities arise and pass away into nonexistence: *Becoming*.

negating the other, each becomes a specific thing. This possibility arises because each of the two entities is simultaneously existing by positing reflection, that is, maintaining itself as an entity in relation to nonexistence. In this sense, the concreteness of discrete entities arises from and subsumes the inner tension of positing reflection (existence vs. nonexistence). The quality of discreteness is possible because each entity maintains a relationship with the background (nonbeing) and also with another entity.

III. Determining Reflection: The Unity of Positing Reflection and External Reflection

Hegel's third level of ontology exists as a relationship between the first two levels. This level addresses the questions: "How can there be anything new under the sun?" and "How can there be at the same time both change and continuity?" By relating the first level of ontology to the second level of ontology, a new level arises: Being is transformed into *Becoming*, or coming to be. Time and change are present at this stage of the analysis.

The relationship of negation and reflection at this level is a relationship of relationships. This third level of relationship provides a context for the second level, within which simple beings enter into relationships and are discrete entities. The third level derives from the relationship between each entity's inner tension with nonexistence (being vs. nonbeing: the first level), and each existent's inner tension with another existent (this vs. that: the second level). It is the relationship of simple being (e = not [not e]) to discrete being (e_1 = not e_2) that transforms them together into a process of change over time. When opposites are sublated, "this unity now remains their base from which they do not again emerge in the abstract significance of being and nothing" (Hegel, 1812/1969, p. 107). The dialectical outcome of this relation of relations is a new dimension, a temporal dimension of change.

These three levels of ontological tension form the emerging reality we experience in time, by Hegel's philosophy. The third level of ontology brings about the possibility of change and transformation, an appropriate starting point for developmental analysis. Hegel writes of this level that: "It is the determinate [third level] that has brought into subjection its transitoriness and its mere positedness, or has bent back its reflection into other into reflection into self" (Hegel, 1812/1969, p. 407).

The possibilities for change are represented in this way, in Hegel's account: "Quality, in its relation, passes over into an other; in its relation its alteration begins. The determination of reflection, on the other hand, has taken its otherness back into itself. It is *positedness*, negation, which however bends back into itself the relation to other, and negation which is equal to itself, the unity of itself and its other, and only through this is an *essentiality*. It is, therefore, positedness, negation; but as reflection-into-self it is at the same time the sublatedness of this positedness, infinite self-relation" (Hegel, 1812/1969, p. 407: See Figure 4). Hegel's concept of "infinite self-relation" and "reflection-into-self" will provide a link to the discussion below of fractal forms in dynamical systems.

In this Hegelian system, ambiguity in some form will be present because the process of reflection and negation is indeterminate; the reflection of e as (not e) is ambiguous because (not e) is undefined except in relation to the existent e. For that reason, e is always becoming. The universe of this logic is continually expanding (in levels) and not fixed. Hegel's use of language is open-ended and not a bounded system. The opposition of dynamics vs. form is resolved through a process of negation by which new form is produced, new articulation; a process which also preserves the original elements within the new context.

Levins and Lewontin discuss the third level in this way:

> What characterizes the dialectical world, in all its aspects as we have described them, is that it is constantly in motion. Constants become variables, causes become effects, and systems develop, destroying the conditions that gave rise to them. Even elements that appear to be stable are in a dynamic equilibrium that can suddenly become unbalanced, as when a dull gray lump of metal of a critical size becomes a fireball brighter than a thousand suns. Yet the motion is not unconstrained and uniform. Organisms develop and differentiate, then die and disintegrate. Species arise but inevitably become extinct. Even in the simple physical world we know of no uniform motion. Even the earth rotating on its axis has slowed in geologic time. The development of systems through time,

then, seems to be the consequence of opposing forces and
opposing motions (Levins & Lewontin, 1985, p. 279).

Change and the Dialectical Moment

The unit of dialectical theory is the moment, an infinitesimal measure. The Hegelian ontology yields a dynamic tension
producing activity at the core of a succession of moments, in
time and over levels of complexity. Kosok (1976) specifies that
the temporal activity of transcendence, or negation-and-reflection, generates a coupling relation from which form appears, so
that an immediate unformed element becomes formal in relationship to other elements. Kosok adds that this activity "acts as
a recursive formula producing a sequence of self-expanding
terms." In this sense, then, dialectics is not a first-order logic, but
rather a modal or tense logic.

This dynamic core of activity is similar to oriental views of
reality: Richard Wilhelm (1979) writes of the Chinese concept of
a world of polarity (Yin and Yang) and their union: "This union,
however, is not a mixing, but a formation of polar tension that
causes, in turn, a type of *rotation* . . . The rotating movement at-
tracts the elements, shaping them into forms that correspond to
its nature. The characteristic of all life is this basic duality"
(emphasis added). In Figure 4, the processes of rotation are
represented by circles or cycles at all three levels. One might
speculate that in the third level, relations of relations, the
rotations of the first level and the second level could reinforce
each other's activity (if they rotate in the same direction) or, if
they rotate in opposite directions, could oppose each other (or, to
extend the metaphor, create friction and heat, throw off sparks or
start a fire). More concisely, "the multiplication of two rotations
generally is another rotation" (Lauwerier, 1991).

This emergence of rotation (discussed below in relation to
complex numbers), and the emergence of movement or change
in time follows from a basic duality, and leads to a discussion in
the next section of the uses of temporal or successive order in
self-reflexive mathematical analyses. Interestingly, in physics,
one meaning of the concept of "moment" refers to the physical

production of rotation. The moment is the maximum *torque* in an electrical or magnetic system of positive and negative charges that any system can experience in a uniform field, as in "dipole moment" (Oxford English Dictionary). The discussion of dynamical systems below will build on this notion of rotation to link dialectical and dynamical systems theory. This link is constructed from the fact that "in dynamical systems theory we are interested in *motion* itself, in the dynamics, in the way points move . . ." (Barnsley, 1988).

Dynamical Systems and Fractal Forms in Behavior

Dynamical systems theory and applications to developmental psychology were presented in a series of lectures and workshops held in pre-conference sessions at the 1989 national meeting of the Society for Research in Child Development. Points of congruence between the assumptions of the two perspectives were elaborated in an opening address by Esther Thelen (1989): both dynamical systems and developmental theories focus on process, in both theories the assumption of nonlinear change is primary, and both include the assumption of multiple levels of causation, with a focus on patterns of variability and phase transitions. In particular, Thelen (1989) noted that "No pre-existing instructions instantiate the end-state" or the outcome in dynamical models of developmental processes, because the process is self-organizing. Dynamical systems researchers from different areas of psychology challenged us to imagine, for example, that "New behavioral forms emerge in development as a series of phase shifts, leading to complex multistable states," and that "Behavior is assembled ad hoc by what's available and what fits the task," in an assembly process that is self-organizing and self-correcting (Huber, 1989). Newtson (1989) spoke of social interactions as a Lewinian behavioral field containing coupled oscillators—the social partners. Scott Kelso (1989) invoked a consideration of the fact that in dynamical systems, it is the boundary between two domains, between chaotic and deterministic regions, that generates forms never before imagined: that boundary produces fractal forms. (See Smith & Thelen, 1993, for these discussions and others. Also see Barton, 1994; Vallacher & Nowak, 1994.)

It seemed to me that the future had arrived. In particular, it seemed that Waddington's wish had come true. In *The Strategy of the Genes* (1957) he asked: "how does development produce entities which have Form, in the sense of integration or wholeness?" "What we seem to meet in embryology are situations in which small initial differences lead to large divergences in later development. To account for this, we need something more complicated than the very simple system we have . . ." Using metaphors from geometry, he proposed that proper analyses would require open systems of differential equations designed to model coupled autocatalytic processes: a simple form of a feedback mechanism. Waddington concluded that "Unfortunately, the mathematical apparatus does not yet seem to have been developed which could enable one to discuss in any detail the conditions necessary to give rise to such states."

Dynamical systems theory appropriates a set of mathematical procedures to do just that, using procedures that are designed to fit with assumptions of change and continuous process, mathematical systems with time as an inherent component. For all of these reasons, dynamical systems are uniquely well suited for the study of organismic growth and change. These systems are "systems of difference or differential equations in which the dependent variables (states) evolve in time and/or space according to nonlinear laws" (Molenaar, in press; also see Molenaar & Oppenheimer, 1985). "The types of equilibrium in a nonlinear system may change abruptly under continuous variation of the system parameters. If this occurs, the system's ongoing behavior becomes organized in a qualitatively new way which is only determined by its own dynamics and therefore called self-organization" (Molenaar, in press). The simultaneous interaction of relationships defined in a set of coherent equations may produce an order of complexity in the output, the dependent variable, that is unpredictable, random, chaotic behavior. The production of unpredictability from a deterministic system implies that unpredictable novelty can follow from combinations of elements that in themselves are completely predictable. This empirically observed leap from deductive to novelty-producing systems can be viewed as reflecting a theoretical shift in developmental psychology from genetic determinism to an open system of epigenetic developmental change.

The possible advantages of modeling from such a set of starting assumptions are tantalizing for developmental scientists who have struggled to represent change using static statistical models. For example, the analysis of variance is designed to test group differences. The compromise attained in the repeated measures analysis of variance as a method for studying change provides only a halting approach to a dynamic conception of development (Buss, 1979, discusses these points). The hope is that by starting from a different place, from a mathematics of change, developmental theory will be set free to flow unimpeded.

Applications of Dynamical Systems Theory to Behavior

Several applications of dynamical theory to behavioral or biological systems have already been accomplished. The study of attractors, which are regions in the dynamic field that draw or repel data points, offers a dynamic method for modeling form as an alternative to static measures of central tendency. Thelen and Ulrich (1991) have modelled the development of walking and Thelen and others have modelled emotional expression in infants (see references in Thelen and Ulrich, 1991; also see Fogel, Nwokah, Dedo, Messinger, Dickson, Matuson & Holt, 1992). Dynamical analyses of cycles and the structure of variability within cycles have yielded novel interpretations of the function of randomness in biological systems. Skarda and Freeman (1987) have proposed such an analysis of brain electrical activity. The study of cyclic motor behavior in dynamical systems perspective yields domains of unpredictability and phase shifts in predictable behavior: Kugler (1986) and Kugler, Kelso, and Turvey (1982) have studied rhythmic movement. Gregson (1988; 1992) has made extensive application of dynamical systems to psychophysics. Other investigators have explored neuronal axon branching, language, and cognitive development, all using dynamical systems perspectives. Thelen and Ulrich (1991) contains references to much of this work in psychology: also see Barton (1994), Smith and Thelen (1993), Vallacher and Nowak (1994), and Metcalfe and Merrill (1988). In biology, see Degn, Holden, and Olsen (1987) for some technical treatments. Population biology is dealt with by Asmussan (1986) and others (Odom, 1988). Applications to medicine are discussed by Weiner (1989). None of these, to my knowledge, relates fractal theory to behavioral development.

Experimental Mathematics and the Discovery of Fractals

Fractals are a family of shapes that result from self-recursive iterations of groups of equations. Two points are most intriguing for the purposes of this discussion: 1) The intricate and infinitely self-reflexive forms are generated at the boundary between determinate and chaotic domains in dynamical systems; 2) In the fractal boundary, the two domains do not mix together, but rather interpenetrate in discrete shapes at every level of magnification to create an infinitely long boundary between them.

Mandlebrot in his book *The Fractal Geometry of Nature* (1977/1983) presents "a casebook and a manifesto" using examples of fractals he has discovered by empirically investigating mathematical domains and finding fractals in certain ranges of values for those domains. These "ill-defined zones of transition" (Mandelbrot, 1983) are structured in infinitely regressive scale as self-similar (but not identical) forms. (See Figure 5: also see Lauwerier, 1991.) The inductive and empirical nature of the discovery process for finding fractals is a remarkable aspect of the method. It involves selecting an interesting set of equations (the Mandelbrot fractal uses one equation: $z^2 + c = x$), setting a starting value to begin the computational series, and representing the result of the iterative series on the video screen (or other display). The sets of equations that direct the computations are sequential and self-reflexive: from one starting value, z, the result of a first iteration through the equation set is a new value (x) that is then used as the value of z for the second iteration through the same equation set to produce a third value, which becomes the value of z for the third iteration, and so on for a specific number of iterations, until the result is obtained and displayed as a point in the display, with one axis for starting values and one axis for the results. A range of starting values and intervals might be explored, for example, values from 2.75000 to 2.85000, as starting points for the computations. By this method, the outcomes of the iterative series from some particular set of starting values are represented on the screen.

Quite different outcomes are possible at different numerical ranges. For a particular starting value, some small number of iterations might take the result to a fixed value of 0. In another part of the range of starting values, the iterative series might cycle through a specific set of resulting values, without changes in the cycle, in an infinitely repeating loop. In yet another part of the range of starting values, the result of iterations might seem random or chaotic, because adjacent starting points that differ only in minute proportions (at the *n*th decimal place) produce values as results that are unrelated to each other, and that are unpredictable from the behavior of adjacent starting points. These starting values produce chaotic regions, areas where the equations produce unpredictable results. In another possible outcome, iterations might go on forever (or as long as allowed in the program) without repeating cyclic values, and without converging to a fixed value.

There are various conventions for assigning color to the results of iterative series over a range of starting values. For example, starting values that produce a predictable result might be colored black, and starting values that produce unpredictable or chaotic results might be colored white. Alternatively, one might set a critical number of iterations for any starting value, and plot the result (e.g. black if it exceeds a critical value after the iterative series and other colors depending on the number of iterations required to reach the critical value). This method plots a shape that describes the rate at which the function approaches that critical value, within the range of starting values. Domains of the range can be located in which values produce different kinds of results. The investigator can "zoom in" or tune in to a particular region of a shape by enlarging the scale or resolution, for example, by selecting a subset of the starting values and using additional decimal places for the starting values in that subset, to obtain a more detailed image of the behavior of starting values in that range. This process of tuning or focusing is limited only by

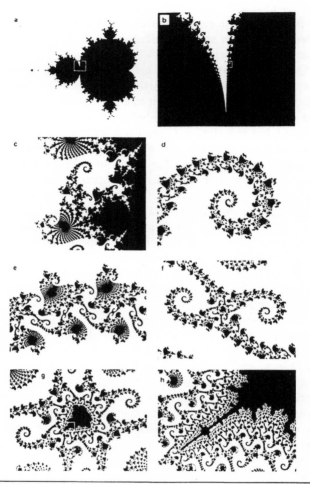

Figure 5. Zoming in on the Mandelbrot fractal. Between determinate space (black) and chaotic space (white) is a region where fractal boundaries occur, infinitely regressive and infinitely complex at every scale of measurement. Here, in successive magnifications of subsets of the region (images a-h), increasingly refined images of detailed regions show the preservation of complexity and self-similarity of form.

the speed of the computer and the degree of resolution available in the display.

Figure 5 illustrates "zooming in" at a boundary of the Mandelbrot fractal. Note that the degree of complexity at the fractal boundary is preserved at every level of magnification.

The Dialectical Power of Imaginary Numbers

The most interesting fractal shapes for biology, the Julia sets (like the Mandlebrot fractal), require a contradiction to exist. In many Julia sets and Mandlebrot fractals, there is a bounded region. The region between determinate and indeterminate regions encloses an area with a fractal boundary. These bounded fractal forms are thought to be most like cellular and biological forms, which are bounded regions enclosed by membranes containing receptors and channels for selective passage of molecules: skin, sense organ receptors, lungs, kidneys, intestines, neurons, and other cells. Interestingly, to generate these biologically relevant fractal forms requires the use of imaginary numbers, which are used to form the complex plane. In the complex two-dimensional plane, one axis of the space, and one component of the recursive equations that generate the space, is a complex number, a number derived using the imaginary number, i. The other axis is associated with the real part of the complex number. The special number i is defined as the square root of -1: $i^2 = -1$.

The contradiction inherent in imaginary numbers gives rise to a powerful ambiguity: the fractal form. In classical mathematics, the process of negation negates itself in multiplication; $-1 \times -1 = 1$. In addition, odd numbers cancel themselves and even numbers do not, in the sense that odd numbers added together produce even numbers. Any real number squared cannot equal a negative number: for this reason i is called an imaginary number. Altering the classical rules of negation to create the possibility of imaginary numbers also permits the generation of a domain of surprising proportions, infinitely complex, containing forms not found elsewhere, not predicted, and not expected: fractal forms.

The concept of imaginary numbers, which originated in antiquity from Arab, Greek and Indian mathematicians, was ridiculed and rejected as an impossible figment of delusion. It was regarded by Western thinkers as a mathematical monstrosity. However, after applications by Italian mathematicians in the sixteenth century, the seventeenth-century mathematician and philosopher Leibniz, who invented calculus and who challenged the mechanistic conceptions of nature of Descartes and Newton, issued the judgement that "Complex numbers are a fine and wonderful refuge of the divine spirit, as if it were an amphibian of existence and nonexistence" (quoted in Solomentser, 1988).

Practice has since proved Leibniz to be sound in the judgement of "fine and wonderful." It turns out that complex numbers are required for obtaining the roots of all possible algebraic equations, and that complex numbers are basic to quantum physics and electromagnetic field theory. The concept of the imaginary number is indispensable in modern mathematics. Interestingly for our discussion, the redefinition of the function of squaring that permits imaginary numbers involves a geometric *rotation* and rescaling (reflection) in the complex plane, with mirroring or *reflection* functions as similarity transformations. These lead to spiral forms (Lauwerier, 1991).

Dialectical and Dynamical Systems

Because the forms in dynamical systems theory most relevant to biological organisms are fractals derived from complex numbers, we might use a Hegelian ontological perspective to consider fractals as entities like Leibniz's amphibian, with one foot in existence and one foot in nonexistence. In Hegel's first level of ontology, the reflection of Being and Nonbeing is the dialectical basis for further levels of reflection in the continuous creation of the world. Might the dialectical interpenetration of Being and Nonbeing result in a generative fractal boundary, that in turn produces an infinity of new forms in unlimited levels of complexity?

Kosok's explication of Hegel's ontology highlights the parallels in the two philosophical domains. Like the self-referential iterative dynamical system, dialectical logic is a type of temporal logic (Kosok, 1976). The "synthesis" concept of Becoming for Hegel is "the indeterminate *state* of transition between that which is and is not . . . a single 'boundary zone' . . . distinguishing yet connecting two mutually opposed 'regions' called (e) and (not-e). This boundary zone can be regarded as a mathematical *limit relation* between two *distinct although inseparable* spaces . . . a boundary condition expressing a state of transition and transcendence" (Kosok, 1976, p. 335 ff., emphasis in original). Furthermore, the Hegelian analysis presents an infinite regress, like a fractal boundary does: "It would be possible . . . to extend the analysis indefinitely, each time increasing the subtlety and complexity present by a more *detailed* explication in depth of the ever-present Absolute of infinite interpenetrability. Thus Hegel's system would have to be regarded as essentially *open*, subject to continually higher modes of reflection" (Kosok, 1976, p. 349). The theme of interpenetrability runs through these discussions, and here the infinite regress of the fractal is implicit as an infinite series of "more detailed explication."

In the *Science of Logic* (1812/1969) Hegel writes of the "self-similar" form of reality, that it represents "an infinitely *determinable* receptivity" of "absolute porosity" in which two entities interpenetrate yet do not touch. The two entities depend on "infinite self-relation" and the result is an "in-dwelling pulsation of self-movement and spontaneous activity" (p. 442). As in the fractal forms of infinite depth, "The action . . . is *bent round* and becomes an action that returns into itself, an *infinite reciprocal action*" (p. 569). In particular, he asserts that the state of matter is "not only a matter and *also* its negation, . . . but also that in *this* thing it has, *in one and the same point,* (1) *self-subsistent* matter, and (2) its *negation* or porosity and the other *self-subsistent* matter, and that this porosity and the independent subsistence of the matters in one another as in a single point is a reciprocal negation and a penetration of the penetration" (p. 497).

Does Hegel's view anticipate the structure of fractals as a "penetration of the penetration?" Any opinion on these points would be highly conjectural, and the state of ambiguity in this synthesis will perhaps function to draw some clever analysts into the puzzle. An intriguing clue is suggested in the discussion by LeMehaute (1991) that "The fractal object is basically an intricate intermingling . . . the very complex frontier that separates each of two domains . . . [may contain] the thermodynamic significance of the fractal object . . ." which may constitute "a degree of freedom by means of which the [open] system may adjust its free energy."

Fractal Boundaries as Models for Behavioral Development

The bewitching beauty of fractal forms has assured their pre-eminence as magazine covers and graphic illustrations. There are even more astonishing features within the systems that generate these illustrations, in the mathematical properties that produce the fractal forms, and in what these properties imply about the possible nature of biological organization. These uniquely complex levels of representation may yield new ways to model the intricacies of behavior at multiple levels of scaling.

I propose that this boundary of fractal forms be conceived as an orthogonal dimension to the generating regions, as a dimension of interior depth and complexity that is potentially infinite. In particular, I propose that in the developmental analysis of some behaviors, the boundary between approach and withdrawal (as in Figure 1) might be imagined as a fractal boundary or a fractal attractor between the graded, determinate space of the A response and the nondimensional domain of the W response. At this boundary, where A and W are transformed into each other, complex species-typical forms of behavior may originate. If this is true, then perhaps the most appropriate analytical tool for investigating those origins is fractal geometry. The surprising shapes and infinite complexity of fractal forms might serve to represent the infinite regression of levels of organization of biology and behavior over time, and the possible mirroring of relationships between levels.

The application of fractal forms to behavioral development might be well suited to address the fact that behavior is itself composed of levels of analysis or causation: each act, such as touching a novel conspecific, consists of multiple levels of organization: neural impulses, muscle movements, neural integration of sensory input and motor feedback, motor adjustments in relation to sensory stimulation, and the integration of these sequences over time. Within a behavior episode, events transpire at the scale of nanoseconds (corticosterone occupies receptor complex). Over repeated episodes, patterns (such as latency to attack) change over hours, days, or over the life-span of the organism. One construction of these levels of biological and psychological and social interactions as dynamic relationships is presented in Mandell's notion of "vertical integration." He proposes that changes in electrical, chemical, and experiential components of the brain/organism may be synchronized by rate or frequency characteristics at each level and across levels (Mandell, 1980).

The realization of these ideas as scientific accounts may not yet be an immediate prospect. Barnsley (1988), in his discussion of the "lair of the wild fractals," as he likes to call them, notes that "At the present stage of development of science and mathematics, the idea of a fractal is most useful as a broad concept. Fractals are not defined by a short legalistic statement, but by the many pictures and contexts that refer to them." It may be too soon to expect an integrated application of these fields. Mandelbrot offers this critique: "The theory should ideally focus upon intrinsically interesting and realistic (but simple) dynamical systems, whose attractors are understood as fractals. The strange attractors literature—though extremely important—is far from this ideal: its fractals are usually incompletely understood, few are intrinsically compelling, and most fail to be solutions to well-motivated problems." (1983, p. 195). Future efforts in these very active areas may increasingly specify the appropriate applications of fractal theory to behavioral domains.

Representing Activity in Dynamical Systems

Lauwerier (1991) recommends that an excellent way to appreciate fractals is to watch them as they come into being on the screen in a field of values. His recommendation suggests to me that a useful approach to integrating dynamical systems and developmental theory may result from a higher-level set of algorithms that describe that developmental process. To date, representations of fractal forms show the final outcome of series of iterations. It may be that representations of the successive patterning and sudden shifts that result in the process of realizing fractal forms will offer the most appropriate level of description for applications to behavioral development. To describe the activity, rather than the outcome, of a model that changes over time might show the way to capture the complexity of organismic developmental processes. To a similar end, Abraham and Shaw's (1988) elegant figural representations of activity in three-dimensional dynamical systems show the possibility of illustrating complex moving systems. In their three-dimensional representations of cyclic behaviors, some look like bagels and some look like balls with twists and loops, externally or internally, and points of exit to other structures. These shapes may prove to be useful in modeling activity in neural circuits, which involve feedback loops at many levels of the brain. Beyond modeling activity in established patterns, the challenge of modeling the development of those loop patterns may require an additional level of abstraction in representation.

In the meantime, we can note that not all behavioral phenomena are dialectical. For detecting promising areas for dialectical analysis, ambiguity serves as a marker; it is where ambiguity prevails that dialectical processes may occur. Alternatively, where linear accounts are sufficient for addressing a question, dialectical analyses may not be required. Not all dynamical systems generate fractal boundaries. Not all behaviors are multiply determined, at any given level. One might object that these vague recommendations describe what many scientists already do. Yet the possibility of a synthesis of dialectical/dynamical analysis and developmental analysis may prove sufficiently interesting to support the labor of testing its usefulness. In the end, it is by this method that "Scientific knowledge destroys itself in order to *become* the world" (Sartre, 1960/1976).

The Practical Significance of Theory

In these wide-ranging discussions, an attempt has been mounted to articulate points of complementarity among three different theoretical sources. The risk of such an ambitious project is that one might feel, in the end, like the proverbial seeker who got on a horse and rode off in all directions. The product of this particular speculative excursion is a strong directive to empirical research for testing any new conceptions. Schneirla's A/W theory, dialectical theory and fractal theory each require specific experimental contexts for their applications. To fit them together into a conceptual model will require additional specification and experimentation. The attempted application to aggressive behavior illustrates some of these complexities.

The reconceptualization of interaction as a fractal boundary (between two social partners, between physiology and behavior, between opposed approach and withdrawal tendencies) offers several new possibilities. This new idea of interaction is not a mixing of factors in the middle ground of a continuum, but an interpenetration of the two distinct factors. The interaction is composed of directional movements, vectors or rotating forms, and the combined effects of the movements of parts can produce unexpected changes in the outcome.

Mathematical methods for modeling these forms are yet in development, but some relevant applications are available. The elegant discussion of insect social organization by Deneuborge (in Kugler, 1976) is one such application: by a dynamical systems approach, high levels of organization can be understood without recourse to instinct. (Also see Franks, Wilby, Silverman, & Tofts, 1992.) Theoretical discussions by Fentress (1976, 1991) and by Scott (1983) set the stage for applications to proximal factors in individual development. In human development, Lerner (1991) has proposed understanding development as relations of relations. Rychlak (1982) has applied a dialectical analysis to lives that evokes Block's (1971) factor analyses of change patterns over time. (Also see Ford, 1987; Ford & Lerner; 1992; Freedle, 1977; Magnusson & Allen, 1983; Cairns, 1979; Sameroff & Harris, 1979.) Interpretations of evolutionary change from a process orientation are available, in Gottlieb's reconfiguration of the

sources of evolutionary novelty (Gottlieb, 1992), and in other
extensions (Cairns, 1979; Cairns, Gariépy & Hood, 1990; Dean,
1992; Oyama, 1985; Salthe, 1985).

In considering the application of A/W theory, Tobach sets
limits on the claims made for Schneirla's theory. "The concepts
offered by Schneirla may be useful in breaking the set in which
modern-day experimentalists function. These concepts are not
offered as theories to be tested as deductive experiments, and
thus "proved" or "disproved"; they offer, instead, a means of
organizing existing data, and asking questions about the data in
such a way as to formulate further inductive types of studies"
(Tobach, 1970, p. 239). A/W theory challenges scientists to
pursue a developmental analysis that explains behavioral
development in parsimonious and general terms. Schneirla's
theory is radical because it offers an analysis of the fundamental
elements of development, and the processes that animate them,
that posits no invisible entities: no innate sign-stimuli, no
engram in the brain, no instinct to produce a fixed action pattern,
and no genetic program. Rather, it proposes that form arises
from process. "The logical alternative to nativism is neither to
minimize the weight of genomic influences underlying development, nor is it compatible with shifting the emphasis to
"experience" by interpreting this term incorrectly as synonymous with conditioning and learning. Nativists typically
underestimate the subtlety, indirectness, and variety of relationships prevalent in development between the complexes denoted
by the terms "maturation" and "experience," which are not
simply interrelated but constitute a fused system in each stage
(Schneirla, 1957). This theory, then, is much more than "interactionism" (Schneirla, 1965, p. 352). Is a "fused system" one that
supports interpenetration?

Machine or Motion

A useful approach to understanding the practical significance of theory may be to contrast the perspective that results
from taking alternative views. Analyses of aggressive behavior
from the perspective of ethology and from the developmental
perspective will make the contrast. If we concur with Campbell

(1974) that "One of the lessons of evolutionary epistemology is that there exists no literal language for describing truth; all language, including mathematics being metaphorical rather than literal or direct when used as in science for descriptive functions," then why does it matter, in practical terms, which metaphor for truth we use—machine or motion? The most direct way to evaluate this question may be to examine the practical results of adopting alternative metaphors: machine (the ethological view) or process (the developmental view).

The Nobel Prize-winning ethologist Niko Tinbergen wrote in 1968 of an "attack-withdrawal" behavior system that maintains territorial boundaries in animals. Citing the Nazi era specifically, he notes that under Hitler, "the 'attack fighting' was set ablaze by playing the myth of the Herrenvolk." He concludes with his view of our own "unfortunate" species, which has created the danger of human self-annilihation by nuclear war:

> "We scientists will have to sublimate our aggression into an all-out attack on the enemy within . . . I should like to conclude by saying a few words to my colleagues of the younger generation . . . It is no use denying that the chances of designing the necessary preventive measures are small, let alone the chances of carrying them out. It is difficult for my generation to know how seriously you take the danger of mankind destroying his own species. But those who share the apprehension of my generation might perhaps, with us, derive strength from keeping alive the thought that has helped so many of us in the past when faced with the possibility of imminent death. Scientific research is one of the finest occupations of our mind. It is, with art and religion, one of the uniquely human ways of meeting nature, in fact, the most active way. If we are to succumb, and even if this were to be ultimately due to our own stupidity, we could still, so to speak, redeem our species. We could at least go down with some dignity, by using our brain for one of its supreme tasks, by exploring to the end. (Tinbergen, 1968, p. 1418)

The trenchant despair in the ethologist's conclusion follows from his positing of the source of evil in our own hearts: "the enemy within" is the genetic architecture of our emotions,

hopelessly outmoded by the rapid pace of cultural-technical evolution. Our cortex and our brainstem are at loggerheads, he says.
They are at war. The brain is its own enemy. Tinbergen concurs
with Lorenz that "elimination, through education, of the internal
urge to fight will turn out to be very difficult, if not impossible"
(Tinbergen, 1968).

Interestingly he notes that "I now agree (however belat-
edly) with Schneirla that we must extend our interest to earlier
stages of development and embark on a full-scale program of
experimental embryology of behavior" (Tinbergen, 1968). Yet
clearly he imagines a mechanistic system, mixing metaphors to
ask "How does the behavior machinery develop as the individual grows up?" Why, like constructing a car in a factory, he says.
He posits an endless chain of Sollwerte or templates to account
for human learning. These are programs for behavior that arise
from unknown sources to direct the flow of experience. Early in
his essay he notes that "Ethologists tend to believe that we still
carry within us a number of behavioral characteristics of our
animal ancestors, which cannot be eliminated by different ways
of upbringing, and that our group territorialism is one of those
ancestral characters" (Tinbergen, 1968). He assumes his conclusion without presenting further evidence.

The alternative view from a developmental perspective asserts that behavior arises from the interaction of organisms with
environments of predictable specific qualities. The result is an
optimistic array of myriad possibilities, including the possibility
that by reflecting on ourselves, using scientific and other means,
we may transcend many limits in the present situation. "The
essence of dialectic analysis lies in the fact that it forces reformu-
lations and transformation of presently accepted and artificially
fixed conceptualizations. It is opposed to any type of fixed-
substance notion, whether the concepts apply to the self, world,
or self-world interaction" (Kosok, 1976, p. 341). Levins and
Lewontin present a succinct description of the mindset of a di-
alectician: "First, it accepts as primary the heterogeneity of
individual life histories and of social developments. Far from
seeing the variations as obscuring or even illuminating the
underlying uniform ideal, it assumes the contradictions within
and between societies to be the motive force of human history, so

that the heterogeneity itself becomes the proper object of study. Second, a dialectical analysis does not ascribe intrinsic properties either to individuals or to societies, but stresses the interpenetration of individual and social properties and forces" (1985, p. 258).

By the careful articulation of social science as social action embedded in societal meaning systems, scientists act as social agents. An excellent example of this creative process is Richard Lerner's analysis of the political misuses of biological determinism (Lerner, 1992). Other valuable perspectives are discussed in Hunter (1991), in the edited volumes by Rose (1982a; 1982b), and in the new theoretical integrations by Wittig (1985) and Gowaty (1992).

It seems fitting to end this discussion not with an attempt at premature closure, not with smashing clashes or exhortations, but rather to exit the hall of mirrors and turn to a gentler style from another era with a statement on scientific interpretation and intersubjectivity by a process-oriented mathematician/philosopher, Alfred North Whitehead (1929, p. 162):

> Thus, estimates of quantity in space and time, and, to some extent, even estimates of order, depend on the individual observer. But what are the crude deliverences of sensible experience, apart from that world of imaginative reconstruction which for each of us has the best claim to be called our real world? Here the experimental psychologist steps in. We cannot get away from him. I wish we could, for he is frightfully difficult to understand. Also, sometimes his knowledge of the principles of mathematics is rather weak, and I sometimes suspect— No, I will not say what I sometimes think: probably he, with equal reason, is thinking the same sort of thing of us.

NOTE

*Important support for the preparation of this article was provided by Richard M. Lerner, Ethel Tobach, Gary Greenberg, Robert B. Cairns,

Joseph C. Flay, Michael Vicario, Vladimir Skorikov, Peter C. M. Molenaar, David Eastzer, Donald H. Ford, Paul Cornwell, and Anne C. Petersen.

REFERENCES

Abraham, R. H., & Shaw, C. D. (1988). *Dynamics: The geometry of behavior.* Santa Cruz, CA: Aerial Press.

Allen, G. E. (1987). Materialism and reductionism in the study of animal consciousness. In G. Greenberg & E. Tobach (Eds.), *Cognition, language and consciousness: Integrative levels.* Hillsdale, NJ: Erlbaum.

Archer, J. (1976). The organization of aggression and fear in vertebrates. In P. P. G. Bateson & P. H. Klopfer (Eds.), *Perspectives in ethology,* Vol. 2. New York: Plenum.

Asmussan, M. A. (1986). Regular and chaotic cycling in models from population and ecological genetics. In M. F. Barnsley & S. G. Demko (Eds.), *Chaotic dynamics and fractals.* New York: Academic Press.

Barnsley, M. (1988). *Fractals everywhere.* New York: Academic Press.

Barton, S. (1994). Chaos, self-organization, and psychology. *American Psychologist, 49,* 5–14.

Baltes, P. B., & Cornelius, S. W. (1977). The status of dialectics in developmental psychology: Theoretical orientation versus scientific method. In N. Datan & H. W. Reese (Eds.), *Life-span developmental psychology: Dialectical perspectives in experimental research.* New York: Academic Press.

Bengtsson, H. (1983). The approach and preference behavior of chicks in relation to the intensity of neural-input effects. *Animal Behaviour, 31,* 490–496.

Blanchard, R. J., Blanchard, C. D., & Hori, K. (1989). An ethoexperimental approach to the study of defense. In R. J. Blanchard, P. F. Brain, C. D. Blanchard, & S. Parmigianni (Eds.), *Ethoexperimental approaches to the study of behavior.* Boston: Kluwer.

Block, J. (1971). *Lives through time.* Berkeley, CA: Bancroft.

Buss, A. R. (1979). *A dialectical psychology*. New York: Wiley.

Cairns, R. B. (1973). Fighting and punishment from a developmental perspective. In J. K. Cole & D. D. Jensen (Eds.), *Nebraska Symposium on Motivation* (Vol. 20). Lincoln: University of Nebraska Press.

Cairns, R. B. (1979). *Social development: The origins and plasticity of interchanges*. San Francisco: Freeman.

Cairns, R. B., Gariépy, J.-L., & Hood, K. E. (1990). Development, microevolution, and social behavior. *Psychological Review*, *97*, 49–65.

Cairns, R. B., Hood, K. E., & Midlam, J. (1985). On fighting in mice: Is there a sensitive period for isolation effects? *Animal Behaviour*, *33*, 166–180.

Cairns, R. B., MacCombie, D. J., & Hood, K. E. (1983). A developmental-genetic analysis of aggressive behavior in mice: I. Behavioral outcomes. *Journal of Comparative Psychology*, *97*, 69–89.

Cairns, R. B., & Scholtz, S. D. (1973). On fighting in mice: Dyadic escalation and what is learned. *Journal of Comparative and Physiological Psychology*, *85*, 540–550.

Campbell, D. T. (1974). Downward causation in hierarchically organized biological systems. In F. J. Ayala & T. Dobzhansky (Eds.), *Studies in the philosophy of biology: Reduction and related problems*. Berkeley, CA: University of California Press.

Datan, N., & Reese, H. N. (1977). *Life-span developmental psychology: Dialectical perspectives on experimental research*. New York: Academic Press.

Dean, D. (1992). The interpretation of dialectic and hierarchy theory: A hominoid paleobehavioral example. In E. Tobach & G. Greenberg (Eds.), *Levels of social behavior: Evolutionary and genetic aspects*. Wichita, KS: T. C. Schneirla Research Fund.

Degn, H., Holden, A. V., & Olsen, L. F. (1987). *Chaos in biological systems*. NY: Plenum.

Devaney, R. L. (1986). Exploding Julia sets. In M. F. Barnsley & S. G. Demko (Eds.), *Chaotic dynamics and fractals*. New York: Academic.

Engels, F. (1880/1940). *Dialectics of nature*. Translated by C. Dutt. NY: International Publishers.

Fentress, J. C. (1976). Dynamic boundaries of patterned behaviour: Interaction and self-organization. In P. P. G. Bateson & R. A Hinde

(Eds.), *Growing points in ethology*. New York: Cambridge University Press.

Fentress, J. C. (1991). Analytical ethology and synthetic neuroscience. In P. P. G. Bateson (Ed.), *The development and integration of behaviour*. New York: Cambridge University Press.

Flay, J. C. (1984). *Hegel's quest for certainty*. Albany, NY: SUNY Press.

Fogel, A., Nwokah, E., Dedo, J. Y., Messinger, D., Dickson, K. L., Matuson, E., & Holt, S. (1992). Social process theory of emotion: A dynamic systems approach. *Social Development*, *1*, 123–150.

Ford, D. H. (1987). *Humans as self-constructing living systems: A developmental perspective on behavior and personality*. Hillsdale, NJ: Erlbaum.

Ford, D. H., & Lerner, R. M., (1992). *Developmental systems theory: An integrative approach*. Newbury Park, CA: Sage.

Franks, N. R., Wilby, A., Silverman, B. W., & Tofts, C. (1992). Self-organizing nest construction in ants: Sophisticated building by blind bulldozing. *Animal Behavior*, *44*, 357–375.

Freedle, R. (1977). Psychology, Thomian topologies, deviant logics, and human development. In N. Datan & H. W. Reese (Eds.), *Life-span developmental psychology: Dialectical perspectives in experimental research*. New York: Academic Press.

Gottlieb, G. (1992). *Individual development and evolution: The genesis of novel behavior*. New York: Oxford University Press.

Gowaty, P. A. (1992). Evolutionary biology and feminism. *Human Nature*, *3*, 217–249.

Gray, J. A. (1987). *The psychology of fear and stress* (2nd ed.). New York: Cambridge University Press.

Gregson, R. A. M. (1988). *Nonlinear psychophysical dynamics*. Hillsdale, NJ: Erlbaum.

———. (1992). *n-Dimensional nonlinear psychophysics: Theory and case studies*. Hillsdale, NJ: Erlbaum.

Guthrie, E. R. (1935). *The psychology of learning*. New York: Harper & Row.

Hailman, J. P. (1970). Comments on the coding of releasing stimuli. In L. K. Aronson, E. Tobach, D. S. Lehrman, & J. S. Rosenblatt (Eds.), *Development and evolution of behavior: Essays in memory of T. C. Schneirla*. New York: Freeman.

Hegel, G. W. F. (1812/1969). *Science of logic*. (A. V. Miller, Trans.). London: George Allen & Unwin.

————. (1830/1970). *Encyclopaedia of the philosophical sciences*. (Tr. by A. V. Miller). Clarendon: Oxford.

Heshka, S. (1986). Counter examples, boundary conditions, and research strategy in social psychology. In K. S. Larsen (Ed.), *Dialectics and ideology in psychology*. Norwood, NJ: Ablex.

Hood, K. E. (1988). Female aggression in [albino ICR] mice: Development, social experience, and the effects of selective breeding (*Mus musculus*). *International Journal of Comparative Psychology, 2*, 27–41.

————. (1992). Contextual determinants of menstrual cycle effects in observations of social interactions. In A. J. Dan & L. L. Lewis (Eds.), *Menstrual health in women's lives* (pp. 83–97). University of Illinois Press.

Hood, K. E., & Cairns, R. B. (1988). A developmental-genetic analysis of aggressive behavior in mice: II. Cross-sex inheritance. *Behavior Genetics, 18*, 605–619.

————. (1989). A developmental-genetic analysis of aggressive behavior in mice: IV. Genotype-environment interaction. *Aggressive Behavior, 15*, 361–380.

Hood, K. E., & Jones, B. C. (in preparation). Hormone-behavior relationships in selectively bred lines of mice: Aggressive behavior and motivational state.

Hunter, A. E. (1991). *On peace, war, and gender: A challenge to genetic explanations*. (Vol. VI in the series *Genes and Gender*, edited by B. Rosoff and E. Tobach). NY: The Feminist Press.

Johnston, T. D. (1987). The persistence of dichotomies in the study of behavioral development. *Developmental Review, 7*, 149–182.

Kelso, J. A. S. (1989). *A tutorial on dynamical systems and applications to behavioral studies*. Presentation in the pre-conference workshop in Dynamical Systems in Development, Society for Research in Child Development, Kansas City, MO.

Kosok, M. (1976). The systematization of dialectical logic for the study of development and change. *Human Development, 19*, 325–350.

————. (1984). The dynamics of Hegelian dialectics and non-linearity in the sciences. In R. S. Cohen & M. W. Wartofsky (Eds.), *Hegel and the sciences*. Boston: Reidel (Kulwer).

Kugler, P. N. (1986). A morphological perspective on the origin and evolution of movement patterns. In Wade, M. G., and Whiting, H. T. A. (Eds.), *Motor development in children: Aspects of coordination and control*. Boston: Nijhoff.

Kugler, P. N., Kelso, J. A. S., & Turvey, M. T. (1982). On the control and coordination of naturally developing systems. In Kelso, J. A. S., and Clark, J. E. (Eds.), *The development of movement control and coordination.* New York: Wiley.

Kuo, Z.-Y. (1976). *The dynamics of behavior development: An epigenetic view.* New York: Plenum.

Lauwerier, H. (1991). *Fractals: Endlessly repeated geometrical figures.* Princeton, NJ: Princeton University Press.

LeMéhauté, A. (1991). Fractals, materials and energy. In G. Cherbit (Ed.), *Fractals.* New York: Wiley.

Lehrman, D. S. (1970). Semantic and conceptual issues in the nature-nurture problem. In L. K. Aronson, E. Tobach, D. S. Lehrman, & J. S. Rosenblatt (Eds.), *Development and evolution of behavior: Essays in memory of T. C. Schneirla.* New York: Freeman.

Lerner, R. (1986). *Concepts and theories of human development* (2nd ed.). Random House.

Lerner, R. M. (1991). Changing organism-context relations as the basic process of development: A developmental contextual perspective. *Developmental Psychology, 27,* 27–32.

———. (1992). *Final solutions: Biology, prejudice, and genocide.* University Park, PA: Penn State Press.

Levins, R., & Lewontin, R. (1985). *The dialectical biologist.* Cambridge, MA: Harvard University Press.

Lewis, M. H., Gariépy, J. L., Gendreau, P., Nichols, D. E., & Mailman, R. B. (1994). Social reactivity and D_1 dopamine receptors: Studies in mice selectively bred for high and low levels of aggression. *Neuropsychopharmacology, 10,* 115–122.

Magnusson, D., & Allen, V. L. (Ed.). (1983). *Human development: An interactional perspective.* New York: Academic Press.

Mandelbrot, B. B. (1983). *The fractal geometry of nature.* New York: Freeman.

Mandell, A. J. (1980). Vertical integration of levels of brain function through parametric symmetries within self-similar stochastic fields: From brain enzyme polymers to delusion. In H. M. Pinsker & W. D. Willis, Jr. (Eds.), *Information processing in the nervous system.* New York: Raven.

Meacham, J. A. (1977). A transactional model of remembering. In N. Datan & H. W. Reese (Eds.), *Life-span developmental psychology:*

Dialectical perspectives on experimental research. New York: Academic.

Metcalfe, J., & Merrill, J. (1988). 1987 Conference on dynamic patterns in complex systems. *Psychobiology, 16*, 75–78.

Molenaar, P. C. M. (in press). On the viability of nonlinear dynamics in psychology. In F. van den Vijver & M. Croon (Eds.), *Viability of mathematical models in the social sciences*. Lisse: Swets & Zeitlinger.

Molenaar, P. C. M., & Oppenheimer, L. (1985). Dynamic models of development and the mechanistic-organismic controversy. *New Ideas in Development, 3*, 233–242.

Newtson, D. (1989). *Social action systems*. Presentation in the pre-conference workshop in Dynamical Systems in Development, Society for Research in Child Development, Kansas City, MO.

Odom, H. T. (1988). Self-organization, transformity, and information. *Science, 242*, 1132–1139.

Oyama, S. (1985). *The ontogeny of information: Developmental systems and evolution*. New York: Cambridge University Press.

Rappoport, S. (1986). Renaming the world: On psychology and the decline in positive science. In Larsen, K. S. (Ed.), *Dialectics and ideology in psychology*. Norwood, NJ: Ablex.

Riegel, K. F. (1976). The dialectics of human development. *American Psychologist, 31*, 689–700.

Rose, S. (Ed.) (1982a). *Against biological determinism*. London: Allison & Busby.

———. (1982b). *Towards a liberatory biology*. London: Allison & Busby.

Rychlak, J. F. (1976). *Dialectic: Humanistic rationale for behavior and development*. Basel, Switzerland: S. Karger.

———. (1982). *Personality and life-style of young male managers: A logical learning theory analysis*. New York: Academic Press.

Salthe, S. N. (1985). *Evolving hierarchical systems: Their structure and representation*. New York: Columbia University Press.

Sameroff, A. J. (1982). Development and the dialectic: The need for a systems approach. In W. A. Collins (Ed.), *The Concept of Development: Minnesota Symposium on Child Psychology*, Vol. 15. Hillsdale, NJ: Erlbaum.

———. (1983). Developmental systems: Context and evolution. In W. Kessen (Ed.), *History, theory and methods* (Vol. 1) of P. M. Mussen (Ed.) *Handbook of Child Psychology*. New York: Wiley.

Sameroff, A. J., & Harris, A. E. (1979). Dialectical approaches to early thought and language. In M. H. Bornstein & W. Kessen (Eds.), *Psychological development from infancy: Image to intention*. Hillsdale, NJ: Erlbaum.

Sartre, J-P. (1960/1976). *Critique of dialectical reason*. London: NLB.

Schneirla, T. C. (1939; 1972). A theoretical consideration of the basis for approach-withdrawal adjustments in behavior. *Psychological Bulletin*, *37*, 501–502. Reprinted in 1972 in *Selected writings of T. C. Schneirla*, L. R. Aronson, E. Tobach, J. S. Rosenblatt, & D. S. Lehrman (Eds.). New York: Freeman.

———. (1949; 1972). Levels in the psychological capacities of animals. In R. W. Sellars, V. J. McGill, M. Farber, & MacMillan (Eds.), *Philosophy for the future: The quest of modern materialism*. Reprinted in 1972 in *Selected writings of T. C. Schneirla*, L. R. Aronson, E. Tobach, J. S. Rosenblatt, & D. S. Lehrman (Eds.). New York: Freeman.

———. (1959; 1972). An evolutionary and developmental theory of biphasic processes underlying approach and withdrawal. In M. R. Jones (Ed.), *Nebraska Symposium in Motivation*, Vol. 7. University of Nebraska Press. Reprinted in 1972 in *Selected writings of T. C. Schneirla*, L. R. Aronson, E. Tobach, J. S. Rosenblatt, & D. S. Lehrman (Eds.). New York: Freeman.

———. (1965; 1972). Aspects of stimulation and organization in approach-withdrawal processes underlying vertebrate behavioral development. In D. S. Lehrman, R. Hindo, & E. Shaw (Eds.), *Advances in the study of behavior*, Vol. 1. New York: Academic. Reprinted in 1972 in *Selected writings of T. C. Schneirla*, L. R. Aronson, E. Tobach, J. S. Rosenblatt, & D. S. Lehrman (Eds.). New York: Freeman.

———. (1966). Behavioral development and comparative psychology. *Quarterly Review of Biology*, *41*, 283–302.

Schneirla, T. C., & Rosenblatt, J. S. (1963). "Critical periods" in the development of behavior. *Science*, *139*, 1110–1115. Reprinted in 1972 in *Selected writings of T. C. Schneirla*, L. R. Aronson, E. Tobach, J. S. Rosenblatt, & D. S. Lehrman (Eds.). New York: Freeman.

Scott, J. P. (1983). A systems approach to research on aggressive behavior. In E. C. Simmel, M. E. Hahn, & J. K. Walters (Eds.), *Aggressive behavior: Genetic and neural approaches*. Hillsdale, NJ: Erlbaum.

Skarda, C. A., and Freeman, W. J. (1987). How brains make chaos in order to make sense of the world. *Behavioral and brain sciences*, *10*, 161–195.

Smith, L. B., & Thelen, E. (1993). *A dynamic systems approach to development: Applications*. Cambridge, MA: MIT Press.

Solomentser, I. V. (1988). Complex numbers. In M. Hazewinkel (Ed.), *Encyclopaedia of Mathematics*. Dordrecht; Boston.

Solomon, R. L. (1980). The opponent-process theory of acquired motivation. *American Psychologist*, *35*, 691–712.

Taylor, G. T. (1979). Reinforcement and intraspecific aggressive behavior. *Behavioral and Neural Biology*, *27*, 1–24.

Thelen, E. (1989). *Conceptualizing development from a dynamical systems perspective*. Presentation in the pre-conference workshop in Dynamical Systems in Development, Society for Research in Child Development, Kansas City, MO.

Thelen, E., & Ulrich, B. D. (1991). *Hidden skills: A dynamic systems analysis of treadmill stepping during the first year*. Monograph of the Society for Research in Child Development, *56*, 1–102.

Tinbergen, N. (1968). On war and peace in animals and men. *Science*, *160*, 1411–1418.

Tobach, E. (1970). Some guidelines to the study of the evolution and development of emotion. In L. K. Aronson, E. Tobach, D. S. Lehrman, & J. S. Rosenblatt (Eds.), *Development and evolution of behavior: Essays in memory of T. C. Schneirla*. New York: Freeman.

Tobach, E., and Schneirla, T. C. (1968). The biopsychology of social behavior in animals. In R. R. Cook (Ed.), *The biological basis of pediatric practice*. New York: McGraw-Hill. Reprinted in 1972 in *Selected writings of T. C. Schneirla*, L. R. Aronson, J. S. Rosenblatt, & D. S. Lehrman (Eds.). New York: Freeman.

Vallacher, R. R., & Nowak, A. (1994). *Dynamical systems in social psychology*. New York: Academic.

Van der Poel, A. M., Mos, J., Kruk, M. R., & Olivier, B. (1984). A motivational analysis of ambivalent actions in the agonistic behavior of rats in tests used to study effects of drugs on aggression. In K. Miczek, M. R. Kruck, & B. Olivier (Eds.), *Ethopharmacological aggression research*. New York: Alan Liss.

Waddington, C. H. (1957). *The strategy of the genes*. London: George Allen & Unwin.

Weerts, E. M., Miller, L. G., Hood, K. E., & Miczek, K. A. (1992). Increased $GABA_a$-dependent chloride uptake in mice selectively bred for low aggressive behavior. *Psychopharmacology, 108,* 196–204.

Weiner, H. (1989). The dynamics of the organism: Implications of recent biological thought for psychosomatic theory and research. *Psychosomatic Medicine, 51,* 608–635.

Whitehead, A. N. (1929). Space, time, and relativity. *The aims of education.* New York: Mentor.

Wilhelm, R. (1979). *Lectures on the I Ching: Constancy and change.* Bollingen Series XIX:2. Princeton, NJ: Princeton University Press.

Wittig, M. A. (1985). Metatheoretical dilemmas in the psychology of gender. *American Psychologist, 40,* 800–811.

CHAPTER 3

Approach/Withdrawal Theory and Comparative Psychology

Howard Topoff

After 20 years of teaching animal behavior, I'm more than a bit tired of lecturing on those concepts—instinct, territory, dominance, aggression—that were heated topics of discussion during my own graduate training. Each semester, however, I manage to muster just enough enthusiasm to get the job done, because every new generation of graduate students comes to my classes with little appreciation of the complex historical and theoretical issues underlying the study of behavioral processes in diverse animal species. The most recent piece of evidence for my assumption was supplied by a first-year doctoral student, whose thorough undergraduate training in evolutionary biology and ethology prompted the following question: "I don't understand Schneirla's point of view. Exactly why didn't he *believe* in instincts?"

It is true that instinctive, or innate, behavior was one of the key concepts of classical ethology (summarized by Lorenz, 1965). By applying the methods and principles of comparative anatomy to behavioral studies, ethologists turned their attention from the mechanisms underlying behavior, and concentrated instead on evolutionary issues. The two most important of these were: (1) the role of behavior in promoting survival and reproductive success (i.e., the adaptive value of behavior); and (2) the changes in behavior during speciation (i.e., the phylogeny of behavior). Because these considerations began their analyses with patterns of behavior in adult organisms, the entire developmental process

by which species-typical behavior emerged was simply subsumed under the concept of "instinct." It makes little sense, of
course, to debate whether concepts such as instinct, territoriality,
or even imprinting are right or wrong, nor is it particularly relevant who believes in them. Concepts should be judged instead
by the degree to which they adequately reflect actual processes
occurring in nature. In a book dedicated to the memory of T. C.
Schneirla, Lehrman (1970) resolved at least one protracted problem in the study of instinctive behavior:

> When opposing groups of intelligent, highly educated,
> competent scientists continue over many years to
> disagree, and even to wrangle bitterly, about an issue
> which they regard as important, it must sooner or later
> become obvious that the disagreement is not a factual one,
> and that it cannot be resolved by calling to the attention of
> the members of one group (or even the other!) the exis-
> tence of new data which will make them see the light.
> Further, it becomes increasingly obvious that there are no
> possible crucial experiments that would cause one group
> of antagonists to abandon their point of view in favor of
> that of the other group.

Classical ethology, primarily because it focused on adaptive behavior of adult organisms, relied on qualitative perceptual
and motivational processes, including the now famous sign
stimuli, fixed action patterns, and innate releasing mechanisms.
Schneirla's objection was that patterns of species-typical behavior in adult organisms might develop out of simpler, quantitative
processes. It was in this ontogenetic context that Schneirla
sought to substitute quantitative aspects of the organism's stimulus environment for qualitative aspects. This, I think, is the
essence of A/W theory. For Schneirla, A/W theory was an extension of his view that only developmental studies could provide an objective evolutionary perspective of the similarities and
differences in the processes underlying species-typical behavior.
For Schneirla, therefore, behavioral ontogeny is the cornerstone
of comparative psychology, and A/W theory proposed a particular developmental process by which behavioral responses to
quantitative aspects of stimuli early in development could eventually become elicited by the type of qualitative stimuli that

ethologists typically studied. As in Lehrman's comments about Schneirla's views of instinctive behavior, A/W theory was never meant to suggest a definitive, falsifiable, experiment. Instead, it is a model for a research program in behavioral development that seeks to find quantitative antecedents for the complex responses that often dominate patterns of adult behavior. Accordingly, it can't be emphasized enough that A/W theory is not simply about reactions of adult organisms to stimulus intensities. Schneirla (1939, 1956, 1959) stated repeatedly that A/W theory is "based on the utilization, through development, of the animal's *inclusive* resources for adaptive behavior." Simply put, the threshold and response to any stimulus may change as a function of age, experience, trophic state, temperature, hormonal state, or any other factor(s) that alter levels of arousal. For all animal species, according to A/W theory, these modifications are minimal *early in development*, so that physiological processes of organ systems, and taxis- and kinesis-type responses of organisms, are guided by the quantitative parameters of stimulation. During ontogeny, however, species representing different levels of evolutionary history have correspondingly different capabilities for developmental plasticity, and therefore for perceptual and social development. The theory of levels of organization, which is an integral part of A/W theory, thus provides the rationale for a truly evolutionary, comparative psychology. Depending on the nature of their neurophysiological systems, and the habitat in which they evolved, species differ in the degree to which developmental processes permit A/W responses to surpass being a reaction to quantitative stimuli. This is precisely why Schneirla warned that, in adult stages of many animal species, the application of A/W theory must consider "modifications, occlusions, and reversals that arise inevitably through perceptual and social development" (Schneirla, 1959). Generally speaking, the magnitude and range of such modifications would be proportional to the complexity of the species, so that adult stages of vertebrates should be expected to exhibit more of these behavioral changes than invertebrates. But complexity, I think, is a thorny issue. The inductive nature of A/W theory dictates that predictions about behavioral plasticity across species be replaced by empirical studies that take into account the ecological and evolutionary history of the species, in addition to anatomical specializations. Although I do not think it productive to engage in a "complexity" contest between invertebrates and vertebrates, the degree of behavioral modification displayed by social insects is quite impressive. Here are several examples.

1. Cyclic Behavior of Army Ants

The periodic shifting of nesting sites by tropical army ants was well known to many early naturalists, and they usually postulated food exhaustion as the proximate cause of nomadism. This "random drift" hypothesis was tested by Schneirla, in which he concentrated on the two most surface-adapted army ant species, *Eciton hamatum* and *E. burchelli*. Schneirla concluded that both species of *Eciton* exhibit regular cycles of activity, with each cycle consisting of a distinct nomadic and statary phase. The nomadic phase, lasting just over two weeks, is a period of high colony activity, in which large daily predatory raids are typically followed by an emigration to a new temporary nest or bivouac. The nomadic phase is followed by a statary interval lasting almost three weeks, and is characterized by a lower intensity of raiding and the absence of emigrations (Schneirla, 1957).

According to Schneirla's theory of brood stimulation, the behavioral cycle in both *Eciton* species is regulated by stimulative interactions between the large developing broods and the adult worker ants. At the start of a nomadic phase, a mature pupal brood completes its development and emerges from cocoons as lightly-pigmented callow workers. The callows are highly excitatory to the adult population. This sudden and intensive social stimulation, originating through callow-adult interactions and transmitted throughout the bivouac by communication among the mature adults, starts the colony off on a new nomadic phase. As the callows mature, however, their chemotactual excitatory effects decline. Nomadic activities in the colony are now maintained by equivalent stimulation imparted to the adults by a brood of developing larvae, hatched from eggs laid by the queen shortly after the onset of the previous statary phase. Later, as this maturing larval brood ceases feeding prior to pupation, the adult workers receive only minimal stimulation, and the colony lapses into the statary phase. The queen lays a new batch of eggs which hatch into larvae at approximately the same time that the present pupal brood ecloses. The eclosion of the callows initiates a new nomadic phase, and the cycle is repeated.

2. Raiding Behavior of Socially Parasitic Ants

For comparative psychologists, parasitism provides information about the evolution and development of social bonds between different species of organisms. Strictly speaking, parasitism is a form of symbiosis, a broad ecological concept which also includes mutually beneficial associations, such as between a cow and the intestinal microorganisms that aid its digestion. But parasitism is decidedly one-sided, with the parasite living at the expense of its host, and sometimes even killing it. People are most familiar with physiological parasites, small creatures like viruses or fleas, which attach themselves to the skin or internal organs of larger-sized organisms. But an even more fascinating interspecific relationship among animals is known as social parasitism. Among vertebrates, the best known of these symbionts are avian brood parasites, such as cuckoos and cowbirds. In these species, the female parasite lays an egg in the nest of another species, and leaves it for the host to rear, typically at the expense of the host's young. Less known but more varied, are dulotic (from the Greek word for servant) species of insects in the order Hymenoptera (comprising bees, wasps, and ants). Consider, for example, the unusual behavior of parasitic ants belonging to the genus *Polyergus*, which have lost the ability to care for themselves. The workers do not forage for food, feed their brood or queen, or even clean their own nest. To compensate for these deficits, *Polyergus* has become specialized at obtaining workers from the related genus *Formica* to do these chores for them. This is accomplished by a slave raid, in which several thousand *Polyergus* workers travel up to 150 meters, penetrate a *Formica* nest, disperse the *Formica* queen and workers, and capture the resident's pupal brood (Topoff et al., 1984). Back at the *Polyergus* nest, some raided brood is consumed. But a portion of it is reared through development, and the emerging *Formica* workers then assume all responsibility for maintaining the permanent, mixed-species nest. They forage for nectar and dead arthropods, and regurgitate food to colony members of both species. They also remove wastes and excavate new chambers as the population increases.

During slave raids, the level of arousal of *Polyergus breviceps* raiders is extremely high. By contrast, their activity level is greatly reduced during the nest-circling that typically precedes slave raids, and during the homeward trip after a successful raid. Recently, we conducted a field study to demonstrate that recruitment by *Polyergus* (to the same stimulus) differs among these three behavioral contexts (Topoff et al., 1989). The procedure consisted of placing 100 *Formica* adult workers, with 100 pupae, into a small plastic box containing a single entrance hole at the bottom of one wall. In the first experimental condition, the box containing *Formica* adults and brood was taken to the field and placed on the ground, alongside a *Polyergus* raiding swarm. In the second condition, the box containing *Formica* adults and pupae was placed in front of the leading edge of ants returning from a slave raid. Finally, for the third condition, the box was placed near the entrance to a *Polyergus* nest, during the period of pre-raid circling. Each condition was repeated five times, on a different afternoon.

As expected, the mean cumulative number of *Polyergus* workers entering the experimental box among the three behavioral contexts was significantly different. In the "raiding" condition, initial contact with *Polyergus* set off a wave of panic-alarm, as adult *Formica* workers scurried around inside the box. This resulted in a burst of recruitment, with a mean of 250 *Polyergus* workers entering the box during the eight-minute test period, and the removal of all *Formica* pupae.

In contrast to the "raid" condition, the magnitude of recruitment by *Polyergus* during the "circling" condition was significantly lower. Thus for the five trials during "circling," an average of only 12 *Polyergus* workers entered the box during the entire eight-minute test, and those that exited resumed circling without recruiting nestmates. Even more interesting was the observation that the *Formica* adults inside the box exhibited aggressive behavior instead of panic-alarm. They grasped the legs of the intruding *Polyergus* and often prevented them from leaving the box. Of the 100 *Formica* pupae present in each box, a mean of only 14 were removed during the five trials.

When *Polyergus* workers returning from a raid encountered the experimental box, their response was quite similar to the "circling" condition. The mean number of ants entering the box was 28, there was no attempt by *Polyergus* to recruit nestmates, and the resident *Formica* exhibited aggressive behavior instead of panic-alarm. Many *Polyergus* walked over *Formica* pupae without picking them up, and the mean number of pupae removed during the five trials was 21.

3. Social Control of Behavioral Development in Ants

Most studies of behavioral ontogeny have been conducted with vertebrate species. Behavior in insects, by contrast, was largely viewed as emerging according to a rigid, invariable genetic blueprint, chained to biological maturation. In recent years, however, investigators have shown a key role of early experience in the development of social behavior in many species of ants, since olfactory experience during larval or pupal stages can influence both intra- and inter-specific social-bond formation.

We recently conducted a laboratory study of the social regulation of behavioral development in the arid-land ant, *Novomessor albisetosus* (McDonald and Topoff, 1985). Worker ants are considered mature when they spend more than half the time outside the nest (foraging for food), and no longer tend either the brood or queen. For control colonies, the mean time to maturity after eclosion (i.e., emergence from the pupal stage) was 68 days (range, 51–82 days). In experimental colonies, however, in which the mature foragers were removed, our criterion of maturity was reached in only 19 days (range, 14–24 days). Conversely, when immature brood tenders were removed from inside the nest, the mature foragers immediately reverted to feeding brood and queen, although they had not touched either for four to six months prior to the manipulation.

The Experimental Embryology Model of Development

As an alternative to instinctivist views, A/W theory regards behavioral development as a sequence of progressive, changing relationships between organism and environment. Schneirla was often accused of being outside the "zeitgeist" of psychology, but few recognized the reason for this: he was usually out in front of it! In my opinion, his greatest contribution (frequently not recognized by psychologists) was equating his formulation of behavioral development to that of experimental embryology. For while both comparative psychologists and ethologists continue the gene-environment argument to the present day, experimental embryologists diffused the issue more than 30 years ago. They did it by giving new (and true) meaning to the concept of "interaction."

Consider, in this exceedingly simplified example, a fertilized egg, having a nuclear-bound genome and a surrounding cytoplasm (the genes' environment, at this level of organization). Now, it is well known that the activation of genes (i.e., their transcription into RNA and eventual translation into protein molecules) is ultimately regulated by chemical processes originating in the genes' environment. And because the distribution of these chemicals is not uniform throughout the cytoplasm, slight differential gene activation occurs even during the first cleavage division. The result of this differential transcription and translation is that the cytoplasms of the resulting two cells now have an even greater chemical disparity. And because of this difference, the magnitude of differential gene activation will be heightened during the next round of cell division, resulting in still greater environmental variation surrounding each nucleus. Note how different this process is from the traditional nature-nurture argument, which is conceptualized by the *static* idea that genes set the developmental limits, while the environment simply determines the extent to which the genomic limits will be realized. In this model, which empirical evidence shows to be the one that works in nature (De Pomerai, 1985), the functioning (activation) of a portion of the genome, owed to the action of its environment, alters the very environment surrounding that gene sequence. The genes thus create a new milieu, and the new environment effects the activation (and, of course, repression) of still other genes. This is an interaction! And this is why Schneirla (1965) envisaged behavioral development as a process of "progressive, changing relationships between organism and environment in which the contributions of growth are always inseparably interrelated with those of the effects of energy changes in the environs." Simply put, genes don't just react to an environment. They are part of it, they change it, and by doing so, they effect changes in their own functioning at later stages of development.

In employing the embryological model of differential gene expression to describe behavioral development, Schneirla could just as easily have opened a different (but related) window, one that could provide new insight into our conceptualization of behavioral evolution. Because each cell in a multicellular organism is ultimately derived from a single fertilized egg, the cells of differentiated organs contain the same set of genes (barring mutations and nondisjunctions that occur after fertilization). Although no one would confuse the extensive anatomical and physiological differences among epidermal cells, neurons, muscle cells, or lymphocytes, it has been known for many years that these variations are due to differential gene functioning, so that only about 10 percent of the genes are active in any given mature cell. No one seems concerned that cell differentiation which, for all intensive purposes, is permanent, does not require a different set of structural genes for each cell type. To embryologists, a genuine *developmental event* can occur even though contrasting cell "phenotypes" have the same set of structural genes (i.e., the same genotype). If nature produces adaptive cell phenotypes through the process of selective gene activation, that's good enough for the embryologist. But when the issue shifts from a group of cells with a common ancestor, to a group of species with a common ancestor (e.g., a monophyletic genus), the analogy does not seem to be good enough for most evolutionary biologists. Speciation is typically conceptualized as resulting from a genuine evolutionary event only when phenotypic changes *can* be attributed to changes in the frequency of structural genes. But if cell differentiation demonstrates the enormous phenotypic variability (in both structure and function) possible from a single genotype, who knows how immense the phenotypic potential is from a given gene pool. Given the close (structural) genetic similarity between humans and pongid apes, it is clear that phyletic differentiation can also involve alterations in the temporal activation of existing genotypes. Many years ago, Kuo (1967) called attention to this issue, by suggesting that psychologists take a serious look at what he termed behavioral neo-phenotypes. To illustrate, here is a brief quote from the epilogue of his insightful book.

> We must not forget that even animals such as arthropods, particularly the social insects, shifting from one ecological niche to another, may induce changes in certain behavior patterns. As long as the general nature of the new environmental context remains relatively unchanged, despite inevitable variations, we may expect that the newly induced behavior patterns, or behavioral neo-phenotypes of the group as a whole would be carried on from generation to generation. In such cases there is hardly any need to assume any change in the gene pool.

Despite Kuo's perceptive understanding of behavioral evolution, his reputation as an ardent Watsonian behaviorist undoubtedly impeded critical examination of his views. Schneirla and Kuo might be considered examples of intellectual "parallel evolution," because Schneirla's theoretical contributions about behavioral ontogeny, levels of behavioral organization, and A/W theory were intended to provide a comparative framework for elucidating how the evolutionary process produced the observed variation in behavioral processes among animal species. Perhaps this important issue can be more fully explored at a future meeting of the T. C. Schneirla Conference Series.

REFERENCES

De Pomerai, D. (1985). *From genes to animal*. Cambridge: Cambridge University Press.

Kuo, Z. Y. (1967). *The dynamics of behavior development*. New York: Random House.

Lehrman, D. S. (1970). Semantic and conceptual issues in the nature-nurture problem. In L. Aronson, E. Tobach, D. Lehrman, and J. Rosenblatt (Eds.), *Development and evolution of behavior*. San Francisco: Freeman, 17–52.

Lorenz, K. (1965). *Evolution and modification of behavior*. Chicago: University of Chicago.

McDonald, P., and Topoff, H. (1985). Social control of behavioral development in the ant *Novomessor Albisetosus* (Mayr). *Journal of Comparative Psychology*, 99, 3–14.

Schneirla, T. C. (1939). A theoretical consideration of the basis for approach-withdrawal adjustments in behavior. *Psychological Bulletin*, 37, 501–502.

———. (1956). Interrelationships of the "innate" and the "acquired" in instinctive behavior. In P. P. Grasse (Ed.), *L'instinct Dans Le Comportement Des Animaux Et De L'homme*. Paris: Masson, 387–452.

———. (1957). Theoretical consideration of cyclic processes in doryline ants. *Proceedings of the American Philosophical Society*, 101, 106–133.

———. (1959). An evolutionary and developmental theory of biphasic processes underlying approach and withdrawal. In M. R. Jones (Ed.), *Current Theory and Research on Motivation*, Vol. 7. Lincoln: University of Nebraska, 1–42.

———. (1965). Aspects of stimulation and organization in approach-withdrawal processes underlying vertebrate behavioral development. In D. Lehrman, R. Hinde, and E. Shaw (Eds.), *Advances in the Study of Behavior*, Vol. 1. New York: Academic Press, 1–74.

Topoff, H., Lamon, B., Goodloe, L., and Goldstein, M. (1984). Social and orientation behavior of *Polyergus Breviceps* during slave-making raids. *Behavioral Ecology and Sociobiology*, 15, 273–279.

Topoff, H., Cover, S., and Jacobs, A. (1989). Behavioral adaptations for raiding by the slave-making ant *Polyergus Breviceps*. *Journal of Insect Behavior*, 2, 545–556.

CHAPTER 4

Schneirla's A/W Biphasic Processes Theory

Jay S. Rosenblatt

Several topics touched upon in this volume have not been adequately discussed in my view, and other issues of importance have not been discussed at all. In this brief discussion section I would like to deal with these in order.

1. Circularity in Schneirla's Formulation of A/W Biphasic Processes Theory

Schneirla's theory of biphasic A/W processes rests on the concepts that weak stimuli elicit approach responses and strong stimuli elicit withdrawal responses in neonates and in many lower animals throughout life. This aspect of the theory has been criticized as circular in its logic. Weak and strong stimuli are determined by noting the response they evoke—approach or withdrawal. Then, in a circular manner, weak stimuli are said to evoke approach responses and strong stimuli withdrawal responses. The consequence of this criticism, left unanswered, is that many have discarded the theory without further investigation of other characteristics that might otherwise recommend it to them. We must, therefore, present a procedure for determining weak and strong stimuli and their relationship to approach and withdrawal responses that avoids the criticism of circularity.

It is not uncommon for an animal's response to a stimulus to be used to characterize that stimulus (e.g., eating defines a stimulus as food). However, in these instances we are specifically asking the animal to tell us what the stimulus *means* to it, not what the stimulus is in objective, physical terms. Weak and strong stimuli refer to measurable physical characteristics of the stimuli (e.g., visual, auditory, chemical, tactile) that can be converted to measures of energy in some form. Stimuli can be ranged along a gradient from weak or low intensity to strong or high intensity. Schneirla's theory proposes that if this gradient of stimuli from weak to strong intensity is presented to an animal its responses will not simply increase in scope or amplitude, but rather, over a narrow range of the gradient, the response will change from approach to withdrawal in relation to the stimulus gradient. A single stimulus cannot, therefore, be called weak or strong unless it has previously been tested as part of a gradient of stimulation and response to it noted.

I believe through this procedure we can avoid the criticism of circularity in Schneirla's formulation of A/W biphasic processes theory and at the same time provide a test of both its validity and generality.

2. Translation of Qualitative Stimuli into Quantitative Terms

Closely related to the problem of avoiding circularity in defining weak and strong stimuli in terms of approach and withdrawal responses is the problem of characterizing qualitative stimuli (e.g., visual shape, movement pattern, object quality) in quantitative terms of stimulus intensity. It is the problem of avoiding a priori attribution to other species and to neonates of our own perceptual abilities, particularly when there is a strong likelihood that they are responding to these stimuli in less advanced ways, based upon simpler stimulus characteristics that are more quantitative than qualitative in nature. Schneirla provided several examples in which he showed how qualitative stimuli could be translated into quantitative stimuli (Schneirla, 1965).

The first example was the approaching and fleeing response of goslings to the same visual model with a long tapered neck, wings spread wide and a short stubby tail swooping down on them in one direction, which Lorenz labeled the goose shape, and in the opposite direction, which he labeled the hawk, the short stubby tail now leading with the wings spread wide and the tapered neck trailing behind (Schneirla, 1965). Schneirla proposed that the approaching goose shape could be viewed as a triangle with the narrow-angled apex (the extended neck) leading and the wide base (formed by the spread wings) following. The gradual increase in visual stimulation over the retina of the goslings when moving in the "goose" direction contrasted with the abrupt increase in stimulation in the "hawk" direction when the wide base of the triangle was the leading edge followed by the tapered apex of the triangle. The slow rate of change of visual stimulation provided weak intensity stimulation while the rapid rate of change provided strong intensity of stimulation that could account for the approach and withdrawal responses of the goslings. Lorenz had viewed the model in the qualitative terms of an adult human rather than considering the possibility that the goslings were responding to it on the basis of stimulus intensity. Of course this interpretation of the model in terms of stimulus intensity requires a knowledge of visual neurophysiology and makes several assumptions about the visual capacities of the goslings.

Another example provided by Schneirla (1965) involved Tinbergen and Perdeck's (1950) study of the feeding response of herring gull chicks that pecked at a red spot on the parent's yellow bill to obtain a piece of food regurgitated by the parent. The bill was moved up and down in an arc with its pivot at the head and was held just above the chick's head, silhouetted against the sky. The width of the bill, the location and color of the spot, the movement of the bill and its height above the chicks, all proved to be important aspects of the stimulus that increased or decreased the chicks' pecking at it. Each feature of the stimulus was viewed as a releasing stimulus for the pecking response which was seen as a response to a complex stimulus. Underlying this interpretation was the perception of these releasing stimuli as qualitative stimuli of bill, contrasting spot and pattern of movement.

Schneirla interpreted these several features of the bill as contributing to a single quantitative stimulus consisting of the rate of movement of the two edges of the bill across the chicks visual field. At the same rate of bill movement, narrow bills were more effective than thicker bills because they produced a greater frequency of edge stimulation; more contrast of the bill against the sky was also more effective and a contrasting spot on the bill added to this effect. The height of the bill from the chick determined how much of the visual field of the chick was stimulated by the movement of the bill and the location of the pivot of the bill movement determined the arc traversed by the bill and, therefore, the stimulus repetition rate. Weidman and Weidman's (1958) and Hailman's (1962, 1967) studies confirmed many of the predictions that Schneirla made on the basis of this theory.

The analysis of quantitative features of stimulation requires a knowledge of sensory physiology of the various sensory modalities. This provides us with the parameters of stimulation that the neonate is capable of responding to and enables us to translate qualitative aspects of stimulation into quantitative variations in stimulus intensity.

3. Characterizing Approach and Withdrawal Responses

Approach responses consist of those responses that initiate or maintain an animal's contact with a weak stimulus source and include turning towards, moving towards, and continuing to follow an object as it moves. Withdrawal responses consist of turning away from, moving away from, withdrawing the stimulated part, among other kinds of responses. There are more subtle forms of withdrawal such as interrupting an approach response or becoming immobile and subtle approach responses may consist of individual limb movements such as reaching towards a stimulus. The core meaning of approach responses is to initiate and maintain contact with the stimulus and the core meaning of withdrawal responses is to remove the effect of the stimulus upon the animal. Until I realized these core meanings I was puzzled by Schneirla's inclusion of defensive aggression as a withdrawal response. However, this response occurs among rats when they are prevented from fleeing a predator; they attack it as a means of ridding themselves of the stimulus. Predatory aggression, on the other hand, appears to be a specialized approach response in the service of feeding.

Because of their different characteristics approach and withdrawal responses provide quite different bases for learning. Approach responses continue to be guided by the stimuli which initiated the approach while withdrawal responses, which terminate contact with the stimulus, are no longer guided by it unless it is applied repeatedly.

4. Lifelong Application of A/W Biphasic Processes Theory

Schneirla intended that A/W biphasic process theory apply to all stages of development, not just the neonatal stage. Modifications are required, however, in the form of approach and withdrawal responses and in the nature of the stimuli that elicit them. Increasingly, meaningful aspects of stimulation replace stimulus intensity in eliciting approach and withdrawal responses. With development, approach responses become seeking, and withdrawal processes, avoiding stimulation. The forms of these responses become modified and specialized and often are internalized in the form of attentional processes and attitudes, mediated by language and laden with emotion.

5. Integration of Approach and Withdrawal Responses

There are few situations in real life in which only approach or only withdrawal responses are elicited by a stimulus. More often objects or situations arouse both approach and withdrawal responses simultaneously and at times conflicts between these responses arise that need to be resolved. This aspect of A/W theory has been least developed but would repay further theoretical study. What appear to be threshold phenomena (i.e., by increasing stimulation a response appears) can often be shown to be hidden conflict situations in which the additional stimulation resolves the conflict in one direction or the other. This concept has helped us to understand the emergence of maternal behavior in nonpregnant females exposed to newborn pups which we have analyzed in Approach/Withdrawal conflict resolution terms. In adulthood approach and withdrawal responses form intricate patterns of thoughts and feelings which are the result of the lifelong need to integrate approach and withdrawal responses in adaptive patterns of behavior.

6. Levels of Integration and Levels of Psychological Functioning

The terms "levels of integration (or organization)" and "levels of psychological functioning" have been used during our discussion in ways that need to be clarified, I believe. The term "levels of integration" will be used to refer to the analysis of behavioral capacities by various means whereas the terms "levels of psychological functioning" will be used to refer to a comparison of the behavioral capacities of various species (Schneirla, 1949, 1959).

Behavioral capacities can be characterized by studying the perceptual, motor, motivational-emotional, and integrative (i.e., conditioning, learning, memory, problem solving) abilities of animals. These abilities are based upon a functioning nervous system and specific neural processes. These processes, in turn, involve cellular and subcellular mechanisms that also include biochemical and molecular processes. Each of these subdivisions requires special methods of study and concepts appropriate to the subject matter that differ from other related subdivisions. One of the difficulties that exists is relating concepts in one of these subdivisions to those in another; often when the same concepts are used in two subdivisions they mean different things (e.g., refractory, activation, threshold, inhibited—as used in psychology and neurophysiology). When concepts from neurophysiology are used to refer to behavioral processes this is labeled "reductionism" and when behavioral processes are described in neurophysiological terms this is labeled "neurologizing" in recognition of the difficulty of bridging these fields in valid ways. Each subdivision is itself an integrated field; since these subdivisions can be ordered from the more inclusive, such as psychology, to the less inclusive, such as cellular neurophysiology, each is often thought of as representing an underlying "level of analysis" with respect to the more inclusive subdivision to which it is related. Cellular neurophysiology is a less inclusive subdivision than "network" neurophysiology and therefore is viewed as an underlying level of analysis while both are less inclusive than behavioral science. Because molecular processes are included in all of the more inclusive subdivisions, discoveries made in this subdivision have important implications and a strong impact on these subdivisions. On the other hand, behavioral science, because it is more inclusive than these less inclusive subdivisions, often provides a guiding framework for research in these subdivisions and for integrating their discoveries.

The terms which characterize psychological functioning refer to the behavioral capacities of animals listed above (e.g., perceptual, motor, motivational-emotional and integrative capacities). Instead of comparing species with respect to these capacities, they are often compared with respect to their adaptation to their natural habitats. Since all animals are more or less adapted to their natural habitats, to order animals according to their adaptations requires that their habitats be scaled according to complexity, severity, regularity, etc. In the end this does not lead to characterizing behavioral capacities nor does it enable us to compare these capacities in different animals. This kind of enterprise has led to the conclusion that all animals have specialized behavioral capacities related to the habitats in which they evolved and cannot therefore be compared to one another in any meaningful way.

Yet the behavioral functioning of organisms represents an integrated whole that can be compared with that of other organisms. These comparisons often reveal important differences such as those described by Schneirla when ants and rats learn mazes and in describing the early socialization capacities of ants and kittens (Aronson, Tobach, Rosenblatt, and Lehrman, 1972). These differences arise from specific component processes of the overall integration, e.g., perceptual integrative capacities, learning abilities, etc. Empirical analyses of many species suggests that integrative functions are the key to the evolutionary progression from simpler to more complex organisms and that it is with respect to these capacities that levels of psychological functioning among animals are to be found. Since these capacities are also important in the more inclusive level of social behavior and organization among animals, which involves trophallactic relationships among individuals based upon stimulation of mutual approach responses, A/W biphasic processes theory can provide a key to the study of levels of social behavior among those animals.

REFERENCES

Aronson, L. R., E. Tobach, J. S. Rosenblatt, and D. S. Lehrman (Eds.). (1972). *Selected Writings of T. C. Schneirla*. San Francisco: Freeman.

Hailman, J. P. (1962). Pecking of laughing gull chicks at models of the parental head. *Auk* 79: 89–98.

————. (1967). The ontogeny of an instinct. *Behaviour Suppl.* 15.

Schneirla, T. C. (1949). Levels in the psychological capacities of animals. In R. W. Sellars, V. J. McGill, and M. Garber (Eds.), *Philosophy for the future: the quest of modern materialism*. New York: Macmillan.

————. (1959). An evolutionary and developmental theory of biphasic processes underlying approach and withdrawal. In M. R. Jones (Ed.), *Nebraska Symposium on Motivation* 7: 1–42. Lincoln: University of Nebraska Press.

————. (1965). Aspects of stimulation and organization in approach-withdrawal processes underlying vertebrate behavioral development. In D. S. Lehrman, R. Hinde, and E. Shaw (Eds.), *Advances in the study of behavior*, vol. 1. New York: Academic Press.

Tinbergen, N., and Perdeck, A. C. (1950). On the stimulus situation releasing the begging response in the newly hatched Herring Gull chick (*Larus argentatus argentatus Pont*). *Behaviour* 3: 1–39.

Weidman, R., and Weidman, U. (1958). An analysis of the stimulus-situation releasing food begging in the black-headed gull. *Animal Behavior* 6: 114.

SECTION II

Approach/Withdrawal—
Biochemical and Neural Processes

Cellular and Network Processes Involved in Biphasic Responses to Noxious Stimulation in *Aplysia*

Prospects for a Reductionist Analysis

Edgar T. Walters
Andrea L. Clatworthy

Comparative psychology has attracted the interest of behavioral and brain scientists who hope that fundamental, phylogenetically general principles of behavioral organization can be identified and applied to the study of human behavior and brain function. T. C. Schneirla, one of the seminal comparative psychologists, discerned a pattern common in adults of simpler species and in the early ontogenetic stages of more complex species, namely that "low intensities of stimulation tend to evoke approach reactions, high intensities withdrawal reactions" (Schneirla, 1959). He elaborated this general observation into a biphasic approach/withdrawal theory which was applied primarily to problems in behavioral development, such as the nature-nurture controversy. Schneirla's observations of biphasic responses to environmental stimulation raise three interesting neurobiological questions, aside from the question of the developmental roles of such response patterns. Are intensity-dependent, biphasic response patterns common in the animal kingdom, as Schneirla claimed? How can an animal generate opposite responses to qualitatively similar stimuli? How does an organism change its choice of responses as a consequence of behavioral experience? As described below, recent investigations of the gastropod mollusc, *Aplysia californica*, address these questions, and pose a fourth question. How can we balance the promises and pitfalls of reductionist analysis in our efforts to understand neuronal substrates of behavior?

Intensity-Dependent Approach/Withdrawal Patterns Are Displayed by *Aplysia*

The biphasic pattern described by Schneirla (1959) of approach to weak stimuli and withdrawal to intense, qualitatively similar stimuli is exhibited by *Aplysia* in response to mechanical stimulation during feeding behavior. When the animal is searching for seaweed to eat, weak tapping or brushing of the tentacles causes the animal to turn towards the source of stimulation (e.g. Preston & Lee, 1973). Similarly, gentle handling by the experimenter or weak pinch of the tail increases the rapidity with which the animal subsequently ingests food (Kupfermann & Weiss, 1981). In contrast, strong cutaneous stimulation causes immediate withdrawal of the stimulated region, rapid (at least by snail standards) escape locomotion, and suppression of feeding behavior (Kupfermann & Pinsker, 1968; Walters & Erickson, 1986). An analogous pattern is seen with photic stimuli: *Aplysia* show positive phototaxis towards a moderate intensity light, but withdraw from intense light (Cook & Carew, 1989).

The mechanisms underlying intensity-dependent approach/withdrawal patterns are not known in *Aplysia*, but should be amenable to study in neural circuits controlling head withdrawal and feeding since these circuits have been partially characterized (e.g. Fredman & Jahan-Parwar, 1977; Weiss, Chiel, Koch, & Kupfermann, 1986; Teyke, Weiss, & Kupfermann, 1989). However, some insights into possible mechanisms contributing to biphasic responses may be obtained by considering neuronal processes involved in two other forms of response regulation in *Aplysia* which are discussed below.

Biphasic Sensory Responses to Noxious Stimulation

In general, more is known about neural mechanisms of withdrawal than approach. Fast withdrawal responses to noxious or threatening stimuli often involve relatively simple circuits and large, accessible neurons. In addition, it has been far easier to obtain simple withdrawal responses than more complex approach responses in surgically reduced preparations suitable for intracellular recording. Neural substrates of rapid responses that withdraw an animal from a threatening stimulus have been probed most extensively in gastropod molluscs (such as *Aplysia*) and several other animals presenting advantages for concurrent analysis of neuronal and behavioral properties, including crayfish (Krasne & Wine, 1984), leech (Kristan, McGirr, & Simpson, 1982), cockroach (Ritzmann, 1984), and fish (Eaton & Hackett, 1984). In these animals, rapid withdrawal and escape responses involve neural networks which share several features. The withdrawal or escape circuits are usually activated by sensory neurons that are either nociceptors (tuned to injurious stimuli) or that respond selectively to signals that warn of predators. For example, rapid withdrawal and escape behavior in *Aplysia* are triggered reliably by activation of nociceptors, while in another gastropod, *Tritonia*, similar behaviors can be triggered by gentle contact of the tube feet of a voracious sea star, *Pycnopodia*, within the receptive field of chemosensitive mechanoafferents (Getting, 1976). Such "early warning" sensory neurons and nociceptors are often connected by relatively short pathways (having few synaptic relays) to a small number of executive neurons ("response-dedicated trigger neurons"; Krasne & Lee, 1988) that can control the withdrawal or escape response (e.g. siphon with drawal, tail flip, crawling, swimming). These circuit components provide simple "labeled lines" between sufficiently intense stimuli and appropriate defensive responses. Additionally, more complex pathways also contribute to withdrawal responses (e.g. Krasne & Wine, 1984, and see below).

In *Aplysia* withdrawal responses of the gill, siphon, and tail are activated by sensory neurons that have their receptive processes in the skin and body wall, and their cell bodies and many of their synaptic terminals within central ganglia (Byrne,

Castellucci, & Kandel, 1974; Walters, Byrne, Carew, & Kandel, 1983a). The mechanosensory neurons in identified clusters in the pleural and abdominal ganglia are wide-dynamic-range nociceptors; i.e. they respond weakly with one or two action potentials to moderate cutaneous pressure, and show a progressively increasing number and frequency of action potentials as the pressure is increased. They are considered nociceptors because maximal firing occurs to pressures that, if sustained, cause tissue damage (Walters et al., 1983a; Clatworthy & Walters, 1993a). These sensory neurons make synaptic connections to various types of interneurons (see below) and also make direct connections to motor neurons which mediate withdrawal responses. Normally four to six sensory neurons are activated by a punctate cutaneous stimulus, but one can sometimes trigger a withdrawal response by artificially stimulating the cell body of just a single sensory neuron (Byrne, Castellucci, & Kandel, 1978; Walters, Byrne, Carew & Kandel, 1983a).

Withdrawal responses in *Aplysia* undergo a biphasic change in sensitivity and intensity following a noxious stimulus, and this behavioral modulation is paralleled by a change in sensory neuron properties. It was initially observed that moderate intensity or noxious mechanical stimuli delivered to one part of the body could *sensitize* withdrawal responses to test stimuli delivered to another part of the body (Carew, Castellucci, & Kandel, 1971; Walters, Byrne, Carew, & Kandel, 1983b), with sensitization defined as an increase in the amplitude of the test response following the sensitizing stimulation. Reflex sensitization can begin within seconds after a noxious stimulus and can last for days or weeks if the noxious stimulation is severe (Pinsker, Hening, Carew, & Kandel, 1973; Frost, Castellucci, Hawkins, & Kandel, 1985; Walters, 1987a, 1991). Sensitization has been associated with changes in several types of neurons in withdrawal circuits (Frost, Clark, & Kandel, 1988), with changes in sensory neurons being particularly profound and long-lasting (Carew, Castellucci, & Kandel, 1971; Walters, Byrne, Carew, & Kandel, 1983b; Frost, Castellucci, Hawkins, & Kandel, 1988). There are a number of parallel sensory neuron changes, all tending to enhance the sensitivity and output of the sensory neuron: transmitter release is increased (Castellucci & Kandel, 1976), excitability of the central (Klein, Hochner, & Kandel, 1986; Clatworthy & Walters, 1993a) and peripheral (Billy & Walters, 1989a,b) regions of the cell is increased, and sensory cell growth is triggered in its central (Bailey & Chen, 1983) and possibly peripheral (Billy & Walters, 1989a) regions. These functional changes have been linked to a large number of biophysical and biochemical events in the sensory neuron (e.g., depression of K^+ conductances, activation of protein kinases, phosphorylation of ion-channel-associated proteins, regulation of specific gene elements; alteration of protein synthesis) (reviewed by Kandel & Schwartz, 1982; Sweatt, Volterra, Siegelbaum, & Kandel, 1988; Castellucci & Schacher, 1990; see also Eskin, Garcia, & Byrne, 1989; Dash, Hochner, & Kandel, 1990).

Noxious stimulation causes both *general* sensitization, reflected by an enhancement of defensive responses tested anywhere on the body surface, and *stimulus-specific* sensitization, in which certain test stimuli become much more effective than others. Stimulus-specific sensitization in *Aplysia* has been produced with two different paradigms which in mammals are used to produce 1) classical conditioning and 2) primary hyperalgesia. In *Aplysia* the stimulus specificity from both paradigms occurs, at least in part, because of properties of the wide-dynamic range nociceptors. As described above, facilitation of the signalling effectiveness of these sensory neurons contributes to general sensitization. These sensory neurons are normally silent and thus are not firing action potentials during the initiation of general sensitization; they only fire action potentials when their peripheral receptive field is stimulated by a tactile stimulus of at least moderate intensity. A very interesting finding was that the mechanisms of general sensory facilitation are amplified if a sensory neuron fires action potentials at the time that neuromodulatory messengers released by a noxious stimulus are received by the sensory neuron. If a sensory neuron is activated by a conditioned stimulus (CS) shortly before a noxious stimulus presented elsewhere on the body (in a classical conditioning paradigm), this activity-dependent sensory facilitation can contribute to the encoding of a memory of the CS, expressed as CS-specific sensitization (Hawkins, Abrams, Carew, & Kandel, 1983; Walters & Byrne, 1983). Perhaps more important in mechanosensory neurons of

Aplysia, the presentation of the noxious unconditioned stimulus (US) causes intense activation of wide-dynamic range nociceptors innervating the US site. These sensory neurons undergo strong activity-dependent facilitation, and this enhanced facilitation represents a memory of the noxious US in those cells (Walters, 1987a, b, and Figure 1). Under natural conditions this site-specific sensitization enhances the sensitivity around a wound, similar to the effect of primary hyperalgesia in humans (Woolf and Walters, 1991). Presumably the heightened sensitivity serves to protect a vulnerable wounded area during recuperation.

More recently it was discovered that a phase of reflex inhibition sometimes precedes the sensitization phase. Inhibition of withdrawal reflexes by noxious tail stimulation was first described by Marcus, Nolen, Rankin, & Carew (1988), Mackey, Glanzman, Small, Dyke, Kandel, & Hawkins (1987), and Krontiris-Litowitz, Erickson, & Walters (1987). Like sensitization, inhibition is likely to be associated with changes in several types of neurons (Wright, Marcus, & Carew, 1991). Siphon sensory neurons appear to show classical presynaptic inhibition for brief periods after noxious stimulation, probably releasing less transmitter from their terminals (Mackey et al., 1987). We have focused our recent analysis of biphasic modulation of sensory neurons on another manifestation of inhibition—suppression of action potential initiation and conduction (Clatworthy & Walters, 1993b). Figure 2 illustrates representative responses recorded in the cell body of a tail sensory neuron before, during, and after noxious stimulation. The test responses were evoked by stimulating the tail with a train of weak shock. A noxious "training stimulus" was used to produce high frequency activation of afferents from the tail, similar to activation produced by traumatic cutaneous stimulation. In this case the training stimulus was intense electrical stimulation of the nerve innervating the tail, a stimulus which causes the same defensive responses and modulatory effects, but avoids the complications of tissue destruction that usually occur when the tail is traumatized. We have conducted many experiments with a variety of different test and training stimuli and found similar effects in

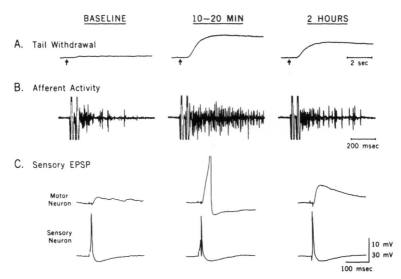

Figure 1. Facilitatory effects of noxious stimulation on the tail withdrawal reflex and tactile sensitivity of *Aplysia* (from Walters, 1987b, Figure 3). A 45-second train of intense shock was delivered to the tail following the baseline test. Part A. Enhancement of reflex contraction measured with an electronic tension transducer attached to the tail. A brief, weak test shock was delivered to another part of the tail at each arrow. Part B. Enhancement of extracellularly recorded activity of afferent neurons in the nerve from the tail. Efferent activity in the nerve at the recording site was reversibly blocked by superfusing a solution lacking Na^+ over a section of the nerve between the recording electrode and the central ganglia. Part C. Enhancement of an excitatory postsynaptic potential (EPSP) at a synapse between a tail sensory neuron and tail motor neuron (sensory neurons also make parallel synaptic connections to various interneurons, some of which in turn project to motor neurons). The effectiveness of the synaptic connection was tested by artificially activating the sensory neuron, by briefly passing electrical current through the intracellular recording electrode. The resulting action potential in the sensory neuron led to neurotransmitter release, which produced the EPSP monitored with a second intracellular electrode in the motor neuron. The EPSP observed 10–20 minutes after tail shock was facilitated so much that it reached the threshold for triggering an action potential (which has been clipped in the figure) in the motor neuron. Facilitation of the EPSP is still clear two hours after the tail shock. Reprinted by permission from *The Journal of Neuroscience*.

each case. Prior to the noxious training stimulus, test stimuli (brief trains of eight pulses) to the tail reliably caused the conduction of five to six action potentials to the soma of the illustrated sensory neuron. Ten intense trains of shock were then delivered at five second intervals to the nerve from the tail, which contained the sensory neuron's axon. As can be seen, ten seconds after the last train the same test stimulus gave rise to no action potentials in the cell body, and after five minutes the number of action potentials was still reduced compared to before training. The test response returned to the pre-training level (five spikes) at ten minutes, and then showed facilitation (eight spikes) at 40 minutes. The inhibition of sensory spike conduction was greater in sensory neurons, such as this one, which were

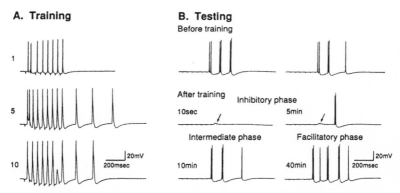

Figure 2. Biphasic modulation of action potential conduction in a tail sensory neuron by noxious stimulation. Part A. Responses to noxious training sequence. Ten trains of strong shock were delivered to the nerve to the tail. The resulting action potentials were conducted to the sensory neuron soma where the recordings were made (only the responses to the first, fifth, and tenth trains are shown). Notice the afterdischarge following the later trains. Part B. Test responses to weak tail shock before and after training. Two tests are shown before training and four tests are shown after training. Note the absence of conducted action potentials ten seconds after training. The arrows indicate attenuated spikes which were probably blocked near the sensory neuron's synaptic terminals onto motor neurons in the adjacent pedal ganglion. Reprinted by permission from *The Journal of Neuroscience*.

activated during training than in sensory neurons which did not fire action potentials. This suggested that one of the signals for inhibition of spike conduction may normally be the action potentials evoked in sensory neurons by noxious stimulation of their receptive fields. This possibility was confirmed by demonstrating significant inhibition of sensory spike conduction following selective intracellular stimulation of single sensory neurons through the recording electrode. This selective suppression indicates that high frequency activation of the cell can transiently block conduction of subsequent action potentials, even in the absence of inhibitory inputs from other cells. Recent data suggests that brief, activity-dependent inhibitory effects are generated peripherally, near the sensory receptors and along the axon, as well as centrally, near the cell's soma and synaptic terminals.

In summary, noxious stimulation of *Aplysia* activates wide-dynamic range mechanosensory neurons which 1) trigger withdrawal responses and 2) cause biphasic modulation of their own signalling effectiveness. A brief, strong inhibitory phase of sensory modulation is followed by a long-lasting facilitatory phase. Both phases can occur in sensory neurons that are not activated by the noxious stimulus, but both phases are enhanced in sensory neurons active during the noxious stimulus (i.e. sensory neurons activated by either the noxious US or a paired CS).

Expression of Alternative Motor Responses to Noxious Stimulation

In addition to studying intensity-dependent approach and withdrawal reactions, Schneirla was concerned with the effects of prior experience on an organism's approach or withdrawal to a given stimulus. The question of how qualitatively different response alternatives are selected during behavior is fundamental to psychology and neuroscience, and has begun to be approached at the cellular level in invertebrate preparations (e.g. Kovac & Davis, 1977). Furthermore, some of these preparations may soon provide answers to the question of how behavioral choice is influenced by prior experience (e.g. London & Gillette, 1986). With these questions in mind, we are examining processes

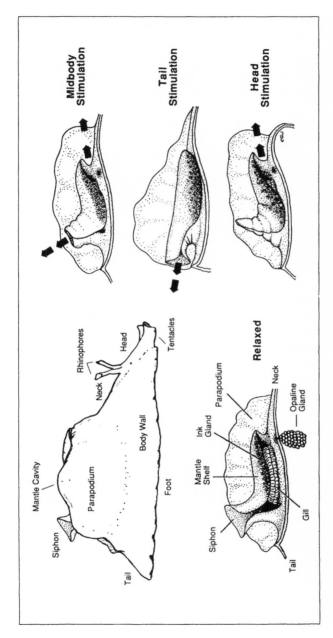

Figure 3. Different siphon responses of *Aplysia*. Left. Diagram of an intact animal at rest, and cutaway view of the mantle organs and siphon in the relaxed animal. Right. Cutaway views of three qualitatively distinct siphon responses evoked by stimulation of different parts of the body. The arrows indicate the direction of water currents (which carry ink, opaline, and other secretions out of the mantle cavity) during each response. The different responses serve to direct these secretions towards the source of noxious stimulation. Modified from Walters and Erickson, 1986, Figure 7. Copyright© Springer-Verlag. Reprinted with permission.

contributing to experience-dependent selection of alternative siphon responses in *Aplysia*. The siphon is a soft, contractile funnel through which water is expelled from the mantle cavity after it has passed over the gill (Figure 3). The siphon also has an important role in directing ejections of the defensive secretions, ink and opaline, from the mantle cavity following noxious stimulation (Walters & Erickson, 1986). Thus far, we have only examined *withdrawal* and withdrawal-like responses of this organ. Siphon movements are also involved in nondefensive behavior, such as defecation (the siphon contains the anus). Any direct involvement in *approach* behavior has not been described, although there is a remote possibility that siphon responses could aid in directing pheromones to conspecifics during mating and egg laying (Audesirk, 1977; Lederhendler, Herriges & Tobach, 1977).

As shown in Figure 3, mechanical stimuli applied to different regions of the body surface evoke qualitatively different siphon responses, each of which causes mantle secretions to be directed towards the site of stimulation. An interesting finding was that noxious stimulation of one site can change the type of siphon response evoked by subsequent stimulation of another site. For example, strong head or tail stimulation can change the response to weak midbody stimulation so that the response to the midbody stimulus is transformed to the same type as that evoked by the strong stimulus to the head or tail (Erickson & Walters, 1988). An example of transformed siphon responses in a surgically reduced siphon/mantle preparation is illustrated in Figure 4. In this particular experiment a classical conditioning procedure was used to see whether response transformation would show any specificity to the pairing of a weak CS, delivered to the mantle shelf, with a strong US, delivered to nerves from the tail. Following five CS-US pairings the CS evoked flaring conditioned responses (CRs) like those produced by the US (URs), rather than the constricting alpha responses it had evoked prior to pairing.

Neural models which have been proposed to explain the appearance of such CRs have been dominated by the idea of "Hebbian synapses." In these models, individual synapses are strengthened if the presynaptic neuron, activated by the CS, and the postsynaptic neuron, activated by the US, fire

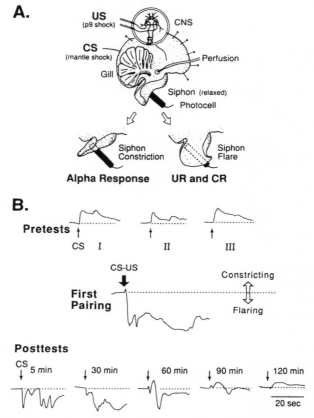

Figure 4. Surgically reduced siphon/mantle preparation used to examine qualitative transformation of siphon responses (Walters, 1989, Figure 1). Part A. The test stimulus or CS was a weak shock delivered to the dorsal surface of the mantle. The US was an intense shock delivered to both nerves (p9) innervating the tail. Arrows indicate defensive siphon responses observed before training (alpha response), during training (UR), and after training (CR). Part B. Examples of siphon responses measured with the photocell in the surgically reduced preparation before, during, and after training. Training causes the transformation of one defensive siphon response into another defensive response that involves opposite movements.

conjunctively (Hebb, 1949; Sejnowski & Tesauro, 1989). However, we concluded that a different model may better account for the behavioral and cellular data of siphon conditioning (Walters, 1989). Of particular importance was the finding that the US alone, in the absence of pairing with the CS, could sometimes cause a siphon response transformation (pseudoconditioning), although the transformation of CS responses was significantly less likely following training with the US alone or unpaired training than after paired training. This observation led to a "concatenation model" (Figure 5), in which mechanisms of stimulus-specific facilitation observed in *Aplysia* sensory neurons (see above) and mechanisms of response-specific facilitation observed in identified motor neurons (Frost et al., 1988; Hickie & Walters, 1991) are triggered independently in sensory neurons and motor neurons during conditioning. Stimulus-specific sensory facilitation causes the CS to show the largest increase in effectiveness in eliciting motor responses; i.e. the sensory system becomes tuned to the CS. Response-specific motor facilitation causes the unconditioned response (UR) to the US to show the largest increase in responsiveness to sensory stimulation in general; i.e. the motor system becomes biased towards the UR. Together, these simultaneous but independent cell-wide effects may lead to the appearance of new responses to the CS that resemble the responses to the US.

A somewhat different mechanism, involving synapse-specific or branch-specific facilitation of sensory neuron synapses in the CS pathway, has been suggested by Hawkins, Lalevic, Clark, & Kandel (1989) to explain similar changes in siphon responses seen in behavioral studies of the intact animal. However, true synapse-specific neuronal plasticity has not been reported thus far in *Aplysia* or in other invertebrates during learning-related manipulations. The advantage of concatenating cell-wide plasticity mechanisms is that novel stimulus-response associations can be created in simple networks using common mechanisms that remain available for other, nonassociative uses. The disadvantage of concatenation models is that, unlike synapse-specific models (e.g. Hebbian models), they have a low information storage capacity—they cannot readily store multiple associations in the same network (e.g. linking several CSs with different CRs).

However, it is intriguing to consider the possibility that primitive concatenation mechanisms might be involved in fundamental modifications of behavior such as a transformation of a withdrawal response into an approach response or vice-versa.

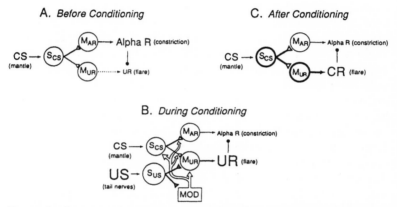

Figure 5. Concatenation model of conditioned response transformation in *Aplysia* (Walters, 1989, Figure 3). S, sensory neuron; M, motor neuron; MOD, modulatory interneurons. Part A. Before conditioning the connection from S_{CS} to M_{AR} is stronger than the connection to M_{UR}. The CS evokes the preexisting "alpha" response, which inhibits (filled circle) incompatible responses such as the UR (see Illich et al., 1994). Part B. During conditioning S_{CS} undergoes activity-dependent modulation, facilitating all of its synaptic outputs, and M_{UR} (but not M_{AR}) undergoes activity-dependent modulation which facilitates its responsiveness to all of its synaptic inputs. Part C. After conditioning, concatenation of CS-specific sensory facilitation in S_{CS} with UR-specific motor facilitation in M_{UR} results in the greatest facilitation of signals from S_{CS} to M_{UR}. Facilitated signalling strength is indicated by thickened lines. With sufficient pre- and postsynaptic facilitation, S_{CS} excites M_{UR} more than M_{AR}, and the CS evokes a novel CR resembling the UR.

Could Neuronal Mechanisms Found in *Aplysia* Contribute to Intensity-Dependent Biphasic Processes?

In a highly speculative exercise, one can extrapolate from the mechanisms involved in biphasic modulation of sensory neurons and in the transformation of siphon responses in *Aplysia* to consider potential mechanisms for Schneirla's intensity-dependent approach-withdrawal processes. The simplest model would be to have sensory neurons in a given modality be divided into separate populations coding for innocuous and threatening stimuli. In this model, approach responses would be triggered by low-threshold receptors and withdrawal responses by high-intensity receptors (nociceptors). Although this organization is seen in many somatosensory systems (and has been implicated by the apparent existence of unidentified low-threshold mechanosensory neurons in the somatosensory system of *Aplysia*, see Cohen, Henzi, Kandel, & Hawkins, 1991) it seems unlikely for most other modalities (e.g. chemosensory, auditory, visual), where there is little if any evidence for intensity-dependent specificity in primary sensory neurons or sensory interneurons. While the mammalian somatosensory system does make use of separate populations of low- and high-threshold primary sensory neurons, at the next level (spinal interneurons) many of the cells show graded responses to a broad range of stimulus intensities (e.g. Woolf & King, 1987). Interestingly, wide-dynamic-range sensory neurons in *Aplysia* display a number of functional similarities to wide-dynamic-range sensory interneurons in the spinal cord (Walters, Byrne, Carew, & Kandel, 1983a; Woolf & Walters, 1991). In both systems noxiousness is represented, at least in part, by elevated firing rates of cells that fire less intensely to innocuous stimuli. Biphasic approach-withdrawal behavior could be produced by sensory input from such cells if 1) some wide-dynamic-range sensory interneurons were to make parallel connections to separate populations of executive neurons controlling approach and withdrawal responses, 2) executive neurons in the approach system had lower thresholds than executive neurons in the withdrawal system, and 3) the approach and withdrawal systems were mutually inhibitory, but the withdrawal system produced stronger inhibitory effects when it was activated than did the approach system, as may be the case in *Aplysia* (Walters, Carew, & Kandel, 1981; Lukowiak, 1987).

Many other models for approach-withdrawal behavior can be constructed from the cellular properties observed in *Aplysia*. For example, the same behavioral pattern could be produced if sensory neurons or executive neurons controlling approach behavior were more responsive at low-stimulus intensities than cells controlling withdrawal behavior, but were also more prone to activity-dependent synaptic depression or inhibition of spike conduction (as seen in *Aplysia* sensory neurons). While we don't yet know the underlying mechanisms, the biphasic approach-withdrawal pattern emphasized by Schneirla points to interesting neural processes that should be amenable to direct cellular investigation in *Aplysia* and perhaps in other relatively simple organisms.

Reductionist Analysis of Behavioral Mechanisms in *Aplysia:* Promises and Pitfalls

As just indicated, the ability to examine identified neurons and networks in *Aplysia* during relatively normal behavior offers considerable promise for relating cellular properties to behavioral function. Indeed, the analysis of cellular and molecular mechanisms of sensitization and classical conditioning of siphon and gill withdrawal in *Aplysia* is widely acclaimed as a triumph of the reductionist approach to the study of behavior. Therefore, it is instructive to consider some of the limitations of reductionist analysis that are being encountered in this analytically favorable system. These limitations may, in part, be consequences of the complex interactions among genetic, developmental and experiential factors emphasized by Schneirla. They also reflect other sources of biological complexity, technological limitations and, perhaps, what has been an excessive reliance on concepts and paradigms derived from traditional mammalian psychology.

A consideration of pitfalls in reductionist approaches to behavior seems particularly timely today when neuroscientists are engaged in what may be the ultimate reductionist exercise, searchng for individual genes controlling specific behavioral traits and behavioral diseases.

A popular reductionist recipe for explaining mechanisms of learning was pioneered in *Aplysia* and other invertebrate "model systems" (e.g. Kandel & Schwartz, 1982; Byrne, 1987; Alkon, 1988), and can be described as follows.

1) Begin at the behavioral level. Define and characterize the behavioral features of a response, such as gill withdrawal, and its modifiability during learning. Do this both in the intact animal and in the surgically reduced preparations that will be necessary for studying neuronal correlates of behaviorally expressed learning.

2) In surgically reduced preparations identify sensory, motor and interneurons making major contributions to the behavior and find out which cells show alterations during learning.

3) In identified neurons within isolated ganglia, or dissociated cell culture, find specific ionic conductances (e.g. to K^+) and other cellular processes (e.g. neurotransmitter mobilization) whose alterations may contribute to the expression of altered neuronal function during learning in the surgically reduced preparations.

4) Using pharmacological methods (extracellular application of neuromodulators and neuromodulator antagonists) search for extracellular messengers (e.g. serotonin) involved in altering neuronal function in the reduced preparations.

5) Inject second and third messenger candidates (e.g. cAMP and protein kinase A, Ca^{2+} and Ca^{2+}-dependent kinases) and specific blockers into identified neurons to mimic or block the effects of learning or (more commonly) plasticity produced by spike activity and/or extracellular messengers implicated as learning signals.

6) Apply molecular biological techniques in order to identify genes and gene products regulated by neural activity and by the implicated extracellular and intracellular messengers.

Well-known discoveries resulting from this approach in *Aplysia* include the discovery of novel mechanisms of short- and long-term plasticity (e.g. heterosynaptic facilitation, depression of specific K^+ conductances), and the involvement in these plastic mechanisms of various second messengers (cyclic AMP, Ca^{2+}, protein kinase C, arachidonic acid metabolites), altered protein synthesis, the regulation of particular genes and growth of synaptic terminals (e.g. Kandel & Schwartz, 1982; Bailey & Chen, 1983; Sweatt, Volterra, Siegelbaum, & Kandel 1988; Castellucci & Schacher, 1990).

On the other hand, three general limitations have become evident in the application of this reductionist approach to learning in *Aplysia*. First, because of the interest in analyzing general learning processes, behavioral paradigms (notably sensitization and classical conditioning) were imported from the mainstream of the American animal learning field, a field which emphasized behaviorist approaches to learning in select vertebrate species (primarily rodents and pigeons). Little effort was made to test the functional significance of mechanisms activated by these behavioral paradigms in molluscs, which have very different life styles from mammals and which are only very distantly related to mammals. For example, it was not realized until recently that the sensory neurons proposed to be the major sites of memory and learning in *Aplysia* function as nociceptors and that their greatest plasticity is not exhibited during learning about a CS as originally proposed (Hawkins, Abrams, Carew, & Kandel, 1983; Walters & Byrne, 1983), but instead is most dramatic after injury of their peripheral receptive fields (Walters, 1987a,b; Billy & Walters, 1989a). As described earlier, this potent plasticity takes the form of short-term, activity-dependent suppression of nociceptive signals from the injured region (preventing the elicitation of protective reflexes that might interfere with the more important business of escape) and long-term, activity-dependent enhancement of the same nociceptive signals (similar to hyperalgesia). This revised functional interpretation of sensory plasticity in *Aplysia*, while not contradicting the mechanisms revealed by the reductionist experiments, showed that it is important to ask appropriate questions of one's experimental data. In this case, some of the experiments (e.g. Walters & Byrne, 1983; Hawkins et al., 1983) ostensibly answered the question of how a sensory neuron learns that it represents a CS during classical conditioning. But the experiments may have answered another question: How does a sensory neuron remember that its receptive field has been traumatized? Although functionally distinct, these two questions may be evolutionarily related—a mechanism that was initially selected in evolution to represent sites of peripheral injury might have been co-opted later in evolution to encode memories of innocuous CSs that are paired with injury (Walters, 1987a; Walters, 1991; Walters, Alizadeh & Castro, 1991; Walters, 1994). It should by emphasized that questions about the behavioral functions of cellular mechanisms are very difficult to answer. Indeed, while the memory-of-injury function for activity–dependent sensory plasticity in *Aplysia* explains current data and has produced useful experimental predictions, alternative or additional functions for this plasticity need to be considered.

A second limitation of reductionist analyses of learning mechanisms is the large number of neurons that may be involved in these processes, even in relatively simple organisms such as *Aplysia*. Intracellular recording, stimulation, and injection methods have provided the clearest and most detailed information in these analyses, but such methods can only be used on a few neurons at a time (typically one to four cells). *Aplysia* may have about 10,000 neurons in its CNS, and recent data indicate that a much larger number of neurons than had been expected show some kind of involvement in behavioral modifications. Indeed, the neural network underlying siphon responses has not been completely identified and much remains to be learned about the cellular properties of the interneurons and motor neurons that have been identified. At least some of these neurons are known to be additional loci of plasticity contributing to sensitization of siphon withdrawal (Kanz, Eberly, Cobbs, & Pinsker, 1979; Frost et al., 1988). The potential complexity involved in regulating even these "simple" reflexes is suggested by recent recordings of the abdominal ganglion using optical methods and voltage-sensitive dyes. Initial observations suggest that a large number of neurons, perhaps 15 to 40 percent of the approximately 1,000 neurons in the ganglion, may be activated by siphon stimuli which elicit siphon and gill withdrawal (Zecevic, Wu, Cohen, London, Hopp, & Falk, 1989;

Nakashima, Yamada, Shiono, & Maeda, 1989 and personal communication). While most of these neurons probably make little or no contribution to the reflex under observation, it will still be a very large task to map all of the synaptic interconnections among these cells and to determine which of the many thousands of connections may be altered during learning.

This problem is illustrated by difficulties encountered in defining the afferent limb of the siphon and gill reflexes used in many learning studies in *Aplysia*. The primary mechanisms of sensitization and classical conditioning of these reflexes were initially assumed to lie in the siphon sensory neurons (e.g. Kandel & Schwartz, 1982) because there was often an apparent isomorphism between sensory plasticity and aspects of the behavioral changes (e.g. Hawkins, Abrams, Carew, & Kandel, 1983). However, further studies revealed conditions in which there is little or no correlation between alterations of identified siphon sensory neurons and siphon or gill behavior (Lukowiak, 1986; Wright, Marcus, & Carew, 1991). Moreover, it was found that responses of mantle organs and their motor neurons can be elicited by stimuli that are too weak to activate identified sensory populations whose alterations have been central to analyses of reflex plasticity in *Aplysia* (e.g. Kupfermann, Carew, & Kandel, 1974; Cohen, Henzi, Kandel, & Hawkins, 1991; Illich & Walters, unpublished observations). These results indicated that other, as yet unidentified sensory populations exist, making unknown contributions to siphon responses and their modifiability. Although several interneurons in the siphon control circuit have been identified and examined during sensitizing stimulation (e.g. Frost, Clark, & Kandel, 1988), the problem of identifying all the major interneurons contributing to learning-related alterations of siphon responses should be even more severe. To make matters worse, the functional identification of neurons and networks can be confused by the dependence of neuronal and network functions on different states produced by neuromodulators and hormones. For example, in the lobster stomatogastric ganglion where *all* synaptic interactions have been examined (e.g. Miller & Selverston, 1982), the dramatic dependence of network properties upon neuromodulators and hormones has made the analysis of network function extremely difficult (Harris-Warwick, 1988).

Even if all the sites of plasticity contributing to learning could be found and each cellular alteration described, there would still be a third problem confronting a reductionist analysis of learning mechanisms. This is the difficulty of assessing the relative contributions of particular mechanisms to the behavior of the organism. In very simple networks one can test the contribution (i.e. relative necessity and/or sufficiency) of a particular neuron or small set of neurons to a given behavioral feature by using intracellular electrodes to artificially hyperpolarize it (reversibly removing it) from the network during the behavior, and by artificially activating it to try to mimic aspects of the behavior. However, few biological networks have been found in which specific behavioral functions are concentrated in few enough experimentally accessible neurons for this type of test to cause any discernible effects (e.g. Getting, 1989). Other currently available methods (e.g. multiunit extracellular recording, optical recording) are limited to showing correlations between behavioral features and activity patterns in particular neurons or sets of neurons. Even without the complexity of multiple states due to the action of neuromodulators, computer models of simplified, generalized networks and electrophysiological recordings from "simple" biological networks reveal complex, nonlinear properties which are not obvious in the properties of individual synapses and neurons in the network (e.g. Sejnowski, Koch, & Churchland, 1988; Getting, 1989). It now seems clear that detailed quantitative simulations will be required to begin to make sense out of even the simplest biological networks. However, the impossibility of obtaining *complete* empirical descriptions of such networks, and the extraordinary difficulty in testing quantitative contributions of particular circuit elements in biological experiments, insure that we can never be completely confident of mechanistic interpretations based on these simulations. Although I have focused on the cellular and neural network levels, similar problems confront analyses at the intracellular and molecular levels. For example, the growing number of second and third messengers and their increasingly complex interactions make such analyses within a single cell very difficult (e.g. Dash,

Hochner, & Kandel, 1990; Dash, Karl, Colicos, Prywes, & Kandel, 1991; O'Dell, Kandel, & Grant, 1991).

Thus, three pitfalls have been encountered in reductionist analyses of learning mechanisms in *Aplysia* : 1) excessive reliance on experimental and theoretical paradigms which sometimes have questionable significance for the behavioral alterations and species under investigation; 2) problems in finding and manipulating cellular and molecular elements that may be important for the behavioral alterations under investigation; and 3) even bigger problems in assessing the contributions of individual elements (cells, synapses, ion channels, enzymes) to behaviorally expressed learning. These problems suggest that a *complete* reductionist explanation of behaviors such as withdrawal may prove impossible, even in relatively simple brains such as *Aplysia*'s. Nevertheless, an informative perspective onto the organization, regulation, and evolution of behavior is available from cellular and network studies of relatively simple, behaving nervous systems. In the case of *Aplysia*, neurobiologists have learned a great deal about cellular processes involved in both transient and long-lasting changes in sensory and motor responsiveness. At the same time, one of the most significant outcomes of these efforts is the continued appearance of surprising results that overturn simplistic experimental assumptions and continue to challenge neurobiologists' bid to explain the neural bases of behavior and learning, even in "simple model systems."

Evolutionary Perspectives on Cellular and Network Processes

The complex processes neuroscientists seek to understand through reductionist analysis are the products of evolution. Thus it seems likely that clues about the biological history of neuronal processes can inform and balance the reductionist analyses, and, conversely, that knowledge derived from reductionist analyses may shed light on the evolution of neuronal properties. Coordination between reductionist and evolutionary approaches might begin to answer some of the most difficult questions about brain,

behavior and evolution. For example, how does natural selection, which largely acts at the level of behavior, interact with
the potentialities and constraints imposed by fundamental neuronal properties? The accessibility to scientists of neuronal
mechanisms having relatively clear links to behavioral function
in *Aplysia* and various molluscs suggests that a beginning might
be made with this group of animals in attempting to answer this
kind of question. Molluscs offer a rare opportunity to compare
specific neuronal mechanisms contributing to behavior across a
wide range of species, and to relate differences and similarities in
these neuronal mechanisms to phylogenetic relationships and
differences in behavioral ecology (e.g. aquatic vs. terrestrial, soft-
bodied vs. heavily armored, carnivorous vs. herbivorous, specialized feeder vs. generalized feeder, short life span vs. long life
span). Conversely, knowledge of the phylogenetic variation and
functional significance of specific neuronal mechanisms within
experimentally convenient groups of animals such as molluscs
can indicate which mechanisms are highly specialized and which
are likely to be general. In arguing for the fundamental importance of approach-withdrawal processes, Schneirla invoked the
evolutionary significance of processes that are widespread and
of clear adaptive value. For the neurophysiologist, the existence
of widespread behavioral and neuronal processes justifies the
use of relatively simple organisms to probe potentially general
(homologous or analogous) mechanisms underlying behavior.

To test the generality and evolutionary significance of particular neuronal mechanisms, explicit comparative studies must
be made across a broad range of species, using multidisciplinary
methods (Bullock, 1984). Thus far, mechanisms of learning and
memory have probably received the most comparative attention
from behavioral neurobiologists (e.g. Kandel, 1976; Sahley,
Rudy, & Gelperin, 1981; Bitterman, 1986). We suggest that the
relatively neglected phenomenom of nociceptive memory offers
considerable promise for interesting phylogenetic comparisons
at both the behavioral and neuronal levels. Behavioral responses
to peripheral injury occur in virtually all organisms, and adaptive changes in behavior persisting long enough for an injury to
heal probably appeared very early in evolution (Walters, 1991;
1994). As described above, preliminary comparisons of *Aplysia*

and mammals suggest that such changes in behavior may often be associated with long-lasting alterations in the excitability of primary and secondary mechanosensory and nociceptive neurons (Woolf & Walters, 1991). Because sensory neurons are easier to identify than many types of neurons and are relatively accessible for neurophysiological analysis, it should be feasible to conduct systematic comparative studies of nociceptive memory in these types of neurons in many animal groups. Furthermore, explicit hypotheses about evolutionary relationships among different forms of plasticity can be framed and examined. For example, similarities in *Aplysia* between activity-dependent mechanisms of classical conditioning and wound-specific sensitization ("primary hyperalgesia") suggest that some processes involved in associative learning might have evolved from more primitive mechanisms of nociceptive sensitization (Walters, 1987b; 1991). And similarities between cellular mechanisms of nociceptive sensitization and cellular alterations produced by axonal injury suggest that mechanisms of long-lasting sensitization might have evolved from even more primitive adaptive reactions of sensory neurons to injury of their peripheral branches (Walters, Alizadeh, & Castro, 1991; Walters, 1994). A comparative analysis of behavioral processes at the behavioral and neuronal levels may illuminate the interplay of functional demands and available neuronal mechanisms in the evolution of nervous systems, and provide some clues about the evolution of some mechanisms of memory. Such a broad-based, comparative approach fits well with the ideas of T. C. Schneirla, and might eventually prove useful for understanding the approach-withdrawal processes that he emphasized.

REFERENCES

Alkon, D. L. (1988). *Memory traces in the brain.* Cambridge University Press, Cambridge, England.

Audesirk, T. E. (1977). Chemoreception in *Aplysia californica* III. Evidence for pheromones influencing reproductive behavior. *Behavioral Biology*, 20, 235–243.

Bailey, C. H., & Chen, M. (1983). Morphological basis of long-term habituation and sensitization in *Aplysia*. *Science*, 220, 91–93.

Billy, A. J., & Walters, E. T. (1989a). Long-term expansion and sensitization of mechanosensory receptive fields in *Aplysia* support an activity-dependent model of whole-cell sensory plasticity. *Journal of Neuroscience*, 9, 1254–1262.

Billy, A. J., & Walters, E. T. (1989b). Modulation of mechanosensory threshold in *Aplysia* by serotonin, small cardioactive peptideB (SCPB), FMRFamide, acetylcholine, and dopamine. *Neuroscience Letters*, 105, 200–204.

Bitterman, M. E. (1986). Vertebrate-invertebrate comparisons. In H. J. Jerison & I. Jerison (Eds.), *Intelligence and Evolutionary Biology* (pp. 251–276) Berlin: Springer-Verlag.

Bullock, T. H. (1984). Comparative neuroscience holds promise for quiet revolutions. *Science*, 225, 473–478.

Byrne, J. H. , Castellucci, V. F., & Kandel, E. R. (1974). Receptive fields and response properties of mechanoreceptor neurons innervating siphon skin and mantle shelf in *Aplysia*. *Journal of Neurophysiology*, 37, 1041–1064.

Byrne, J. H., Castellucci, V. F., & Kandel, E. R. (1978). Contribution of individual mechanoreceptor sensory neurons to defensive gill-withdrawal reflex in *Aplysia*. *Journal of Neurophysiology*, 41, 418–431.

Carew, T. J., Castellucci, V. F., & Kandel, E. R. (1971). An analysis of dishabituation and sensitization of the gill-withdrawal reflex in *Aplysia*. *International Journal of Neuroscience*, 2, 79–98.

Castellucci, V. F., & Kandel, E. R. (1976). Presynaptic facilitation as a mechanism for behavioral sensitization in *Aplysia*. *Science*, 194, 1176–1181.

Clatworthy, A. L., & Walters, E. T. (1993a). Rapid amplification of mechanosensory discharge in *Aplysia* by noxious stimulation. *Journal of Neurophysiology*, 70, 1181–1194.

———. (1993b). Activity-dependent depression of mechanosensory discharge in *Aplysia*. *Journal of Neurophysiology*, 70, 1195–1209.

Cohen, T. E., Henzi, V., Kandel, E. R., & Hawkins, R. D. (1991). Further behavioral and cellular studies of dishabituation and sensitization in *Aplysia*. *Society for Neuroscience Abstracts*, 17, 1302.

Cook, D. G., & Carew, T. J. (1989). Operant conditioning of head-waving in *Aplysia*. II. Contingent modification of electromyographic activity in identified muscles. *Journal of Neuroscience, 9*, 3107–3114.

Dash, P. K., Hochner, B., & Kandel, E. R. (1990). Injection of the cAMP-responsive element into the nucleus of *Aplysia* sensory neurons blocks long-term facilitation. *Nature, 345*, 718–721.

Dash, P. K., Karl, K. A., Colicos, M. A., Prywes, R., & Kandel, E. R. (1991). cAMP response element-binding protein is activated by Ca^{2+}-calmodulin as well as cAMP-dependent protein kinase. *Proceedings of the National Academy Sciences of the U.S.A., 88*, 5061–5065.

Eaton, R. C., & Hackett J. T. (1984). The role of the Mauthner cell in fast-starts involving escape in teleost fishes. In R. C. Eaton (Ed.), *Neural mechanisms of startle behavior* (pp. 213–266). New York: Plenum.

Erickson, M. T., & Walters, E. T. (1988). Differential expression of pseudoconditioning and sensitization by siphon responses in *Aplysia*: Novel response selection after training. *Journal of Neuroscience, 8*, 3000–3010.

Eskin, A., Garcia, K. S., & Byrne, J. H. (1989). Information storage in the nervous system of *Aplysia*: Specific proteins affected by serotonin and cAMP. *Proceedings of the National Academy of Science of the U.S.A., 86*, 2458–2462.

Fredman, S. M., & Jahan-Parwar, B. (1977). Identifiable cerebral motoneurons mediating an anterior tentacular withdrawal reflex in *Aplysia*. *Journal of Neurophysiology, 40*, 608–615.

Frost, W. N., Castellucci, V. F., Hawkins, R. D., & Kandel, E. R. (1985). Monosynaptic connections made by the sensory neurons of the gill- and siphon-withdrawal reflex in *Aplysia* participate in the storage of long-term memory for sensitization. *Proceedings of the National Academy of Science of the U.S.A., 82*, 8266–8269.

Frost, W. N., Clark, G. A., & Kandel, E. R. (1988). Parallel processing of short-term memory for sensitization in *Aplysia*. *Journal of Neurobiology, 19*, 297–334.

Getting, P. A. (1976). Afferent neurons mediating escape swimming of the marine mollusc, *Tritonia*. *Journal of Comparative Physiology, 110*, 271–286.

Getting, P. A. (1989). Emerging principles governing the operation of neural networks. *Annual Review of Neuroscience, 12*, 185–204.

Goelet, P., Castellucci, V. F., Schacher, S., & Kandel, E. R. (1986). The long and the short of long-term memory—a molecular framework. *Nature, 322,* 419–422.

Harris-Warwick, R. M. (1988). Chemical modulation of central pattern generators. In A. H. Cohen, S. Rosiggnol, S. Grillner (Eds.), *Neural control of rhythmic movements* (pp. 285–332). New York: Wiley.

Hawkins, R. D., Abrams, T. W., Carew, T. J., & Kandel, E. R. (1983). A cellular mechanism of classical conditioning in *Aplysia*: Activity-dependent amplification of presynaptic facilitation. *Science, 219,* 400–404.

Hawkins, R. D., Lalevic, N., Clark, G. A., & Kandel E. R. (1989). Classical conditioning of the *Aplysia* siphon-withdrawal reflex exhibits response specificity. *Proceedings of the National Academy of Science of the U.S.A., 86,* 7620–7624.

Hebb, D. O. (1949). *The organization of behavior.* New York: Wiley.

Illich, P. A., Joynes, R. L., & Walters, E. T. (1994). Response-specific inhibition during general facilitation of defensive responses in *Aplysia. Behavioral Neuroscience,* 614–623.

Kandel, E. R. (1976). *Cellular basis of behavior.* San Francisco: Freeman.

Kandel, E. R., & Schwartz, J. H. (1982). Molecular biology of learning: Modulation of transmitter release. *Science, 218,* 433–444.

Kanz, J. E., Eberly, L. B., Cobbs, J. S., & Pinsker, H. M. (1979). Neuronal correlates of siphon withdrawal in freely behaving *Aplysia. Journal of Neurophysiology, 42,* 1538–1556.

Klein, M., Hochner, B., & Kandel, E. R. (1986). Facilitatory transmitters and cAMP can modulate accommodation as well as transmitter release in *Aplysia* sensory neurons: Evidence for parallel processing in a single cell. *Proceedings of the National Academy of Science of the U.S.A., 83,* 7994–7998.

Getting, P. A. (1976). Afferent neurons mediating escape swimming of the marine mollusc, *Tritonia. Journal of Comparative Physiology, 110,* 271–286.

Krasne, F. B., & Lee, S. C. (1988). Response-dedicated trigger neurons as control points for behavioral actions: Selective inhibition of lateral giant command neurons during feeding in crayfish. *Journal of Neuroscience 8,* 3703–3712.

Krasne, F. B., & Wine, J. J. (1984). The production of crayfish tailflip escape responses. In R. C. Eaton (Ed.), *Neural Mechanisms of Startle Behavior* (pp. 179–211). New York: Plenum.

Kristan, W. B., McGirr, S. J., & Simpson, G. V. (1982). Behavioral and mechanosensory neurone responses to skin stimulation in leeches. *Journal of Experimental Biology, 96,* 143–160.

Krontiris-Litowitz, J. K., Erickson, M. T., & Walters, E. T. (1987). Central suppression of defensive reflexes by noxious stimulation and by factors released from body wall. *Society for Neuroscience Abstracts, 13,* 815.

Kupfermann, I., Carew, T. J., & Kandel, E. R. (1974). Local, reflex, and central commands controlling gill and siphon movements in *Aplysia. Journal of Neurophysiology, 37,* 996–1019.

Kupfermann, I., & Pinsker, H. M. (1968). A behavioral modification of the feeding reflex in *Aplysia californica. Communications in behavioral biology, A,* 2, 13–17. Kupfermann, I., & Weiss, K. R. (1981). Tail pinch and handling facilitate feeding behavior in *Aplysia. Behavioral and Neural Biology, 32,* 126–132.

Lederhendler, I. I., Herriges, K., & Tobach, E. (1977). Taxis in *Aplysia dactylomela* (Rang, 1828) to water-borne stimuli from conspecifics. *Animal Learning & Behavior, 5,* 355–358.

London, J. A., & Gillette, R. (1986). Mechanism for food avoidance learning in the central pattern generator of feeding behavior of *Pleurobranchaea californica. Proceedings of the National Academy of Science of the U.S.A., 83,* 4058–4062.

Lukowiak, K. (1986). In vitro classical conditioning of a gill withdrawal reflex in *Aplysia*: Neural correlates and possible neural mechanisms. *Journal of Neurobiology, 17,* 83–101.

Lukowiak, K. (1987). A blood-borne factor from food-satiated *Aplysia* suppresses the gill withdrawal reflex in in vitro preparations from unsatiated animals. *Neuroscience Letters, 77,* 205–208.

Mackey, S. L., Glanzman, D. L., Small, S. A., Dyke, A. M., Kandel, E. R., & Hawkins, R. D. (1987). Tail shock produces inhibition as well as sensitization of the siphon-withdrawal reflex of *Aplysia*: Possible behavioral role for presynaptic inhibition mediated by the peptide Phe-Met-Arg-Phe-NH2. *Proceedings of the National Academy of Science of the U.S.A., 84,* 8730–8734.

Marcus, E. A., Nolen, T. G., Rankin, C. H., & Carew, T. J. (1988). Behavioral dissociation of dishabituation, sensitization, and inhibition in *Aplysia. Science, 241,* 210–212.

Miller, J. P., & Selverston, A. I. (1982). Mechanisms underlying pattern generation in lobster stomatogastric ganglion as determined by selective inactivation of identified neurons. IV. Network properties of the pyloric system. *Journal of Neurophysiology*, 48, 1416–1432.

Nakashima, M., Yamada, S., Shiono, S., & Maeda, M. (1989). A 448-channel optical monitoring of neural signals from *Aplysia* ganglion. *Society for Neuroscience Abstracts*, 15, 1046.

O'Dell, T. J., Kandel, E. R., & Grant, S. G. (1991). Long-term potentiation in the hippocampus is blocked by tyrosine kinase inhibitors. *Nature*, 353: 558–560.

Pinsker, H. M., Hening, W. A., Carew, T. J., & Kandel, E. R. (1973). Long-term sensitization of a defensive withdrawal reflex in *Aplysia*. *Science* 182, 1039–1042.

Preston, R. J., & Lee, R. M. (1973). Feeding behavior in *Aplysia californica*: Role of chemical and tactile stimuli. *Journal of Comparative and Physiological Psychology*, 82, 368–381.

Ritzmann, R. E. (1984). The cockroach escape response. In R. C. Eaton (Ed.), *Neural mechanisms of startle behavior* (pp. 93–131). New York: Plenum.

Sacktor, T. C., & Schwartz, J. H. (1990). Sensitizing stimuli cause translocation of protein kinase C in *Aplysia* sensory neurons. *Proceedings of the National Academy of Science of the U.S.A.*, 87(5), 2036–9.

Sahley, C., Rudy, J. W., & Gelperin, A. (1981). An analysis of associative learning in a terrestrial mollusc I. Higher-order conditioning, blocking and a transient US pre-exposure effect. *Journal of Comparative Physiology*, 144, 1–8.

Schneirla, T. C. (1959). An evolutionary and developmental theory of biphasic processes underlying approach and withdrawal. In M. R. Jones (Ed.), *Current Theory and Research on Motivation* (pp. 1–42). Lincoln, Nebraska: University of Nebraska Press.

Sejnowski, T. J., Koch, C., & Churchland, P. S. (1988). Computational neuroscience. *Science* 241, 1299–1306.

Sejnowski, T. J., & Tesauro, G. (1989). The Hebb rule for synaptic plasticity: Algorithms and implementations. In J. H. Byrne, W. O. Berry (Eds.), *Neural Models of Plasticity: Experimental and Theoretical Approaches* (pp. 94–103). New York: Academic Press.

Sweatt, D., Volterra, A., Siegelbaum, S. A., & Kandel, E. R. (1988). Molecular convergence of presynaptic inhibition and presynaptic facilitation on common substrate proteins of individual sensory neurons of *Aplysia*. *Cold Spring Harbor Symposium on Quantitative Biology*, 53, 395–405.

Walters, E. T. (1987a). Site-specific sensitization of defensive reflexes in *Aplysia*: A simple model of long-term hyperalgesia. *Journal of Neuroscience, 7,* 400–407.

———. (1987b). Multiple sensory neuronal correlates of site- specific sensitization in *Aplysia*. *Journal of Neuroscience 7,* 408–417.

———. (1989). Transformation of siphon responses during conditioning of *Aplysia* suggests a model of primitive stimulus-response association. *Proceedings of the National Academy of Science of the U.S.A., 86,* 7616–7619.

———. (1991). A functional, cellular, and evolutionary model of nociceptive plasticity in *Aplysia*. *Biological Bulletin, 180,* 241–251.

———. (1994). Injury-related behavior and neuronal plasticity: an evolutionary perspective on sensitization, hyperalgesia, and analgesia. *International Review of Neurobiology, 36,* in press.

Walters, E. T., Alizadeh, H., & Castro, G. A. (1991). Similar neuronal alterations induced by axonal injury and learning in *Aplysia*. *Science, 253,* 797–799.

Walters, E. T., & Byrne, J. H. (1983). Associative conditioning of single sensory neurons suggests a cellular mechanism for learning. *Science, 219,* 405–408.

Walters, E. T., Byrne, J. H., Carew, T. J., & Kandel, E. R. (1983a). Mechanoafferent neurons innervating tail of *Aplysia*. I. Response properties and synaptic connections. *Journal of Neurophysiology, 50,* 1522–1542.

Walters, E. T., Byrne, J. H., Carew, T. J., & Kandel, E. R. (1983b). Mechanoafferent neurons innervating tail of *Aplysia*. II. Modulation by sensitizing stimulation. *Journal of Neurophysiology, 50,* 1543–1559.

Walters, E. T., Carew, T. J., & Kandel, E. R. (1981). Associative learning in *Aplysia*: Evidence for conditioned fear in an invertebrate. *Science, 211,* 504–506.

Walters, E. T, & Erickson, M. T. (1986). Directional control and the functional organization of defensive responses in *Aplysia*. *Journal of Comparative Physiology A, 159,* 339–351.

Weiss, K. R., Chiel, H. J., Koch, U., & Kupfermann, I. (1986). Activity of an identified histaminergic neuron, and its possible role in arousal of feeding behavior in semi-intact *Aplysia*. *Journal of Neuroscience 6,* 2403–2415.

Woolf, C. J., & King, A. E. (1987). Physiology and morphology of multi-receptive neurons with C-afferent fiber inputs in the deep dorsal horn of the rat lumbar spinal cord. *Journal of Neurophysiology*, 58, 460–479.

Woolf, C. J., & Walters, E. T. (1991). Common patterns of plasticity contributing to nociceptive sensitization in mammals and *Aplysia.*, 14, 74–78.

Wright, W. G., Marcus, E. A., & Carew, T. J. (1991). A cellular analysis of inhibition in the siphon withdrawal reflex of *Aplysia*. *Journal of Neuroscience*, 11(8), 2498–509.

Zecevic, D., Wu, J.-Y., Cohen, L. B., London, J. A., Hopp, H.-P., & Falk, C. X. (1989). Hundreds of neurons in the *Aplysia* abdominal ganglion are active during the gill-withdrawal reflex. *Journal of Neuroscience* 9, 3681–3689.

ACKNOWLEDGMENTS

Preparation of this article was supported by grants from the National Institute of Mental Health and National Science Foundation. We are grateful to Chris Hickie and Dr. Kathryn Hood for their comments on an earlier draft of the article, and to Jim Pastore for preparing the illustrations.

CHAPTER 6

Nerve Growth Factor and Cholinergic Development
Biochemical Levels in Approach/Withdrawal Processes

Gemma Calamandrei and Enrico Alleva

In discussing theoretical issues based on approach/withdrawal (A/W) adjustments in behavior, Schneirla (1939; 1965) pointed out that properties of stimulation at different intensities account not only for quantitative differences, but also for qualitative differences in the adjustment to the environment. We, therefore, center our discussion on the development of a specific central nervous system (CNS) neurotransmitter system, the cholinergic system, because of its well-known role in behavioral regulation through central cholinergic processes. We consider specifically a developmental phenomenon described as a two-phase ontogenetic progression in cholinergic maturation. We also focus on a polypeptide neurotrophic factor, Nerve Growth Factor (NGF), that appears to play a specific regulatory role in such a series of developmental stages. These biphasic developmental processes may be related to stage-dependent biphasic A/W regulations.

Evidence for a Biphasic Process Underlying the Ontogenesis of the Brain Cholinergic System: Behavioral Pharmacology and Biochemistry Studies

It is generally thought that the CNS cholinergic system of developing rodents undergoes a two-stage maturation, the first occurring between birth and postnatal day 18–20 and the second one starting at the time of weaning, i.e., around postnatal day 21. The first maturational stage shows a good level of adrenergic "arousal system" maturation, but a still poorly developed level of cholinergic "inhibitory system" maturation. The cholinergic system matures abruptly around the age of weaning (Campbell et al., 1969; Fibiger et al., 1970).

In general, behavioral tasks requiring inhibition of a loco-motor response are affected by blockage of cholinergic transmission. It is not until weaning that rodents respond in the adult fashion to cholinergic antagonists such as scopolamine with a dramatic increase in locomotor activity and impaired habituation to a novel environment. The ability to withhold a punished response parallels the development of the cholinergic system, since adult-like performances in a passive avoidance task are displayed by weaning rodents. These behavioral responses during early stages of development are reviewed by Alleva & Bignami (1985) and by Laviola et al. (1988). In general, these findings seem to support a two-phase process, and the maturation of the brain's cholinergic system is very likely linked to the progressive ability of young rodents to withhold a behavioral response.

However, a clear distinction between an early adrenergic regulation of behavior and a late-developing cholinergic "inhibitory" system may be somewhat simplistic. Behavioral development involves both small changes and sudden transitions. At each developmental stage different neural systems, even though not yet fully functional, are likely to interact in regulating behavioral patterns. Thus, a number of developmental studies suggest that some portions of the cholinergic system are already functional well before weaning. Specifically, scopolamine produces a paradoxical depressant effect on response latency to choice in a T-maze task in rat pups as young as seven days (Smith, Spear, & Spear, 1982) and impairs suckling behavior in five-day-old rats and mice (Williams, Rosenblatt, & Hall, 1979; Ristine & Spear, 1984; Calamandrei, Valanzano, & Alleva, 1991).

Other views of developmental phenomena may be equally simplistic, such as that there is a gradual increase of adult-like competence and "completeness," irrespective of stage-dependent functional "revolutions" actually occurring during ontogenesis (Bateson, 1981; D'Udine & Alleva, 1982; Alleva & D'Udine, 1988; D'Udine & Alleva, 1988a; D'Udine & Alleva, 1988). For example, using the comparative method stressed by Schneirla, a comparison of the development of altricial and precocial rodents is helpful. The maturational trend just described is actually prototypic only for the rat and the mouse, two muroid rodents exhibiting an altricial developmental style (Alleva & Bignami, 1985; Campbell & Mabry, 1972; Ray & Nagy, 1978). In the case of precocial species such as guinea pigs (Campbell & Mabry, 1972), and the Spiny mouse (*Acomys cahirinus*), the development of cholinergic inhibition of adrenergic arousal appears to be a much more complex phenomenon than a simple, evolutionary conserved pattern of neurobehavioral development. Gestation in *A. cahirinus*, belonging to the same subfamily as rats and mice, is about twice as long as the length of mice and rats and twice as long as a corresponding altricial *Murinae* species of similar body size and habitat preference (Pintor, Alleva, & Michalek, 1986). A detailed analysis of the development of the central cholinergic systems of *A. cahirinus* shows a mixture of biochemical markers of postnatal development that proceed at about the same pace as in rat/mouse development, and markers of cholinergic development that are triggered by the birth event (Birke, D'Udine, & Albonetti, 1985; D'Udine & Alleva, 1982).

A Regulating Role for the Nerve Growth Factor (NGF) Protein in the Postnatal Development of CNS Cholinergic Systems

Neurotrophic factors are protein molecules endowed with prominent and sometimes specific effects on neuronal growth in the developing nervous system. It has been suggested recently that these factors are also involved in a multitude of other aspects of neural development, such as axonal guidance and regulation of neurotransmitter synthesis, leading to strong statements such as "the emerging generality of the neurotrophic hypothesis" (Davies, 1988). NGF is a specific neurotrophic factor for developing sensory and sympathetic neurons of the peripheral nervous system, which require NGF for development, survival, and maintenance of function (Levi-Montalcini, 1987; Levi-Montalcini & Angeletti, 1968; Thoenen & Barde, 1980). More recent data indicated that NGF also exerts its trophic action on neurons of the central nervous system (Buck et al., 1988; Johnston et al, 1987; Mobley et al., 1985; Springer, 1988; Taniuchi et al., 1988). NGF appears to be involved in cholinergic regulatory functions of the CNS of altricial rodents. Both NGF and mRNA NGF are particularly evident in zones with dense cholinergic innervation. High NGF levels have been found both in regions innervated by the magnocellular cholinergic neurons of basal forebrain (hippocampus, olfactory bulbs, neocortex) and in regions containing the cell bodies of these neurons, such as the septum (Korshing et al., 1985; Shelton & Reichardt, 1986; Whittemore et al., 1986). NGF has been detected only in the hippocampus and neocortex, but not in the septum (Shelton & Reichardt, 1986). This observation, together with several studies using fimbria/fornix transection, strongly support the view that adult cholinergic neurons of the basal forebrain are continuously supplied with NGF by retrograde axonal transport from their target cholinergic regions (Korshing, 1986; Seiler & Schwab, 1884; Whittemore et al., 1986; Whittemore & Seiger, 1987).

The developmental dynamics of NGF are noteworthy. It has been shown that NGF accumulation in the basal forebrain parallels that in the hippocampus and neocortex, while preceding an increase in Choline-Acetyl-Transferase (ChAT) activity, suggesting that the neurochemical differentiation of magnocellular cholinergic neurons is regulated by retrogradely transported NGF (Gnahan et al., 1983; Large et al., 1986). Moreover, NGF receptor distribution in the CNS resembles the distribution of cholinergic neurons of the forebrain (Richardson, Verge Issa, & Riopelle, 1986; Taniuchi et al., 1988). Finally, a marked increase in ChAT activity was observed in the septum, hippocampus, nucleus basalis, neocortex, and caudate-putamen of neonatal rats upon intracerebroventricular (icv) NGF administration (Mobley et al., 1985; Johnston et al., 1987).

Cholinergic areas in the CNS of developing rats appear to respond with high regional specificity to exogenous NGF administration. For example, a single icv administration on postnatal day two almost immediately affects ChAT activity in the caudate-putamen, which increases up to about fourfold of normal levels, while septal and hippocampal ChAT levels only double their values, and with regionally-specific timing and duration. More interestingly, repeated NGF administration is necessary to observe a long lasting ChAT increase in septal and hippocampal tissues, while exposure limited to single or double daily injection fails to maintain a persistently high level of ChAT activity. Increasing ChAT activity levels are considered a reliable marker of cholinergic system maturation, and exogenous NGF administration at the brain level somehow mimics endogenous NGF production from target cholinergic areas. As a result, the rapidly changing regionally-specific NGF sensitivity of cholinergic tissues can be easily explained in terms of interference with on-going maturational processes occurring among different brain areas, which use NGF to promote and to guide neuronal growth and/or phenotypic cholinergic expression (Alleva & Calamandrei, 1990; Davies, 1988).

It is now clear that NGF is one of the most important regulators of cholinergic development. But how is NGF involved in the two-stage developmental process evidenced by the above cited behavioral pharmacology studies? In other words, what is the role played by the NGF molecule in promoting such a rapid maturational transition in altricial rodents around weaning time? Despite the fact that most of the NGF studies aimed at characterizing its developmental role in cholinergic ontogenesis were carried out during the first two postnatal weeks, sufficient evidence indicates that brain regulatory processes involving endogenous NGF production (and release) can explain the stage-transition occurring at weaning. This evidence is fully provided by studies showing that NGF mRNA production peaks around day 20 (Large et al., 1986; Whittemore et al., 1986). Both mRNA NGF

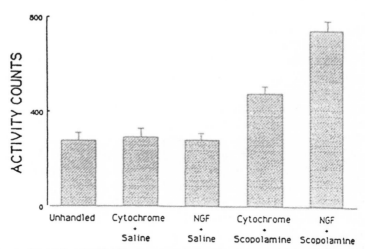

Fig. 1: Proactive NGF effects on scopolamine hyperactivity in weaning mice. The hyperactivity response to the muscarinic cholinergic blocker scopolamine (2 mg/kg) is enhanced after a single NGF injection (20 μg) given intracerebroventricularly 24 hrs before testing. The data are activity levels (means + SEM) as measured in Varimex Activity Meter apparatus during a 5-min session (Alleva, Aloe, & Laviola, 1986).

expression and NGF protein synthesis have developmental course which fits very well with a two-step model of cholinergic development.

As assessed by specific molecular probes, NGF shows a peak around the age of weaning in rats. It is then conceivable that endogenous NGF expression from CNS target areas (or, at least, growth- and/or differentiation-promoting brain regions) send a maturational input (the high level of NGF expressed) to appropriate cholinergic "responders." Accordingly, we were able to show an anticipation of scopolamine responding around weaning upon NGF pre-exposure (Alleva, Aloe & Laviola, 1986), and this is shown in Figure 1.

More recent data from our lab (Calamandrei, Valanzano, & Alleva, 1991) show a much more dramatic advancement of the scopolamine-induced hyperkinesia, since upon extended icv NGF treatment (which somehow mimics endogenous NGF release at the CNS level), specific subportions of the cholinergic system appear to undergo rapid stage transition, involving neonatal differentiation of muscarinic receptor bearing cells. We found that NGF icv administration on postnatal days two and four enhanced the scopolamine-blocking effect on suckling behavior on day five, while anticipating the appearance of scopolamine hyperactivity syndrome at this same early stage. In much simpler terms, it is possible to shift backwards the first appearance of the second (postweaning) period of cholinergic maturation by simply exposing the developing mouse brain to an unnaturally high amount of exogenous NGF (Fig. 2). We predict that this is only one among a number of possible developmental shifts which could occur following exposure to appropriate quantities of specific growth factors at critical stage of neuronal sensitivity.

Adrenal Products and Thyroid Hormone Involvement in Cholinergic Developmental Processes under NGF Control

Some phenotypic transformation of cholinergic cells emerges relatively late in normal development of both precocial and altricial mammals (Pintor, Alleva, & Michalek, 1986), supplanting earlier properties (Vaca, 1988). Some cholinergic cells, in fact, retain a catecholamine uptake system and can be eliminated by neonatal treatment with the adrenergic neurotoxin 6-hydroxydopamine or by a very limited neonatal exposure to NGF antibodies. It can be suggested that at least some of these late-developing components of cholinergic differentiation are involved in (i) the organization of early developmental stages and ontogenetic pathways leading to *individual* behavioral differences (the "alternative tactics" of Caro & Bateson, 1986); (ii) the emergence of a series of functional loops, where both neurotransmitter and growth factor production is enhanced (Hanley, 1989), resulting in accelerated maturation of some specific elements of the developing CNS, most likely at the expense of other CNS and non-CNS elements (Calamandrei & Alleva, 1989); (iii) in developmental interactions between important regulatory

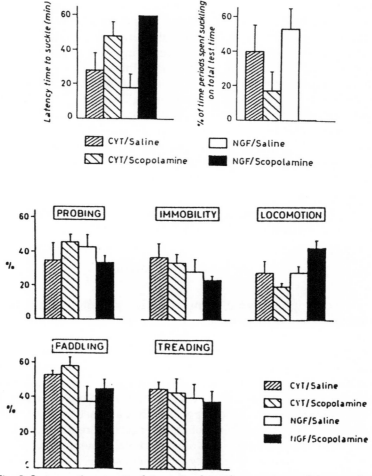

Fig. 2: Latency time to attach to a nipple and percentage of time periods spent suckling by 5-day-old mice given NGF or cytochrome c on post-natal days 2 and 4 and either scopolamine or saline 15 min. before the suckling test on day 5 (top); effects of this same NGF pretreatment and of scopolamine given before testing on day 5 on probing, paddling, treading, immobility, and forward locomotion. Note that NGF-treated animals receiving scopolamine were more active than the corresponding controls (bottom). (Calamandrei, Valanzano & Alleva, 1991).

systems, such as those involving adrenal products (Aloe, 1989) and thyroid hormones (Patel, Hayashi, & Hunt, 1988; Wion et al., 1985). These two latter aspects are crucial for the understanding of some important behavioral phenomena occurring during early developmental stages.

As a first example, we can focus on adrenal control of hippocampal NGF regulation. In rat CNS, the hippocampus contains one of the highest levels of NGF and of mRNA specifically encoding NGF (Ayer-LeLievre et al., 1988). Several lines of evidence indicate that NGF is synthesized within the hippocampal area, taken up selectively by cholinergic neurons of the septal lateral band terminals, and eventually transported retrogradely to the cell of origin. Intrahippocampal administration of NGF antibodies causes granule cell loss, suggesting an on-going trophic supporting role of NGF for granular cells. At the same time, the hippocampal area is a major target site for glucocorticoid hormones, particularly corticosterone, and early administration of glucocorticoids influences both CNS and somatic growth. More recent studies have shown that glucocorticoids have a profound influence on the survival of hippocampal neurons. Aloe (1989) was able to show that adrenalectomy of young adult rats reduces both hippocampal NGF level and ChAT immunoreactivity in lateral bands of the septal area. A recent report showed that thyroid hormones modulate the distribution of NGF receptors in neuronal elements of the basal forebrain (Patel, Hayashi, & Hunt, 1988), exerting a rather sophisticated regulatory role. Moreover, Hayashi & Patel (1987) reported an interaction between thyroid hormone and nerve growth factor in the regulation of ChAT activity in neuronal cultures derived from the septal-diagonal band region of the developing rat brain.

NGF and Mouse Neurobehavioral Development

While the morphological and biochemical effects of neonatal NGF exposure have been well characterized in the past years, only limited data are available about the repercussions of these effects on behavioral regulation during early developmental stages.

    Repeated systemic NGF administration during the first ten
days of postnatal life has been found to affect the neurobehavioral maturation of mice (Alleva, Aloe, & Calamandrei,
1987; Calamandrei & Alleva, 1989). Figure 3A shows the
accelerating NGF effects we reported for a number of early
neonatal responses such as the righting reflex, while
later-developing behavioral responses, such as the full-fledged
emission of ultrasonic calls (Figure 3B), which emerges around
the end of the first postnatal week, were not altered significantly.
It should be mentioned that other polypeptidic growth factors,
such as Epidermal Growth Factor (Alleva & Calamandrei, 1989;
Gomez-Pinilla, Knower, & Nitre-Sampedro, 1988; Hoath, 1986;
Werner et al., 1988), basic Fibroblast Growth Factor (Morrison,
Keating, & Moskal, 1988; Santucci, Calamandrei, & Alleva, 1993),
truncated forms of Insulin-like Growth Factor type I (Sara &
Carlsson- Skwirut, 1988) also exert specific (in some cases,
blocked by antibodies) growth-promoting or growth-inhibiting
effects on neuronal cells, which are also stage- and re-
gion-dependent. For more complete reviews aimed at explaining
how such a mixture of protein molecules could affect vertebrate
and invertebrate development, see Alleva & Calamandrei, 1990;
Calamandrei & Alleva, 1992; Mercola & Stiles, 1988; and Sporn &
Roberts, 1988.

Cholinergic Neuron Development in Behavioral Ontogeny

    An overview of the pre- and postnatal development of the
cholinergic neurons has to take into account a number of either
general or specific events which may affect the individual fate of
any single cell (Vaca, 1988). Some cell lines among the cholinergic ones appear to have a high degree of rigidity in phenotypic
expression, while others seem more sensitive to the effects of environmental factors. Among these, growth factors play a major
role, as shown in a variety of in vitro experiments. It should be
pointed out that NGF exerts pronounced phenotype-shifting
activities, particularly on adrenomedullary chromaffin cells

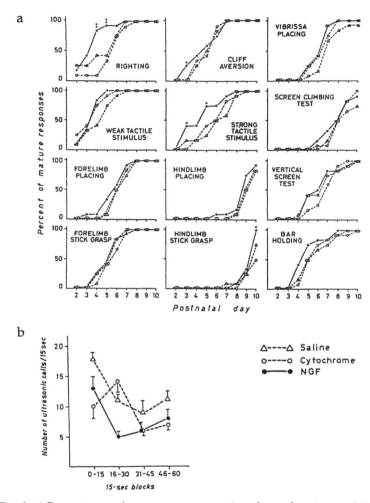

Fig. 3: a) Percentages of mature responses given by male mice receiving from day 2 to day 10 a daily subcutaneous injection of either saline solution, 5 mg/kg cytochrome c, or 5 mg/kg murine NGF. $^* = p < 0.05$ $^{**} = p < 0.01$; b) pattern of ultrasonic vocalization of 7-day-old mice injected daily from postnatal day 2 with either saline solution, cytochrome c, or murine NGF. Cytochrome c is used as an additional control treatment since it is physicochemically similar to NGF, but lacks its neurotrophic activity (Alleva, Aloe & Calamandrei, 1987).

(Levi-Montalcini, 1987), and that its specific action on cholinergic cell elements seems to be counterbalanced by adrenal hormones, both in vitro and in vivo (Aloe, 1989). New molecular biology techniques are expected to lead to new insights about cholinergic system development. For example, Vaca (1988) suggests two classes of genetic control elements which could possibly be important for cholinergic ontogenesis, namely homeotic genes and proto-oncogenes. The former are, in fact, expressed late in development, and are mostly limited to cellular elements of CNS lines. Initial expression of cholinergic properties, early innervation of the appropriate target tissue, synaptogenesis, pre-programmed or environmentally-directed cell death, synapse elimination, growth cone shaping, axon guidance, are all important aspects of the maturation of cholinergic funtion. NGF, as well as some other growth factors, such as Epidermal Growth Factor, Fibroblast Growth Factor (Gomez-Pinilla, Krauer, & Nieto-Sampedro, 1988; Hoath, 1986; Morrison, Keating, & Moskal, 1988), Insulin Growth Factor (Sara & Carlsson-Skwirut, 1988; Sara et al., 1986), and TGFs (Massague, 1987), endowed with either specific or nonspecific neuroregulatory functions, exert biological roles for each of these components of neural maturation. (For NGF and EGF localization at the human brain level, see also Hefti & Mash (1987) and Werner et al. (1988), respectively.) Since some of the most striking NGF effects (e.g., its prominent activity on cholinergic cell lines of the CNS) have been discovered recently (Johnston et al., 1987; Mobley et al., 1985), we still lack a comprehensive theoretical frame and providing a synthetic explanation for understanding GF roles in giving directions to both vertebrate and invertebrate development (Alleva & Calamandrei, 1990; Mercola & Stiles, 1988; Sporn & Roberts, 1988).

Finally, it has to be stressed that in adult rodents mRNA NGF expression and/or NGF release, both at periphery and CNS level, occur within minutes, and are reportedly caused by psychosocial stress (Aloe et al, 1986; Spillantini et al., 1989) or by limbic seizures (Gall & Isackson, 1989). This raises a whole series of questions about behavioral regulation of neuronal developmental events through NGF expression at specific CNS sites. Whether the exposure to external stimuli at a specific time in de-

velopment can trigger NGF expression in the brain, thus inducing either transient or long-lasting changes in neural connectivity
and morphology is an interesting possibility, deserving further
investigation (for an extensive review of NGF role in adult
neuroendocrine regulations in rodents see Alleva & Aloe, 1991).

Some science-fiction-like experiments aimed at manipulating NGF expression at the CNS level have been already reported:
very recent studies used fibroblasts genetically modified to
secrete NGF by infection with a retroviral vector, and then im-
planted into the brain of adult rats receiving surgical lesions of
the fimbria fornix. The NGF molecules secreted by the grafted
cells prevented retrograde cholinergic degeneration and induced
axonal sprouting (Hempstead, Schleifer, & Chao, 1989; Rosenberg et al., 1988). The extension of such a powerful and specific
technique to the understanding of developmental phenomena
where NGF (as well as other growth factors) play a biological
role does promise to be quite fruitful.

A/W Theory and Inhibition of Behavioral Arousal During Rodent Development

The involvement of CNS cholinergic pathways in learning
and memory processes has suggested a role for NGF in cognitive
functions (Fisher et al., 1987). We know that, following NGF
pre-exposure, the level of "curiosity" of an immature mouse
toward a novel stimulus set is unaffected (Alleva, Aloe &
Laviola, 1986). NGF administration at the early postnatal stage,
however, does not modify the rather poor retention performances of neonatal mice in an odor-aversion learning task
(Alleva & Calamandrei, 1986; Calamandrei et al., 1988). In other
studies (Calamandrei, Ricceri & Alleva, 1990), we found that
neonatal exposure to NGF affects imprinting-like phenomena,
since it reduces neophobic reactions to an odor CS upon a CS
pre-exposure following icv NGF pretreatment. Other attempts
have to be conducted, using a much wider variety of learning
tests, as well as more than one CS and one US, at several developmental stages. The use of a passive avoidance task, where an-

imals have to withhold a locomotor response to avoid being punished, showed that NGF pretreatment facilitates response inhibition in developing mice, thus favoring learning and retention of this specific learning task (Ricceri, Calamandrei, Chiarotti, & Alleva, 1992, submitted). These results support the hypothesis that NGF plays a role in the maturation of cholinergic mechanisms involved in response inhibition. As a whole, the effects of early NGF exposure on learning deserve much more extended investigation.

General Discussion

The evidence presented above on the role of NGF and other polypeptidic growth factors on ontogeny and activation of specific cell lines of the peripheral and central nervous systems (particularly those underlying sympathetic reactivity and cholinergic inhibition of behavioral arousal) make those growth factors very good candidates for regulating developmental changes in the relative amount of stimulation necessary to elicit either A or W responses. Interestingly, the NGF molecule appears to be strongly conserved in evolution, from invertebrates such as cephalopods and snails to humans.

The ubiquity and the persistence of the identical (or nearly identical) polypeptidic form in such different species of living organisms as humans, rodents, reptiles, amphibians, molluscs, worms, and insects (Levi Montalcini, 1987; Mercola & Stiles, 1988), support the growth factor molecules as good candidates for explaining some basic features of cell-to-cell communication systems across species.

Increasing evidence suggests that the action of specific trophic molecules on receptive neuronal population might form an ontogenetic substrate for phylogeny. As Black pointed out, (Black, 1986; Black et al., 1987), NGF-controlled bioregulations can be one of the pivotal axes around which evolution has shaped the different living forms, particularly in regard to nervous system form and function. Most observed differences in shape and functioning of different organisms can in fact be due to relatively slight changes in their developmental pathways.

The timing and the sensitivity of a particular cell line to a specific growth factor could in fact result in dramatic developmental alterations, and random combinations of these teratogenic events could possibly produce new adaptive forms. Black provides fascinating examples of the phylogenetic role that NGF may be endowed with, particularly for neural functions.

Finally we want to celebrate one of the secondary aspects of Schneirla's contribution to developmental biology. One of the most important contributions of Schneirla's work is its dictionary of biopsychological terms. His whole work is in fact actually filled with epistemological considerations, whose flavour has been totally lost in the subsequent decades. Towardness and awayness, in developmental terms, can be fruitfully used as indicators of neophobic reactions, such as those we reported about imprinting-like phenomena in neonatal mice. Some terms are established through oppositions: avoidance vs. seeking, adaptive vs. purposive, beniception vs. nociception, acceptance vs. rejection (Schneirla, 1965). More importantly, Schneirla never forgot the comparative method (see examples in Aronson et al., 1972) while describing a specific biological term, attributing to it appropriate limitations in its phyletic value. After 11 years of rampant sociobiology, and the massive destruction of the biobehavioral sciences by both cellular and molecular neurosciences, T. C. Schneirla's contribution to contemporary biology stands as a pyramid in the African desert, a landmark of lost civilization.

REFERENCES

Alleva, E., & Aloe, L. (1991). Nerve growth factors effects on neuro-immunoendocrine system: A biobehavioral perspective. *International Symposium on Biotechnology of Growth Factors*, 80–86.

Alleva, E., Aloe, L., & Calamandrei, G. (1987). Nerve growth factor influences neurobehavioral development of newborn mice. *Neurotoxicology and Teratology, 9*, 271–275.

Alleva, E., Aloe, L., & Laviola, G. (1986). Pretreatment of young mice with nerve growth factor enhances scopolamine-induced hyperactivity. *Developmental Brain Research, 28,* 278–281.

Alleva, E., & Bignami, G. (1985). Development of mouse activity, stimulus reactivity, habituation, and response to amphetamine and scopolamine. *Physiology & Behavior, 34,* 519–523.

Alleva, E., & Calamandrei, G. (1986). Odor-aversion learning and retention span in neonatal mice. *Behavioral and Neural Biology, 46,* 348–357.

Alleva, E., & Calamandrei, G. (1990). On the functional role of polypeptide growth factors in rodent neurobehavioural development. *Acta Neurobiologiae Experimentalis, 50,* 341–352.

Alleva, E., & D'Udine, B. (1978). Early learning capability in rodents: A review. *International Journal of Comparative Psychology,* Winter, 107–125.

Aloe, L. (1989). Adrenalectomy decreases nerve growth factor in young adult rat hippocampus. *Proceedings of the National Academy of Sciences (USA), 86,* 5636–5640.

Aloe, L., Alleva, E., Bohm, A., & Levi-Montalcini, R. (1986). Aggressive behavior induces release of nerve growth factor from mouse salivary gland into blood stream. *Proceedings of the National Academy of Sciences (USA), 83,* 6187–6190.

Aronson, L. R., Tobach, E., Rosenblatt, J. S., & Lehrman, D. S. (Eds.) (1972). *Selected Writings of T.C. Schneirla.* San Francisco: Freeman.

Ayer-LeLievre, C., Olson, L., Ebendal, T., Seiger, A., & Persson, H. (1988). Expression of the beta-nerve growth factor gene in hippocampal neurons. *Science, 240,* 1339–1344.

Bateson, P. P. G. (1981). Ontogeny of behaviour. *British Medical Bulletin, 37,* 159–164.

Birke, L. I. A., D'Udine, B., & Albonetti, M. E. (1985). Exploratory behavior in two species of Murid rodents, *Acomys cahirinus* and *Mus musculus:* A comparative study. *Behavioral and Neural Biology, 43,* 143–161.

Black, I.B. (1986). Trophic molecules and evolution of the nervous system. *Proceedings of the National Academy of Sciences (USA), 83,* 8249–8252.

Black, I., Adler, J. E., Dreyfus, C. F., Friedman, W. F., LaGamma E. F., & Roach, A. H. (1987). Biochemistry of information storage in the nervous system. *Science, 236,* 1263–1268.

Buck, C. R., Martinez, H. J., Chao, M. V., & Black, I. B. (1988). Differential expression of the nerve growth factor receptor gene in multiple brain areas. *Developmental Brain Research, 44*, 259–268.

Calamandrei, G., & Alleva, E. (1989). Epidermal growth factor has both growth-promoting and growth-inhibiting effects on physical and neurobehavioral development of neonatal mice. *Brain Research, 477*, 1–6.

Calamandrei, G., & Alleva, E. (1994). Growth factors in neurobehavioral development. In E. V. Cosmi, G. C. Di Renzo, & D. H. Hawkins (Eds.), *Recent advances in perinatal medicine*. London: Hartwood Academic Press.

Calamandrei, G., Alleva, E., & Ricceri, L. (1990). Nerve Growth Factor, olfactory learning and imprinting-like processes in newborn mice. European Science Foundation Network Conference on Neural Mechanisms of Learning and Memory, Abstract book, p. 3.

Calamandrei, G., Cirulli, F., Alleva, E., & Aloe, L. (1988). Nerve growth factor does not ameliorate the infantile forgetting syndrome of neonatal mice. *Monitore Zoologico Italiano* (Italian Journal of Zoology), *22*, 235–243.

Calamandrei, G., Valanzano, A., & Alleva, E. (1991). NGF and cholinergic control of behavior: Anticipation and enhancement of scopolamine effects in neonatal mice. *Developmental Brain Research, 61*, 237–241.

Campbell, B. A., Lytle, L. D., & Fibiger, H. C. (1969). Ontogeny of adrenergic arousal and cholinergic inhibitory mechanisms in the rat. *Science, 166*, 635–637.

Campbell, B. A., & Mabry, P. D. (1972). Ontogeny of behavioral arousal: A comparative study. *Journal of Comparative and Physiological Psychology, 81*, 371–379.

Caro, T. M., & Bateson, P. (1986). Organization and ontogeny of alternative tactics. *Animal Behaviour, 34*, 1483–1489.

Davies, A. M. (1988). The emerging generality of the neurotrophic hypothesis. *Trends in Neuroscience, 11*, 243–244.

D'Udine, B., & Alleva, E. (1982). Early experience and sexual preferences in rodents. In P. P. G. Bateson (Ed.), *Mate Choice* (pp. 311–327). Cambridge, U.K.: Cambridge University Press.

D'Udine, B., & Alleva, E. (1988a). The *Acomys cahirinus* (Spiny mouse) as a new model for biological and neurobehavioural studies. *Polish Journal of Pharmacology and Pharmacy, 40*, 525–534.

D'Udine, B., & Alleva, E. (1988b). The ontogeny of learning capability in rodents: Comparative models. In J. L. McGaugh (Ed.), *Contemporary psychology: Biological processes and theoretical issues* (pp. 131–144) Amsterdam: Elsevier.

Fibiger, H. C., Lytle, L. D., & Campbell, B. A. (1970). Cholinergic modulation of behavioral arousal in the developing rat. *Journal of Comparative and Physiological Psychology, 72,* 384–389.

Fisher, W., Wictorin, K., Bjorklund, A., Williams, M. R., Varon, S., & Gage, F. (1986). Amelioration of cholinergic neuron atrophy and spatial memory impairments in aged rats by nerve growth factor. *Nature, 329,* 65–68.

Gall, C. M., & Isackson, P. J. (1989). Limbic seizures increase neuronal production of messenger RNA for nerve growth factor. *Science, 245,* 758–761.

Gnahan, H., Hefti, F. Heumann, R., Schwab, M. E., & Thoenen, H. (1983). NGF mediated increase of choline acetyltransferase (ChAT) in neonatal rat forebrain: Evidence for a physiological role of beta-NGF in the brain? *Developmental Brain Research, 3,* 229–238.

Gomez-Pinilla, F., Knauer, D. J., & Nieto-Sampedro, M. (1988). Epidermal growth factor receptor immunoreactivity in rat brain: Development and cellular localization. *Brain Research, 438,* 385–390.

Hanley, M. R. (1989). Mitogenic neurotransmitters. *Nature, 340,* 97.

Hayashi, M., & Patel, A. J. (1987). An interaction between thyroid hormone and nerve growth factor in the regulation of choline acetyltranferase activity in neuronal cultures, derived from the septal-diagonal band region of the embryonic rat brain. *Progress in NeuroPsychopharmacology and Biological Psychiatry, 11,* 109–130.

Hefti, F., & Mash, D. C. (1987). Localization of nerve growth factor receptors in the human brain. In E. G. Jones (Ed.), *Molecular Biology of the Human Brain* (pp. 119–132). New York: Alan Liss.

Hempstead, B., Schleifer, L. S., & Chao, M. V. (1989). Expression of functional nerve growth factor receptors after gene transfer. *Science, 243,* 373–375.

Hoath, S. B. (1986). Treatment of the neonatal rat with epidermal growth factor: Differences in time and organ response. *Pediatric Research, 20,* 468–472.

Johnston, M. V., Rutkowski, J. L., Wainer, B. H., Long, J. B., & Mobley, W. C. (1987). NGF effects on developing forebrain cholinergic neurons are regionally specific. *Neurochemical Research, 12,* 985–994.

Korshing, S. (1986). Nerve growth factor in the central nervous system. *Trends in Neuroscience, 11/12,* 570–573.

Korshing, S., Auburger, G., Heumann, R., Scott, J., & Thoenen, H. (1985). Levels of nerve growth factor and its mRNA in the central nervous system of the rat correlate with cholinergic innervation. *European Molecular Biology Organization Journal, 4,* 1389–1393.

Large, T. H., Bodary, S. C., Clegg, D. O., Weskamp, G., Otten, U., & Reichardt, L. F. (1986). Nerve growth factor gene expression in the developing rat brain. *Science, 234,* 352–355.

Laviola, G., Renna, G., Bignami, G., & Cuomo, V. (1988). Ontogenetic and pharmacological dissociation of various components of locomotor activity and habituation in the rat. *International Journal of Developmental Neuroscience, 6,* 431–438.

Levi-Montalcini, R. (1987). The nerve growth factor: Thirty-five years later. *Science, 237,* 1154–1162.

Levi-Montalcini, R., & Angeletti, P. U. (1968). The nerve growth factor. *Physiological Review, 48,* 534–569.

Massague, J. (1987). The TGF-beta family of growth and differentiation factors. *Cell, 49,* 437–438.

Mercola, M., & Stiles, C. D. (1988). Growth factor superfamilies and mammalian embryogenesis. *Development, 102,* 451–460.

Mobley, W. T., Rutkowsky, J. L., Tennekoon, G. I., Buchanan, K., & Johnston, M. V. (1985). Choline acetyltranferase activity in striatum of neonatal rats increased by nerve growth factor. *Science, 229,* 284–287.

Morrison, R. S., Keating, R. F., & Moskal, J. R. (1988). Basic fibroblast growth factor and epidermal growth factor exert differential trophic effects on CNS neurons. *Journal of Neuroscience Research, 21,* 71–79.

Patel, A. J., Hayashi, M., and Hunt, A. (1988). Role of thyroid hormone and nerve growth factor in the development of choline acetyltransferase and other cell-specific marker enzymes in the basal forebrain of the rat. *Journal of Neurochemistry, 50(3):* 803–811.

Pintor, A., Alleva, E., & Michalek, H. (1986). Postnatal maturation of brain cholinergic systems in the precocial murid *Acomys cahirinus*: Comparison with the altricial rat. *International Journal of Developmental Neuroscience, 4,* 375–382.

Ray, D., & Nagy, Z. M. (1978). Emerging cholinergic mechanisms and ontogeny of response inhibition in the mouse. *Journal of Comparative and Physiological Psychology, 92*, 335–349.

Richardson, P. M., Verge Issa, V. M. K., & Riopelle, R. J. (1986). Distribution of neuronal receptors for nerve growth factor in the rat. *The Journal of Neuroscience, 6*, 2312–2321.

Ristine, L. A., & Spear, L. P. (1984). Effects of serotonergic and cholinergic antagonists on suckling behavior of neonatal, infant, and weaning rat pups. *Behavioral and Neural Biology, 41*, 99–126.

Rosenberg, M. B., Friedmann, T., Robertson, R. C., Tuszynski, M., Wolff, J. A., Breakefield, X. O., & Gage, F. H. (1988). Grafting genetically-modified cells to the damaged brain: Restorative effects of NGF expression. *Science, 242*, 1575–1577.

Santucci, D., Calamandrei, G., & Alleva, E. (1993). Neonatal exposure to bFGF exerts NGF-like effects on mouse behavioral development. *Neurotoxicology and Teratology, 15*, 131–137.

Sara, V. R., & Carlsson-Skwirut, C. (1988). The role of insulin-like growth factors in the regulation of brain development. *Progress in Brain Research, 73*, 87–99.

Sara, V. R., Carlsson-Skwirut, C., Andersson, C., Hall, E., Sjogren, B., Holmgren, A., & Jornvall, H. (1986). Characterization of somatomedins from human fetal brain: Identification of a variant form of insulin-like growth factor I. *Proceedings of the National Academy of Science (USA), 83*, 4904–4907.

Schneirla, T. C. (1939). Theoretical consideration of the basis for approach-withdrawal adjustments in behavior. *Psychological Bulletin, 37*, 501–509.

––––––. (1965) Aspects of stimulation and organization in approach-withdrawal processes underlying vertebrate behavioral development. In D. S. Lehrman, R. Hinde, & E. Shaw (Eds.), *Advances in the study of behavior, 1* (pp. 344–412). New York: Academic Press.

Seiler, M., & Schwab, M. E. (1984). Specific retrograde transport of nerve growth factor (NGF) from neocortex to nucleus basalis in the rat. *Brain Research, 300*, 33–39.

Shelton, D. L., & Reichardt, L. F. (1986). Studies on the expression of beta nerve growth factor (NGF) gene in the central nervous system: Level and regional distribution of NGF mRNA suggest that NGF functions as a trophic factor for several distinct populations of neurons. *Proceedings of the National Academy of Science (USA), 83*, 2714–2718.

lations of neurons. *Proceedings of the National Academy of Science (USA)*, *83*, 2714–2718.

Smith, G. J., Spear, L. P., & Spear, N. E. (1982). Detection of cholinergic mediation of behavior in 7-, 9-, and 12-day-old rat pups. *Pharmacology, Biochemistry & Behavior*, *16*, 805–809.

Spillantini, M. G., Aloe, L., Alleva, E., Goedert, M., & Levi-Montalcini, R. (1989). Nerve growth factor mRNA and protein increase in hypothalamus in a mouse model of aggressive behavior. *Proceedings of the National Academy of Sciences (USA)*, *86*, 8555–8559.

Sporn, M. B., & Roberts, A. B. (1988). Peptide growth factors are multifunctional. *Nature*, *332*, 217–219.

Springer, J. E. (1988). Nerve growth factor receptors in the central nervous system. *Experimental Neurology*, *102*, 354–365.

Taniuchi, M., Clark, H. B., Schweitzer, J. B., & Johnson, E. M. Jr. (1988). Expression of nerve growth factor receptors by Schwann cells of axotomized peripheral nerves: Ultrastructural location, suppression by axonal contact and binding properties. *Journal of Neuroscience*, *8*, 664–681.

Thoenen, H., & Barde, Y. A. (1980). Physiology of nerve growth factor. *Physiological Review*, *60*, 1284–1335.

Vaca, K. (1988). The development of cholinergic neurons. *Brain Research Reviews*, *13*, 261–286.

Werner, M. H., Nanney, L. B., Stoscheck, C. M., & King, L. E. (1988). Localization of immunoreactive epidermal growth factors receptors in human nervous system. *Journal of Histochemistry and Cytochemistry*, *36*, 81–86.

Whittemore, S. R., Ebendal, T., Larkfors, L. Olson, L., Seiger, A., Stromberg, I, & Persson, H. (1986). Developmental and regional expression of nerve growth factor messenger RNA and protein in the rat central nervous system. *Proceedings of the National Academy of Sciences (USA)*, *86*, 817–821.

Whittemore, S. R., & Seiger (1987). The expression, localization, and functional significance of beta-nerve growth factor in the central nervous system. *Brain Research Reviews*, *12*, 439–464.

Williams, C. L., Rosenblatt, J. S., & Hall, W. G. (1979). Inhibition of suckling in weanling-age rats: A possible serotonergic mechanism. *Journal of Comparative and Physiological Psychology*, *93*, 414–429.

Wion, D., Barrand, P., Dicou, E., Scott, J., & Brachet, P. (1985). Serum and thyroid hormones T3 and T4 regulate nerve growth factor mRNA levels in mouse L cells. *FEBS Letters, 189*, 37–42.

CHAPTER 7

What and Where Are Memories?*

*Steven P. R. Rose***

I have been impressed by the concept of the Schneirla conferences for many years now and feel privileged to have been
invited to participate in one. However, I should say that I have
been beset by doubts as to what contribution I, as a neurobiologist whose laboratory practice is buried in the microstructure of
cells and their molecular constituents, can make to a meeting
whose prime concern lies in theoretical constructs such as ap-
proach/withdrawal and whose main subject/object of study is
the human infant. This session is entitled "biochemical/genetic/
molecular level" and perhaps the most useful thing I can do is to
offer some reflections on the issue of "levels" in the context of
my own primary research interest in the hope that these may
strike some chords with you.

---

*This chapter is dedicated to the memory of John Hambley, develop-
mental biologist and neurobiologist, who died 27th October, 1989. John
Hambley, whose research as graduate and post-doctoral student with
me in the early 1970s helped lay the foundations for the empirical data I
present here, consistently refused to see the brain as isolated from the
multitude of biological systems, hormonal and immunological, within
which it functioned, any more than he was prepared to see science as an
activity divorced from its social context and social function. I salute his
memory.

My central concern is an attempt to understand the "translation rules" (Rose, 1987) that define the relationship between levels of explanation and levels of organisation in the brain and behavioural sciences. The processes of choice for the study of such rules are, for me, the phenomena of learning and memory. The reasons for this are twofold. First, I find the phenomena themselves of profound interest, both subjectively and objectively, because of the way in which we humans, to such a great extent, *are* our memories. Second, because as a general scientific principle it is easier to measure change than stasis. When an organism learns, its behaviour changes in a reasonably predictable and adaptive manner. In order for such change in behaviour to occur, something must also have changed in the organism's biology—by which we mean, largely though not exclusively, its brain. Studying those phenomena that change in the brain when learning occurs, and which are necessarily, sufficiently and exclusively the cellular correspondents of that behavioural change may offer us a Rosetta stone by which we can decode the translations of behaviour into brain phenomena (Rose, 1981, 1988).

At what level should we look for such correspondents? Although there was a brief flurry of enthusiasm in the 1960s and 1970s for the idea that there were specific molecular codes for memory—an enthusiasm that has not entirely vanished—it is probably fair to say that most conceptual models assume that memory is encoded in some way in the form of changed connections between cells, an idea most clearly enunciated by Donald Hebb in 1949, when he proposed in his well-known book *The Organisation of Behavior,* that memory depended on an association between two neurons firing contiguously, such that:

> When an axon of Cell A is near enough to excite a Cell B and repeatedly or persistently takes part in firing it, some growth process or metabolic change takes place in one or both cells such that A's efficiency, as one of the cells firing B, is increased (Hebb, 1949, p62).

Hebb synapses are now part of the stock-in-trade of all neural modellers concerned either with the workings of real brains or with the current revived enthusiasm for artificial intelligence as reflected in computers operating along principles described as parallel distributed architecture.

But before considering further the reality or otherwise of such synapses I want to reflect a little further on the issue of levels. Margaret Masterman once critically analysed Thomas Kuhn's use of the term "paradigm" in his discussion of normal and revolutionary science and identified more than twenty different ways in which this single author used the term. The same I suspect is true for the idea of a level in the brain and behavioural science. Here are some of the ways in which we find ourselves using the term:

(1) To define different scales of organised complexity which possess ontological distinction. Churchland and Sjenowski's (1988) recent hierarchy (which some, though perhaps not the authors, will recognise follows Engels) runs:

CNS → systems → maps → networks → neurons → synapses → molecules
1m   10cm   1cm   1mm   100μm   1μm   1Å

(2) To define different structures in the CNS, as in the sequence:

cortex → midbrain → brain stem

(3) To describe phylogeny, as in the sequence:

human → primate → mammal → vertebrate → invertebrate

(4) To define different scientific discourses each with a distinct history, methodology and style of partitioning the universe; that is, an epistemology, as in:

psychology → organ physiology → cellular physiology →
biochemistry → molecular biology

(5) To define different classes of analytical question about a phenomenon as proposed by Marr and Poggio's three levels of analysis:

(i)   Computational level of abstract problem analysis

(ii) Algorithmic level specifying the formal procedures required to perform a task from given inputs

(iii)   Implementation level defining the physical (biological) structures instantiating the algorithmic procedures.

(In Marr's view these three levels can all be studied separately.)

So when we use the term here, do we imply an ontological state of organisation of the material world which is somehow radically distinct from other ontological states—so that, for instance, there are discontinuities between the universe studied by physiologists and that studied by behaviourists which demand we seek different laws and organising principles? Or are the levels purely epistemological, referring to our mode of study of them? In either case, what is the relationship between data collected and theories made at one level to that at another? (If the idea of level is purely a statement of epistemology, then we should probably abandon the term in favour of the idea of *discourse*.) I suspect that some of the ways in which we use the term level are no more than epistemological—they reflect specific research traditions and languages and are more an inherent consequence of the history of our science than of the way the material world is ordered. But most of us believe, I guess, that the issues are not purely epistemological, that our concept of a level is also—or at least sometimes—intended to reflect the way the material world is organised, in which increasing degrees of complexity result in sharp transitions into new modes of organisation in which qualitatively new types of relationship appear. Psychologists, albeit dealing with the electrical properties of a single cell whilst biochemists deal with the properties of homogenates of many millions, are nonetheless working in this sense at a "higher" level.

So what is the right level to study the mechanisms of learning and memory? Although the molecular reductionism of the 1960s is, as I have said, largely discredited, there is still a powerful school of thought, especially within the U.S., typified by the research programmes of the schools founded by Kandel (Hawkins and Kandel, 1984) and by Alkon (1987) that it will be possible to discover what Kandel has called a "cellular alphabet" for memory. In this model, the modification of a single synapse will be sufficient to store an alteration in behaviour or an association. By contrast, many neural modellers seek to find

Hebb synapses distributed in a small ensemble or network of neurons, which is a higher organisational level than the single synapse, for sure. But is even this level adequate—perhaps memories are stored not in a discrete location at all, but in a widely distributed manner across large regions of the nervous system? This idea finds expression in two very different research traditions—within the Soviet Union in the form of Anokhin's concept of "functional systems" (Anokhin, 1974) and more recently in the chaos models developed by Skarda and Freeman (1987).

This comment on levels is concerned with the scale of cellular organisation, from synaptic to cerebral. But one might also wonder whether, phylogenetically, it is appropriate to assume identity of process and mechanism—a concern which Schneirla would certainly have recognised. For instance, are we right to expect that habituation and sensitisation in sea slugs are appropriate models for the subtleties of vertebrate—or still more human—learning? Is long-term potentiation—a change in the firing properties of hippocampal cells as a result of a train of high-frequency impulses—really to be regarded as a model or even a mechanism for what happens when we recall the face of a friend? Is there indeed a single phenomenon at the behavioural level which we are right to call memory? Psychologists distinguish a wide variety of antithetic pairs—short- and long-term, working and storage, learning how and learning that, procedural and declarative, and many others. Further, there are memories in multiple modalities—visual, auditory, olfactory, kinaesthetic. Must we assume underlying identity of mechanisms for all? (There are some fascinating suggestions that olfactory memory, unlike other forms of animal memory, is protein synthesis-independent.) And yet a further issue of levels especially relevant— are there ontogenetic differences in memorial processes? There is some evidence that in early childhood eidetic (visual) memory predominates, to be superceded during development by the more linear forms of verbal memory. I have speculated elsewhere on the potential adaptive significance of this transition (Rose, 1976; 1989c)—but what does it imply about mechanism?

Perhaps there are enough question marks in these paragraphs to abandon the rest of my discussion, to decide that the phenomena of human memory are better left to the novelist and autobiographer than to the neurobiologist. Is Proust more relevant than biochemistry to our understanding of ourselves and the world around us? Let me turn from theoretical questioning to empirical data in an attempt to persuade you otherwise.

I will first describe two recent experiments from our laboratory, which seem to me not only to be of interest in their own right but also to have heuristic value in the context of the theme of this book. The first experiment raises problems for models which assume that memory is formed in a series of stages between short- and long-term, in which synaptic connections in a single ensemble of neurons are progressively altered in weights so as to form a neural representation of the novel information. The second presents some interesting difficulties for theories based on the contiguous-firing hypothesis derived from Hebb.

Our research approach is to study the biochemical, morphological and physiological processes occurring during memory formation in the day-old chick. We work with the young chick because, as a precocial animal, it needs to learn a great deal about its environment within the hours and days after hatching—for instance, to recognise its mother, and to distinguish good- from bad-tasting food. Also, as a precocial animal, it has on hatching a well-developed brain with a reasonably full complement of neurons and synapses. Teaching chicks relatively simple tasks results in long-lasting modifications of many neuronal properties, and in order to present the experiments I wish to discuss I need to spend a little time summarising these results (full recent reviews, and the primary references to the work summarised below are to be found in Rose, 1989a, 1991; Stewart, 1989).

In the training task we use, chicks are offered a small bright bead which they will peck at spontaneously within a few seconds of presentation. If the bead is dipped into a bitter-tasting substance (we use methylanthranilate), the chick will peck once, shake its head vigorously in a disgust reaction and subsequently avoid pecking a similar but dry bead. The chick will remember this one trial passive avoidance (surely an appropriate example of approach/withdrawal!) for many days afterwards, and the simplicity and strength of the training task makes it an excellent model in which to study the cellular correlates of memory formation. Chicks trained on the bitter bead may be compared with controls which have pecked a water-coated bead, which they will continue to peck on subsequent test. To summarize briefly a decade of analysis of the cellular sequelae of passive-avoidance training, one of the first goals was to identify the regions of the chick brain involved in responses to the training procedure by use of the radioactively labelled glucose analogue 2–deoxyglucose (2–DG). As neurochemists will know, systemically injected 2–DG is taken up into neurons as if it were glucose and is there converted to 2–deoxyglucose 6–phosphate, but cannot be metabolised further. It is thus accumulated intracellularly, and the radioactivity in the cell can be taken as a surrogate measure for neuronal metabolic activity, itself an index of synaptic activity and cell firing. Neurons whose activity is enhanced during training on the passive avoidance task will accumulate increased radioactivity from 2–DG. Mapping the entire forebrain by serial autoradiography and comparing maps derived from trained and control chicks will enable one to identify regions of interest.

This method reveals three cellular regions from the chick forebrain in which neuronal activity is increased by pecking at the methylanthranilate-coated bead. These are the intermediate medial hyperstriatum ventrale (IMHV), lobus parolfactorius (LPO) and paleostriatum augmentatum (PA). Although both right and left hemispheres are involved in the response to training, there is evidence of lateralisation, with left IMHV in particular being especially implicated.

The enhanced metabolic activity in the three nuclei is followed by a cascade of biochemical processes summarised in Table 1. You will doubtless be relieved to learn that I do not intend to discuss the intricacies of, or evidence for, these effects. Briefly, in the minutes following training on the passive avoidance task, there are transient increases in muscarinic cholinergic transmission. Probably triggered by antidromic signals from the post-synaptic side and the opening of Ca^{2+} channels, a membrane-bound form of a ubiquitous protein kinase enzyme, protein kinase C (PKC), is mobilised, and this alters the rate of phosphorylation of a presynaptic membrane protein, a 52kD polypeptide which under a variety of names (B50, GAP 43, F1) has now been shown to be involved in a range of phenomena of neural plasticity running from regeneration of crushed nerves to long-term potentiation. Taken together, these changes in cholinergic transmission and the membrane phosphorylation steps activate cellular events in both pre- and post-synaptic neurons.

It is known that PKC-dependent membrane phosphorylation can result, probably by regulation of intracellular Ca^{2+} levels, in signals originating at the cell membrane being transmitted to the nucleus, and as a consequence triggering genomic activation, probably by way of another rather universal mechanism, the eukaryotic oncogene c-fos (for review of these mechanisms, see e.g. Chiarugi, Ruggiero and Corradetti, 1989). The result is the synthesis of new proteins, and, for up to 24 hours following training the chick on the passive avoidance task, there is an increased *de novo* synthesis of a variety of intracellular proteins, including the microtubular protein tubulin, and, of most importance for what follows, synaptic membrane glycoproteins. Again by way of reminder for non-biochemists, glycoproteins, which are combinations of proteins with "tails" made of sugars like galactose and fucose, are major membrane constituents and play a crucial role in cell-cell recognition and adhesion.

Transported to the synapse, the new and post-translationally modified glycoproteins are inserted into both pre- and post-synaptic membranes, resulting in a lasting modification of their dimensions and shape. It is here that our biochemical measures have been supplemented by morphological analysis, using the methods of quantitative morphometry and stereology at light and electron microscope levels. In the context of the ideas and models which have suggested that synaptic efficacy can be modified by the transition from shaft to spine synapses and changes in the diameter of the spine head (Perkel and Perkel [1985] and Pongracz [1985]), we have paid particular attention to the size and shape of the dendritic spines on neurons of the IMHV. Twenty-four hours after training chicks on the passive avoidance task, there is a 60 percent increase in the number of spines on dendrites of the multipolar projection neurons of the left IMHV, and a 15 percent increase in their average spine head diameter.

This remarkable postsynaptic structural change is coupled with presynaptic changes in synapse structure identified in the electron microscope. In particular there is a substantial increase in the number of synaptic vesicles per synapse in the left IMHV and LOP. Finally, to complete the picture neurophysiologically, within the hours following training on the passive avoidance task, there is a massive (four-fold) increase in the rate of high-frequency neuronal firing ("bursting") recorded as multi-unit activity from the IMHV of anaesthetised birds (we don't yet know whether this effect can be found in LPO as well).

The cellular changes so far described have been sequelae of training chicks by way of a single peck at a bitter-tasting bead. It has been important to our research goals to demonstrate that these are more than mere correlates, but may be demonstrated to be necessary and sufficient aspects of the memory-formation process (Rose, 1981). Thus we have shown that if the birds are trained on the methylanthranilate bead, but are then rendered amnesic, the biochemical, structural and physiological responses do not occur; the taste of the bead alone, together with the disgust responses it produces, does not result in the cellular phenomena. Further, if the biochemical processes which occur after training are inhibited by the use of appropriate blockers, memory formation cannot occur. Importantly for one of the experiments I now wish to describe, a metabolic analogue of the sugar fucose, the substance 2–deoxygalactose, which prevents glycoprotein synthesis, also blocks long-term memory formation if injected intracerebrally at around the time of training.

Everything I have described so far is perfectly in accord with standard memory-formation models; that is, of Hebb-type contiguous firing of pre- and post-synaptic neurons, one driven by sight of or peck at the bead, the other by the registration of the bitter taste, modifying connectivity by selective dendritic growth or synaptic sprouting. As a result of the contiguous firing, a linear sequence of events in a single cell ensemble then results in a transition between the earlier, short-term phases of memory and long term, permanent engram formation; the new pattern of connections is the brain representation of the association between beadpeck and aversive taste.

Having set this model up, let me now describe the paradoxical results of two recent experiments. First, the concept of a localisable memory store. If, as I described above, the cells of the

Table 1. Temporal Processes in Vertebrate Memory Storage, Based Mainly on Chick Studies

Timescale	Processes	Region
Very short term sec → min	Pre/post depolarizations?, Ca^{2+} flux? transmitter release? Increased glucose utilization	**IMHV, LPO, PA**
Short term min → h	Pre/post antidromic signals **Translocation of PKC**	**Left IMHV**
	C-fos expression	**Left IMHV**
	Presynaptic phosphorylation of B50	**IMHV**
	Transient increases in receptor binding	**IMHV**
	Increased neuronal bursting	**IMHV**
Long term h → days	**Changed neuronal connectivity via:**	**IMHV**
	Protein synthesis, including tubulin	"roof"
	Pre and Post-synaptic membrane glycoprotein synthesis	**IMHV, LPO**
	Presynaptic increases in synaptic vesicle numbers	**Left IMHV +Left LPO**
	Postsynaptic increases in synaptic apposition zone length	**Left IMHV +Left LPO**
	Increased dendritic spine density on IMHV projection neurons	**Left IMHV**
	Increased spine head diameter on IMHV projection neurons	**Left IMHV**

Bold face = results established in chick

left IMHV show increased metabolic and physiological activity, and ultimately structural changes, consequent on training on the bead, and they are therefore to be regarded as the locus of the engram, it should follow that lesioning the IMHV will result in amnesia for the passive avoidance task. Accordingly, we lesioned IMHV bilaterally in new hatched chicks, and 24 hours later trained them on the task. They evinced the expected disgust reaction and early avoidance, but when tested on a dry bead three hours later they pecked at it; as predicted, without their IMHV, the chicks could learn, but not remember the task. The next experiment repeated the study, but lesioned the IMHV only unilaterally. Again, the results matched prediction; chicks with right hemisphere IMHV lesions learned the task well and showed no amnesia; chicks with left hemisphere lesions learned but were amnesic. The conclusion is clear and unproblematic (Patterson, Gilbert & Rose, 1991; to learn and remember the task, chicks need their left IMHV.

Now for the problem. Our next experiment reversed the sequence of operations, day-old chicks were trained on the task, and one hour later were given bilateral IMHV lesions. The prediction from the previous experiment is that they should show amnesia when tested later, as the memory store is, as we have shown, located in the IMHV. However, this was not the outcome; the lesioned chicks showed no memory loss. Somehow the brain region necessary for memory formation to take place, and in which we had found so many cellular changes, was no longer necessary an hour after training.

Where could the trace have gone? [Incidentally, rather similar results have been found for IMHV lesions in imprinting by Horn (1985).] Recalling our 2–DG data and the evidence for some metabolic activity consequent on training in the LPO as well as IMHV, we turned our attention there. Lesioning the LPO bilaterally in newly hatched chicks, training and testing 24 hours later, gives no impairment; unlike the IMHV, the LPO is therefore not required for memory formation to occur. However, if we trained the day-old chicks, and lesioned the LPO one hour later, the chicks were once more amnesic. The LPO is thus required for storage, but not formation of memory.

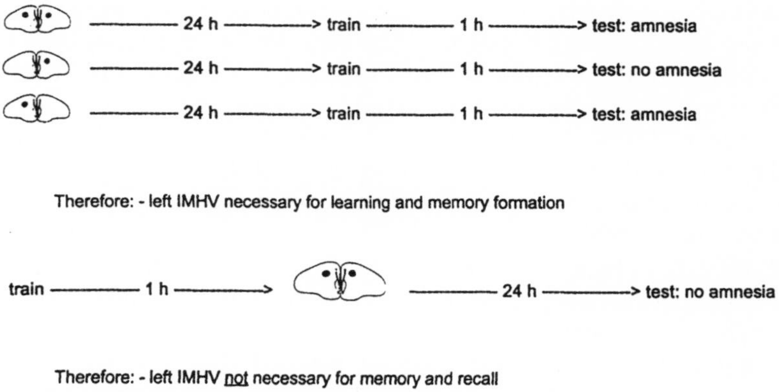
24 h → train — 1 h → test: amnesia
24 h → train — 1 h → test: no amnesia
24 h → train — 1 h → test: amnesia
Therefore: - left IMHV necessary for learning and memory formation
train — 1 h → — 24 h → test: no amnesia
Therefore: - left IMHV not necessary for memory and recall

Figure 1. IMHV Lesions and Memory

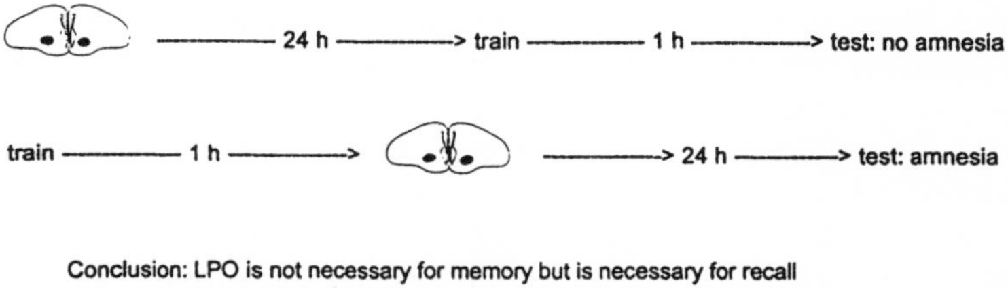
24 h → train — 1 h → test: no amnesia
train — 1 h → → 24 h → test: amnesia
Conclusion: LPO is not necessary for memory but is necessary for recall

Figure 2. LPO Lesions and Memory

Within the hour following training, the memory trace, the neural representation of the beadpeck-aversive taste pairing, has been redistributed from IMHV to other brain regions, including the LPO—perhaps only the LPO, although these experiments cannot yet say for sure. However the memory for this task is stored in the chick brain, it clearly *isn't* in the form of a simple, small ensemble of cells in the IMHV in which a linear sequence of events following the initial pairing results in modified synapses.

Now for the second paradoxical result. One of the phenomena which has puzzled orthodox associationist psychologists for a number of years, since its first description by Garcia,

Ervin and Koelling (1966) has been that of delayed sickness aversion. In the original description, animals were presented with a novel-coloured or -tasting food, or food located in a novel place. Some considerable time after eating it, they were injected with lithium chloride, which produces sickness which lasts for up to several hours. When offered the same coloured, tasting or located food subsequently, the animal would avoid it, clearly having concluded that it was the food which produced the sickness. Whilst such a result makes good sense to animal behaviourists, as it is obviously of survival value, it is a problem to account for within a psychological theory which demands a close temporal association between CS and US for learning to occur. The standard way of saving the theory has been to assume that ingesting the food leaves a long-lasting internal trace, for instance, the presence of the food in the stomach, which can subsequently be paired with the sickness.

I have never found this account very convincing, but in any event, because there was evidence that chicks too would show delayed sickness aversion (Gaston, 1977), I was interested to see whether they could be trained to show the effect to a beadpeck. We (Barber, Gilbert and Rose, 1989) therefore trained chicks by allowing them to peck at a dry chrome bead or a small green light (an LED). Half an hour later they were injected intraperitoneally with lithium chloride, and after three more hours, when they had recovered from the sickness, they were offered the bead or light. Sure enough, they avoided the object they had previously seen and pecked, though they did not avoid the novel one. Only after this initial experiment did I realise that, as the bead the chicks have pecked is dry, tasteless and apparently neutral, the standard associationist explanation for the pairing, that a residue of the ingested material remains in the stomach, cannot account for the learning. However, this was not the main point of the experiment. We wanted to know whether the metabolic inhibitors which we had earlier shown produced amnesia for the pairing of beadpeck and methylanthranilate would have any effect on the chick's ability to pair beadpeck with subsequent sickness. So we repeated the delayed sickness experiment, but injected the chicks, at the time of the initial beadpeck, with the inhibitor of glycoprotein synthesis,

2–deoxygalactose, discussed above. When, following recovery from the lithium chloride-induced sickness, the chicks were tested with the chrome bead or green light, they now pecked indifferently at each; that is, they no longer made the association between the initial beadpeck and subsequent sickness. The 2–deoxygalactose only produced the amnesia if it was injected at the time of the beadpeck, not if its injection was delayed to match that of the lithium chloride (Fig 3).

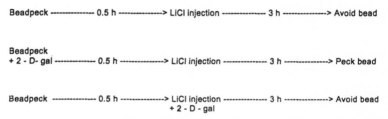

Figure 3. Glycoprotein Synthesis and Delayed Sickness Learning

The implications of this experiment are quite interesting. First, chicks can hold a memory of an apparently neutral stimulus, the bead, for at least half an hour before associating it with sickness. Second, in order to hold this memory, or representation, it is necessary for the chick to be able to synthesise membrane glycoproteins which we know to be involved in modulation of synaptic connectivity. In the orthodox associationist model, into which the data I described above could be fitted, the signal for new glycoprotein synthesis and synaptic modification was assumed to come from the contiguous, Hebb-type pairing of two neuronal pathways associated respectively with the sight of the bead and its taste. But what could be the two contiguously-firing pathways in the case of this delayed-sickness learning experiment? Forming an internal representation of the bead seems to be important enough for the chick to devote metabolic resources to the manufacture of new glycoproteins to make the representation of the bead even in the absence of an obvious pairing mechanism with a specific aversive US. With some trepidation, I would suggest that this could be described as a non-Hebbian memory mechanism—at least insofar as Hebbian mechanisms are regarded as synonymous at the cellular level with associationist ones at the behavioural.

What are the implications of this perhaps excessively empirical presentation of data to the theme of our discussion? Perhaps one may be that in biology, which deals with very complex phenomena, as opposed to physics, which deals with simpler but more exact ones, theory is much harder to make than experiments. A large number of mathematical models and computer simulations have been published based on assumptions about Hebbian mechanisms and involving transitions within an individual cell ensemble between short- and long-term memory, yet the empirical grounds for assuming that these are indeed the memory-storage processes which require modelling are clearly fragile.

Modelling the brain is appealing because one powerful mode of scientific advance has been by trying to explain one type of phenomenon or system in terms derived metaphorically from another. Such transfers are certainly not illegitimate—the question is about their utility. The history of science shows that sometimes they are helpful, sometimes not. One can usefully distinguish between three types of analogy in science (Wall and Safran, 1986). The first is *poetic*—Wall and Safran's example is Rutherford's description of electrons in orbit around the atomic nucleus as if they were planets revolving around the sun. In using this analogy he did not mean that the nucleus and electrons were *like* the sun and planets nor that the forces which related them were gravitational; all that the analogy provides is a useful visual image. The second analogic mode is *evocative*, in which a principle from one sphere is transferred to another. Thus until the Middle Ages and the Newtonian revolution, everything that moved seem to be pushed and pulled by something else. Hence to explain the movement of the sun around the earth, metaphor spoke of horse-drawn fiery chariots. Finally, one has the metaphor as a statement of structural or organisational identity. Thus when Harvey discovered the circulation of the blood and described the heart as a pump, his metaphor had a precise meaning which distinguishes it from the previous two categories. Within the circulatory system, the heart indeed functions *as* a pump, and organisationally its structure, with valves and emptying and filling phases, resembles at least those pumps which were being mechanically contrived at the time of Harvey's discovery. Treating the heart *as* a pump enables mathematical models of its action to be made which accurately describe many of its properties.

In the history of theory-making in the biological sciences, the heart-pump example is paradigmatic. A biological structure and mechanism was explained by analogising it to a piece of relatively advanced technology. In the three centuries since Descartes, brains and nervous systems have been hydraulic pumps and valves, clockwork, magnetic, electrical, telegraph and telephone exchanges, and, most recently, computers. Until now this flow of model-making has been unidirectional, from technology to biology. Just why this has been the case is not clear; it may reflect the contingent fact that in the history of western science the physical sciences developed prior to the bio-logical ones and have been seen as more "fundamental."

It may also be a more deep-seated aspect of the reduc-tionist mode of thinking which has characterised the way that our science has developed (Rose, Lewontin and Kamin, 1984). In any event at the present time it is just possible that this direction of metaphor transfer may be changing and becoming more of a two-way flow. For me as a neurobiologist, however, the important question is not whether one can make computers work more like brains or develop artificial intelligence. Mathe-matical modelling of "systems with memory" is of interest only if the systems in some way approach real brains. I simply don't accept what I might describe as the new cognitivist scholasticism which argues that, if one can identify appropriate mind proper-ties and processes, then one can model these properties and processes in abstract *gedankenexperiments* and subsequently incarnate them (or, perhaps more accurately, *inmachinate* them) into sets of silicon components, optical switches or magnetic monopoles just as well as into the complex bits of carbon chemistry that evolutionary processes have generated. As Boden has put it "you don't need brains to be brainy" (Boden, 1986). This process is well-exemplified in Minsky's recent book

(Minsky, 1987) in which he sees "mind" as a "society" of arbitrarily defined and hierarchically arranged "agents," or "memory," "anger," "sleep," "more" or what-you-will. To me this is a classic example of the top-down approach of the cognitive scientist, an approach which has the capacity to generate an infinite number of models capable of passing the test of theory whilst being wholly indifferent to the reality-test that the material biological world imposes upon more empirically based science (Rose, 1987). It is precisely the type of evocative analogy we neurobiologists do *not* need if we are to be helped to understand real brains and real behaviour.

In what ways then are brain memories *not* like computer memories? The analogy, while of potent fascination to many, has always been suspect amongst biologically grounded neuroscientists, on both structural and organisational grounds. Structurally of course the properties of chips, AND/OR gates, logic circuits or whatever, do not at all resemble neurons, if indeed it is neurons that are to be regarded as the relevant units of exchange within the nervous system. The units of which the computer is composed are determinate, with a small number of inputs and outputs, and the processes that they carry out with such impressive regularity are linear and error-free. They can store and transform information according to set rules. One consequence of this, for computer brain-modellers, has been the persistent tendency to attempt to reify certain types of process in which real minds/brains participate, and turn them into fixed machine properties—for instance in the very concept of "artificial intelligence" itself—as if intelligence were simply the property of the machine itself. I would indeed argue that such a reification is not even appropriate to brains, let alone computers.

The brain/computer metaphor fails because neurons and the systems they compose, unlike computers, are radically indeterminate. Central nervous system neurons each have many thousands of synaptic inputs of varying weights and origins (perhaps 10^4–10^5 in the human brain); they show developmental and experiential plasticity to a striking degree, yet also manifest redundancy and extraordinary resilience of functionally appropriate output despite injury and insult. They carry out linear computations relatively slowly yet judgmental functions with an extreme ease that baffles the modellers. Brains are complex, richly interconnected, open systems, and are indeterminate in the crucial sense that, unlike computers, they (or the humans or other animals in which they are embedded) determine their own future, albeit in circumstances not of their own choosing. One important difference between computer memory and brain memory is that computers are error-free, they can only succeed or fail in a task. By contrast brain memory is error-full, and uses multiple different modalities.

Von Foerster (1969) offers a restaurant analogy which may be helpful here. Offered a menu with a multiple choice of dishes, one reads it, chooses and eats a meal. Information in the printed text of the menu is considered in the light of recollections of earlier tastes, then the spoken order to the waiter, and then the material reality of the food and its actual taste. And when one subsequently describes the experience again and says, last night I ate salmon and salad, one neither offers the listener the printed menu nor the food—still less does one expect the listener to taste it directly. Instead the previous night's experience is further modified by translating it into spoken words. At each point in this sequence there has been more than just a switch in the modality in which the information is expressed: there has been an input of work on that information which has irreversibly transformed it (and this of course says nothing about the work that each listener does in subsequently further transforming, working on and interpreting the data). The point is that brains do not work with *information* in the computer-sense, but the *meaning*. And intelligence, as I understand and wish to use the term, is not a fixed property locked inside a brain, as the crude Anglo-Saxon psychometric tradition maintains (Rose, 1987)—still less locked inside a machine—but a historically and developmentally shaped process, expressed by individuals in interaction with their natural and social environment. Indeed, one of the problems of studying memory is precisely that it is a dialectical phenomenon. Each time we remember, we in some senses do work or and transform our memories; they are not simply being called up from store and, once consulted, replaced unmodified. Our memories are recreated each time we remember.

To exemplify from the history of so-called artificial intelligence, Wall and Safran (1986) call it *artefactual*, consider the contrast between the relative ease with which programmers were able to develop chess-playing programs to grand master level and the difficulty in developing a robot system which can laboriously pile an orange pyramid onto a blue cube. Compare this with the accuracy with which an untrained human can toss an apple (or Apple) core into a waste basket three metres away, or, for that matter, play poker. Sure, you can devise a program that can calculate the odds of drawing a flush against three-of-a-kind, but poker involves a type of competitive psychology, of bluff, and it requires the appreciation and assessment of non-cognitive inputs for which, I would argue, there can be no effective machine analogy. Humans might derive some pleasure from playing chess against a program, none from betting against a computer in poker—so perhaps the poker test should replace the Turing test?

To return, not before time, to the issue of memory. The starting point, for modellers and cellular neurobiologists alike, must be the phenomenology of the behaviour. One must concede, for instance, that the aspects of animal learning and memory studied in the *Aplysia* gill withdrawal reflex, rats swimming through water mazes or pressing levers in Skinner boxes, or even chicks pecking beads, are likely to be but a poor shadow of the competences of even relatively small-brained animals in their natural environments, and that the mechanisms we so meticulously endeavour to elucidate with scintillation counters, electrodes and image analysis are a small and perhaps misleading part of a larger picture. (The difficulties that biologically "obvious" phenomena like imprinting or delayed-sickness aversion seem to present to psychological theory-builders underscores my point.) To begin to see the scale of this larger picture we might consider returning to human experience of memory, studied experimentally or even (a blasphemous suggestion?) introspectively.

Let me conclude with one final very simple experimental example, yet one which, I suggest, presents profound problems of explanation, and this is the well-known distinction between recall and recognition memory. When shown an ensemble of articles or list of words and then asked to *recall* what has been seen, humans (and, in analogous experiments, other primates) find it very hard to go accurately beyond about 10–20 items. Yet when Standing (1973) briefly showed subjects a series of pictures, and later asked them to choose between pictures they had seen before and a novel set, their memory was to all intents and purposes unsaturable—even after being shown ten thousand pictures, subjects still showed an astonishingly high success rate when asked to *recognise* the pictures days later. The biological, adaptive significance of having a huge capacity for recognition memory is obvious, yet how do we begin to account for it in cellular, synaptic terms, or to model this apparently deep distinction between recognition and recall? The richness of the reality of the brain's functional capacities is the real challenge for us all.

**This report was written for a conference that took place in 1989. The empirical results are not updated. However, the main theoretical issues I believe remain valid despite the passage of time.

REFERENCES

Alkon, D. (1982). *Memory traces in the brain*. University Press, Cambridge.

Anokhin, P. K. (1974). *Biology and Neurophysiology of the Conditioned Reflex and Its Role in Adaptive Behaviour*. Pergamon Press.

Barber, A., Gilbert, D., and Rose, S. P. R. (1989). Glycoprotein synthesis is necessary for memory of sickness-induced learning in chicks. *Eur. J. Neurosci. 1*, 673–677.

Boden, M. (1986). In *Science and Beyond*. Rose, S. P. R., and Appignanesi, L., eds. Oxford: Blackwell, 103–114.

Chiarugi, V. P., Ruggiero, M., and Corradetti, R. (1989). Oncogenes, protein kinase C, neuronal differentiation and memory. *Neurochemistry International 14*, 1–9.

Churchland, P., and Sejnowki, T. (1993). Computational neuroscience. MIT Press.

Garcia, J., Ervin, F. R., and Koelling, R. (1966). Learning with prolonged delay of reinforcement. *Psychonom. Sci. 5,* 121–122.

Gaston, K. (1977). An illness-induced conditioned aversion in domestic chicks: one-trial learning with a long delay of reinforcement. *Behav. Biol. 20,* 441–453.

Gilbert, D. B., Patterson, T. P., & Rose, S. P. R. (1991). Dissection of brain sites necessary for regulation and storage of memory for a one-trial passive avoidance task in the chick. *Behavioral Neuroscience, 106,* 465–470.

Hawkins, R. D. and Kandel, E. R. (1984). Is there a cell-biological alphabet for simple forms of learning? *Psychol Rev. 91,* 375–391.

Hebb, D. O. (1949). *The organisation of behaviour.* New York: John Wiley.

Horn, G. (1985). *Memory, imprinting and the brain.* Oxford: University Press.

Minsky, M. (1987). *The society of mind.* London: Heinemann.

Perkel, D. H., and Perkel, D. J. (1985). Dendritic spines: role of active membrane in modulating synaptic efficacy. *Brain Res. 325,* 23–45.

Pongracz, F. (1985). The function of dendritic spines: a theoretical study. *Neuroscience 15,* 933–946.

Rose, S. P. R. (1976, 1989c). *The conscious brain.* New York: Knopf and Paragon House.

——. (1981). What should a biochemistry of learning and memory be about? *Neuroscience 6,* 811–822.

——. (1987). *Molecules and minds: Essays on biology and the social order.* Open University Press, Milton Keynes.

——. (1988). Mind and memory between metaphor and molecule, in *Systems with learning and memory abilities,* eds. Delacour, J., Levy, J. C. S. Elsevier, North Holland, 177–192.

——. (1989). Glycoprotein synthesis and post-synaptic remodelling in memory formation. *Neurochemistry International 14,* 299–307.

——. (1991). Biochemical mechanisms involved in memory formation in the chick. In *The chick as a model for the study of learning and memory.* Andrew. R., ed. Oxford: University Press.

Rose, S. P. R., Lewontin, R. C., and Kamin, L. (1984). *Not in our genes.* Harmondsworth: Penguin.

Squire, L. (1987). *Memory and brain.* Oxford: University Press.

Standing, L. (1973). Learning ten thousand pictures. *Quar. J. Exp. Psychol., 25*, 207–222.

Stewart, M. G. (1991). Changes in dendritic and synaptic structure in chick forebrain consequent on passive avoidance training. In *The chick as a model for the study of learning and memory*. Andrew, R., ed. Oxford: University Press.

von Foerster, H. (1969). What is memory that it may have hindsight and foresight as well? *Atorga*, Feb.-April, Comm 122–124.

Wall, P. D., and Safran, J. N. (1986). Artefactual intelligence. In *Science and Beyond*, eds. Rose, S. P. R. and Appignanesi, L. Oxford: Blackwell, pp. 130–150.

SECTION III

Approach/Withdrawal—Socialization

An Analysis of Approach/Withdrawal Processes in the Initiation of Maternal Behavior in the Laboratory Rat

Jay S. Rosenblatt and Anne D. Mayer

I. Introduction

Tobach and Schneirla (1968) have provided the theoretical context for analysis of the formation, maintenance, and dissolution of the mother-young relationship among animals in terms of approach/withdrawal (A/W) biphasic processes theory. They characterized the formation of the bond between mother and young by emphasizing the predominance of approach responses: "Processes of bond formation on all social levels involve relationships of approach and consequent mutual stimulation" (p. 507). However, they were aware that *both approach and withdrawal processes* are involved in phases of the mother's behavior towards her young, particularly at weaning, and they wrote: "The processes of approach and withdrawal are both essential to the development of social behavior . . . as . . . in such social phenomena as territoriality, aggression, [and] weaning . . ." (p. 507–508). Moreover, they considered that the physiological (i.e., hormonal) processes of reproduction energized and channeled the mother's behavior in relation to her young and in that way

they are "... central in the development of bond formation ..."
between mother and young (Tobach and Schneirla, p. 508).

At the time they wrote, only general statements could be
made about the relationship of processes of reproduction to the
formation of the bond between mother and young. Although
these remain valid as a guiding framework, newer findings reveal more about the organization of A/W biphasic processes
within the female which culminate in maternal behavior with the
consequent formation of the bond between the mother and her
young. In this article we will review these findings in the rat as
a means of presenting our current understanding of how
A/W biphasic processes are involved in the onset of maternal
behavior.

Tobach and Schneirla (1968) proposed that the early mutual attraction of mother and young was based upon their approach responses to the sensory properties each encountered in
the other. For the mother, these consisted of chemoceptive
stimuli of the birth fluids bathing the neonate and the neonate's
tactile, auditory, and visual properties. The neonate, in turn, approached the mother through the effects on it of temperature,
tactile, chemoceptive, visual, and auditory stimuli. These low intensity stimuli in the various sensory modalities directly elicited
mutual approach responses which were, therefore, labelled bio-
taxic responses and the relationship called biosocial. They proposed that within a few hours after parturition the basis of the
mother's approach responses to her newborn changed as a result
of experience gained in interaction with them. Gradually the female expanded the basis of her approach response to the young,
incorporating her experiences with them and their effects upon
her, which modified her motivational/emotional and sensorimotor responses to them. The young underwent corresponding
changes, at a simpler psychological level, in their suckling and
huddling approaches to the female. As Tobach and Schneirla
(1968) described it: "... within the first hours after delivery the
formation of a psychosocial bond between parent and offspring
is well begun" (p. 521).

In an earlier article, one of us (Rosenblatt, 1983) traced the
developmental transition in the young of several altricial species
from stimulus intensity-based A/W responses to responses

based upon experience. It was proposed that olfactory stimulation mediates this transition by being associated with thermotactile stimulation, providing an incentive stimulus that was actively sought by young. The present article continues our interest in extending T. C. Schneirla's A/W biphasic processes theory into areas not yet explored. It is based upon the research on maternal behavior in the rat by many of our colleagues and students. In the course of these studies we were forced to develop our thinking about the organization of maternal behavior, particularly during the onset and early maintenance of this behavior, and this has led us to challenge the earlier "threshold" concept and to adopt the "approach/withdrawal biphasic processes" concept proposed by Schneirla (1959, 1965).

The present article represents the results of such an analysis of maternal behavior in the rat.

We acknowledge the important contribution of other investigators to the concept of approach/withdrawal in the analysis of maternal behavior in the rat. The research and writings of Alison S. Fleming (a former student of the first author) have been particularly influential as will be noted in our many references to her studies and particularly to her theoretical review (Fleming, 1986). We have made extensive use of the studies of Joseph Terkel and his student Moshe Jakubowski (Jakubowski and Terkel, 1984, 1985a, 1985b). The studies of Hansen and his colleagues have also played an important role in providing crucial evidence of fear and timidity in nonpregnant females and their attenuation in lactating mothers (Hansen and Ferreira, 1986; Hard and Hansen, 1985).

The contents of this article are divided into five main sections following the introduction. The first contrasts the theoretic approaches represented by *single system activation threshold theory* and *approach/withdrawal biphasic processes theory*. In the next section we analyze the process of sensitization, as a means of stimulating maternal behavior in nonpregnant females by exposing them to pups, in terms of approach/withdrawal responses. After describing the behavioral events which occur during sensitization, we analyze the underlying perceptual, motivational/emotional, and motor processes. This is followed by tracing the ontogenetic origins of maternal approach/

withdrawal processes. In the next section, we discuss the action of hormones and other reproductive processes on maternal approach/withdrawal processes first during early pre- and postnatal development, puberty and postpuberty, and then during pregnancy and parturition. The last section recapitulates the theoretical argument.

II. Single System Activation Threshold and Approach/Withdrawal Biphasic Processes Theories Contrasted

The initiation of maternal behavior during sensitization of nonpregnant females as well as the onset at the end of pregnancy, can be analyzed in terms either of single system activation threshold theory or *approach/withdrawal biphasic processes theory*. In this section we shall contrast these theories as they apply to sensitization of nonpregnant females. Sensitization consists of exposing nonpregnant females to young pups continuously, exchanging the pups for freshly fed ones daily, and observing the gradual appearance of maternal behavior over a period of five to seven days depending upon various conditions. The two theories are depicted graphically in Figures 1 and 2 and their application to the sensitization process in nonpregnant females is presented in Figure 3.

Threshold theory proposes that the components of maternal behavior are organized within the CNS and each has a threshold of activation, resulting in its performance when suitably stimulated (Figure 1). Descriptive studies of sensitization (Fleming and Rosenblatt, 1974a; Rosenblatt, 1967; Stern, 1983) suggest that anogenital licking has the lowest threshold of arousal and appears earliest during sensitization; nursing and nestbuilding have higher thresholds, appearing several days later, and retrieving, which appears shortly after these two behavior patterns, has the highest activation threshold. Maternal aggression has not been included because it is difficult to elicit from nonpregnant females and its threshold, therefore, is much higher than the thresholds of the other components of maternal behavior (Erskine, Barfield, and Goldman, 1980; Mayer and Rosenblatt, 1987).

The separate interactions of sensory and hormonal factors, and interactions between them, provide the excitation needed to arouse the components of maternal behavior. They are filtered (i.e., selectively passed on to the CNS thresholds for components of maternal behavior) and integrated (i.e., their excitatory effects are summed) by a system designated "perceptual filter and integrator." Once aroused by above-threshold excitation the motor patterns of maternal behavior are organized into sequences of varying components, having different frequencies and durations, in relation to stimuli presented by the pups. There are both internal constraints on the organization of maternal behavior and external eliciting stimulation arising from the behavior of the young.

The various factors which can influence the thresholds of activation of maternal behavior components are not shown in the figure. They will be discussed in this article and include pre- and early postnatal hormones, pubertal and postpubertal hormones, hormones during pregnancy and parturition, maternal experience, and special inhibitory stimuli and emotional states. There are feedback effects of performing maternal behavior (e.g., anogenital licking) which provide additional stimulation that adds to the excitation which activates the behavior pattern as a whole or components of the pattern. At the core of these processes, however, is the concept of thresholds for components of maternal behavior.

Approach/withdrawal biphasic processes theory proposes that the central organization consists of a pattern of approach processes and a pattern of withdrawal processes (Figure 2). When approach processes are stimulated, approach responses to the eliciting stimuli are activated: their specific nature is determined, within the approach processes, by additional factors specific to each situation as shown in the figure. Withdrawal processes may also be stimulated and withdrawal and avoidance responses activated, their specific nature also determined by a subsystem shown in the figure. Under most conditions both approach and withdrawal processes are activated simultaneously. On the left side of the figure, the sensory stimuli and their interactions are

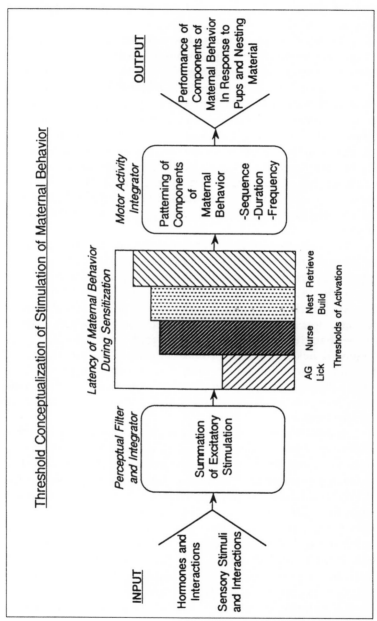

Figure 1

sorted and prioritized into approach-eliciting and withdrawal-eliciting stimuli. It is not the total excitation which is fed into the central processing system but the separate approach and withdrawal excitations, each to its related central system.

Approach and withdrawal processes may be aroused simultaneously but not equally and this may result in the predominance at any given time of either approach or withdrawal processes. Still further, the interaction may result in ambivalence or conflict in which neither approach nor withdrawal processes predominate. The consequences for behavior of these kinds of interactions may be the predominance of approach responses with the occasional intrusion of withdrawal responses, or the opposite, in which withdrawal and avoidance responses predominate with intrusions of approach responses. When approach and withdrawal processes are both strong and balanced, ambivalence or conflict prevails. Then some form of ambivalence or conflict will be observed in the female's behavior. "Stretched attention" (see below) is one form of this behavior; others will include alternating approach and withdrawal responses or immobilization ("freezing").

Hormones and other neuroactive substances (e.g., beta-endorphin) influence the approach/withdrawal system at all points as shown in Figure 2. By acting at peripheral sensory systems they affect the nature of the sensory stimuli that are received by the female. The valence of stimulation may be altered by hormones and other substances so that previously aversive or neutral stimulation becomes attractive. The capacity to resolve conflicts between approach and withdrawal may also be affected as well as the strengthening of approach or withdrawal processes. Finally, hormones and other substances may selectively prime the female within the approach system to perform certain patterns of behavior rather than others. Many of these influences of hormones will be discussed below.

Our studies of sensitization and hormonal stimulation of maternal behavior in the rat were initially based upon the threshold concept of the processes underlying maternal behavior (Rosenblatt, 1967). Discovery of the facilitating effect of anosmia on the initiation of nonhormonal maternal behavior (Fleming and Rosenblatt, 1974b,c; Mayer and Rosenblatt, 1975, 1977) and observation of approach/withdrawal conflict behavior

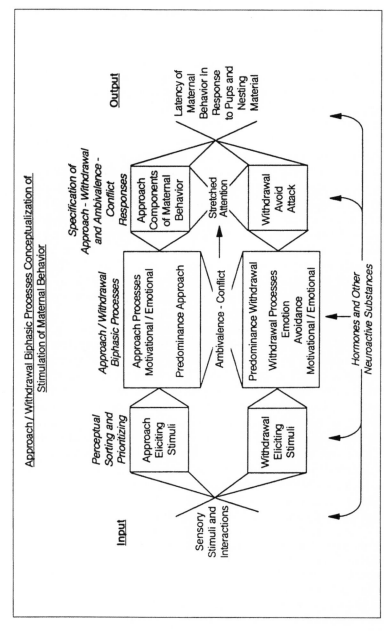

Figure 2

during sensitization (Fleming and Rosenblatt, 1974a; Terkel and Rosenblatt, 1971) led us to re-examine this theory. Our later work has been guided by the concepts of approach and withdrawal and the mechanisms depicted in Figure 2.

We now conceive of the sensitization process as shown in Figure 3 which contrasts the threshold concept with the approach/withdrawal concept. According to the threshold concept (upper part of Figure 3), the absence of maternal behavior during the initial phase of sensitization represents a low level of excitation. Sensitization represents the buildup of excitation from pup stimulation to threshold levels for anogenital licking, about midway through the process. With further increases in excitation, the thresholds for nursing and nestbuilding are reached

Sensitization of Nonpregnant Female Rats
Threshold and Approach / Withdrawal Concepts

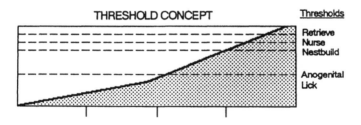

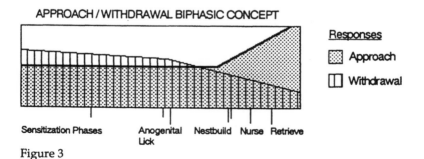

Figure 3

after a delay, then retrieving is stimulated shortly afterward. Each behavior appears abruptly when its threshold of activation has been reached.

Despite the failure to respond maternally towards pups at the start of sensitization when nonpregnant females are first exposed to pups, according to the approach/withdrawal concept (lower part of Figure 3), a high level of maternal approach responsiveness is activated but an even higher level of withdrawal responsiveness is stimulated by the pups. If the olfactory stimulus eliciting withdrawal (among other withdrawal-eliciting stimuli including the novelty of the pups) is removed (e.g., by making the female anosmic) maternal behavior appears very rapidly indicating that excitation does not need to be built up over several days. As withdrawal responsiveness declines due to continuous exposure to pups, approach responses emerge as the predominant factor and they increase as females, now aroused to approach the pups, receive additional approach-eliciting stimulation. Throughout the first half of the sensitization process, females may show ambivalence and conflict in relation to the pups but these responses disappear as withdrawal declines and approach processes grow stronger.

III. Approach/Withdrawal Processes in the Onset of Maternal Behavior

A. Sensitization of Maternal Behavior in the Nonpregnant Female Rat: The Behavioral Substrate

The rediscovery in the mid-1960s by Cosnier (1963), Cosnier and Couturier (1966), and Rosenblatt (1967) of the possibility of inducing maternal behavior in nonpregnant females by the procedure called "sensitization" has enabled us to study maternal behavior in the absence of hormonal stimulation. Earlier Wiesner and Sheard (1933) had shown that by exposing nonpregnant females to young pups continuously, a process which they termed "concaveation," they could stimulate females to exhibit retrieving and nestbuilding. Their success was limited to a small percentage of the females they studied because their procedure was faulty: they did not exchange pups daily for recently fed ones and, since nonpregnant females do not lactate, the pups became weaker and less able to locomote and they deteriorated as stimuli and eventually died. We have found that the ability of pups to crawl into contact with the female, even when she is resistant to approaching them, accelerates the initiation of maternal behavior; anything which retards this delays maternal behavior. Moreover, Wiesner and Sheard did not report on nursing and anogenital licking.

Several procedures have been used to sensitize female rats. Cosnier (1963) exposed females to pups for two hours twice daily and scored their behavior: negative scores represented attacking and cannibalizing young or simply withdrawing from them; positive scores, approaching them and exhibiting three components of maternal behavior—nursing, retrieving and nestbuilding. The procedure introduced by Rosenblatt (1967) and later utilized in a more detailed study by Fleming and Rosenblatt (1974a) has now become standard and is used widely with modifications. Pups three to ten days of age are introduced into the female's cage at a distance from the female's resting mat. Females are observed for the appearance of anogenital licking, an early appearing behavior pattern during sensitization, adopting the nursing posture over the young, nestbuilding and, finally, retrieving the pups to the "nest site." Latencies in days are recorded for each of these behavior patterns. The pups are exchanged daily for fresh pups so that the stimuli remain optimal throughout the period of sensitization.

The procedure of sensitization has had an important influence upon research on maternal behavior in the rat. For one, sensitization provides a means of inducing maternal behavior in females, without the intervention of endogenous pituitary or ovarian hormones. Hypophysectomized or ovariectomized females can be sensitized as rapidly as intact females (Rosenblatt, 1967). In addition, the analysis of the female's behavior during the sensitization process has enabled us to understand the behavioral substrate upon which the hormones of pregnancy act to stimulate the rapid onset of maternal behavior. This involves study of how the behavior of the nonpregnant female is altered by the hormones of pregnancy and the process of giving birth and lactation. For example, Kinsley and Bridges (1990) found that virgin females exhibited less than chance preference for bedding soiled by young pups whereas lactating females preferred them at 33 percent above chance level.

Using the procedure of sensitization we have also been able to study the development of A/W processes during the ontogeny of maternal behavior and this has been especially advantageous in the adolescent period before females and males develop the capacity for reproduction.

What we have learned from the studies using the sensitization procedure no longer allows us to conceive of maternal behavior in simple terms. We will propose that the appearance of maternal behavior at parturition represents the resolution of approach/withdrawal processes present in the nonpregnant female in relation to the stimulus of newborn young. The actions of hormones and other reproductive processes are not simply to enable the neural network to reach a threshold of activation of maternal behavior, which is a longstanding view with respect to many hormone-dependent behavior patterns. This view has its origins in Steinach's concept of hormonal erotization of the nervous system which was contemporaneous with Freud's concept of the libido (Beach, 1948). Rather, hormones and other reproductive processes play a role by influencing the resolution of conflicts between approach and withdrawal processes underlying maternal behavior.

1. Nonhormonal Induction of Maternal Behavior

The induction of maternal behavior by sensitization has been shown to be independent of endogenously released pituitary and ovarian hormones. Latencies for sensitization are no different in recently hypophysectomized or ovariectomized females than in intact ones: nearly all females exhibit the full pattern of maternal behavior (Cosnier and Couturier, 1966; Rosenblatt, 1967). Moreover, increasing circulating levels of prolactin does not alter sensitization latencies (Baum, 1978) and cross-transfusing blood from a sensitized female to a non-maternal one does not shorten sensitization latencies as cross-transfusion of blood from a parturient maternal female does

(Terkel and Rosenblatt, 1971, 1972). Although Leon, Numan, and Moltz (1973) reported that ovariectomy facilitates sensitization, we have not been able to replicate their findings (Mayer and Rosenblatt, 1979c; Siegel and Rosenblatt, 1975b).

2. Descriptive Analysis of Behavioral Changes
During Sensitization

Cosnier's (1963) records indicated that females started with negative scores (i.e., attacking and cannibalizing pups) and slowly, over the next 15 days, their scores crossed the zero or indifference line then became increasingly positive (i.e., nursing posture, retrieving, nestbuilding). It is not always possible to know from these records what the latencies were for the individual components of maternal behavior and the order in which these components appeared. Nevertheless, this was the first indication that nonpregnant females are not simply indifferent to pups but strongly avoid them—often taking the form of attacking them. Jakubowsky and Terkel (1985) also found that nonpregnant females of their strain initially killed five- to ten-day old pups in all instances, but by the fourth day of exposure killing had declined to only 25 percent of the females and, after that time, maternal behavior increased rapidly during the next six days until nearly all females exhibited retrieving, crouching over the young in the nest, and licking the young.

Our strain of rat, Sprague-Dawley, is tamer than the Sherman strain used by Cosnier (1963) and the strain used by Jakubowski and Terkel (1985), and we see less attacking and cannibalizing of pups by nonpregnant females. There are, however, clear indications that their initial responses to pups include strong avoidance and withdrawal from them. Fleming and Luebke (1981) described the initial responses of nonpregnant nulliparous females to pups on the basis of their own observations and earlier ones by Terkel and Rosenblatt (1971) and Fleming and Rosenblatt (1974a). They wrote: "When the pups are placed in the nulliparous animal's cage, she approaches and intensively sniffs the pups and then rapidly hops or runs away. Subsequent approaches to the pups tend to be slower and more cautious with the female stretching towards the pups and sniffing them from a distance. After a series of approach and with-

drawal responses, the female settles at a distance from the pups
... [T]he female seems to treat the pups as aversive stimuli and
in their presence she engages in a variety of behaviors which
function to increase the distance between herself and the pups"
(Fleming and Leubke, 1981, p. 863). As exposure to the pups continues for several days, the female undergoes a gradual change
in her behavior which eventuates in the abrupt onset of the maternal responses: she adopts a nursing posture, exhibits nestbuilding, and, finally, retrieves pups to the nest, all within a few
hours (Fleming and Rosenblatt, 1974a). Stern and Mackinnon
(1978) have shown that very young pups, neonates up to two
days of age, elicit less avoidance than older pups and
sensitization occurs more rapidly.

Stretching towards the pups, described above, is exhibited
by rats in a situation which arouses "... a behavioural conflict
between exploratory (approach) and flight (avoidance) tendencies," according to Van der Poel (1979, p. 446), Grant (1963) and
Silverman (1965). This behavior pattern has been referred to as
"stretched attention" by Grant and Mackintosh (1963). Pinel,
Mana, and Ward (1989) have described a stretched approach
response, resembling stretched attention, as "... a response to
aversive stimulation that is most prevalent in situations in which
the source of aversive stimulation is both well defined and inanimate, situations in which neither flight nor freezing are likely to
be particularly adaptive" (p. 141). Pups qualify as inanimate
objects insofar as they are stationary and also they are a well-
defined source of aversive stimulation. One behavior described
by these authors was the rat pushing a pile of bedding down the
alley towards the source of aversive stimulation (i.e., electric
shock) which resembles nonpregnant rats pushing bedding
towards pups to cover them when they are initially exposed to
them during sensitization.

During stretched attention the female may be unusually
sensitive to olfactory, visual, and auditory stimuli, indicated by
head scanning and sniffing movements. This is normally shown
by exploring animals that exhibit orientation to a visual stimulus,
and selective responsiveness to auditory stimulation. The
approach/withdrawal conflict is believed to reflect opposing
motivational processes and associated perceptual and motor

processes. Resolution of the conflict has consequences for each of these processes. In the situation of the nonpregant female exposed to pups, described above, the period of vacillation was followed by near-complete withdrawal from the young and avoidance of them.

Phases in the sensitization process have been described by Terkel and Rosenblatt (1971). Following the female's initial investigation of the pups and her avoidance of them by resting at a distance from them (Fleming and Leubke, 1981), the pups become active and crawl into contact with the female and remain there. The female stiffly tolerates their contact but otherwise takes no interest in them and does not adjust to their nuzzling and huddling against her body. After a time, the female begins to show an interest in them and at this time she begins to lick them, focusing her licking on the anogenital region, stimulating pup elimination which she ingests. The initiation and rise in anogenital licking anticipates the abrupt appearance of the other components of maternal behavior (Fleming and Rosenblatt, 1974a; Stern, 1983). At the end of this process the female can be seen resting in contact with the pups where she remains for long periods, in contrast to her earlier behavior when she moved her resting site each time pups were placed in it (Fleming and Leupke, 1981).

The process of sensitization can be accelerated or delayed (or even prevented) by confining females with pups in smaller or larger cages (Terkel and Rosenblatt, 1971). Female sensitization latencies increased from 2.8 days to 11.6 days as cage area increased from 36 to 468 sq. in. In the smallest cages females were forced to be in continuous contact with the pups, and, as a consequence the avoidance phase of sensitization did not appear. In the largest cages females could entirely avoid contact with the pups and the pups could not reach the females except in a few cases; two of the five females tested in the largest cages did not undergo any change in their initial avoidance behavior as a consequence.

B. Analysis of Underlying Perceptual, Motivational/Emotional, and Motor Processes during Sensitization

The process of sensitization reveals the behavioral substrate upon which hormones and sensory stimuli act to stimulate the onset of maternal behavior during pregnancy and parturition. These changes, which are shown by changes in the female's behavior, occur in slow motion in the sensitized female with the various phases drawn out in time. By analyzing the perceptual changes which occur, through experiments that directly or indirectly alter either the female's sensory capacities or the stimuli to which she is exposed, we can specify these changes underlying sensitization.

Underlying motivational/emotional changes can be analyzed experimentally by comparing the reactions of nonpregnant females to fear- and anxiety-provoking stimuli before and after sensitization; their responses can also be compared to those of postparturient females exhibiting maternal behavior. Nonpregnant females can also be compared in their ability to resolve motivational/emotional conflicts as they undergo changes during sensitization and they can be compared in this ability to postparturient females.

Motor responses also undergo changes during sensitization as consequences of the perceptual and motivational/emotional changes described above. Pups evoke changes in the female's behavior: total body approach responses be followed by specific sniffing, mouthing, licking and forepaw manipulation responses to pup stimuli. Of particular importance is tactile stimulation the female receives through the snout and perioral region: deprivation of this stimulation in lactating females has serious consequences for the performance of nursing and licking behavior (Stern and Joyhnson, 1989, 1990; Stern and Kolunie, 1991). Withdrawal/avoidance responses may develop into aggressive attack behavior which results in cannibalizing the young, removing, therefore, the source of disturbing stimulation. By comparing the behavior of nonpregnant females before and after sensitization, these changes can be analyzed and by testing females with a variety of stimuli in addition to pups, the nature of their specific responses to pups can be determined.

1. Perceptual Processes

Although they are attracted to young at a distance, non-pregnant females withdraw after approaching and sniffing them; their stretched attention posture, facing towards the pups, but at a distance with sniffing and head scanning movements, indicates they are still responding to pup odors. When bilateral olfactory bulbectomies (BOB) were performed on nonpregnant females, half of the females responded by cannibalizing the young while the remaining half exhibited maternal behavior almost immediately (Fleming and Rosenblatt, 1974b). These results were the first indication that anosmia accelerated the onset of maternal behavior during sensitization; the cannibalism was attributed to the irritability that is produced by BOB (Cain, 1974; Cain and Paxinos, 1974). In subsequent studies anosmia was produced by zinc sulfate injected intranasally, or by sectioning the lateral olfactory tracts without involvement of the olfactory bulbs (Fleming and Rosenblatt, 1974c). Irritability was no longer present (Cain and Paxinos, 1974) and all of the females, responding to the anosmia, became sensitized in less than two days, many initiating maternal behavior in a few hours. Subsequent studies have implicated elimination of both the main olfactory system and the vomeronasal system in the accelerated maternal response to pups by nonpregnant females (Fleming, Vaccarino, Tambosso, and Chee, 1979). Fleischer, Kordower, Kaplan, Dicker, Smerling, and Ilgner (1981) also reported significant cannibalism (38 percent of group) by nonpregnant females following olfactory bulbectomy as well as the accelerated onset of retrieving, although not all aspects of maternal behavior were accelerated.

Until recently, direct evidence of the aversive nature of pup odors was not available. Kinsley and Bridges (1989), as noted above, have shown that, unlike postpartum females that approach and remain in the vicinity of bedding containing pup odors, ovariectomized, nonpregnant females do not approach pup odors. It may be a semantic problem as to whether they exhibit an aversion to these odors or fail to exhibit a preference for them over clean shavings, as the authors propose. We have seen that even when an aversion for pup odors is clearly evident in the later behavior of nonpregnant females during their first test, they initially explore them and return repeatedly before remaining away (Fleming and Luebke, 1981).

The strength of the aversion to pup odors and its role in the delayed onset of maternal behavior during sensitization in nonpregnant females was demonstrated in a study by Mayer and Rosenblatt (1975). Nonpregnant females were treated with an intranasal injection of zinc sulfate which made them anosmic for several days. They initiated short-latency maternal behavior then were permitted $1^1/2$ days of additional contact with the pups. Pups were then removed and over the next 17 days, while they were without pups, the females regained the olfactory function they had lost as a result of the zinc sulfate treatment. They were then exposed once again to pups for sensitization. In a previous study Fleming and Rosenblatt (1974a) had found, upon reinduction, that nearly all nonpregnant females not previously treated with zinc sulfate showed reduced latencies for retrieving and adopting a nursing posture. In the present study latencies to retrieve pups remained low during reinduction but latencies to retrieve and attend them in the nest (i.e., adopt a nursing posture and lick them) increased from a mean of 1.1 days during the original sensitization while the females were anosmic to a mean of 2.6 days during their resensitization. Because they had not overcome their aversion to pup odors, the zinc sulfate-treated females, once they regained smell, were delayed in resuming maternal behaviors which they had been performing $2^1/2$ weeks earlier and the maternal behaviors most affected were those requiring close contact and exposure to pup odors in the nest.

The implication of these studies is that during sensitization the nonpregnant female must overcome her aversion to pup odors in order to respond to those pup stimuli which are not aversive. These stimuli evoke the specialized approach responses associated with maternal behavior. The earliest evidence of this development during sensitization is seen in the initiation of anogenital licking of pups beginning well before other components of maternal behavior appear (Fleming and Rosenblatt,

1974a). Stern (1983) reported similar findings: she compared the effects on later sensitization of prior continuous exposure to the odors, vocalizations, and appearance of pups placed beneath the cage floor in a wire mesh basket as against actual contact with them for 15 minutes per day during which, among other behavior patterns, females could perform anogenital licking. Among the females that had experienced brief contacts with pups, only those that had licked pups exhibited accelerated sensitization latencies: latencies of all other groups were an average of three times longer. Jakubowski and Terkel (1985b) confirmed these findings in a more aggressive strain of rats. Nonpregnant females were permitted presensitization contact with pups contained within a wire mesh container that allowed them to smell the pups but not lick them. These females were not less aggressive and cannibalistic during sensitization and they did not show maternal behavior any more rapidly than females without such pre-exposure (Jakubowski and Terkel, 1985b). All attempts to facilitate sensitization by exposing females to pup stimuli but not to pups themselves have failed to have an appreciable effect on sensitization latencies. Jakubowski and Terkel (1986) found in their unresponsive strain that distance stimuli were not effective in sensitizing females and that proximal stimuli need not include suckling but only ventral stimulation to elicit maternal behavior. Stern (1983) has suggested, as we have (Fleming and Rosenblatt, 1974a), that the crucial behavior for initiating the full maternal complex may be anogenital licking of the pups.

These findings suggest that once females adapt to the olfactory stimulus and they begin to lick the pup's anogenital region, additional stimuli, very likely taste and tactile stimuli, begin to play a role in stimulating maternal behavior. Support for the role of taste comes from studies by Charton, Adrien, and Cosnier (1971) and Kristal, Whitney, and Peters (1981). In the former study, covering the pups' perineal region with collodion significantly reduced the female's perineal licking to less than one third that of pups with perineal secretions still available to the female. It is likely that taste rather than olfaction or any other signals was involved since nonpregnant females drank significantly more water containing perineal secretions, obtained by wiping the perineal region of the newborn, than pure water. In the latter study, applying amniotic fluid to pups' bodies accelerated the onset of maternal behavior in nonpregnant females.

There may be a tongue tactile component to licking in addition to its taste component since anesthetizing the tongue in strongly motivated postparturient females, thereby reducing feedback tactile stimulation as well as taste, significantly reduces the duration of pup licking (Stern and Johnson, 1989).

The importance of tactile stimulation of the perioral region for the elicitation of maternal responses in postparturient females—stimulation that would also be received during licking of pups—has only recently been studied extensively (Stern, 1989; Stern and Johnson, 1989, 1990; Stern and Kolunie, 1991). Presumably, nonpregnant females would receive this stimulation during sensitization when they began anogenital licking of pups; Rosenblatt (1975) has shown that, presented with a single pup, nonpregnant females not exhibiting maternal behavior will nevertheless approach it, sniff it, and lick it several times before turning away from it. In a more strongly motivated lactating female depriving her of perioral stimulation may disrupt her readiness to adopt a nursing posture and to retrieve pups (Stern and Johnson, 1989).

2. Motivational/Emotional Processes

The "timidity" of nonpregnant females in response to newborn pups, described by Fleming and Luebke (1981), consisted of leaving the area in which pups had been placed and remaining at a distance until the females had been sensitized. When sensitized they no longer avoided the pups and in fact exhibited maternal behavior towards them. Their initial timidity extended beyond their response to pups: they were also fearful when placed in a novel area. They required three times longer than parturient females to enter the novel area, and were highly restricted in their movements in it. Moreover they reared much less frequently, a sign of reduced exploratory behavior. Their social responses to a female intruder also reflected timidity: they tended to run away from the intruder and, when chased by the intruder, tried to escape by climbing the cage wall. Since sensitized females were not compared to nonsensitized females in open-field and intruder tests we do not know to what extent these aspects of timidity had been reduced as a result of sensitization.

There are marked strain differences with respect to the timidity of nonpregnant females towards pups. In several strains of rats, females attack and kill pups upon first encountering them and they may continue to kill them until they initiate maternal behavior (Cosnier, 1963; Jakubowski and Terkel, 1985a, 1985b). Pup attack and killing may be an extreme form of the fear which underlies the timidity observed in less aggressive strains since not all attacking and killing is an expression of predatory behavior. Adams (1983) has suggested, among rodents that even in the aggression shown by lactating females there ". . . appears to be the simultaneous activation of both offense and defense" (p. 224).

Hansen and his colleagues have utilized the freezing response of females to auditory stimulation (i.e., doorbell sound at 95 dB) as a measure of fear (Härd and Hansen, 1985). In response to the bell, estrous cycling females remained immobilized about seven times longer than lactating females with pups.

While sensitization reduces some of the fearfulness of nonpregnant females, it does not eliminate it and sensitized females, although they display maternal behavior, remain more fearful than their lactating counterparts. One measure of their fearfulness is their unwillingness to retrieve pups placed in an unfamiliar runway extending from their cages (Bridges, Zarrow, Gandelman, and Denenberg, 1972; Quadagno, Debold, Gorzalka, and Whalen, 1974). The task requires that they emerge from their cages into the apparatus, then walk to its end to retrieve pups placed there. They all retrieve pups inside the home cage but only in 20 percent of the tests do sensitized females retrieve pups from the runway as compared to 100 percent retrieval by lactating females.

Lactating females are faced, on occasion, with the conflict between remaining with their litters to protect them from intruders and fleeing the threatening intruder. This is, in essence, an approach/withdrawal conflict; it is almost always resolved by the female attacking the intruder, driving it away or immobilizing it (Erskine, Barfield, and Goldman, 1978). Ferreira, Hansen,

Nielsen, Archer, and Minor (1989) compared the ability of non-pregnant and lactating females with pups to handle approach/withdrawal conflicts of two kinds: the first involved the conflict between approaching a water spout to drink, when water deprived, in the face of electric shock punishment for drinking, and the second, feeding in an unfamiliar area by food-deprived females, something rarely done by rats because of the anxiety provoked by the novel area. Even when matched for thirst motivation and responsiveness to electric shock, nonpregnant females made more than 90 percent fewer licks at the water spout, and in the novel area ate about half the amount of food they otherwise consumed. Lactating mothers with pups licked more than ten times more frequently than nonpregnant females and ate nearly twice as much food.

3. Motor Processes

The appearance of specialized maternal approach responses in sensitized and postpartum females, and aggressive nest defense responses in the postparturient female, are consequences of perceptual and motivational/emotional changes associated with maternal responsiveness. How these responses arise has been studied with respect to only a few maternal responses.

Nonsensitized females approach, sniff, lick and only occasionally pick up newborn pups placed in their cages (Jakubowski and Terkel, 1984; Rosenblatt, 1975). They distinguish between pups and other objects (e.g., a small plastic toy, rubber dropper-bulbs) and respond differently to these objects, mouthing them and carrying them to various places outside the nest (Gray and Chesley, 1984) . When they become sensitized or give birth, the transition from licking to picking up occurs more frequently; licking, in fact, may drop out of the sequence, and sniffing lead directly to picking up (Gray and Chesley, 1984; Rosenblatt, 1975). This change may be facilitated by changes in the sensitivity of the snout-vibrissae region (Kenyon, Cronin, and Keeble, 1981, 1983; Stern and Johnson, 1989; Stern and Kolunie, 1989). Both retrieving and adopting the hunched nursing posture over the pups appear to be sequences initiated by perioral stimulation.

IV. Ontogenetic Origins of Maternal Approach/Withdrawal Responses

Additional information about the approach-withdrawal organization of maternal behavior has been obtained by studying the ontogeny of maternal behavior. Using the sensitization procedure, juvenile young are exposed to pups, observations are made of their behavior towards them and of their ability to exhibit maternal behavior (Bridges, Zarrow, Goldman, and Denenberg, 1974; Mayer, 1983). These studies have revealed an initial period during which juveniles exhibit predominantly approach responses to young pups, which include aspects of maternal behavior seen in the adult animal. This period comes to an end abruptly when withdrawal responses arise and juveniles reduce their approach responses and begin to avoid pups. After pubertal onset, a balance between approach and withdrawal responses to pups is established. The pubertal hormones (estrogen and progesterone) continue to play a role in tonically maintaining this balance in adulthood.

Differences between females and males in responsiveness to newborn pups are absent or minimal throughout the juvenile period and arise only after puberty (Bridges et al., 1974; Mayer and Rosenblatt, 1979b). In one study, differences were found at 24 days (males were more responsive than females) (Gray and Chesley, 1984). Postpubertally, males are less responsive to newborn pups than females and have longer latencies for sensitization. Underlying this change are several factors including hormonal influences during pre- and early postpartum, and experience.

A. Prepubertal Origins of Approach/Withdrawal Organization of Maternal Behavior

The components of maternal behavior, as seen in the adult female, are not organized into a coherent pattern in the prepubertal female and male (Bridges, et al., 1974; Brunelli, Shindledecker, and Hofer, 1985; Mayer and Rosenblatt, 1979b).

Brunelli et al. (1985) have suggested that not until after puberty do the various components of maternal behavior, i.e., retrieving, nursing posture, anogenital licking, and nestbuilding (excluding maternal aggression), appear simultaneously and consistently in individual females (Fleming and Rosenblatt, 1974; Slotnick, 1967). Nevertheless, prepubertal females and males respond to pups by approaching them and exhibiting the most advanced forms of maternal behavior, often picking them up and retrieving them to one region of their home cage and by exhibiting nestbuilding (Mayer and Rosenblatt, 1979a); less often do they exhibit anogenital licking (Brunelli et al, 1985), and crouching or draping themselves over the young (Gray and Chesley, 1984).

Over the period from 18 to 22 days, Mayer and Rosenblatt (1979a) observed a high frequency of contacts with pups during initial exposure by both males and females and an increase over these five days. These contacts consisted of behavior sequences in which the pups performed sniffing, nosing, and licking the pups, manipulating them while licking them, grooming them, and also lying in contact with them. With the rise in aversive responses to pups around day 24, juvenile contacts with pups declined abruptly and remained low through day 30. The 24- to 30-day-old juveniles tended to investigate the pups during the first few minutes of the tests, then they withdrew: few of them licked the pups, while none lay in contact with them.

The decline in approach responses to pups could be forestalled for nearly a week by initially exposing females to pups before day 24. Juveniles that exhibited approach responses when first exposed on days 18 to 22 continued to do so after day 24 at levels approximating their previous levels. By 30 days, however, they too had declined in their approach responses to pups (Mayer and Rosenblatt, 1979a).

The stimulus properties of the pups which attract the approach responses of the younger juveniles (20–21 days of age) were also studied by Mayer and Rosenblatt (1979a). The "live" properties of the pups were approached more frequently than their thermal or contact properties and eight-day-old pups were somewhat more attractive than two-day-old pups which, in turn, were more attractive than an empty warm bowl or similar-sized mouse pups. The older juveniles (24–25 days of age) also preferred live pups to otherwise attractive thermal and contact stimuli and, interestingly, they preferred the younger two-day-old pups to the older eight-day-olds. Adult females also show the shortest sensitization latencies when exposed to one- to two-day-old pups (Stern and Mackinnon, 1978).

The younger juveniles, who were less fearful than the older ones, preferred the livelier stimulation provided by 8-day-old pups over the younger ones, but older juveniles preferred the less active and, therefore, less frightening younger pups. They preferred to associate with their age mates even more when given the opportunity to do so (Mayer and Rosenblatt, 1979a).

Sensitization of 22-day-old juveniles was attempted by Mayer and Rosenblatt (1979a) with results that do not differ substantially from those of Bridges et al. (1974), Brunelli, et al. (1985), and Gray and Chesley (1984). Nearly all juveniles retrieved pups at least once and several retrieved them regularly with latencies to initiate retrieving that ranged from one to three days. Nestbuilding was performed by nearly all juveniles after exposure to young, but well-defined patterns of nursing or anogenital licking were not observed although, as indicated, licking and lying in contact with pups was very frequent.

Using a different strain of rats, Brunelli et al. (1985) found few juveniles of 18 days capable of retrieving pups but by 24 days nearly 80 percent retrieved; by 30 days, after withdrawal responses to pups had emerged, only 24 percent performed this behavior. This study examined play behavior towards the pups, since play behavior consists of rapid changes in approach/withdrawal responses and is very likely, therefore, to share underlying mechanisms with components of maternal behavior. The authors summarize their findings in the following terms: "...
[T]hese data indicate that an association exists between retrieving behaviors and play behaviors regardless of age and show the emergence of an association between crouching and licking in the older juveniles. However, the data point overall to a fragmentation of maternal behaviors during the juvenile period" (p. 320).

The rather abrupt change in the responses of older juveniles to pups from predominantly approach to predominantly withdrawal is an expression of a broad change in their behavior, which is also seen in their responses in an open field and in the presence of novel objects. Mayer and Rosenblatt (1979a) characterized this change in the following way:

> [O]lder juveniles avoid pups rather than simply lose interest in them. This change in response to pups is associated with a dramatic increase, during the weaning-postweaning period, in reactivity to a range of extero-ceptive stimuli which provoke defensive reactions in adults, but to which younger juveniles show relatively little response. For example, older juveniles and adults ambulate significantly less in an open field, when exposed to high intensities of light and noise, than younger juveniles which move about as freely as when light and noise are low (Livesey and Egger, 1970). Defecation in a novel area, reflecting fear or emotionality, increases greatly between 23 and 30 days of age (Candland and Campbell, 1962). Older juveniles (and adults) show more prolonged as well as greater immediate responses to specific aversive stimuli than do younger juveniles when each is confined in a cage in which it has experienced brief foot shock or was exposed to a predator. Older animals (40 to 50 days of age) freeze more and ambulate less than 20-day-olds and when exposed to a suddenly moving object, the older animals (30 to 40 days of age) startle more frequently than 20-day-olds (Bronstein and Hirsch, 1976) . . . These varied findings suggest that between 20 and 30 days of age a rapid maturation of defensive reactivity to external threats occurs (Bronstein and Hirsch, 1976), and that the appearance of aversive reactions to pups is a manifestation of this broader change. (p. 420–421)

B. Postpubertal Development of Approach/Withdrawal Responses in Relation to Maternal Behavior

With the advent of puberty, hormonal influences begin to play a role in the maternal responsiveness of females and males as measured by sensitization latencies. These hormonal effects have been labelled *tonic* influences as contrasted with the *phasic* influence of hormones which trigger the onset of maternal behavior in late-pregnant females. A characteristic level of maternal responsiveness is maintained by hormones which, by themselves, are unable to stimulate the performance of maternal behavior. Built upon this basic level of responsiveness is the non-hormonal stimulation of maternal behavior during sensitization. In this section we will not be concerned with how hormones produce their effects on maternal behavior—this will be discussed in the next section. We shall be concerned with how maternal responsiveness, as measured by sensitization latencies, changes as a result of puberty and other factors which affect the balance of approach and withdrawal processes during the postpubertal period.

Gender differences in maternal responsiveness are not of primary concern in this article. To the extent that they reveal underlying processes governing maternal responsiveness, they are of interest. Therefore, we shall discuss these gender differences where appropriate.

The relatively short sensitization latencies of the younger prepubertal animals, similar in both males and females (except Kinsley and Bridges, 1978a and Stern, 1987—studies in which males had shorter latencies than females), increase sharply in prepubertal, 30-day-old animals (Bridges, et al., 1974; Brunelli, et al., 1985; Mayer, Freeman, and Rosenblatt, 1979b; Stern, 1987). Female and male latencies before puberty do not differ, nor do the sexes differ in the percentage of animals that became sensitized (Bridges, et al., 1974; Mayer and Rosenblatt, 1979b). After puberty at 45 days, latencies are reduced in females, compared to 30-day latencies, but are increased in males (Mayer and Rosenblatt, 1979b; Moretta, Paclik, and Fleming, 1986; Stern and Rogers, 1988). Strains differ in this respect and postpubertal males and females may have similar sensitization latencies in other strains (Bridges, et al., 1974). After 45 days female sensitization latencies remain low into adulthood while male latencies remain high and increase at least through 90 days of age (Mayer and Rosenblatt, 1979b).

Sensitization latencies increase when aversive responses delay female or male approaches to pups and prevent approach-eliciting stimuli from exerting their effects on them. The behavior of late prepubertal animals suggests that their fear and timidity contribute to this delay. A second factor could be their aversion to pup odors.

Systematic handling, particularly during prepuberty, appears to reduce timidity; handled animals are more active and defecate less in a novel area (Thompson and Lippman, 1972; Wild and Hughes, 1972). The timidity of females and males was reduced by removing them from their home cages, stroking them gently on the back, then returning them to their home cages. This was done daily from day 21 until they were presented with pups for sensitization at four different ages, 30, 45, 60, and 90 days. This brief handling reduced 30-day latencies of females by two-thirds and of males by one-third (Mayer and Rosenblatt, 1979b; Thompson and Lippman, 1972; Wild and Hughes, 1972). With additional handling for five minutes daily, 30-day male latencies were further reduced to half that of unhandled males.

Handling was ineffective in reducing female latencies at the later ages, which indicates that timidity becomes a less important factor impeding female sensitization. In males, however, handling continued to be effective in reducing latencies at 45 and 60 days; handled males were not tested at 90 days. Male latencies were affected by their timidity well into adulthood.

Olfactory aversion to pup odors played little role in the long sensitization latencies of 30-day-old females but making females anosmic with intranasally infused zinc sulfate on day 45 reduced latencies by half and the effect was even greater on day 60 when latencies were reduced from four days to one day or less (Mayer and Rosenblatt, 1979b). In males, anosmia significantly reduced sensitization latencies at 45 days and 60 days.

Social factors may also affect females' timidity and fear and thereby affect the development of maternal responsiveness. Moretta, Paclik, and Fleming (1986) restricted sibling exposure from day 10 to 20 postpartum thereby increasing 20-day-old female latencies to lie over pups and to nestbuild and this was correlated with longer latencies to emerge into a novel area, evidence of increased timidity. Exposure to colony odors and sounds from nearby mothers rearing their young reduced the timidity of the 20-day-olds but this had no effect on maternal behavior.

In adulthood these social factors had effects on both maternal behavior and fear and timidity (Moretto et al., 1986). Early rearing with a full complement of siblings and exposure to colony odors and sounds also reduced the latencies for nearly all aspects of maternal behavior in 75-day-old females but had little effect on their performance in a novel area.

Brunelli, Shindledecker, and Hofer (1989) examined the effects of early weaning and social isolation on sensitization latencies prepubertally and again postpubertally in adulthood. Both early weaning and social isolation reduced the number of males and females retrieving; group rearing ameliorated this effect somewhat. Prepubertal sensitization affected their adult behavior: as a consequence of this experience adult females were more responsive to pups than males and also more responsive than nonsensitized females in all aspects of maternal behavior. In addition, early weaned, isolate-reared animals persisted in play behavior (which consists of rapidly alternating approach and withdrawal behavior and the associated underlying emotional responses) toward pups during sensitization well into adulthood; it had previously been found that this pattern of approach/withdrawal social behavior alternated with maternal responses towards pups in prepubertal animals (Brunelli, Shindledecker, and Hofer, 1985).

Experience also plays a role in sensitization latencies during adulthood. Exposing 22- to 32-day-old juveniles to pups and sensitizing them facilitated resensitization at 78 days of age (Gray and Chesley, 1984). Stern and Rogers (1988) also provided juveniles with experience with their younger siblings, born of postpartum mating before the juveniles had been weaned. During their contacts with their younger siblings, the juveniles performed components of maternal behavior such as crouching over them, retrieving, and licking them. When they were subsequently sensitized at 42 days they exhibited shorter latencies for the performance of these behavior patterns than pups that had not had the juvenile experience.

Experience may fixate withdrawal responses to pups, as expressed in attacks on pups and cannibalism (see above), as well as approach responses. In a study by Fleming and Rosenblatt (1974b) the usual maternal approach responses to pups at parturition were replaced by cannibalism. This was the result of an earlier bilateral bulbectomy while females were non-pregnant which had stimulated cannibalism in several females instead of the more common rapid onset of maternal behavior. When these females were mated and gave birth they cannibalized their litters while other bulbectomized females displayed normal maternal behavior. The hormonal stimulation which normally stimulates maternal behavior in parturient females was unable to override the effects of the earlier performance of cannibalism.

Similarly Rosenberg and Sherman (1975a) showed that prior pup-killing experience or lack of it in males determined how they would respond to androgen stimulation which usually stimulates males to engage in infanticide behavior. Males were castrated at 30 days of age and half were given androgen over the next two months which stimulated pup killing while half were treated with oil and therefore did not exhibit pup killing. Hormone treatments were reversed and at 120 days of age, those that had killed pups continued to kill even though they were without androgen. The males that had previously not killed pups, even though they now received androgen, still did not kill pups. In one group pup killing had been fixated as the response to pups and in the other, nonkilling behavior had been fixated. In a second study, similar to the first, males that exhibited pup-killing before castration at 90 days of age remained pup killers at 122 days of age even without androgen treatment; those that had not killed pups earlier continued to be inhibited even when given androgen to stimulate pup killing.

The predominance of either approach or aggressive responses to pups can be established in early development to emerge in adulthood as an important influence on sensitization latencies and responses to newborn at parturition.

V. Hormonal Action on the Neuroendocrine Substrate of Maternal Behavior

Hormones act upon the neuroendocrine substrate of maternal behavior during three distinct but closely related periods of development. 1) During the late prenatal and early postnatal period, gender differences in maternal responsiveness are established that first appear at puberty and persist into adulthood; these are revealed during sensitization. 2) From puberty onward hormones maintain different tonic levels of maternal responsiveness in females and males. 3) During pregnancy the hormones of pregnancy and parturition trigger the rapid onset of a high level of maternal responsiveness in females.

A. Pre- and Early Postnatal Hormonal Influences on Basal Levels of Maternal Responsiveness of Females and Males

In the differentiation of *sexual behavior* in rats and other mammals, two very different mating patterns are involved: the male mounting and intromission pattern and the female immobility and lordosis pattern. Prenatal and early postnatal hormones act in males to influence the relative strength of these patterns. The male pattern becomes predominant and the female pattern is either eliminated or its elicitation in adulthood is made more difficult. In the female, development of the female pattern does not depend upon the action of hormones; it differentiates on the basis of genotype. The female mating pattern predominates, but the male pattern can come to dominate by introducing the appropriate hormone.

The gender differentiation of *maternal responsiveness* among rats is quite different from that of sexual behavior in several respects: first, only a single pattern of behavior, having several components, occurs in both males and females. Males differ from females in their postpubertal latencies for sensitization and in several more subtle features of the organization of approach/withdrawal responses (Mayer, Freeman, and Rosenblatt, 1979b). They also differ in being less responsive to the combination of hormones that stimulates maternal behavior in females (Bridges, Zarrow, and Denenberg, 1973).

The pre- and postnatal effects of hormones on maternal responsiveness in males and females are mainly determined by the ease or difficulty of sensitizing males and females in adulthood. A second method has been to compare their responsiveness to a combination of hormones known to stimulate short-latency maternal behavior in adults. Both methods present the difficulty that sensitization latencies in adulthood do not reflect the influence of perinatal hormones alone. The hormones present at the time of testing also influence sensitization latencies and may also influence the response to the combination of hormones that stimulate maternal behavior. It is therefore necessary either to eliminate these hormones, in the former instance, and their previous influence in the latter case, or to determine their influence on sensitization latencies in both sexes.

Until recently it was believed that prepubertal maternal behavior in males and females was not under hormonal control despite the fact that both sexes have low circulating levels of progesterone and high levels of estradiol as well as FSH, LH, and prolactin during prepuberty (Dohler and Wuttke, 1975). Moreover, Koranyi, Lissak, Tamasy, and Kamaras (1976) and Brunelli, Shindledecker, and Hofer (1987) showed facilitatory effects on maternal behavior of injected blood plasma from parturient females indicating that prepubertal females, at least, are capable of responding to hormones with an acceleration or prolongation of maternal behavior. Kinsley and Bridges (1988) have shown that male sensitization latencies are reduced by prolactin and increased when its release is blocked. Female sensitization latencies, however, do not appear to be responsive to the presence of prolactin.

Ovarian secretions are necessary to maintain the relatively short sensitization latencies in females undergoing puberty between 30 and 45 days of age (Mayer and Rosenblatt, 1979c). After puberty, ovarian hormones are also required to maintain adult latencies. Ovariectomy of 21- or 32-day-old females, to prevent the hormonal changes of puberty, results in nearly doubling their latencies at $1^1/2$, 2 and 3 months of age compared to sham-ovariectomized females (7.5 to 4.0 days) but still well below latencies of intact males (10 and >14 days). Nestbuilding also was of poorer quality in ovariectomized females, a behavioral characteristic usually associated with males (Rosenblatt, 1967). In a different strain Stern (1986) also found an increase in sensitization latencies from pre- to mid- and postpuberty but was unable to find any effect of gonadectomy or hypophysectomy on these latencies.

The ovarian hormone estrogen, rather than progesterone, maintains the short sensitization latencies of females during puberty and postpuberty. In the 32-day ovariectomized females described above, a single injection of estradiol benzoate given 24 hours before the beginning of sensitization restored the original latency of four days. As noted, at 45, 60 and 90 days, ovariectomy also increased latencies significantly in tests conducted three to four months later. Again, estradiol restored the original shorter latencies in all age groups (Mayer and Rosenblatt, 1979c).

Among males, prepubertal castration on day 25 or 30 and postpubertal castration on day 70 do not affect sensitization latencies which are longer than those of females (Quadagno, Debold, Gorzalka, and Whalen, 1974; Quadagno and Rockwell, 1972; Rosenberg and Herrenkohl, 1976). No studies have administered estrogen to late-prepubertal or postpubertal castrates to see whether sensitization latencies can be reduced.

The conclusion to be drawn from these studies on pubertal hormonal influences on maternal responsiveness, thus far, is that a residual gender difference in sensitization latencies exists after females have been ovariectomized from prepuberty onward and males have been castrated either pre- or postpubertally. It is likely that this difference in maternal responsiveness is based upon earlier hormonal influences during prenatal and early postnatal life.

Turning to the studies of prenatal and early postnatal hormonal effects on maternal responsiveness, we find that investigators have attempted to modify female responsiveness by administering androgen to fetuses and neonates and male responsiveness by castrating males early postnatally.

Quadagno and his colleagues (Quadagno, DeBold, Gorzalka, and Whalen, 1974; Quadagno, McCullough, Ho, and Spevak, 1973; Quadagno and Rockwell, 1972) were unable to find any effect of androgen administered early postnatally (i.e., days one through 12) on sensitization latencies or proportion of females that are sensitized in adulthood despite an earlier report from that laboratory of such an effect. Ichikawa and Fujii (1982) found it was necessary to administer androgen directly to fetuses one to three days before birth in order to significantly suppress all components of maternal behavior in females in adulthood. Retrieving was somewhat reduced by androgen injections given on the day of birth and day one postnatally. One problem in interpreting these findings is that the prenatal androgen also affected puberty in these females. The prenatally- and early postnatally-treated females were severely disturbed in undergoing puberty and in their estrous cycling, raising the possibility that some of the difficulties in performing maternal behavior in adulthood could be attributed to the hormonal deficiencies associated with these conditions at puberty. Bridges, Zarrow and Denenberg (1973) could find only a minor effect of androgen treatment four to six hours after birth in females that were later administered a hormone treatment to stimulate short latency maternal behavior. These females were more hesitant to retrieve pups from the maze extending from their cages than neonatally-untreated females.

McCullough, Quadagno, and Goldman (1974) and Quadagno and Rockwell (1972) eliminated the influence of androgens in neonatal males by castrating them or inhibiting the action of the gonadotrophins on the testes and found an increase in the percentage of males sensitized at 70 days above that of intact males and nearly equal to that of intact females. Latencies were also comparable to those of the females. Rosenberg and Herrenkohl (1976) explored the range of the critical period for influencing male maternal responsiveness by castrating males at 1, 5, 10, and 25 days prepubertally and testing them at 70 days following treatment with androgen. They found that day one castration was most effective in increasing maternal responsiveness in adulthood but effects were still evident in five and ten-day neonatal castrates. Androgen treatment in adulthood of these castrates did not have any effect on their sensitization latencies or the percentage exhibiting maternal behavior.

Androgen exposure during the late prenatal and early postnatal period is capable of suppressing maternal responsiveness in females tested in adulthood. However, Leboucher (1989) found that androgen reduction of maternal behavior in females treated early postnatally was significant only at 50 days of age and then it gradually disappeared over the next 30 days. Male maternal responsiveness was also suppressed by androgen treatment in the neonatal period, extending to the tenth day.

Males and females of certain rat strains differ in their tendency for attack and infanticidal behavior in adulthood. Males are nearly all infanticidal while few females kill pups and eat them. Rosenberg and his colleagues have studied the influence of androgen on infanticide in males and females during neonatal, prepubertal and postpubertal periods of development. Infanticide is an extreme behavior pattern falling within the withdrawal system: during withdrawal the animal removes itself from the source of stimulation or removes the stimulus from its behavioral environment. Neonatal castration up to 30 days of age reduces male infanticide behavior to the low levels seen in adult females and treatment with androgen in adulthood does not reverse this effect indicating that the neonatal treatment plays a role in the organization of this behavior pattern (Rosenberg, 1974; Rosenberg, Denenberg, Zarrow, and Frank, 1971; Rosenberg and Sherman, 1975). On the other hand, androgen replacement before 30 days restores high levels of infanticide in adulthood. Castration in adulthood also produces a low level of male infanticide behavior which is reversed by androgen, suggesting an adult activational effect of androgen in addition to its early organizational effect. Androgen also increases infanticidal behavior in females when given during the neonatal period in combination with treatment in adulthood or when given in adulthood only, following ovariectomy (Rosenberg, Denenberg, Zarrow, and Frank, 1971; Rosenberg and Sherman, 1974). Infanticide behavior appears to be dependent upon androgen in both sexes, therefore.

Pup killing is correlated with fearfulness and timidity as measured by reduced locomotion and increased defecation in a novel area (Rosenberg et al., 1971). Neonatal castration which reduces infanticidal behavior in males also makes them less timid as measured by an increase in locomotion in a novel area but not, however, by a decrease in defecation. Conversely, androgen given to neonatal females makes them more timid in adulthood (i.e., increase in locomotion and defecation in a novel area; Rosenberg et al., 1971). Handling from birth onward which reduces timidity also reduces pup killing significantly in 30-day castrated males tested in adulthood (Rosenberg and Sherman, 1975).

B. Hormonal and Other Reproductive Influences on Approach/Withdrawal Processes during Pregnancy and Parturition

During pregnancy sensitization latencies are gradually shortened below the basal latencies of postpubertal nonpregnant females (Rosenblatt and Siegel, 1975). As parturition approaches latencies become even shorter and by 24 hours prepartum females often respond immediately to newborn pups and at $3^{1/2}$ hours prepartum they respond to slightly older pups. They exhibit nestbuilding, retrieving, nursing and anogenital licking and when tested with conspecific intruders they exhibit aggression towards the intruder (Mayer and Rosenblatt, 1984). These behavioral changes are caused by the action of hormones and by stimulation arising during other aspects of reproduction. In this section we shall review how approach/withdrawal responses undergo changes during this period resulting in the onset of maternal behavior at parturition.

The pregnant female undergoes perceptual changes as pregnancy approaches. The growing importance of perioral stimulation of approach responses to neonates is already evident at parturition and preventing females from snout contact with pups interferes with parturitive behavior as well as early retrieving and nursing (Stern and Johnson, 1990; Stern and Kolunie, 1991). Estrogen-induced changes in the perioral somatic receptive field may underlie the increase in sensitivity of this region and its involvement in maternal behavior (Bereiter and Barker, 1975). Ventral sensitivity to tactile stimulation is basic for the establishment of maternal care: exposing females to pups enclosed in wire mesh baskets is not as effective as presenting pups to females directly, even when the females are thelectomized (Jakubowski and Terkel, 1986). This is supported by the finding that late-pregnant Caesarean-sectioned females deprived of exteroceptive sensory systems, singly and in combinations, nevertheless showed an essentially normal onset of maternal behavior in response to tactile stimulation and the performance of licking behavior (Herrenkohl and Rosenberg, 1972). Preliminary study of somatosensory cortex representation reported by Stern (1991) indicates that during lactation there is nearly a twofold increase in its representation and a more detailed representation of the ventrum by cortical somatosensory receptive fields that are often centered around nipples.

Late pregnant females develop a special sensitivity to pup vocalizations and approach them in preference to other sounds when pups are placed at a distance on a runway (Koranyi, Lissak, Tamasy, and Kamaras, 1976).

Aversive or indifferent responses to pup odors by nonpregnant females undergo a dramatic change shortly before parturition. The 22-day pregnant female begins to prefer the odors of pups and, presented with a choice of bedding from a lactating female and her litter or nonlactating female, she prefers the odor of the lactating females (Bauer, 1983). Kinsley and Bridges (1989) have proposed that the rise in endogenous opioids at the end of pregnancy produces this change in olfactory responses. More than olfactory preference may be involved, however, since Mayer, Faris, Komisaruk, and Rosenblatt (1985) found that parturient females administered the opiate blocker naltrexone or made morphine-tolerant did not clean the fetuses nor eat the placentas.

Pregnancy hormones impose upon females excessive heat production which could jeopardize the survival of the fetuses and maintenance of pregnancy (Wilson and Stricker, 1979). Females are particularly sensitive to the thermal environment and seek cool environments. They reduce their activity and this persists after parturition, based upon the action of adrenal cortical hormone and prolactin, and determines their approaches to their young for nursing and the termination of nursing bouts

(Leon, Croskerry, and Smith, 1978; Woodside and Jans, 1988; Woodside, Leon, Attard, Feder, Siegel, and Fischette, 1981).

The short sensitization latencies of nonpregnant females, made anosmic by zinc sulfate nasal infusion, have led to the conclusion that pup stimuli are capable of stimulating maternal behavior rapidly but for the female's neophobic timidity and her aversion to pup odors. Normally, at the initiation of the sensitization process and during the early phase of exposure to pups, the female is involved in a conflict between approach and withdrawal processes aroused by pups (Figures 2 and 3). Unless the female is made anosmic the withdrawal responses predominate. Fleming, Vaccarino, and Luebke (1980) have expressed this in the following terms: "[T]he concaveation (i.e., sensitization-authors) process actually involves two distinct phases: the first phase involves the animal becoming habituated to the aversive properties of pups; the second phase is manifest when the female is no longer avoiding pups and involves the development of 'motivation' to respond maternally" (p. 738). Since parturient females immediately respond to their pups by exhibiting maternal behavior, the hormones which stimulate maternal behavior must also reduce their fearfulness and alter their aversion to pup odors (Fleming and Cheung, 1989; Hansen and Ferreira, 1986; Kinsley and Bridges, 1979). The fearfulness or timidity of virgin females towards young pups has been described by many investigators (Fleming, Cheung, Myhal, and Kessler, 1989; Fleming and Luebke, 1981; Hansen, Ferreira, and Selart, 1985; Terkel and Rosenblatt, 1971) and contrasted with the absence of fear and, indeed, the attraction to pups shown by immediately postparturient mothers (Hard and Hansen, 1985). This fearfulness is evidenced also in the virgin's hesitancy to enter a runway to retrieve pups located in one arm at the far end of a T-maze projecting from the home cage. Lactating females have much less hesitancy in performing this task. Sensitized virgin females, exhibiting maternal behavior but not previously stimulated by hormones, also hesitate to enter the runway indicating that, in this respect, they resemble nonmaternal virgins more than hormonally-stimulated lactating mothers (Bridges et al., 1972). When they are tested in the dark, however, they retrieve pups from the runway much more readily, probably because they are less fearful (Mayer and Rosenblatt, 1979c).

Behavioral tests, not directly involving responses to pups, have revealed the virgin's fearfulness and, by contrast, the change in emotional responsiveness which the lactating mother has undergone. Lactating mothers are more likely than virgins to emerge from a starting box with home cage shavings into a novel area, and once they enter it, to locomote more and more frequently in the central area rather than along the walls. While in the novel area, lactating mothers "freeze" much less in response to a loud noise and/or bright light than virgins and they are more likely to eat while in the novel area than virgins who are too fearful to engage in eating. Also, mothers are better able to tolerate the conflict, when thirsty, between drinking from a nozzle from which they receive an electric shock than are virgins who avoid the nozzle (Ferreira, Hansen, Nielsen, Archer, and Minor, 1989; Fleming and Cheung, 1989; Hansen and Ferreira, 1986; Hansen, Ferreira, and Selart, 1985; Härd and Hansen, 1985).

Treatment with estradiol and progesterone, which induces maternal behavior in ovariectomized nulliparous females, also reduces their fearfulness when they are exposed to a loud sound in a novel area (Hansen and Ferreira, 1986). It also speeds their emergence into the novel area, enables them to cross more inside squares, and reduces their tendency to run away from an intruder (Fleming, Cheung, Myhal, and Kessler, 1989). Estradiol alone increased retrieving pups at the end of the T-maze (a task which requires that the female overcome her fear of leaving the cage to enter a runway) by ovariectomized females that were also stimulated to exhibit maternal behavior (Mayer and Rosenblatt, 1979c). This finding supports an earlier study by MacKinnon and Stern (1977) in which maternal behavior was induced hormonally by terminating pregnancies after mid-gestation and this was accompanied by retrieving pups from a T-maze.

Despite the fact that maternal behavior can be elicited before parturition, parturition plays an important role in the onset of maternal behavior. Females delivered by Caesarean section shortly before normal parturition differ behaviorally in several respects from those that have given birth normally. They continue to exhibit infanticide in 20 percent of the cases whereas infanticide is absent in postparturient females and Caesarean-sectioned dams do not show a preference for zero-to-two-day-old pups as do normally delivering females (Stern, 1986). Bridges (1977) has shown that as little as 15–30 minutes of contact with pups during parturition is sufficient to enable them to sensitize more rapidly nearly a month later. Depriving parturient females of this experience by removing pups as they are delivered or delivering females by Caesarean section prevents this long-term experience effect. This suggests that females gain experience during normal parturition which plays a role in their subsequent maternal behavior.

This was shown in another kind of study. Prepartum maternal behavior was blocked by brain implants of an antiestrogen two days before parturition. Females then delivered their pups and 24 hours later they were able to exhibit maternal behavior. We could prevent this postpartum maternal behavior in a significant proportion of the mothers by delivering the pups by Caesarean section. This showed that even the short period of contact with pups during parturition is able to stimulate maternal behavior in females that are otherwise inhibited by an antiestrogen (Ahdieh, Mayer, and Rosenblatt, 1988).

Apart from the hormonal changes females undergo at parturition, other aspects of reproduction during parturition may account for the important effect of parturition on the onset of maternal behavior. Cervical-vaginal stimulation applied to estrogen-primed nonpregnant females elicited the rapid onset of maternal behavior not shown by females that were simply handled; the effect was dependent upon prior experience in maternal behavior (Yeo and Keverne, 1986). Uterine distention of pseudopregnant inexperienced females also significantly reduced onset latencies for maternal behavior (Graber and Kristal, 1977). Moreover, during parturition among rats, females are attracted to the placentas attached to pups and to the amniotic fluid bathing them and they consume the placentas and lick the pups clean. Placenta and amniotic fluid applied to newborns stimulates licking and this, in turn, shortens sensitization latencies of nonpregnant females (Kristal, Whitney, and Peters, 1981).

As these authors suggest, "[T]he immediate attraction of the female to the skin of pups during delivery would have a much more potent effect on the initiation of maternal behaviour because of the hormonal condition of the other at that time" (p. 84).

Of interest are other treatments that reveal the underlying emotional changes in the lactating mother. When virgin females were subjected to corticomedial amygdaloid lesions they became maternal more rapidly than nonlesioned control animals and this was accompanied by a reduction in their fearfulness in several of the fear-mediated tasks described above (Fleming, Vaccarino, and Luebke, 1980). When the lesioned females were exposed to pups that were placed in their preferred sleeping corners, unlike unlesioned females that left the area to avoid the pups, the lesioned animals remained in place and allowed the pups to crawl under them. The reduction in the above measures of fearfulness is therefore closely correlated with their lack of withdrawal from pups. As the authors suggest, "Estradiol may normally facilitate maternal responding by suppressing amygdaloid activation in response to novel pup odors (as well as other pup cues) and in doing so it would decrease the animal's tendency to avoid pups" (p. 742). The same decrease in latencies to show maternal behavior when sensitized females (and males) was produced by lesions of the bed nucleus of the accessory olfactory tract which interrupts the fear-inducing effect of vomeronasal system stimulation by pup odors (del Cerro, Izquierdo, Collado, Segovia, and Guillamón, 1991).

Fearfulness in rats, measured by freezing in response to a loud noise, can be reduced by pharmacological agents, such as benzodiazepine, which act on GABA receptors in the brain. Virgins treated with benzodiazepine behave like lactating mothers in the feeding and drinking conflict situations described above, however, only when pups are present (Ferreira et al., 1989). They have not been shown to be more responsive to pups nor to become sensitized more rapidly than untreated virgins.

Among sheep, vaginal-cervical stimulation complements hormonal stimulation in eliciting maternal behavior and also enables females to inhibit their rejection of alien newborn and to promote their acceptance (Keverne, 1988; Krehbiel, Poindron, and Levy, 1987; Poindron, Levy, and Krehbiel, 1988). Moreover, vaginal-cervical stimulation alters the ewe's initial avoidance response to amniotic fluid, enabling her, thereby, to lick the fluid-covered lamb. This change from withdrawal to approach responsiveness in relation to the amniotic fluid and the lamb is based on the release of oxytocin in the brain and noradrenergic stimulation of the main olfactory system (Kendrick, Keverne, Chapman, and Baldwin, 1988; Krehbiel, Poindron, Lévy, and Prud'homme, 1987; Lévy, Keverne, Piketty, and Poindron, 1990).

VI. Recapitulation

Approach/withdrawal biphasic theory is able to deal with the complexity of the phenomena related to the onset of maternal behavior in the rat more comprehensively than the single system activation threshold theory. According to the latter theory the nonpregnant female's initial fearfulness and timidity towards pups and her aversion to pup odors is viewed as a low point on a scale of maternal responsiveness. This is implied in the Cosnier's (1963) and Cosnier and Couturier's (1966) scoring of maternal responses along a scale from low to high, with the appearance of all items of maternal behavior as the high point of the scale. According to approach/withdrawal theory, fear and timidity are evidence of a withdrawal system (often manifest as attacking and killing pup as explained earlier). An approach system stands in opposition to this withdrawal system. The approach system consists of the components of maternal behavior in which the female approaches pups to lick them, crouch over them in the nursing posture and retrieve them; nestbuilding also has a strong approach component since it involves the female carrying nest material to the pups in the nest.

Single system activation threshold theory proposes that once the negative responses to pups are overcome during sensitization, positive maternal responses can be aroused by contact with pups. Until then these positive maternal responses are at a low level of excitation. This is controverted by the effects on sensitization latencies of making nonpregnant females anosmic. Their short latencies for initiating maternal behavior indicate that their maternal responsiveness was already highly aroused at the same time that they avoided pups because of their aversion to pup odors. The concept that both the approach and withdrawal systems can be aroused simultaneously is central to A/W biphasic theory but presents a problem for single system activation threshold theory. According to this theory negative and positive stimuli summate: when the female withdraws from pups, as occurs early during sensitization, arousal of maternal behavior is low and removing olfaction only removes a source of negative stimulation but does not add to the excitation. A/W theory proposes, on the other hand, that both systems may be stimulated but one will normally predominate. Removal of olfaction may reduce withdrawal responses and consequently approach responses will dominate and short-latency maternal behavior will appear.

We have proposed that the sensitization process enables us to characterize the behavioral substrate upon which hormones act during pregnancy and parturition to stimulate maternal behavior. This substrate consists of the perceptual, motivational/emotional, and motor processes which characterize the approach/withdrawal systems of the nonpregnant female. We have analyzed each of these areas of function by comparing nonmaternal, nonpregnant females with sensitized females and with lactating mothers.

Approach/withdrawal systems underlying maternal behavior can be traced during ontogeny as they develop in females and males. Until early weaning around $3^{1}/_{2}$ weeks of age juveniles of both sexes show only approach responses to the live stimulus properties of newborns. These early maternal responses do not form a coherent pattern of behavior. They alternate with play behavior, and not all of the adult behavior patterns are exhibited. The development of neophobia and fearfulness in juveniles at $3^{1}/_{2}$ weeks of age gives rise to withdrawal responses which appear suddenly and predominate over approach responses to newborns. From then on influences which affect approach or withdrawal responses determine the sensitization latencies of each of the sexes.

Among the factors during ontogeny which affect approach/withdrawal systems related to maternal behavior are experiences which reduce fearfulness, timidity, anxiety, and aversion to pup odors, and, in addition, the action of hormones during pre- and postnatal life, puberty, adulthood, and pregnancy and parturition. Handling postpubertal animals or making them anosmic was effective in significantly reducing sensitization latencies. Experience with young pups also contributes to reduced fearfulness and perhaps reduced aversion to pup odors and reduces sensitization latencies postpubertally.

Hormonal influences occur at three periods during ontogeny and have different effects. In the perinatal period androgen increases adult sensitization latencies in males and females; estrogen has no effect in females and its effect in males has not been examined. Postpubertally males and females maintain basal levels of maternal responsiveness; male levels are considerably lower than females' and castration does not increase these levels. Female sensitization levels are maintained by estrogen, however, and are increased by ovariectomy. Estrogen effects on adult males have not been studied.

Hormonal effects on maternal responsiveness during pregnancy are built upon these basal levels of responsiveness. These effects are twofold: estrogen and progesterone and prolactin prime the female to respond to the pattern of hormonal changes at the end of pregnancy (i.e., decline in progesterone and increases in estrogen and prolactin) which triggers the onset of maternal behavior. Throughout pregnancy these hormones also increase the level of maternal responsiveness above that of nonpregnant females.

Hormones act on maternal approach/withdrawal systems, on the perceptual processes which activate these systems and on the motor responses of maternal behavior. In general, their effect on these systems is to reduce withdrawal by reducing fear and timidity and by enabling conflicts between approach and withdrawal responses to be resolved in favor of approach responses. Perceptual processes are altered and approach-eliciting stimuli from the pups are favored over those which elicit withdrawal. As a consequence of these two types of effects, behavior sequences that form the components of maternal behavior are performed.

NOTE

After this chapter was submitted an excellent article appeared (Pryce, 1992) which also proposes dual maternal motivational systems similar to the biphasic approach/withdrawal processes proposed in the present chapter. This article extends the application of this concept to all mammals. See Pryce, C. R. (1992). A comparative systems model of the regulation of maternal motivation in mammals. *Animal Behavior, 43,* 417–441.

ACKNOWLEDGMENT

The research referred to in this article from the author's laboratory was supported by NIMH Grant MH-08604 and an NSF Grant to JSR. We wish to acknowledge the collaboration of a number of graduate and undergraduate students and the secretarial and graphic art work done by Winona Cunningham and Cindy Banas. This is contribution number 505 of the Institute of Animal Behavior.

REFERENCES

Adams, D. B. (1983). Hormone-brain interactions and their influence on agonistic behavior. In B. B. Svare (ed.) *Hormones and aggressive behavior* (pp. 223–245). New York: Plenum Press.

Bauer, J. H. (1983). Effects of maternal state on the responsiveness to nest odors of hooded rats. *Physiology and behavior, 30,* 229–232.

Baum, M. J. (1978). Failure of pituitary transplants to facilitate the onset of maternal behavior in ovariectomized virgin rats. *Physiology and Behavior, 20,* 87–89.

Beach, F. A. (1948). *Hormones and Behavior*. New York: Paul B. Hoeber Inc.

Bereiter, D. A., and Barker, D. J. (1975). Facial receptive fields of trigeminal neurons: increased size following estrogen treatment in female rats. *Neuroendocrinology*, 18, 115–124.

Bridges, R. S. (1977). Parturition: Its role in the long-term retention of maternal behavior in the rat. *Physiology and Behavior*, 18, 487–490.

Bridges, R. S., Zarrow, M. X., and Denenberg, V. H. (1973). The role of neonatal androgen in the expression of hormonally induced maternal responsiveness in the adult rat. *Hormones and Behavior*, 4, 315–322.

Bridges, R., Zarrow, M. X., Gandelman, R., and Denenberg, V. H. (1972). Differences in maternal responsiveness between lactating and sensitized rats. *Developmental Psychobiology*, 5, 127–137.

Bronstein, P. M., and Hirsch, S. M. (1976). Ontogeny of defensive reactions to Norway rats. *Journal of Comparative and Physiological Psychology*, 90, 620–629.

Brunelli, S. A., Shindledecker, R. D., and Hofer, M. A. (1985). Development of maternal behaviors in prepubertal rats at three ages: Age-characteristic patterns of response. *Developmental Psychobiology*, 18, 309–326.

———. (1987). Behavioral responses of juvenile rats (*Rattus norvegicus*) to neonates after infusion of maternal blood plasma. *Journal of Comparative and Physiological Psychology*, 101, 47–59.

———. (1989). Early experience and maternal behavior in rats. *Developmental Psychobiology*, 22, 295–314.

Cain, D. P. (1974). Olfactory bulbectomy: Neural structures involved in irritability and aggression in the male rat. *Journal of Comparative and Physiological Psychology*, 86, 213–220.

Cain, D. P., and Paxinos, P. (1974). Olfactory bulbectomy and mucosal damage: Effects on copulation, irritability, and interspecific aggression in male rats. *Journal of Comparative and Physiological Psychology*, 86, 202–212.

Candland, D. K., and Campbell, B. A. (1962). Development of fear in the rat as measured by behavior in the open field. *Journal of Comparative and Physiological Psychology*, 55, 593–596.

Charten, D., Adrien, J., and Cosnier, J. (1971). Déclencheurs chimiques du comportement du léchage des petits par la ratte parturiente. *Revue de Comportement Animale*, 5, 89–94.

Cosnier, J. (1963). Quelques problèmes posés par le comportement maternel provoqué chez la Ratte. *Psychophysiologie Compte Rendu Société Biologie*, 157, 1611–1613.

Cosnier, J., and Couturier, C. (1966). Comportement maternel provoqué chez les rattes adultes castrées. *Compte Rendu Société Biologie*, 160, 789–791.

Del Cerro, M., Cruz, R., Izquierdo, M. A., Collado, P., Segovia, S., and Guillamón, A. (1991). Bilateral lesions of the bed nucleus of the accessory olfactory tract facilitate maternal behavior in virgin female rats. *Physiology and Behavior*, 50, 67–71.

Dohler, K. D., and Wuttke, W. (1975). Changes with age in levels of serum gonadotropins, prolactin, and gonadal steroids in pre-pubertal male and female rats. *Endocrinology*, 97, 898–907.

Erskine, M. S., Barfield, R. J., and Goldman, B. D. (1980). Postpartum aggression in rats: II. Dependence on maternal sensitivity to young and effects of experience with pregnancy and parturition. *Journal of Comparative and Physiological Psychology*, 94, 495–505.

Ferreira, A., Hansen, S., Nielsen, M., Archer, T., and Minor, B. G. (1989). Behavior of mother rats in conflict tests sensitive to antianxiety agents. *Behavioral Neuroscience*, 103, 193–201.

Fleischer, S., Kordower, J. H., Kaplan, B., Dicker, R., Smerling, R., and Ilgner, J. (1981). Olfactory bulbectomy and gender differences in maternal behaviors of rats. *Physiology and Behavior*, 26, 957–959.

Fleming, A. (1986). Psychobiology of rat maternal behavior: How and where hormones act to promote maternal behavior at parturition. In B. R. Komisaruk, H. I. Siegel, M.-F. Cheng, and H. H. Feder (eds.)., *Reproduction: A Behavioral and Neuroendocrine Perspective* (pp. 234–251). New York: New York Academy of Science.

Fleming, A. S., Cheung, U., Myhal, N., and Kessler, Z. (1989). Effects of maternal hormones on "timidity" and attraction to pup-related odors in female rats. *Physiology and Behavior*, 46, 449–454.

Fleming, A. S., and Luebke, C. (1981). Timidity prevents the virgin female rat from being a good mother: emotionality differences between nulliparous and parturient females. *Physiology and Behavior*, 27, 863–868.

Fleming, A. S., and Rosenblatt, J. S. (1974a). Maternal behavior in the virgin and lactating rat. *Journal of Comparative and Physiological Psychology*, 86, 957–972.

———. (1974b). Olfactory regulation of maternal behavior in rats: I. Effects of olfactory bulb removal in experienced and inexperienced lactating and cycling females. *Journal of Comparative and Physiological Psychology*, 86, 221–232.

———. (1974c). Olfactory regulation of maternal behavior in rats: II. Effects of peripherally induced anosmia and lesions of the lateral olfactory tract in pup-induced virgins. *Journal of Comparative and Physiological Psychology*, 86, 233–246.

Fleming, A. S., Vaccarino, F., and Luebke, C. (1980). Amygdaloid inhibition of maternal behavior in the nulliparous female rat. *Physiology and Behavior*, 25, 731–743.

Fleming, A., Vaccarino, F., Tambosso, L., and Chee, P. (1979). Vomeronasal and olfactory system modulation of maternal behavior in the rat. *Science*, 203, 372–374.

Graber, G. C., and Kristal, M. B. (1977). Uterine distention facilitates the onset of maternal behavior in pseudopregnant but not in cycling rats. *Physiology and Behavior*, 19, 133–137.

Grant, E. C. (1963). An analysis of social behaviour of the male laboratory rat. *Behaviour*, 21, 260–281.

Grant, E. C., and Mackintosh, J. H. (1963). A comparison of the social postures of some common laboratory rodents. *Behaviour*, 21, 246–259.

Gray, P., and Chesley, S. (1984). Development of maternal behavior in nulliparous rats (*Rattus norvegicus*): Effects of sex and early maternal experience. *Journal of Comparative Psychology*, 98, 91–99.

Hansen, S., and Ferreira, A. (1986). Food intake, aggression, and fear behavior in the mother rat: Control by neural systems concerned with milk ejection and maternal behavior. *Behavioral Neuroscience*, 100, 64–70.

Hansen, S., Ferreira, A., and Selart, M. E. (1985). Behavioral similarities between mother rats and benzodiazepine-treated nonmaternal animals. *Psychopharmacology*, 86, 344–347.

Härd, E., and Hansen, S. (1985). Reduced fearfulness in the lactating rat. *Physiology and Behavior*, 35, 641–643.

Herrenkohl, L. R., and Rosenberg, P. A. (1972). Exteroceptive stimulation of maternal behavior in the naive rat. *Physiology and Behavior*, 8, 595–598.

Ichikawa, S., and Fujii, Y. (1982). Effect of prenatal androgen treatment on maternal behavior in the female rats. *Hormones and Behavior*, 16, 224–233.

Jakubowski, M., and Terkel, J. (1984). Pup and object carrying by maternally and nonmaternally behaving female albino rats (*Rattus norvegicus*). *Journal of Comparative Psychology*, 98, 311–317.

————. (1985a). Incidence of pup killing and parental behavior in virgin female and male rats (*Rattus norvegicus*): differences between Wistar and Sprague-Dawley stocks. *Journal of Comparative Psychology*, 99, 93–97.

————. (1985b). Transition from pup killing to parental behavior in male and virgin female albino rats. *Physiology and Behavior*, 34, 683–686.

————. (1986). Establishment and maintenance of maternal responsiveness in postpartum Wistar rats. *Animal Behavior*, 34, 256–262.

Kenyon, P., Cronin, P., and Keeble, S. (1981). Disruption of maternal retrieving by perioral anesthesia. *Physiology and Behavior*, 27, 313–321.

Keverne, E. B. (1988). Central mechanisms underlying the neural and neuroendocrine deteminants of maternal behaviour. *Psychoneuroendocrinology*, 13, 127–141.

Kinsley, C. H., and Bridges, R. S. (1988). Prolactin mediation of the maternal-like behavior displayed by juvenile rats. *Hormones and Behavior*, 22, 49–65.

————. (1989). Morphine treatment and reproductive condition alter olfactory preferences for pup and adult male odors. *Developmental Psychobiology*, 23, 331–347.

Koránya, L., Lissak, K., Tamasy, V., and Kamaras, L. (1976). Behavioral and electrophysiological attempts to elucidate central nervous system mechanisms responsible for maternal behavior. *Archives of Sexual Behavior*, 5, 503–510.

Krehbiel, D., Poindron, P., Lévy, F., and Prud'Homme, M. J. (1987). Peridural anesthesia disturbs maternal behavior in primiparous and multiparous parturient ewes. *Physiology and Behavior*, 40, 463–472.

Kristal, M. B., Whitney, J. F., and Peters, L. C. (1981). Placenta on pups' skin accelerates onset of maternal behaviour in non-pregnant rats. *Animal Behavior*, 29, 81–85.

Leboucher, G. (1989). Maternal behavior in normal and androgenized female rats: effect of age and experience. *Physiology and Behavior*, 45, 313–319.

Leon, M., Croskerry, P. G., and Smith, G. K. (1978). Thermal control of mother-young contact in rats. *Physiology and Behavior*, 21, 793–811.

Leon, M., Numan, M., and Moltz, H. (1973). Maternal behavior in the rat: facilitation through gonadectomy. *Science*, 179, 1018–1019.

Lévy, F., Keverne, E. B., Piketty, V., and Poindron, P. Physiological determinism of olfactory attraction for amniotic fluids in sheep. In D. W. MacDonald, D. Muller-Swarze, and S. E. Natinczuk (eds.), *Chemical Signals in Vertebrates 5* (pp. 162–165). Oxford: Oxford University Press.

Lubin, M., Leon, M., Moltz, H., and Numan, M. (1972). Hormones and maternal behavior in the male rat. *Hormones and Behavior*, 3, 369–374.

MacKinnon, D. A., and Stern, J. M. (1977). Pregnancy duration and fetal number: Effects on maternal behavior in rats. *Physiology and Behavior*, 18, 793–797.

Mayer, A. D. (1983). The ontogeny of maternal behaviour in rodents. In R. W. Elwood (ed.), *Parental Behaviour of Rodents* (pp. 1–21). Chichester: Wiley.

Mayer, A. D., Faris, P. L., Komisaruk, B. R., and Rosenblatt, J. S. (1985). Opiate antagonism reduces placentophagia and pup cleaning by parturient rats. *Pharmacology Biochemistry and Behavior*, 22, 1035–1044.

Mayer, A. D., Freeman, N. G., and Rosenblatt, J. S. (1979). Ontogeny of maternal behavior in the laboratory rat: factors underlying changes in responsiveness from 30 to 90 days. *Developmental Psychobiology*, 12, 425–439.

Mayer, A. D., and Rosenblatt, J. S. (1975). Olfactory basis for the delayed onset of maternal behavior in virgin female rats: Experiential basis. *Journal of Comparative and Physiological Psychology*, 89, 701–710.

———. (1977). Effects of intranasal zinc sulfate on open field and maternal behavior in female rats. *Physiology and Behavior*, 18, 101–109.

———. (1979a). Ontogeny of maternal behavior in the laboratory rat: early origins in 18–27-day-old young. *Developmental Psychobiology*, 12, 407–424.

———. (1979c). Hormonal influences during the ontogeny of maternal behavior in female rats. *Journal of Comparative and Physiological Psychology*, 93, 879–898.

———. (1984). Prepartum changes in maternal responsiveness and nest defense in *Rattus norvegicus*. *Journal of Comparative and Physiological Psychology*, 98, 177–188.

———. (1987). Hormonal factors influence the onset of maternal aggression in laboratory rats. *Hormones and Behavior*, 21, 253–267.

McCullough, J., Quadagno, D. M., and Goldman, B. D. (1974). Neonatal gonadal hormones: Effect on maternal and sexual behavior in the male rat. *Physiology and Behavior*, 12, 183–188.

Moretto, D., Paclik, L., and Fleming, A. S. (1986). The effects of early rearing environments on maternal behavior in adult female rats. *Developmental Psychobiology*, 19, 581–591.

Pinel, J. P. J., Mana, M. J., and Ward, J.-A. A. (1989). Stretch-approach sequences directed at a localized shock source. *Journal of Comparative Psychology*, 103, 140–148.

Poindron, P., Lévy, F., and Krehbiel, D. (1988). Genital, olfactory, and endocrine interactions in the development of maternal behavior in the parturient ewe. *Psychoneuroendocrinology*, 13, 99–125.

Quadagno, D. M., Debold, J. F., Gorzalka, B. B., and Whalen, R. E. (1974). Maternal behavior in the rat: Aspects of concaveation and neonatal androgen treatment. *Physiology and Behavior*, 12, 1071–1074.

Quadagno, D. M., McCullough, J., Ho, G. K.-H., and Spevak, A. M. (1973). Neonatal gonadal hormones: effect on maternal and sexual behavior in the female rat. *Physiology and Behavior*, 11, 251–254.

Quadagno, D. M., and Rockwell, J. (1972). The effect of gonadal hormones in infancy on maternal behavior in the adult rat. *Hormones and Behavior*, 3, 55–62.

Rosenberg, K. M. (1974). Effects of pre- and postpubertal castration and testosterone on pup-killing behavior in the male rat. *Physiology and Behavior*, 13, 159–161.

———. (1975). The role of testosterone in the organization, maintenance and activation of pup-killing behavior in the male rat. *Hormones and Behavior*, 6, 173–179.

Rosenberg, K. M., Denenberg, V. H., Zarrow, M. X., and Frank, B. L. (1971). Effects of neonatal castration and testosterone on the rat's pup-killing behavior and activity. *Physiology and Behavior*, 7, 363–368.

Rosenberg, K. M., and Sherman, G. F. (1974). Testosterone induced pup-killing behavior in the ovariectomized female rat. *Physiology and Behavior*, 13, 697–699.

———. (1975a). Influence of testosterone on pup killing in the rat is modified by prior experience. *Physiology and Behavior*, 15, 669–672.

———. (1975b). Effects of handling on the pup-killing behavior of prepubertally castrated male rats. Paper presented at Meeting of the Psychonomic Society, Denver, Colorado.

Rosenberg, P. A., and Herrenkohl, L. R. (1976). Maternal behavior in male rats: Critical times for the suppressive action of androgens. *Physiology and Behavior*, 16, 293–297.

Rosenblatt, J. S. (1967). Nonhormonal basis of maternal behavior in the rat. *Science*, 156, 1512–1514.

———. (1975). Selective retrieving by maternal and nonmaternal female rats. *Journal of Comparative and Physiological Psychology*, 88, 678–686.

———. (1983). Olfaction mediates developmental transition in altricial newborn of selected species of mammals. *Developmental Psychobiology*, 16, 346–375.

Schneirla, T. C. (1959). An evolutionary and developmental theory of biphasic processes underlying approach and withdrawal. In M. R. Jones (ed.), *Nebraska Symposium of Motivation, Vol. 7* (pp. 1–42). Lincoln: University of Nebraska Press.

———. (1965). Aspects of stimulation and organizaion in approach/withdrawal processes underlying vertebrate behavioral development. In D. S. Lehrman, R. Hinde, and E. Shaw (eds.), *Advances in the Study of Behavior, Vol. 1* (pp. 1–71). New York: Academic Press.

Siegel, H. I., and Rosenblatt, J. S. (1975). Estrogen-induced maternal behavior in hysterectomized-ovariectomized virgin rats. *Physiology and Behavior*, 14, 465–471.

Silverman, A. P. (1965). Ethological and statistical analysis of drug effects on the social behavior of laboratory rats. *British Journal of Pharmacology*, 24, 579–590.

Slotnick, B. M. (1967). Intercorrelations of maternal activities in the rat. *Animal Behavior*, 15, 267–269.

Stern, J. M. (1983). Maternal behavior priming in virgin and Caesarean-delivered Long-Evans rats: Effects of brief contact or continuous exteroceptive pup stimulation. *Physiology and Behavior,* 31, 757–763.

――. (1987). Pubertal decline in maternal responsiveness in Long-Evans rats: Maturational influences. *Physiology and Behavior,* 41, 93–98.

――. (1989). Multisensory regulation of maternal behavior and masculine sexual behavior: A revised view. Presented at conference on reproductive behavior, Skidmore College, Saratoga Springs, New York.

――. (1991). Somatosensory determinants and consequences of nursing behavior in rats. Presented at conference on reproductive behavior, Asilomar, California.

Stern, J. M., and Johnson, S. K. (1989). Perioral somatosensory determinants of nursing behavior in Norway rats (*Rattus norvegicus*). *Journal of Comparative Psychology,* 103, 269–280.

――. (1990). Ventral somatosensory determinants of nursing behavior in Norway rats. I. Effects of variations in the quality and quantity of pup stimuli. *Physiology and Behavior,* 47, 993–1011.

Stern, J. M., and Kolunie, J. M. (1991). Perioral anesthesia disrupts maternal behavior during early lactation in Long-Evans rats. *Journal of Comparative Psychology,* 105, 984–997.

Stern, J. M., and MacKinnon, D. A. (1976). Postpartum, hormonal, and nonhormonal induction of maternal behavior in rats: Effects on T-maze retrieval of pups. *Hormones and Behavior,* 7, 305–316.

――. (1978). Sensory regulation of maternal behavior in rats: Effects of pup age. *Developmental Psychobiology,* 11, 579–586.

Stern, J. M., and Rogers, L. (1988). Experience with younger siblings facilitates maternal responsiveness in pubertal Norway rats. *Developmental Psychobiology,* 21, 575–589.

Terkel, J., and Rosenblatt, J. S. (1971). Aspects of nonhormonal maternal behavior in the rat. *Hormones and Behavior,* 2, 161–171.

――. (1972). Humoral factors underlying maternal behavior at parturition: Cross transfusion between freely moving rats. *Journal of Comparative and Physiological Psychology,* 80, 365–371.

Thompson, R. W., and Lippman, L. G. (1972). Exploration and activity in the gerbil and rat. *Developmental Psychobiology,* 7, 76–79.

Tobach, E., and Schneirla, T. C. (1968). The biopsychology of social behavior in animals. In R. E. Cooke and S. Levin (eds.), *Biologic Bases of Pediatric Practice* (pp. 68–82). New York: McGraw-Hill.

Van Der Poel, A. M. (1979). A note on "stretched attention," a behavioural element indicative of an approach-avoidance conflict in rats. *Animal Behavior*, 27, 446–450.

Wiesner, B. P., and Sheard, N. M. (1933). *Maternal Behaviour in the Rat*. London: Oliver and Boyd.

Wild, J. M., and Hughes, R. N. (1972). Effects of postweaning handling on locomotor and exploratory behavior in young rats. *Physiology and Behavior*, 7, 76–79.

Wilson, N. E., and Stricker, E. M. (1979). Thermal homeostasis in pregnant rats during heat stress. *Journal of Comparative and Physiological Psychology*, 93, 585–594.

Woodside, B., and Jans, J. E. (1988). Neuroendocrine basis of thermally regulated maternal responses to young in the rat. *Psychoneuroendocrinology*, 13, 79–98.

Woodside, B., Leon, M., Attard, M., Feder, H. H., Siegel, H. I., and Fischette, C. (1981). Prolactin-steroid influences on the thermal basis for mother-young contact in Norway rats. *Journal of Comparative and Physiological Psychology*, 95, 771–780.

CHAPTER 9

The Mediation of Aggressive Behavior in Mice
A Discussion of Approach/Withdrawal Processes in Social Adaptations

Jean-Louis Gariépy

Introduction

"The A/W theory seems applicable to behavior in all animals, although the extent to which basic A-responses and W-responses may change from early stages is naturally dependent upon resources for plasticity through experience."

Schneirla (1950), Aspects of stimulation and organization in approach-withdrawal processes underlying vertebrate behavioral development, p. 346.

"Through evolution, higher levels have arisen in which through ontogeny A/W mechanisms can produce new and qualitatively advanced types of adjustments to environmental conditions."

Schneirla (1942), An evolutionary and developmental theory of biphasic process underlying approach and withdrawal, p. 356.

The Approach/Withdrawal theory was formulated in the context of a comparative analysis of psychological capacities across phyletic and developmental levels. Its aim was to stimulate attention to basic mechanisms of adaptation and to their incorporation in higher forms of behavioral adjustment. In its most basic aspect, the theory stipulates that A-processes are activated under conditions of low-intensity stimulation and favor an approach toward the stimulus source, while W-processes are activated at higher intensities and favor withdrawal from the source of stimulation. Research aimed at clarifying how such processes may operate to support adaptive adjustments has focused for the most part on the early stages of behavioral organization, that is, the neonatal period and the lower animal forms. It was one of the objectives of this conference to examine how A/W processes may support adaptations through the adult stages of higher animals including our own species.

The challenge that the theory faces is not so much to demonstrate that A/W processes are common to all animals, but to explicate their *operation* within higher organismic levels. Schneirla emphasizes in the above quotes that new and more advanced forms of adjustments to environmental conditions are created through development and evolution. Depending on the species and the ontogenetic status of the individual, these new forms may consist of enhanced motor and perceptual capacities, capacities for discriminative and associative learning, or enhanced memory and cognitive processing. Accordingly, the analysis of A/W processes beyond the early stages requires a shift from the measurement of stimulus intensity to an analysis of its configurational properties. With reference to the distinction made by Schneirla between the tonic and the phasic aspects of A/W processes, I propose in this chapter a systemic reformulation of an organismic approach to the question. This involves placing the behavioral aspect of A/W theory at the origin of a process whereby external and internal structures are brought into alignment, in ways that support preservation and development. The elucidation of how this alignment is achieved requires a systemic analysis of how, through behavior, novelties are introduced in the organization and coordination of the two structures over time.

In the following sections I report a series of studies on the social adaptations of mice that have been selectively bred over 25 generations for high and low levels of aggression. Issues of theoretical and empirical importance in this work included the role of genetic biases, of maturational changes and experiential input in behavioral adaptation, and the integration of these factors within the developing organism. The questions addressed in this research were central to Schneirla's perspective on behavioral ontogenesis. At this juncture, an A/W reinterpretation of the major findings should profit both the empirical work and the theory. In the first part, I will present an overview of the research program and the evidence obtained on the joint intraorganismic-social ecological support of behavioral adaptations in mice. In the second part I will discuss the relevance of the findings for clarifying two issues concerning the operation of A/W mechanisms beyond the early stages. The first issue concerns the nature and form of A- and W-responses when organic adaptation takes place within social interactions. The second issue is the identification of the new pathways whereby A/W mechanisms sustain organismic adaptations among social animals.

The Selective Breeding Program: The Subject Species

The common white laboratory mouse (*Mus musculus*) is a social mammal which displays a fairly elaborate repertoire of fighting behaviors. Although there is a fair amount of variability among strains, most of them are known to exhibit substantial intraspecific aggression under both natural and laboratory conditions. Beyond its aggressiveness, the albino mouse presents the advantage of a rapid reproductive cycle and large litter sizes. Within a single academic year, two or three consecutive generations can be produced, and lines that differ along desired phenotypic dimensions are rapidly created when appropriate selection procedures are applied. The relatively short life-time of the species also reduces considerably the time investment necessary to complete longitudinal studies and to compare developmental patterns across successive generations. Finally, the small size of the animal makes housing within laboratory facilities relatively inexpensive and simplifies the experimental control of social experiences. The combination of these characteristics in the same species permitted an in-depth investigation of aggressive behavior while maintaining appropriate controls over genetic background, age, and prior individual history at the time of testing.

The research conducted in our laboratory showed that *mus musculus* is capable of highly flexible forms of social adaptation. To better understand the mechanisms underlying this flexibility it was necessary to step beyond the experimental controls and to question its significance for the species under natural conditions. In the wild, mice form colonies of varying sizes. When population densities are not too high, certain males tend to exhibit a high degree of territoriality (Crowcroft, 1963) and functionally isolate themselves by confining other males to a small area of the colony (McIntosh, 1981; Van Oortmerssen, 1989). The females by contrast, are free to roam from one territory to the other and often show a strong preference for well-established or dominant males (McIntosh, 1981; Sandnabba, 1984). On the other hand, when population densities reach a critical level, another form of social organization emerges which involves the temporary formation of dominance hierarchies, a concomitant reduction of aggressiveness and territorial behavior, and early emigration attempts by juvenile males (Van Oortmerssen, 1990). Thus the relevant context for ontogenetic adaptations in mice is primarily social. Of special interest to the present discussion is the fact that the interactions between developmental status, prior history, and the changing social dynamic of the colony as a whole have the potential to generate a substantial diversity in patterns of individual adaptation. Although under laboratory conditions the experimenter generally prevents such complex social organization from taking place, an understanding of its significance for the species is necessary to the interpretation of the phenomena observed in the laboratory.

Selective Breeding and Testing Procedures

The program of genetic selection that served as a basis for the studies reported here was implemented 16 years ago by Robert B. Cairns when he joined the Psychology Department of the University of North Carolina at Chapel Hill. A foundational stock of pregnant female mice of the ICR strain was purchased from a mouse breeder. Three days after delivery, all litters were culled to eight pups (four females and four males) in order to insure uniformity in weight. The animals were weaned at 21 days of age and the males were placed in individual cages without social contact until they reached puberty. At 45 days of age, these males were observed in dyadic interactions with an unfamiliar male. In the foundational generation, the males which attacked most rapidly and frequently were identified, and they were subsequently mated with females who were non-littermates but whose brothers had also been selected for high levels of attack. From the first selection generation onward, the same procedures were duplicated within the initially selected high-aggressive line. This meant that the males who failed to attack were, in each generation, removed from the reproduction colony for that line, along with the females in their litters. Exactly comparable procedures were followed in establishing the low-aggressive line, except that low-aggressive males were selected and high-aggressive ones were eliminated. Thus attack behavior among the males was the only criterion for selection. In the following discussion, "NC100" and "NC900" refers to the low-aggressive and the high-aggressive lines thus produced.

A nonselectively bred line derived from the original ICR stock was also maintained throughout the research program. These animals were reared in groups of four or five males and were used as partners in the dyadic tests. Rearing this line of animals under such conditions dramatically reduced their tendency to initiate attacks, which permitted us to obtain relatively independent measures of agonistic tendencies among the selected subjects. This interesting effect of housing conditions on aggressive behavior will be discussed in a later section. All housing and testing procedures have been continued virtually unmodified since the work began. A full description of these procedures is available in previous publications (see, for instance, Cairns, McCombie, & Hood, 1983; Cairns & Nakelski, 1971; Gariépy, Hood, & Cairns, 1988).

In each generation, two tests were administered on consecutive days when the animals reached the specified age for testing. On the first day, subjects were tested for reactivity to tactile stimulation. Six stimulations were delivered by lightly tapping the subject on its flank with a cotton swab. Reactivity ratings reflected the extent to which the subject responded with any combination of reflexive kicks, vocalizations and jumps. On the second day, a dyadic test was conducted. For this purpose, the subject was placed alone for 5 minutes in one side of a Plexiglas compartment in order to habituate to the test environment, then a sliding sheet-panel wall was removed, exposing the subject to a same-age, randomly selected group-reared male which had been placed in the other half of the compartment. In the succeeding 10 minutes, all social interactions were recorded following a dyadic syntax by an observer who was blind to the experimental condition or genetic background of the subject. These interactions were recorded in successive 5-second blocks on specially prepared sheets containing 120 blocks. The coding categories included various forms of mild (e.g. sniff, climb), and more intense (vigorous grooming) investigative behaviors, agonistic behaviors (bite, feint, attack, chase, box posture, escape), behavioral indices of social reactivity (startle, kick, vocalize, escape and/or jump in response to mild investigative behaviors), and an index of behavioral inhibition (freezing/rigid immobility upon social contact).

The Genetic Component of Aggressive Behavior in Mice

The number of 5-second blocks during which the selected subjects were observed to attack in the dyadic tests is depicted in Figure 1 for 22 consecutive generations of selective breeding. In each generation a total of 20 to 35 animals were observed in each line. This figure shows that the line differentiation began as early as the first generation. Differences in attack frequencies reached statistical significance in S_4, and a clear separation of the lines was maintained thereafter. Note that the outcome of the selective breeding program has been largely unidirectional even though the procedures were bidirectional. In the high-aggressive line attack frequencies did not change from the foundational level across the successive generations of selective breeding. Line differentiation occurred principally as a result of the rapid decrease of attacks in the low-aggressive line and the stabilization of frequencies near zero in the subsequent generations of low-aggressive animals.

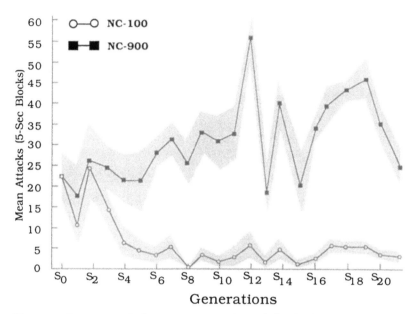

Figure 1: Generational changes in rates of attack for the high-aggression (NC900) and the low-aggression (NC100) lines. The abcissa shows the successive generations of selection, and the ordinate shows attack frequency. Shading indicates standard error.

The subjects observed in the dyadic tests had had no prior experience of dominance or subordination in fighting interactions with other males. At 45 days of age, they were exposed to a conspecific for the first time since weaning. In the absence of prior learning relevant to the dyadic situation, the differences observed between the lines strongly suggested that aggressive behavior in mice is under genetic control. Lagerspetz (1964) and

Van Oortmerssen & Bakker (1981) made the same observation on the basis of their own selective breeding for high and low aggression. The finding that individual differences in aggressiveness among males in mice populations are largely heritable is not a serendipitous one. Reviewing the last fifty years of research in behavior genetics, Fuller & Thompson (1978) showed that most behavioral characteristics, even the most complex, are readily amenable to genetic selection. On this basis, they concluded that all behavior is genetically regulated. Also of interest is the recurring rapidity of the selective breeding effects reported in the same literature. This phenomenon does not support a conservative view of change at the genetic level. Rather, another explanation for the malleability observed at this level is called for.

Susceptibility of Genetic Effects to Age and Experience

In the generations following line differentiation a series of experiments was conducted to verify whether the genetic effects could be attenuated or magnified through maturation and/or experiential input. These experiments permitted us to determine the relative importance of the multiplicative component (gene X environment interaction) in the otherwise additive model of phenotypic variance advocated in classic behavior genetics (for a succinct description of this model, see Plomin, 1988). For this purpose, four males from the same litter were assigned to be tested at different points during ontogeny, with a total of 23 litters represented at each point. One of the males was tested at 30 days of age, and again at 45, 72 and 235 days. The other three males were tested only once either at 45, 72 or 235 days of age. This research strategy was adopted in the 4th generation of selection, S_4, and was designed to evaluate jointly the effects of age and repeated experience on the expression of the underlying line difference in genetic background.

The result reported in Cairns, McCombie, & Hood (1983) showed that the magnitude of the line differences depended upon the age of the subjects at testing. Among prepubertal animals (30 days, first test point), only a few attacks were observed in the dyadic tests and the lines did not differ in aggressive performance. In the single test condition, the large difference appeared around puberty (45 days), was maintained among young adults (72 days), and some convergence between the lines was observed later in adulthood (235 days). The cross-sectional study further confirmed the genetic influence on aggressive behavior, and showed that this influence is itself under maturational control. The repeated testing condition yielded a very different picture on behavioral regulation. It turned out that 4 short 10-minute exposures to a conspecific, with long intertest intervals, were sufficient to wipe out completely the line difference observed among older (235 days of age) animals. Moreover, a clear attenuation of the line difference was already observed at 45 days, even if no attacks had occurred in the previous test. Taken together, the cross-sectional and the longitudinal studies demonstrated that genetic expression is essentially context-dependent, and that the two forces—the genetic-maturational/experiential—collaborate, rather than compete in ontogeny. The findings were entirely consistent with Schneirla's (1966) insistence on the fact that genetic, maturational, and experiential controls do not affect behavior in an additive manner but that these influences are intimately fused within the developing organism (see also Hood & Cairns, 1989).

Although conclusive, the previous study left unanswered a certain number of questions. For instance, it was not clear if the observed experiential effects had been magnified through an interaction with maturational events. Would the same experiential effects take place over intervals of hours or days instead of weeks and months, or even be observable over the course of a single but extended test? In subsequent research we examined this possibility by submitting untrained animals for several consecutive hours to social conditions normally conducive to high frequencies of aggressive interchanges among males. Specifically, extended triadic tests (6 to 8 hours) were conducted in S_{13} and S_{19} which involved placing together in a large enclosure ($2' \times 2'$) a high- and a low-aggressive male and a receptive female (Gariépy, 1991). The goal was to determine whether a single but extended test would be sufficient to actually cancel the genetic constraints on low-aggressive animals, with indications for such a cancellation given by the capacity to achieve a dominance status over a same-age, same-weight, high-aggressive partner.

As we expected for this triadic condition, high-aggressive subjects were invariably the first to attack in every test. What was less expected however, was that in 40 percent (22 out of 54) of these tests, low-aggressive subjects achieved full dominance— generally within two hours—over their high-aggressive opponent. In these cases of line reversal, the behavioral analyses conducted for successive points in time prior to and following the establishment of dominance showed a massive reorganization of interactive patterns. The initial behavioral inhibition/avoidance typical of low-aggressive animals was gradually replaced by more frequent approaches, and attacks were initiated at a higher rate when some of the high-aggressive partners, because they were counterattacked, decreased their own rate of aggressive initiation and became more reactive. After the establishment of social dominance, the high degree of behavioral homogeneity normally found within lines for the dyadic test vanished, and attack measures no longer differentiated the lines.

Taken together, the effects of age, prior experience, and sustained interactions in a challenging context showed that the primary outcome of selection has been to reduce the probability of interactions escalating to attacks in the low-aggressive line, not the capacity to attack. Indeed, even in the dyadic test, when given sufficient provocation, low-aggressive animals often attack. In contrast, only modest contact by the partner (or its mere presence) triggers escalatory sequences in the high-aggression line. As shown by the comparison between the dyadic and the triadic tests, the genetic effects on behavioral organization are more readily discernible in the first minutes of social interaction. This phenomenon points to the importance of the window of time selected for the identification of mechanisms underlying behavioral organization. Indeed, these mechanisms should be expected to differ vastly in nature, as behavioral organization is investigated over the time frames of stimulus appraisal, social interactions, ontogeny, or over successive generations (Cairns, McGuire, & Gariépy, 1993; Griffin, 1958; Rosenblatt, 1965). Such time-bound mechanisms, and their potential to either reinforce or cancel each other out, would explain how otherwise strong and pervasive genetic biases are easily overridden when conditions are encountered that are uncorrelated with those that led to their consolidation over evolutionary time. It is with this perspective in mind that we became interested in the mediational pathways whereby the rapid changes observed at the genetic and ontogenetic levels may take place.

The Mediation of Aggressive Behavior

Three major hypotheses have been formulated on the behavioral mediation of genetic and ontogenetic effects. These hypotheses have implicated respectively behavioral reactivity, behavioral inhibition, or a combination of both. Since our work on this issue was intimately tied to an analysis of the effects of isolation, a preliminary discussion of these effects is called for.

The Effects of Isolation

Social isolation has been a most popular method for inducing fighting in the laboratory mouse. A recurrent critique of this method, however, has been that animals living in the absence of normal stimulation experience stress and exhibit behavioral and physiological deficits not encountered among normally reared animals (e.g. Essman, 1966; Valzelli, 1973). An alternative view describes isolation in mice as the removal of the fighting inhibition developmentally acquired in the presence of male conspecifics (Brain, 1989).

To gain insight on what isolation in mice effectively isolates from, high- and low-aggressive males born in S_{14} were reared either in social isolation or in groups of four animals between the age of 21 and 45 days. Half of the isolated males were handled for 2 minutes every day by a laboratory assistant and the other half was left untouched except for the regular weekly cage cleaning. In the group-rearing condition, half of the males were housed with 3 females of the unselected line and the other half with 3 unselected males. Each of the 15 animals assigned to a given condition had a brother assigned to each of the other three conditions. This design permitted us to determine whether the effects of isolation on social behavior reflect the absence of physical stimulation, the absence of social stimulation in general, or the absence of specific stimulation provided by other males. The various measures taken in the dyadic tests conducted at 45 days showed no effect of handling relative to the complete isolation group. Fighting behavior was not reduced in the high-aggressive line nor was it augmented in the low-aggressive line as a result of handling. Moreover, the social interactions of males reared with females were not different from those of the males reared under the two isolation conditions. Only males reared with other males differed significantly from the other experimental groups. In the dyadic tests involving this last group virtually no attacks were observed.

With respect to its original questions, this study showed that neither removal from physical stimulation nor removal from nonspecific social stimulation is sufficient condition for the observed isolation effects. While it might be debated whether or not human handling provided appropriate or sufficient physical stimulation, it is clear that for the males reared with females an ample supply of such stimulation was provided through exposure to the activities of the cage occupants. Yet these males behaved in the dyadic tests as if they had been reared in isolation. The research rather suggested that isolated males are primarily deprived of the stimulation obtained through fighting with other males and of its inhibiting effects. A related explanation is that isolated males are essentially deprived of exposure to other males' pheromones (Scott, 1966; Benton, Brain, & Goldsmith, 1979).

The isolation-as-stressor viewpoint also predicted that stress hormones would be higher among isolated animals relative to others reared in groups. We tested this prediction by comparing blood levels of circulating corticosterone between animals raised under each condition. No isolation effect was found. The measures obtained for the two conditions were essentially the same and did not support the claim that male mice experience isolation as stressful. A similar study conducted by

Benton, Goldsmith, Gamal-el-Din, Brain, & Huckelbridge (1978) where several strains of mice were investigated, yielded identical results.

To be sure, when measured in conjunction with known stressors corticosterone is a powerful index of stress. For instance, large differences were found in S_{19} between the males that had achieved a dominant or a submissive status in the (6 hr) triadic tests. These differences were very consistent. Corticosterone levels for the submissive member of each dyad (i.e., for 30 pairs of high- and low-aggressive males) were twice as high as that of the dominant member. The same pattern of difference was observed irrespective of selected lines: low-aggressive males that had achieved a dominant status had corticosterone levels as low as high-aggressive animals with the same status. In fact, when the data were analyzed with respect to line instead of social status, no difference was found and virtually the same levels were obtained for the two lines (Gariépy, 1991). In conjunction with the measures obtained across rearing conditions, these results demonstrated that the line difference in attack behavior is not mediated through a line difference in how much stress is experienced under isolation-rearing conditions. On the other hand, the levels measured across line and social status suggested that corticosterone plays an important role (along with other steroids) in supporting ongoing demands for behavioral adjustment.

In a majority of primate species social isolation has devastating effects on subsequent patterns of social adaptation (e.g. Macaques, see Harlow, Harlow, Dodsworth, & Arling, 1954). But there are some interesting exceptions, including the genus Patas, where isolation seems to facilitate rather than hinder social adaptations (Seay, Schlottmann, & Gandolfo, 1972). Examination of these cases shows that the species-specific effects of isolation are generally correlated with important species differences in social structures under natural conditions. For instance, while most species of Macaques are highly cohesive, especially when stressful events occur, Patas monkeys maintain a rather loose social structure at all times which tends to break down in the face of internally or externally generated stress (Chance & Jolly, 1972). In a similar way, the enhanced aggression observed among male mice following isolation may be associated with the characteristic social organization of the species and the kind of attack seen in breeding territorial mice (Brain, 1989). Before puberty, these males migrate to the periphery of the colony where they defend a small territory and functionally isolate themselves from other males. By comparison, isolation rearing in the laboratory seems to recreate some fundamental aspect of the natural condition for the species whereby the development of fighting inhibition is prevented.

Research conducted by Cairns & Nakelski (1971) showed that isolated males also tend to react more strongly to novel stimuli than males reared in groups. In the test of reactivity described above (see *Selective breeding and testing procedures*), isolated nonselected ICR males were easily startled following tactile stimulation while group-reared subjects seemed to simply ignore the same stimulation. A similar effect was observed in the dyadic tests where the isolated males tended to exhibit unusually strong responses to the mild investigatory approaches of the partner. In both the nonsocial and the social tests, reactivity was higher when isolation occurred early, and was directly proportional to the duration of isolation (Cairns, Hood, & Midlam, 1985).

In the NC selected lines both high- and low-aggressive males display strong reactions to mild social stimulation following isolation. Low-aggressive animals, however, also tend to freeze and become immobile upon social contact. In the experiment described above (S_{14}), low-aggressive males that were handled or reared with females froze at the same high rate as that observed among isolated males. By contrast, freezing was almost never observed in the dyadic interactions of low-aggressive males that had been reared with other males. The fact that isolated high-aggressive animals were rarely observed to freeze in their social interactions, irrespective of their rearing histories, demonstrates that differences in genetic background have the potential to constrain the effects of context on behavioral organization. The differences seen in rearing effects between species that differ in social organization or genetic background support a similar conclusion (see for example, Fuller, 1967; Jones & Brain, 1987; Krsiak & Borgesova, 1973). From yet another perspective, the findings demonstrate how the circumstances that prevail during development may serve to either magnify or reduce the expression of genetic differences (see also Fuller, 1967).

Mediation: Reactivity or Behavioral Inhibition?

The analysis of rearing effects suggested that the salient differences in behavior between individually and group-housed male mice were similar to those associated with different forms of social adjustment within the natural colony. This generalization seemed applicable to both attack behavior and social reactivity. As demonstrated by Cairns and Nakelski (1971), the reactive response of the isolated animals to the mild investigatory action of the partner tends to heighten the intensity of social interchanges and to create an interactive context where bites and attacks rapidly follow (see also Banks, 1962). Extending this view to the natural context, Brain (1989) remarked that the high reactivity typical of isolated male mice would not be inappropriate among territory holders in wild colonies because it would serve the same adaptive function. Having seen how social reactivity seems to precipitate the occurrence of attacks in social interactions, Cairns (1973) formulated the hypothesis that the population differences in attack propensity created through selective mating may be mediated by changes in reactivity thresholds. The fact that reactivity levels were easily modifiable through either social experience or selective breeding provided additional support for this hypothesis. Not only did reactivity vary in intensity as a function of rearing conditions, but lines of mice that differed in reactivity thresholds following isolation had been produced when both reactivity and attack behaviors served as selection criteria (Cairns et al., 1983).

If the heightened reactivity hypothesis was correct, the generational emergence and subsequent differentiation of the NC100 and NC900 lines depicted in Figure 1 (where attack was the sole criterion for selection), should have been paralleled by a corresponding change in the propensity to respond reactively to novel stimuli. Specifically, we expected to find progressively higher levels of reactivity in the high-aggressive line across generations, and/or a reduction of reactivity levels in the low-aggressive line. To test this hypothesis, the scores of reactivity to tactile stimulation were plotted for the two lines across the successive generations, and compared to the generational changes observed in aggressive behavior. Contrary to expectations, the cross-generational study showed that the NC100 and NC900 lines did not differ from each other in reactivity measures (Gariépy, et al., 1988). Moreover, reactivity to tactile stimulation across the successive generations did not differ significantly from the foundational level for either line. Similar analyses conducted for indexes of social reactivity (i.e., startle, kick) in dyadic tests yielded the same negative results. Thus, no evidence had been found at this point in support of the hypothesis of mediation through heightened reactivity.

The second hypothesis on mediation was formulated when two basic facts, the outcome of the NC selective breeding program and the line specificity of some of the isolation effects, were brought together. I made the point earlier that the outcome of this program had been largely unidirectional in that only the low line of animals significantly departed from the foundational level of attacks. This outcome suggested that the question of mediation should begin with an examination of the characteristics of the low-aggressive line instead of those of the high-aggressive line. One such characteristic was the peculiar tendency of the low-aggressive animals to freeze upon social contact following isolation. With respect to the question of mediation, freezing was an interesting candidate for two reasons. First, this response was very rarely observed among high-aggressive animals, but was common among the low-aggressive ones. The second reason was that freezing in social interactions seemed to have a de-escalating or inhibitory effect on the course of social interactions which matched the low rates of aggressive encounters observed in the low-aggressive line. The second hypothesis was tested as before by plotting the rates of freezing upon social contact for the successive generations of selective breeding, and by comparing these rates to those of attacks in the dyadic tests for the two lines.

This analysis yielded the first conclusive results on behavioral mediation. The results are presented in Figure 2. As seen in this figure, the foundational level of freezing was low, and the high-aggressive line never changed from that level as a result of the continued selective pressure. By contrast, in the low-aggressive line, the propensity to freeze augmented steadily during the first 15 generations, in spite of the floor values attained much earlier (around S_8) in the tendency to attack. Across the different generations, the correlations between attack and freezing frequencies varied between –0.45 and –0.76, with a median of –0.58. Regression analyses conducted for successive generations systematically showed that freezing was the most powerful predictor of (non)attack in the dyadic tests (Gariépy et al., 1988).

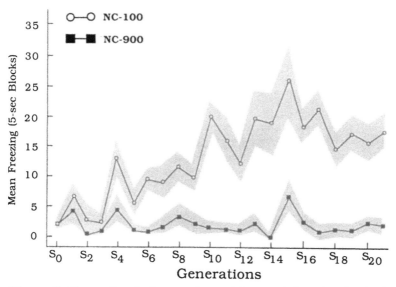

Figure 2: Generational changes in social immobility for the high-aggression (NC900) and the low-aggression (NC100) lines. The abcissa shows the successive generations of selection, and the ordinate shows immobility frequency. Shading indicates standard error.

It is worth noting again that only attacks served as the selection criterion and that freezing upon social contact had not been selected for. This kind of phenomenon is often encountered in research in behavior genetics where selection for one characteristic tends to drive correlated changes in other characteristics as well (Fuller & Thompson, 1978). In the present case, changes in the propensity to freeze upon (novel) social contact seemed to have constituted an optimally efficient pathway for altering the probability that social interactions will escalate to attacks between unfamiliar male mice. The interesting fact that behavioral characteristics tend to be correlated suggests that instead of discrete morphological units (e.g. aggression, maternal behavior, sexual behavior) behaviors may be better conceived of as systems of correlated and mutually supportive functions. In this sense, behavior would be more akin to metabolic processes than to morphological structures (Cairns, 1993).

Development and the Microevolution of Social Inhibition

Was the relationship between the microevolution of aggressive behavior and social inhibition a fortuitous one or was it, as suggested above, indicative of a basic mechanism whereby aggressive behavior is regulated? The functional analysis of social interactions supports the second alternative. Yet another approach to substantiate this view involves examining whether the simultaneous changes induced either by age or repeated experience in both aggressive behavior and the propensity to freeze are correlated. This was examined in the 13th generation using the longitudinal/cross-sectional design implemented in S_4. In this study, 12 litters were represented on each of the test points, with one male tested first at day 30, then repeatedly tested—or tested for the first time—on days 45, 72 and 235. The results obtained for latencies to attack and latencies to freeze are presented respectively in Figure 3 and Figure 4.

On the most basic aspects, this study replicated the effects of age and repeated testing on attack behavior previously reported by Cairns et al. (1983). Low-aggressive animals that were tested only once showed little tendency to attack and their latencies were long for all developmental points. It is interesting to note that by the 13th generation, aging in isolation produced very little change in attack propensity in the low-aggressive line. Repeated testing, however, had a profound effect in that, with accumulated experience, low-aggressive animals exhibited a systematically greater readiness to attack in the dyadic tests. By day 235, these subjects had latency profiles that made them comparable to same-age NC900 subjects. As in the previous (S_4) study, aging in isolation was sufficient to induce substantially faster attacks in the high-aggressive line, and repeated testing had little additional effect.

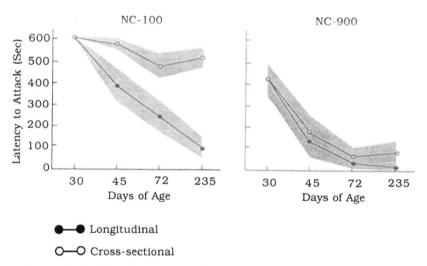

Figure 3: Combined cosibial and longitudinal investigations of attack latency as a function of age in the 13th generation of high-aggressive (NC900: right) and low-aggressive (NC100: left) lines. Shading indicates standard error.

Latency measures for freezing (Figure 4) closely tracked those obtained for attack latencies, except that in this case, the patterns were reversed. Low-aggressive animals that were tested only once entered a freezing mode very early in their social interactions. It is remarkable that in this testing condition, older subjects froze with the same readiness and the same intensity as their prepubertal brothers. Aging without experiential input did not reduce the propensity to freeze. Experienced animals, however, showed across the four tests a progressively lowered tendency to freeze and, as seen in Figure 3, a correspondingly increased readiness to attack. Among high-aggressive animals, latencies were relatively long in the single test condition and exceeded low-aggressive values on all developmental points. Another line difference was that readiness to freeze among high-aggressive animals was relatively high for prepubertal animals but significantly lower for the other three age groups. In this line, aging in isolation induced substantive changes in the propensity to freeze, and repeated testing had little additional effect.

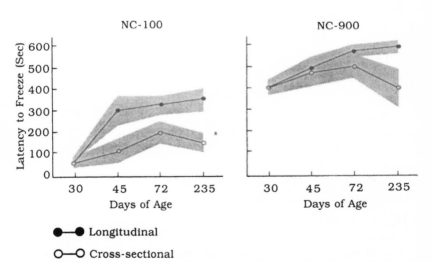

●—● Longitudinal

O—O Cross-sectional

Figure 4: Combined cosibial and longitudinal investigations of latency to become immobile as a function of age in the 13th generation of high-aggressive (NC900: right) and low-aggressive (NC100: left) lines. Shading indicates standard error.

The contrasting effects of aging and repeated experience within each line showed that differences in genetic background can affect the relative power of maturational events and experiential input to induce, maintain, or change the course of behavioral development.

The patterns of changes in social inhibition observed in relation to changes in genetic background, maturation, and experiential input conformed to the different predictions made under the second hypothesis on mediation. When these results are considered jointly, two interesting observations can be made. The first is that whatever the source of change, genetic background, chronological age, or experiential input, a common point of entry for behavioral reorganization was a change in inhibition threshold. The second observation is that the changes measured took place over vastly different time-scales (microevolution, the lifetime of an organism, and the time-course of social interactions), and involved very different mechanisms. Yet the behavioral propensity operated upon was the same. Ever since Waddington (1953), the concept of genetic assimilation has been invoked in discussions concerning the nature of these mechanisms at the genetic level. The essential idea is that what was formerly expressed under certain conditions in the development of some individuals eventually becomes "genetically assimilated" and observable over entire populations. While the parallel drawn between ontogenetic and phylogenetic processes was appealing, the mechanisms proposed to explain this assimilation remained vague and ill-defined (see Cairns, Gariépy, & Hood, 1990; Gottlieb, 1991). On this issue, our results suggested the interesting possibility that genetically-linked differences in behavior may be mediated through alterations in rates of development. Indeed, the major difference between the lines in the cross-sectional study conducted in S_{13} was the amount of change (or departure) from the early stages observed as a result of maturation, or aging.

Several aspects of the results pointed to the possibility that a heterochrony (i.e., a change in developmental rate over successive generations) had been involved in the rapid line differentiation. This possibility was first indicated by Cairns et al. (1983) when the NC selection program was in its 4th generation. At this point, 2 longitudinal studies had been conducted, one in S_1 and the other in S_4, with the intent of comparing the developmental trajectories obtained for attack measures in each line across generations. The first generation showed massive developmental changes (in the direction of a heightened tendency to attack) across the successively older, but inexperienced animals, and depicted essentially the same functions for the two lines. Exactly the same developmental profile was obtained for the 4th generation of high-aggressive animals. The only cross-generational change in developmental function took place in the low-aggressive line. The attack scores of pubertal and older animals in S_4 were then significantly lower than those of the high-aggressive animals, and were also lower than those of the ancestral (S_1) generation of low-aggressive animals.

Cairns et al. (1983) tentatively suggested that the results were consistent with de Beer's (1958) proposal that evolutionary changes may be brought about through changes in rates of development across generations. This interpretation predicted that the initial direction of change observed between S_1 and S_4 would be maintained and accentuated in subsequent generations. The data obtained in S_{13} (Figure 3, cross-sectional data) confirmed the predicted trend. In this generation of low-aggressive males, the tendency to attack over ontogeny showed very little change from the prepubertal level. This trend was in sharp contrast with the 4th and especially the first generations of low-aggressive animals where aging in isolation was sufficient to consolidate a substantial propensity to attack at puberty. As expected, the developmental changes in the 13th generation of high-aggressive animals still closely matched those depicted for the S_1 and S_4 generations (see Figure 5 in Cairns, Gariépy, & Hood, 1990). By reference to de Beer's (1958) categories of heterochrony, the progressive change observed in the developmental trajectory of the low line over generations was described as a neoteny (i.e., the persistence of "immature" features progressively longer in the ontogenies of descendent generations).

The findings on heterochrony had an important implication for the formulation of a consistent model of the mediation of aggressive behavior: If a neotenic trend had been established in the aggressive behavior of the low line, it should be possible to

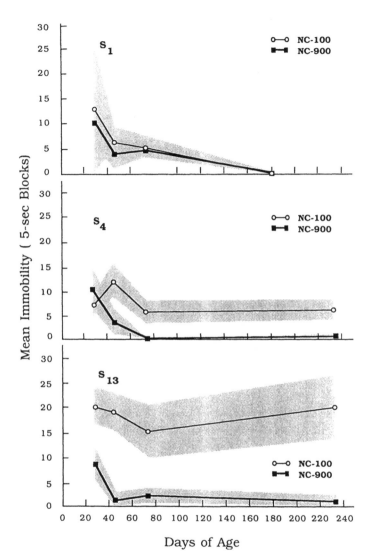

Figure 5: Developmental trajectories for behavioral immobility in three selected generations for the low-aggressive line (NC100: above) and the high-aggressive line (NC900: below). Shading indicates standard error. Note: Data are from Development, microevolution, and social behavior by Cairns, Gariépy, & Hood, *Psychological Review*, 97, p. 60. © 1990 by the American Psychological Association.

demonstrate a similar trend for the tendency to freeze upon social contact. Specifically, it was expected that the developmental extinction of the freezing response would be progressively delayed to later stages of development across the same S_1, S_4 and S_{13} generations. For the convenience of the present discussion, the results published in Cairns et al. (1990) are reproduced here in Figure 5. As seen in this figure, the tendency to freeze in a social context following isolation was fairly high among prebubertal animals (day 30). This was the case for both high- and low-aggressive animals born in S_1, S_4, and S_{13}. According to expectations, the cross-sectional studies indicated a systematic change in the rate of extinction of the freezing response over the ontogeny of low-aggressive animals. Across the successive generations, the propensity to freeze upon social contact was maintained into progressively later stages of development in this line. The heterochronic changes in the propensity to freeze over the generations were inversely correlated to those observed in the propensity to attack. Again, no cross-generational change was observed in the developmental functions of the high-aggressive line.

Further observations were conducted in order to determine the course of the freezing response prior to day 30. Since the propensity to freeze is rarely observed among the young offspring of many mammalian species (Kagan, Reznick, Clarke, & Snidman, 1984; Rothbart, 1988), the goal was to determine whether freezing would be augmented during this early developmental period, and whether its consolidation would occur at the same rate for the two lines. Two separate investigations (S_{15} and S_{23}), where subjects were given only one experience in the dyadic test, either at day 24[1], day 27, or day 30, showed that the tendency to freeze undergoes substantial changes during this seemingly short period. In the high-aggressive line, freezing was well established by day 24, was fully consolidated at day 27, and extinction had already begun by day 30. By comparison, freezing levels were lower among low-aggressive animals at day 24. By day 27 however, they froze at the same high rate as that of high-aggressive animals, and no decline occurred at 30 days of age (Cook & Gariépy, 1991). The line difference in freezing at day 24 did not reach significance but the same trend was replicated for

S_{15} and S_{23}. The independent values obtained for freezing at day 30 in the two studies conformed closely to those obtained in S_{13}, and were consistent with the absence of extinction found in this generation in the subsequent ontogeny of low-aggressive animals. Further research will be needed to determine whether this trend reflects an earlier establishment of the freezing response in the high-aggressive line relative to the low-aggressive one, or a developmental acceleration in the high-aggressive line.

This last piece of developmental information was important in demonstrating that social inhibition was developmentally consolidated to the same extent in the two lines, with the difference that both the establishment and the extinction of this response occurred earlier in the high-aggressive line. As a whole, the studies conducted during this selective breeding program supported the view that a general avenue for change at the genetic level was a modification (in the present case, a neoteny) of the developmental course (establishment, consolidation, and extinction) of a critical component of behavioral organization (see King & Wilson, 1975, for an interesting discussion of the same mechanism in primate evolution).

This research has demonstrated a surprising plasticity in the expression of aggressive behavior. The selective pressure for high and low levels of aggression resulted in a rapid differentiation of the lines. Although firmly established, the differences in genetic background were masked when, even in a minimal amount, appropriate social experience was given. Moreover, behavioral line differences varied in magnitude as a function of age, and the expression of these differences strongly depended upon the rearing history of the subjects. Instead of favoring the view that behavior can be fixed by genes or by experience, these results support the notion that behavior is essentially an adaptive "device" provided with efficient mechanisms enabling rapid change and reorganization.

Except for a slight but significant difference in weight (NC100 is heavier than NC900), the selected lines are not distinguishable from each other in appearance and in the performance of most behavior patterns. Similarly, when these mice attack, they do so in a species-typical, stereotyped fashion regardless of selection line. The line differences arise not in forms of aggressive behavior, but in the thresholds for inhibition/elicitation. Perhaps the most important aspect of the findings is that whatever the time frame considered, transgenerational, maturational, or experiential, quantitative variations in these thresholds seem sufficient to bring about rapid and efficient reorganizations in behavior and social interactions.

The Neurobiological Mediation of Aggressive Behavior

The detailed behavioral characterization of the NC selected lines provided a solid basis for examining the physiological pathways mediating the expression of aggressive behavior. Past research on this question has shown that both gonadal and neurobiological functions are involved. In the first case, the evidence is provided by research linking aggression and gonadal hormones (e.g. Gandelman, 1980; Olweus, 1980; Reinisch, 1976; Rose, Bernstein, & Gordon, 1975), and research in behavior genetics linking aggression and the Y-chromosome (see Michard & Carlier, 1985, for a review). The evidence for neurobiological regulation is supported by research showing that animals that differ in aggressive propensity because of their particular genetic or developmental background show corresponding differences in neurobiological functions (Bernard, Finkelstein, & Everett, 1975; Lagerspetz, Tirri, & Lagerspetz, 1968; Valzelli, 1979; Valzelli & Bernasconi, 1979).

In the context of the NC selection program, the hypothesis of hormonal mediation had several implications. Among them was the prediction that the lines should differ in levels of circulating testosterone and related steroids. The potential involvement of the Y-chromosome also predicted that the line differences would not be observed among the females. Concerning the second prediction, previous research showed that the female descendants of male-selected lines generally do not differ in aggressiveness (Lagerspetz & Lagerspetz, 1971; Van Oortmerssen & Bakker, 1981). Similarly, Hyde & Ebert (1976) reported that selective breeding for female aggressiveness failed to produce parallel differences in the descendent lines of males. According to Fuller & Thompson (1978), the evidence meant that the genetic regulation of aggressive behavior follows different pathways in males and females.

Hood & Cairns (1988) were curious to see if they could verify the same lack of cross-sex inheritance in their selected lines. In doing so, they modified an important aspect of the traditional methodology. Instead of introducing their females to a strange animal in a neutral cage, they used an intruder test where a strange mouse was placed in the home cage of a nursing female (three days postpartum) or a group of virgin females. The goal of this procedure was to create sex-appropriate testing conditions. A new territory may be a strong incentive for fighting among males, but may be irrelevant to females. As shown by Green (1978) and St-John & Corning (1973), female aggression is especially observed in the defense of the brood against an intruder. When they were tested under these conditions, the females exhibited differences that paralleled those observed in the male lines. The NC900 females vigorously attacked intruders while NC100 females did not (Hood & Cairns, 1988). In a related experiment, Lagerspetz and Lagerspetz (1975) showed that early and repeated administration of androgens induced aggression (in a neutral cage) in their high-aggressive line, but not in their low-aggressive line of females. Thus, across different methodologies and selected lines, no evidence was found to support the postulated link between sex differences in aggressiveness and the Y-chromosome. These studies rather suggested that aggressiveness in the two sexes is regulated, at least in part, through a common (autosomal) physiological pathway.

The effects of male selection on female aggression also contradicted the hypothesis that the male lines should differ in levels of circulating testosterone. As expected, our measures of this hormone for pubertal males revealed essentially the same levels for the two lines. Moreover, the developmental functions depicted for the two lines indicated the same augmentation over the prepubertal period and a progression toward the same levels at puberty. The low levels measured at day 24 were consistent with the virtual absence of attack behavior among the animals of either line that were tested at this age (Lewis, Gariépy, & Mason, in preparation). These results, along with those of Lagerspetz and Lagerspetz (1975), demonstrated that gonadal hormones are necessary but not sufficient for the expression of genetic differences in aggressive behavior. As shown by the behavioral research, one mechanism for the expression of these differences was the development of a response (freezing) which is incompatible with the initiation of attacks. There is a large body of evidence suggesting that genetic differences in behavioral inhibition and aggressive behavior are mediated through central brain mechanisms (Adamec, Stark-Adamec, 1986; Kagan, Reznick, Clarke, & Snidman, 1984; Louilot, LeMoal, & Simon, 1986). We have attempted, in collaboration with the neurobiologist Mark Lewis[2] from the Brain Development Research Center at UNC, to unravel some of these mechanisms.

On the basis of the known behavioral line differences and the current literature on the neurobiological substrates for the same behaviors, it appeared promising to conduct neurochemical analyses of the mesolimbic and striatal sensorimotor structures for the two lines. For instance, earlier lesion studies have shown that the nucleus accumbens is an important terminal area and output system of the mesolimbic dopaminergic pathway, and that it plays a key role in the initiation of responses to both social and nonsocial stimuli (Louilot et al., 1986). More specifically, the nucleus accumbens has been shown to be involved in the mediation of the adaptive response toward an aggressive intruder, even though the response to such an intruder was freezing or immobility (Taghzouti, Simon, Louilot, Herman, & LeMoal, 1985). Research also demonstrated a role for the nigrostriatal dopaminergic system in regulating the ability to initiate adaptive responses rapidly (Kelly, Domestik, & Nauta, 1982; Nabeshima, Katoh, Hiramatsu, & Kameyama, 1986). On this issue, there is evidence that dopaminergic activity increases in the preparatory phase of appetitive or instrumental behavior, but not in the following consummatory phase. According to Scheel-Krüger, and Willner (1991), the dopaminergic systems function as motivators to activate and direct behavior toward the goal. In general, both signals predicting reward and approach behavior, and stressors which predict punishment and result in avoidance or escape, activate the mesolimbic and nigrostriatal dopaminergic systems.

In a series of studies that began in the 16th generation of selection, S_{16}, monoamine concentrations (e.g. dopamine, norepinephrine, serotonin, and their acidic metabolites) were determined for several discrete areas of the basal ganglia and striatum for the two selected lines. In addition to these areas, selected limbic regions having important projections to the mesolimbic and/or nigrostriatal dopaminergic systems have been assayed. These regions included the amygdala and the lateral hypothalamus where lesions are known to have effects similar to lesions in the mesolimbic dopaminergic system (Nishino et al., 1987; Yamamoto et al., 1989), and the hippocampus which is involved in the processing of the overall significance of the relationships among multiple stimuli (Eichenbaum et al., 1988).

The initial analyses were conducted using brain tissue of animals that had been sacrificed at day 45 without being tested and which had been in continuous isolation since weaning.[3] Brain samples were obtained using microdissection by punch and were assayed by high performance liquid chromatography. Although a wide range of monoamines has been assayed for each brain area investigated, the line differences that we found were discrete and limited to dopamine concentrations in the nucleus accumbens and the caudate nucleus. These two nuclei are, respectively, important terminal areas of the mesolimbic and nigrostriatal dopaminergic pathways. In these two areas, but especially in the nucleus accumbens, dopamine concentrations and its acidic metabolites were higher in the high-aggressive line. These concentrations are presented in Figure 6 for the nucleus accumbens, and Figure 7 for the caudate nucleus. Exactly the same line differences have been replicated in analyses of the same nuclei conducted over five different generations.

In his research with aging, neonatally isolated monkeys (the Harlow monkeys), Mark Lewis has shown that organisms which by virtue of genetic background or prior experience exhibit low dopamine concentrations also tend to show an increased density, or upregulation, of dopamine receptors. An analysis of these densities has been performed for our two lines by determining the concentrations of recognition sites for

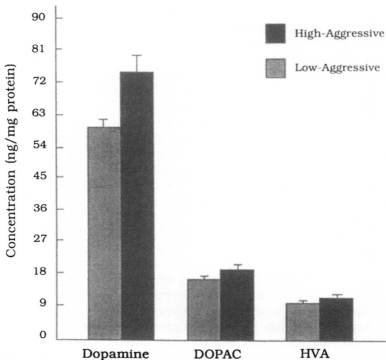

Figure 6: Dopamine concentrations and its acidic metabolites in the nucleus accumbens for the high- and low-aggressive lines. The ordinate indicates dopamine concentration in nanograms per gram of wet tissue.

dopaminergic ligands in both the nucleus accumbens and the caudate nucleus. Quantitative receptor autoradiographic techniques indicated a significantly increased density of these receptors in the low-aggressive line. Specifically, for the two nuclei investigated, D_1 receptor densities were higher among low-aggressive animals. Similar measures obtained for the D_2 receptor revealed higher densities in the rostral caudate nucleus of low-aggressive animals (Lewis, Devaud, Gariépy, Southerland, Mailman, & Cairns, 1992). Additional measures taken at

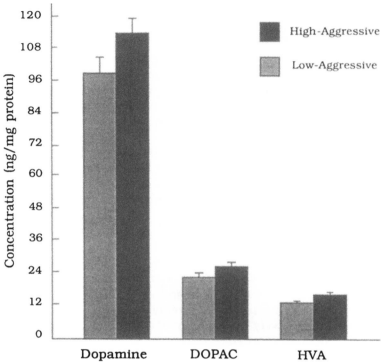

Figure 7: Dopamine concentrations and its acidic metabolites in the caudate nucleus for the high- and low-aggressive lines. The ordinate indicates dopamine concentration in nanograms per gram of wet tissue.

the origin of the two dopaminergic systems showed, by contrast, that the density of D_2 receptors in the substantia nigra and the ventral tegmental area was significantly lower in the low-aggressive line. Since these receptors lie on the bodies of the dopaminergic cells where they act as autoreceptors, the finding suggested that low-aggressive animals have fewer of these cells. Fewer dopaminergic cells at the origin of the mesolimbic and nigrostriatal pathways would explain the reduced dopamine concentrations observed in the terminal areas.

The pattern of line differences observed in neurobiological functions directly paralleled the line differences in behavior. Furthermore, the results were consistent with the proposal that central dopamine is an important mediator of how neocortical and limbic (e.g., amygdala) areas influence complex motor behavior (Louilot et al., 1986). The significance of a line difference in the nucleus accumbens lies especially in the integrative role played by this nucleus as an interface between limbic and striatal sensorimotor structures. As such, this nucleus mediates the integration of emotional responding, motivational states, and the initiation of action.

Although the neurobiological differences between the lines were in the expected direction, and had been identified in the predicted locations, further evidence was needed to demonstrate a functional link between the line differences in neurochemistry and the behavioral line differences. To this end, we investigated the development of mesolimbic and nigrostriatal dopamine concentrations over ontogeny for the two lines, with the goal of verifying a relationship with behavioral development. This study, completed in S_{19}, revealed that the mesolimbic dopaminergic system develops much earlier than the nigrostriatal system. In the two lines, dopamine concentrations in the caudate nucleus augmented massively between day 30 and day 45, and adult levels were not attained before 72 days of age. By contrast, no developmental change was observed for the concentrations measured in the nucleus accumbens. Adult levels were already reached at day 30 when the first measures were taken. Across four life-span developmental points, and for the two nuclei investigated, significant line differences of a nearly constant magnitude were measured, with the highest concentrations observed in the high-aggressive line (Lewis et al., 1991).

A simple comparison between the trends observed in the low-aggressive line in neurochemical and behavioral development was problematic because attack and freezing behaviors maintain in this line the same neotenic level over the life course. On the other hand, the substantial changes taking place in the caudate nucleus matched very well those taking place in the behavioral ontogeny of the high-aggressive line. The absence of such a relationship for the low-aggressive line may reflect dynamic interactions between the nigrostriatal and the mesolimbic dopaminergic systems. For instance, the impact of the developmental changes observed in the caudate nucleus may be masked through an exclusive focus on attacks because dopamine concentrations in the nucleus accumbens remain insufficient to support unprovoked initiations of high-intensity actions. If this view is correct, the behavioral line differences expressed at puberty could be understood in terms of line differences in maturational events taking place fairly early in development.

The difference in developmental rates between the mesolimbic and nigrostriatal dopaminergic systems is important in the present context as it suggests that differences in the timing of social experience may have region-specific effects. With a longer maturation period, the nigrostriatal system may retain more capacity for change through experience than would the mesolimbic system. For instance, the effects of repeated experience on the propensity to attack may be supported by increased turnover rates, increased receptor densities or sensitivities, or a combination of these changes. Research on the neurobiological mediation of experiential effects is still in progress. A preliminary investigation has shown that in both lines repeated social challenges are associated with changes in dopamine turnover rates (but not in concentrations). As expected, these changes also appeared to take place more massively in the most maturationally delayed of the two nuclei, the caudate nucleus (Milko, 1992).

By comparison to the nucleus accumbens, less is known concerning the specific functions of the caudate nucleus (Scheel-Krüger & Willner, 1991). As mentioned earlier, there is evidence that this nucleus is involved in the ability to initiate adaptive responses rapidly (Kelly et al., 1982 and Nabeshima et al., 1986). The dopaminergic activity observed in this nucleus among our repeatedly tested animals would be consistent with this proposal. Without implying advanced cognitive capacities, we can suppose that repeatedly tested and naive animals differ in degree of anticipation and preparedness to stimulation upon entry in the dyadic test. Indeed, a major behavioral difference between the two groups of animals is seen in how rapidly an action is initiated, not in action initiation per se (see Figure 4). Another important difference is that social reactivity and freezing are both

diminished by a factor of two among experienced animals relative to naive animals. These behavioral differences suggest that
the higher metabolic rate seen in the caudate nucleus of experienced animals may reflect the activity of this structure during
the first phases of action initiation. Specifically, this nucleus may
perform important inhibitory functions—including that of self-
regulation of stimulus intensity—which directly or indirectly,
affect the rapidity of behavioral responding. The developmental
trends observed respectively for the caudate and the nucleus accumbens would support such a view. From an adaptationist
standpoint, a fairly early establishment of the capacity to initiate
action effectively should be expected, while the ability to fine
tune this action through greater stimulus control would continue
to develop in conjunction with the developmental emergence of
more complex adaptive demands.

Pharmacological Manipulations of Central Dopamine

The line differences in neurochemistry and the high metabolic rates observed among experienced animals were consistent
with the view that central dopamine mediates the genetic and
maturational/experiential effects on behavior. The findings suggested that decreased dopamine function may contribute to the
marked social inhibition observed in the low-aggressive line of
mice. Accordingly, we verified if a dopamine agonist would
result in a disinhibition of freezing with a consequent increase in
aggression in the low-aggressive line. This was done by challenging high- and low-aggressive animals with variously potent and
site-specific dopamine agonists and antagonists, and by comparing their social interactions in dyadic tests to those of brothers
that served as saline-injected controls.

The most compelling effects on behavior have been ob-
tained in S_{25} using the selective, full-efficacy D_1 receptor agonist
dihydrexidine. In the social interaction tests, reduced aggression
in the high-aggressive line was dose-dependent. Instead of
aggression, these animals displayed a marked reactivity to mild
social stimulation. This reactivity interfered with the attack
behavior typical of this line such that, at the highest doses of

dihydrexidine, no difference in aggression was observed between the two lines. In the low-aggressive line, rather than altering freezing behavior and disinhibiting aggression, the drug also induced strong reactive responses to mild social stimuli, and reduced the rates of nonagonistic approaches (Lewis, Gariépy, Gendreau, Davis, Nichols, & Mailman, 1994). In the two lines, the high reactivity of the experimental subjects made them at least twice as likely to be attacked by the partner mouse than control non-injected animals. We have observed comparable changes in attack patterns and reactivity in an earlier generation (S_{20}) with the direct-acting dopamine agonist, apomorphine. This drug, however, also induced marked stereotypies, and did not affect reactivity as specifically as did dihydrexidine.

The importance of D_1/D_2 interactions in the expression of a variety of behaviors is now widely appreciated (Bordi & Meller, 1989; Braun & Chase, 1986; Mashurano & Waddington, 1986). To gain insight on the role of these interactions in supporting reactive responses, we pretreated mice either with a D_1 or a D_2 antagonist, prior to the administration of dihydrexidine. Pretreatment with a D_1 antagonist (SCH23390), but not with a D_2 antagonist (remoxipride), inhibited the dihydrexidine-induced reactivity in both lines, and suggested that this reactivity is largely D_1-mediated. However, another effect of the D_1 antagonist pretreatment was to reduce the line-characteristic levels of attacks and nonagonistic initiations below that of the respective control groups (Lewis et al., 1994). Since the same D_1 antagonist has been shown to reduce amphetamine-induced locomotion—a behavior believed to be largely mediated by the D_2 receptor (Mailman et. al., 1984)—the reduced rates in agonistic and non-agonistic initiations suggest an interaction between these two receptor types. It may be that administration of the D_1 antagonist affected behaviors (escapes and attacks) that are jointly dependent on the coactivation of both D_1 and D_2 receptors.

So far, none of the dopamine-specific agents that we have used altered significantly the freezing response so characteristic of the low-aggressive line. However, this can not be taken to mean that central dopamine is not involved in the mediation of this behavioral response. In fact, there is abundant evidence in

the literature cited above that the mesolimbic and the nigrostriatal dopaminergic pathways regulate comparable or related responses. The complexity of the structures investigated, including
the multiplicity of monoaminergic systems involved, the bidirectional interactions among these systems, and the importance
of their projections to surrounding structures (e.g. amygdala,
hyppocampus, prefrontal cortex), leaves plenty of room for further investigation. The major behavioral effect of dihydrexidine
was certainly not anticipated and not consistent with our initial
hypotheses. The results forced a re-examination of the basic
working model and called especially for a fresh appraisal of the
question of mediation.

The Question of Mediation Reconsidered

The line difference in mesolimbic and nigrostriatal
dopamine concentrations has been replicated in every generation
since S_{16} when the first neurochemical analyses were undertaken. The direction of these differences also conform to
expectations given the known line differences in behavior
patterns. The question remains: What specific aspect(s) of behavioral organization do the neurochemical differences found
between the lines mediate: stimulus appraisal, reactivity to
stimulative changes, the control/inhibition of action initiation
(which for the moment can not be completely ruled out), the
more general approach-withdrawal orientation of action, or the
dynamic relationship between these different aspects? The latter
proposition would be most likely, given the evidence for the
implication of the long-length dopaminergic systems in all
stages of behavioral responding, from stimulus appraisal, to
motivation, to action initiation. The pharmacological manipulations involving dihydrexidine seemed to interfere more
specifically with the initial phases of this sequence, namely, the
regulation of stimulus intensity and the associated emotional
arousal. If this interpretation is correct, high-aggressive animals,
with higher concentrations of dopamine, should be naturally
predisposed to be more aroused by stimulative changes than

low-aggressive animals and should exhibit more observable reactivity to these changes.

The augmentation (and exaggeration) of social reactivity among the animals that were challenged with dihydrexidine suggested a potential line difference in forms of reactivity. Specifically, animals in the high-aggressive line showed a significantly greater readiness (as measured by shorter latencies) than their low-aggressive counterpart to jump violently and to escape in response to the mild social stimulation provided by the partner mouse. The rates of these responses calculated over the first two minutes of the dyadic test, or prior to the occurrence of the first agonistic initiation, also tended to be higher in the high aggression-line. A similar but reversed trend was identified for a less dramatic form of social reactivity, reflexive kicking while leaving (as opposed to escaping), which tended to occur at a higher rate in the low-aggressive line. Although the line differences in rates did not reach significance for either form of reactivity, the pattern was consistent enough to warrant a similar analysis for nontreated animals.

When the rates of social reactivity were computed in the same way (i.e. prior to the occurrence of attacks, and with the same distinction of forms) across the first 24 generations, a slight but significant line difference in the expected direction was observed. This analysis indicated a tendency among low-aggressive animals to exhibit more reflexive kicking during the preagonistic phase of social interactions than high-aggressive animals which, in turn, showed higher rates of jumping and escaping during the same phase. In the light of these results, the previous failure to identify a line difference in behavioral reactivity (Gariépy et al., 1988), may be attributed to the fact that frequencies were calculated over the entire duration of the dyadic test and that behavioral categories did not include escaping and jumping. In these analyses a confounding factor was that animals of both lines normally tend to become highly reactive following a severe defeat.

The new findings on reactivity were exciting but required a cautious interpretation. First, the magnitude of the line differences for the three forms of reactivity was rather modest across the generations, and was not always significant. A second reason for a cautious interpretation was the large variability of the measures within generations. This variability was such that line differences could be largely attributable to the high scores of a few animals. As indicated by cluster analyses, within each line but especially among high-aggressive animals, reactivity was high for a few individuals, mostly in the form of escapes and jumps, and was almost absent from the behavioral repertoire of the others (Clubb & Gariépy, 1991; Hunsberger, 1992). Approximately 20 percent of the males within each generation are found exhibiting this unusually high reactivity in the high-aggressive line. The freezing response, by contrast, is less variable, is observed to different degrees among a larger proportion of the low-aggressive animals, and it has remained a virtually exclusive characteristic of this line since S_4.

The regular persistence of a sizeable proportion of unusually high reactive animals within each generation is a rather puzzling phenomenon because the continued elimination of animals not qualified for reproduction (between 15 percent and 25 percent in each generation) should have normally precipitated a diminution of this proportion. Recall that these highly reactive animals tend to be attacked, rather than initiating attacks themselves, and that they are often defeated. In the high aggression line, the generally low rate of attack of these animals makes them prime candidates for elimination. Similarly, the aggressive interchanges in which reactive low-aggressive animals are involved often trigger a few counterattacks, a dyadic effect which generally leads to their removal from the reproductive pool for that line. Yet, the proportion of animals that are very reactive to novel social stimulation has remained approximately constant in the two lines across the successive generations, even though this phenotype was actively selected against.

This intriguing selective outcome may be clarified if examined with reference to the view presented earlier (p. 246) that behavior systems consist of correlated and mutually supportive functions. It would be rather surprising if a strong network of correlations would not exist between the various components leading to an action. For instance, mechanisms controlling the perceived intensity of stimulations, the subsequent motivation to attack or flee, and the eventual initiation of an action, should be expected to operate jointly in support of the effective organization of one or the other strategy. Thus, if a strong selective pressure for a high propensity to attack is exerted, mechanisms supporting the autoregulation of stimulus intensity, the corresponding changes in motivational states, and the physiological/behavioral indexes of such changes, should be expected to operate jointly in the service of consolidating agonistic responding.

The same reasoning would explicate the line differences in forms of reactivity. For instance, we would not expect the persistence of violent jumps and escapes in a line where strong selective pressures were exerted for very low levels of attacks. In this case, all phases of behavioral regulation should collaborate in reducing the probability that social interactions will escalate to attacks. The evidence suggests that the system serves this end by facilitating a reduction of the intensity of the stimulation (behaviorally) returned to the (social) stimulative source. This regulative pathway appears to preclude the kinds of physiological/ behavioral changes associated with percepts of high intensity stimulation and the motivation to escape and flee. The reduction of stimulus intensity in this regulative context seems to be achieved through the more quiet action of leaving, or through behavioral immobility which limits even more efficiently the organism's input to the social interaction.

If this view is correct, the systemic support of an agonistic predisposition would involve a propensity to be easily aroused by stimulative changes and a correspondingly high degree of activation. The observation of social interchanges suggest that, when for certain individuals arousal and activation exceed a critical level, the efficient organization of attacks becomes compromised and escape-oriented responses are mobilized. This would explain why escapes and jumps dominate the behavioral repertoire of certain individuals and are virtually absent in other animals. In this case, our measures of reactivity would be more appropriately viewed as reflecting the organism's motivational state for action. Motivational flips orienting the organism toward the source of stimulation (attack), or away from it (escape), would be consistent with the peculiarly skewed distribution of our reactivity measures. We have reasons to think on the basis of the variability observed in dopamine concentrations that the underlying individual differences in autoregulative functions is probably more normally distributed. Considering another level of analysis, the systemic constraints imposed by the linkages between arousal, reaction/activation and the initiation of attacks, in conjunction with the parabolic function relating these components, would explain the unidirectional effects of selective breeding and the large variability observed within and between generations in attack behavior (see Figure 1).

The line differences in reactivity is not only a matter of quantity, but also a matter of quality. As we have seen, the constraints on behavioral organization in the low-aggressive line preclude reactive manifestations in the form of jumping and escaping. Barring these manifestations, under conditions of high arousal, low-aggressive line animals tend to simply move away from the stimulative source (leave). When less aroused by the stimulation, they approach the unfamiliar mouse, and the two animals are rapidly seen exchanging mild investigative actions. Note that we have repeatedly found a positive correlation between rates of kicking and the response of leaving. By contrast, correlations were negative between kicking rates and those of non-agonistic social investigation. Just like the alternative between attacks and escapes is biased in the high-aggressive line by individual differences in arousability, so is the alternative between leaving and social investigation in the low-aggressive line. The notion that stimulus appraisal has a canalizing impact on the organization of a response is empirically supported by the fact that, in both lines, even less reactive animals often tend to be startled on their very first contact with the partner mouse. But this reaction, by itself, is a poor predictor of other forms of behavioral reactivity. Instead of predicting further reactive responses, being startled often leads to the rapid consolidation of attacks in the high-aggressive line, and to sustained investigative behavior in the low-aggressive line.

Taken together, the pharmacological, neurochemical, and behavioral research suggested that the line difference in central dopamine directly affects mechanisms underlying the regulation of stimulus and action intensity. The line difference in behavior arises because of the amplification at the systemic level of a relatively small difference in regulative activity during the initial phase of behavioral responding. Such an effect ultimately constrains, in a line-specific way, the options available for adaptive responding when exposed to novel social stimuli.

The implication of the dopaminergic systems in all stages of action preparation makes it ultimately difficult to envision how the same systems could also regulate the propensity to freeze upon social contact. Mediation through other systems (e.g., opiates, GABA) is more likely. Weerts, Miller, Hood, & Miczek (1992) investigated this possibility using the parallel NC lines maintained at Pennsylvania State University by Kathryn Hood (see Hood, chapter 2). Their work on $GABA_A$-benzodiazepine receptor binding in vivo indicated greater affinities among low-aggressive animals than among high-aggressive animals. Preliminary research conducted in our laboratory on the densities of GABA binding sites similarly showed higher values for the low-aggressive line. The possibility of a linkage between the known inhibitory functions of the GABAergic system and the propensity to freeze in the low-aggressive line is an interesting one, and will continue to be investigated.

The indication that central dopamine regulates all phases of behavioral responding (e.g., Louilot et al., 1986; Scheel-Krüger & Willner, 1991) is entirely consistent with a systemic view of behavioral adaptations. A discussion of how such a view may clarify the ways in which approach-withdrawal processes operate to support social adaptations is the object of the next section.

A/W Processes and Social Adaptation

The distinction made by Schneirla between the tonic and the phasic aspects of approach/withdrawal processes is important as it specifies that observable behavior represents a phasic change in these processes. By definition, phasic refers to the fact that some event took place within a system, rather than referring to the state of that system. During a phase transition, a change in stimulative conditions has occurred with a corresponding increase of activity in the A- or W-systems. Activation within these systems normally supports behavioral responses which create or restore conditions favorable to the continuous, low intensity A-processes that are basic to species-typical development. While behavior and the physiological changes observed during activation are ephemeral, the conditions created internally and externally through action determine the state of the system.

For the isolated male mice exposed for the first time at puberty to an unfamiliar male, the dyadic situation constitutes a sudden and massive change in stimulative conditions. Accordingly, most of what we observe in the dyadic tests reflects an increase of activity in the W-system. By nature, this activity can not be maintained continuously as the predominant tonic state without jeopardizing the well-being of the organism (e.g. decreased immune functions). In fact, it is the temporary removal of conditions which favor the operation of A-processes that activates the W-system. This was well illustrated in the triadic tests, where after fighting to establish its social status, the dominant male was observed copulating with the female and eventually resting with her in a paper nest that they had jointly constructed. While the function of activity in the W-system is always the same, how it operates to support adaptive responses is highly variable, as the options for mediation change with genetic background, developmental-experiential status, and a changing social dynamic.

Hierarchical Organization and Approach/Withdrawal Responding

One of the most difficult concepts in the behavioral sciences is the concept of behavior itself. Traditionally, behavior has been treated as a dependent variable, or a predictable outcome. On this premise, the task of the science has been largely defined as the identification of the causal factors that control behavior. There is a growing consensus that such a framework may impair rather than facilitate our appraisal of behavioral phenomena (e.g. Cairns, 1993; Piaget, 1978; Tobach, 1969). As pointed out by Mayr (1982), the insistence borrowed from the physical sciences on prediction and control may lead to a profound misunderstanding of the distinctive properties of living matter, including its unique capacity to maintain internal organization over time and conditions. Typically, internal organization is maintained through systematic transactions with the environment. These transactions facilitate energetic exchanges, regulate stimulus intensity, and generally serve to establish conditions that support preservation and development (see also Baldwin, 1894 and Preyer, 1893). The question is: "Can we maintain a mechanistic framework which reduces these transactions to their internal and/or external determinants without losing sight of how behavior promotes rapid and reversible adaptations?" It might be of greater heuristic value to place behavior at the origin of a process which functions to bring internal and external conditions into alignment, in a life-preserving way.

The organismic approach in the behavioral sciences advocates the view that living systems owe their functional organization to a developmental process involving both differentiation and hierarchical integration (Werner, 1948). Over the last decades, Gottlieb (1976, 1983, 1992) formalized and expanded this view in a general model describing a hierarchy of systems progressing from the genes to the successively higher levels of neurobiological structures, behavior, and environment. Each level builds upon organization at the lower levels, and with each, new properties and regulative functions emerge. In this model, all components are subordinated to the structural/functional changes taking place in the system as a whole. This is seen in the bidirectional influences that exist throughout ontogeny between the different levels, such that changes in the environment and in behavior influence physiological functions and genetic activity, in the same way that changes at these lower levels contribute further changes in behavior and extraorganismic structures. A logical consequence of this bidirectionality is that behavior, as part of a larger system, is better described in probabilistic terms than in deterministic ones. On the other hand, at the level of the system as a whole, the same bidirectional dependence between structures and functions gives rise over development to a strong network of correlations between genetic activity, neurobiological functions, behavior, and environmental conditions.

The doctrine of psychological levels proposed by Schneirla is similar in many respects to the organismic model formulated by Gottlieb. Although the levels described in the two cases are fundamentally different—levels of psychological functioning in one and organismic levels in the other—both rest on the notions of differentiation, emergent properties, and hierarchical integration. The doctrine of psychological levels is based on the notion that there is in development and in evolution a trend from simple to complex in psychological mediation (Schneirla, 1952). This trend involves a transformation from the primacy of responses based on the sheer intensity of stimulation, to the primacy of configurational patterns. Throughout ontogeny this transformation is guided by forces acting simultaneously from within and from without the organism, such that maturation and experience are essentially fused in development. As a result, it becomes impossible to assess stimulus intensity/configuration without reference to the psychological level attained by the organism. Similarly, an analysis of changes in A/W responding requires a shift from a simple measurement of towardness and awayness to a configural analysis of internal structures for perception and action, and of their relations to the properties of extraorganismic structures.

Beyond their common points, Schneirla's doctrine and Gottlieb's model each bring a unique perspective on the questions of adaptation and development. The view suggested by Schneirla that development within the organism and the parallel changing construction of the environment are intimately fused has important implications. Among them is the implication that the environment develops in a way that parallels organismic development, namely, changing from simple to complex with the successive emergence of higher properties and configural patterns. Sameroff (1983) offered a similar view in a synthetic analysis of developmental systems. On the relation between the developmental changes in the intra- and the extraorganismic systems, he wrote that they are continually "united in new cognitive organizations that serve as the basis for further hierarchical developments" (Sameroff, 1983, p. 269). An important contribution from Gottlieb's model to the question of adaptation and development is the specification that any organismic level can be viewed alternatively as structure or function depending on the direction of influence that one is interested in within the system. If, for instance, the neurobiological and the behavioral levels are considered, the neurobiological level is investigated with respect to its activity, and behavior with regard to structural changes. If the same analysis is conducted at the next higher level of functional relationships, between behavior and environment, behavioral activity is now investigated for its impact on changes in extraorganismic structures. The alternation in the role that each level plays as function or structure provides a comprehensive perspective on how activity within the system induces change in its structural organization.

What is left somewhat unclear, however, in both Schneirla's and Gottlieb's perspectives is the nature and place of behavior within the system as a whole. For Schneirla, approach/withdrawal responses, considered either in their quantitative or configural aspects, constitute behavior. Although A/W processes are believed to be at the origin of adaptive changes, and that the processes guiding intra- and extraorganismic changes are well described, no special properties are specified for behavior. Similarly, in Gottlieb's model, behavior is regarded as one level in a systemic hierarchy of bidirectional influences between levels. But if behavior represents a phasic change in A/W processes, as suggested by Schneirla, then it is by nature ephemeral and elusive, and cannot be reduced to a structural component of the system. Moreover, if behavior is what brings about adaptive change, as suggested by the A/W theory, then behavior should be at the origin of a process whereby novelties are introduced both in internal and external structures, and in their coordination. For behavior to achieve this function, we have to postulate that it cannot be at any point in time completely isomorphic with internal or internal organization. In other words, an understanding of internal and external constraints on behavior does not constitute an understanding of behavior itself.

To be sure, behavioral actions are always correlated with the internal and external configuration of the two systems. This is best seen if it is considered that these systems constitute the two fields within which behavior operates. Hence the possibility to regard the various systemic components as behavioral determinants. In contrast with this view, however, I propose on the basis of the previous discussion that behavior is a life-sustaining device that serves to introduce novelties in the organization of the two systems so as to maintain a state of internal and external organization that promotes self-stabilization and continued adaptation. Behavior itself can not be described as being in a specific state, as can be done for the structures upon which it operates. Rather, behavior is the activity that maintains these states. It follows that behavior is not determined by these systems, not even in a probabilistic sense, but is an active force that exploits their current organization to facilitate a realignment when systemic imbalances arise.

Hierarchical Systems and the Operation of A/W Mechanisms

We have seen in the empirical sections of this manuscript that the social adaptations of mice are flexible and reversible. In spite of genetic and neurobiological constraints on behavioral responding new patterns of adaptation are often achieved which are hardly predictable on the basis of these constraints alone. Rapidity and effective changes in forms of social adaptation were the rule whatever the time frame over which such changes were investigated, transgenerational, ontogenetic, social interactions, or the moment-to-moment adjustments in perception and action. As Cairns, Gariépy and Hood have formulated elsewhere, points of vulnerability exist within both intra- and extraorganismic structures which are exploited to facilitate systemic reorganizations and subsequent adaptation (Cairns et al., 1990). It is an important property of the hierarchical organization of the two structures to offer several points of entry for adaptive reorganization through multiple levels of influence, and the overall dependence of the system as a whole on the state of all of its constituents.

In conclusion, I offer the proposal that behavior as an active interface between internal and external structures exploits the points most vulnerable in the two structures to promote novel forms of adaptation. It is worth noting that some of these points are the same ones that are exploited over vastly different time frames. In the research that I described on the social adaptations of mice, such points of vulnerability involved stimulus perception, and the manipulation of the social source of stimulation itself. The mechanism whereby these points of entry were addressed, however, differed vastly depending on the time frame over which adaptive change was considered. These mechanisms involved changes in the timing of genetic activity, quantitative changes in neurochemical metabolism and in hormonal balance, and quantitative as well as configural changes (e.g., from subordination to dominance) in the stimulative conditions of the social environment. Perhaps the most remarkable aspect of the behavioral function is its capacity to exploit these different mechanisms in such a way that mutual reinforcement or mutual cancellation is always possible. It is precisely because of this capacity that behavior can function as an adaptive device in a system which otherwise tends to conservation and continuity in structure and function.

REFERENCES

Adamec, R. E., & Stark-Adamec, C. (1986). Limbic hyperfunction, limbic epilepsy, and interictal behavior. In Doane, B. K., & Livingston, K. E. (Eds.), *The limbic system*, pp. 129–145. New York: Raven Press.

Baldwin, J. M. (1894). The theory of development. In J. M. Baldwin, *Mental development in the child and the race: Methods and processes*, pp. 170– 220. New York: Macmillan.

Banks, E. M. (1962). A time and motion study of prefighting behavior in mice. *Journal of Genetic Psychology*, 101, 165–183.

Benton, D., Goldsmith, J. F., Gamal-el-Din, L., Brain, P. F., & Huckle-bridge, F. H. (1978). Adrenal activity in isolated mice and mice of different social status. *Physiology and Behavior*, 20, 459–464.

Benton, D., Brain, P. F., & Goldsmith, J. F. (1979). Effect of prior housing on endocrine response to differential caging in male TO strain mice. *Physiological Psychology*, 7, 89–92.

Bernard, B. K., Finkelstein, E. R., & Everett, G. M. (1975). Alteration in mouse aggressive behavior and brain monoamine dynamics as a function of age. *Physiology and Behavior*, 15, 731–736.

Bordi, F., & Meller, E. (1989). Enhanced behavioral sterotypies elicited by intrastriatal injection of D_1 and D_2 dopamine agonists in intact rats. *Brain Research, 504*, 276–283.

Brain, P. F., & Benton, D. (1983). Conditions of housing, hormones, and aggressive behavior. In B. B. Svare (Ed.), *Hormones and aggressive behavior*, pp. 351–372. New York: Plenum Press.

Brain, P. F. (1989). The adaptiveness of house mouse aggression. In P. F. Brain, D. Mainardi, & S. Parmigiani (Eds.), *House mouse aggression*, pp. 1–22. London: Harwood Academic Publishers.

Braun, A. R., & Chase, T. N. (1986). Obligatory D_1/D_2 receptor interaction in the generation of dopamine-agonist related behaviors. *European Journal of Pharmacology, 131*, 301–306.

Cairns, R. B., McGuire, A. M., & Gariépy, J.-L. (1993). Developmental behavior genetics: Fusion, correlated constraints, and timing. In D. F. Hay and A. Angold, *Precursors and causes in development and pathology*, pp. 87–122. London: John Wiley & Son Ltd.

Cairns, R. B., & Nakelski, J. S. (1971). On fighting in mice: Ontogenetic and experimental determinants. *Journal of Comparative and Physiological Psychology*, 74, 354–364.

Cairns, R. B., & Scholz, S. D. (1973). Fighting in mice: Dyadic escalation and what is learned. *Journal of Comparative and Physiological Psychology, 85*, 540–550.

Cairns, R. B. (1973). Fighting and punishment from a developmental perspective. In J. K. Cole & D. D. Jensen (Eds.), *Nebraska Symposium on Motivation, Vol. 20*, pp. 59–124. Lincoln: University of Nebraska Press.

———. (1993). Belated but bedazzling: Timing and genetic influence in social development. In G. Turkewity & D. A. Devenny (Eds.), *Developmental time and timing* (pp. 61–84). Hillsdale, NJ: Erlbaum.

Cairns, R. B., MacCombie, D. J., & Hood, K. E. (1983). A developmental-genetic analysis of aggressive behavior in mice: I. Behavioral outcomes. *Journal of Comparative Psychology, 97*, 69–89.

Cairns, R. B., Hood, K. E., & Midlam, J. (1985). On fighting in mice: is there a sensitive period for isolation effects? *Animal Behaviour, 33*, 166–180.

Cairns, R. B., Gariépy, J.-L., & Hood, K. E. (1990). Development, micro-evolution and social behavior. *Psychological Review, 97*, 49–65.

Chance, M. R. A., & Jolly, C. J. (1970). *Social groups of monkeys, apes and men*. New York: Dutton.

Clubb, P. A., & Gariépy, J.-L. (1991). The effects of rearing conditions on the social behavior of mice (*Mus domesticus*) selectively bred for high and low levels of aggression. Paper presented at the annual meeting of the Animal Behavior Society, Wilmington, June 1991.

Cook, R. M., & Gariépy, J.-L. (1991). The effects of early experience on mice (*Mus domesticus*) selectively bred for high and low levels of aggression. Paper presented at the annual meeting of the Animal Behavior Society, Wilmington, June 1991.

Crowcroft, P. (1966). *Mice all over*. London: Foulis.

de Beer, G. (1958). *Embryos and ancestors*, 3rd Ed. London: Oxford University Press.

Eichenbaum, H., Fagan, A., Mathews, P., & Cohen, N. J. (1988). Hypo-campal system dysfunction and odor discrimination learning in rats: Impairment or facilitation depending on representational demands. *Behavioral Neuroscience, 102*, 331–339.

Essman, W. B. (1966). The development of activity differences in isolated and aggregated mice. *Animal Behaviour, 14*, 406–409.

Fuller, J. L., & Thompson, W. R. (1978). *Foundations of behavior genetics*. St-Louis, MO: Mosby.

Fuller, J. L. (1967). Experiential deprivation and later behavior. *Science, 158*, 1645–1652.

Gandelman, R. (1980). Gonadal hormones and the induction of intra-specific fighting in mice. *Neuroscience & Biobehavioral Reviews, 4*, 133–140.

Gariépy, J.-L. (1991). Genetic biases, experiential constraints, and mechanisms of adaptation. Paper presented at the annual meeting of the Animal Behavior Society, Wilmington, June 1991.

Gariépy, J.-L., Hood, K. E., & Cairns, R. B. (1988). A developmental-genetic analysis of aggressive behavior in mice: III. Behavioral mediation by heightened reactivity or increased immobility? *Journal of Comparative Psychology, 102*, 392–399.

Goldstein, M. (1974). Brain research and violent behavior. *Archives of Neurology, 30*, 1–35.

Gottlieb, G. (1976). Conceptions of prenatal development: Behavioral embryology. *Psychological Review, 83*, 215–234.

———. (1983). The psychobiological approach to developmental issues. In P. H. Mussen (Ed.), *Handbook of child psychology, Vol. 2* (4th ed.), pp. 1–26. New York: Wiley.

———. (1991). Experiential canalization of behavioral development: Theory. *Developmental Psychology, 27*, 3–34.

———. (1992). *Individual development and evolution: The genesis of novel behavior*. New York: Oxford University Press.

Green, J. A. (1978). Experiential determinants of postpartum aggression in mice. *Journal of Comparative and Physiological Psychology, 92*, 1179–1187.

Griffin, D. R. (1958). *Listening in the dark*. New Haven, Conn.: Yale University Press.

Harlow, H. F., Harlow, M. H., Dodsworth, R. O., & Arling, G. L. (1966). Maternal behavior in rhesus monkey deprived of mothering and peer associations in infancy. *Proceedings of the American Philosophical Society, 110*, 58–66.

Hegmann, J. P., & DeFries, J. C. (1970). Are genetic correlations and environmental correlations correlated? *Nature, 226*, 284–286.

Hood, K. E., & Cairns, R. B. (1988). A developmental-genetic analysis of aggressive behavior in mice: II. Cross-sex inheritance. *Behavior Genetics, 18*, 605–619.

———. (1989). A developmental-genetic analysis of aggressive behavior in mice: IV. Genotype-environment interactions. *Aggressive Behavior, 15*, 361–380.

Hunsberger, H. (1992). Internal and cross-contextual consistency of measures of behavioral reactivity in mice selectively bred for high and low levels of aggression. Unpublished Honors Thesis. University of North Carolina at Chapel Hill.

Hyde, J. S., & Sawyer, T. F. (1980). Selection for agonistic behavior in wild female mice. *Behavior Genetics, 10*, 349–360.

Jones, S. E., & Brain, P. F. (1987). *Behavior Genetics, 17*, 87–96.

Kagan, J., Reznick, J. S., Clarke, C., & Snidman, N. (1984). Behavioral inhibition to the unfamiliar. *Child Development, 55*, 2212–2225.

Kelly, A. E., Domestik, V. B., & Nauta, W. H. J. (1982). The amy-dalostriatal projection in the rat: An anatomical study by antero-grade and retrograde tracing methods. *Neuroscience, 7*, 615–630.

King, J. A. (1977). Behavioral comparisons and evolution. In A. Oliverio (Ed.), *Genetics, environment, and intelligence*, pp. 23–36. Amsterdam: Elsevier/North Holland.

King, M., & Wilson, A. C. (1975). Evolution at two levels in humans and chimpanzees. *Science, 188*, 107–116.

Krsiak, M., & Borgesova, M. (1973). Aggression and timidity induced in mice by isolation. *Act. Nerv. Sup., 15*, 21–22.

Lagerspetz, K. (1964). Studies on the aggressive behavior of mice. *Annales Acadamiae Scientiarum Fennicae, Sarja-ser.* B 131, 3, 1–131.

Lagerspetz, K. M. J., & Portin, R. (1968). Simulations of cues eliciting aggressive responses in mice at two age levels. *The Journal of Genetic Psychology, 113*, 53–63.

Lagerspetz, K. M. J., Tirri, R., & Lagerspetz, K. Y. H. (1968). Neuro-chemical and endocrinological studies of mice selectively bred for aggressiveness. *Scandinavian Journal of Psychology, 9*, 157–160.

Lewis M. H., Devaud, L., Gariépy, J.-L., Southerland, S. B., Mailman, R. B., & Cairns, R. B. (1991). Genetic regulation of aggression in mice: Mediation by central dopamine systems. *Brain Research Bulletin.*

Lewis, M. H., Gariépy, J.-L., Gendreau, P. J., Volk, M. A., Nichols, D. E., & Mailman, R. B. (1992). D_1 dopamine receptor activation induces social reactivity in mice selectively bred for aggression (under review).

Lewis, M. H. , Gariépy, J.-L., Gendreau, P. J., Davis, M. S., Nichols, D. E., & Mailman, R. B. (1994). Social reactivity and D_1 dopamine receptors: Studies in mice selectively bred for high and low levels of aggression. *Neuropsychopharmacology, 10*, 115–122.

Louilot, A., LeMoal, M., & Simon, H. (1986). Differential reactivity of dopaminergic neurons in the nucleus accumbens in response to different behavioral situations. An in vivo voltammetric study in free moving rats. *Brain Research, 400*, 397–395.

Mackintosh, J. H. (1970). Territory formation by laboratory mice. *Animal Behaviour, 18*, 177–183.

Mackintosh, J. H. (1981). Behaviour of the house mouse. *Symp. Zool. Soc.* London, 47, 337–365.

Mailman, R. B., Schulz, D. W., Kilts, C. D., Lewis, M. H., Rollema, H., & Wyrick, S. (1986). Multiple forms of the D1 dopamine receptor: Its linkages to adenylate cyclase and psycho-pharmacological effects. *Psychopharmacology Bulletin, 22,* 593–598.

Mashurano, M., & Waddington, J. L. (1986). Stereotyped behavior in response to the selective D2 dopamine receptor agonist RU24213 is enhanced by pretreatment with the selective D_1 agonist SK&F38393. *Neuropharmacology, 25,* 947–949.

Mayr, E. (1982). The place of biology in the sciences and its conceptual structure. In E. Mayr, *The growth of biological thought,* pp. 21–82. Cambridge, MA: Harvard University Press.

Michard, C., & Carlier, M. (1985). Les conduites d'agression intra-spécifique chez la souris domestiques: Différences individuelles et analyses génétiques [Intraspecific aggressive behaviors in the domestic mouse: Individual differences and genetic analyses]. *Behavioral Biology, 10,* 123–146.

Milko, J. E. (1992). Effects of social experience on the dopaminergic systems of mice selectively bred for high and low levels of aggressiveness. Unpublished Honors Thesis, University of North Carolina at Chapel Hill.

Nabeshima, T., Katoh, A., Hiramatsu, M., & Kameyama, T. (1986). A role played by dopamine and opioid neuronal systems in stress-induced motor suppression (conditioned suppression of motility) in mice. *Brain Research, 398,* 354, 360.

Nishino, H., Ono, T., Muramoto, K., Fukuda, M., & Sasaki, K. (1987). Neuronal activity in the ventral tegmental area (VTA) during motivated bar-press feeding in the monkey. *Brain Research, 413,* 302–313.

Olweus, D. (1986). Aggression and hormones: Behavioral relationships with testosterone and adrenaline. In D. Olweus, J. Block, Radke-Yarrow (Eds.), *Development of antisocial and prosocial behavior: Research, theories and issues.* New York: Academic Press.

Piaget, J. (1978). *Behavior and evolution.* New York: Pantheon.

Preyer, W. (1893). *The mind of the child* (2 vols.). New York: Appleton & Co.

Reinisch, J. M. (1976). Effects of prenatal hormone exposure on physical and psychological development in humans and animals: with a note on the state of the field. In E. J. Sachar (Ed.), *Hormones, behavior and psychopathology,* pp. 69–94. New York: Raven Press.

Rose, R. M., Bernstein, I. S., & Gordon, T. P. (1975). Consequence of social conflict on plasma testosterone levels in rhesus monkeys. *Psychosomatic Medicine, 37*, 50–61.

Rosenblatt, J. S. (1965). Effect of experience on behavior in male cats. In F. A. Beach (Ed.), *Sex and Behavior*, pp. 416–439. New York: John Wiley.

Rothbart, M. J. (1988). Temperament and the development of inhibited approach. *Child Development, 59*, 1241–1250.

Sameroff, A. J. (1983). Developmental systems: Context and evolution. In P. H. Mussen (Ed.), *Handbook of child psychology*. Vol 1 (4th ed.), pp. 237–294. New York: Wiley.

Sandnabba, N. K. (1985). Differences in the capacity of male odours to affect investigatory behaviour and different urinary marking patterns in two strains of mice, selectively bred for high and low aggressiveness. *Behavioural Processes, 11*, 257–267.

Scheel-Krüger, L., & Willner, P. (1991). The mesolimbic system: Principles of operation. In P. Willner and J. Scheel Krüger (Eds.), *The mesolimbic dopamine system: From motivation to action*. New York: John Wiley.

Schneirla, T. C. (1966). Behavioral development and comparative psychology. *Quarterly Review of Biology, 41*, 283–302.

———. (1964). An evolutionary and development theory of biphasic processes underlying approach and withdrawal. In N. R. F. Maier and T. C. Schneirla (Eds.), *Principles of animal psychology*, pp. 511–544. New York: Dover.

———. (1952). A consideration of some conceptual trends in comparative psychology. *Psychological Bulletin, 49*, 559–597.

Scott, J. P. (1966). Agonistic behavior of mice and rats: A review. *American Journal of Zoology, 6*, 683–701.

Seay, B. M., Schlottmann, R. S., & Gandolfo, R. (1972). Early social interaction in two monkey species. *Journal of General Psychology, 87*, 37–43.

St. John, R. D., & Corning, P. A. (1973). Maternal aggression in mice. *Behavioral Biology, 9*, 635–639.

Taghzouti, K., Simon, H., Louilot, A., Herman, J. P., & LeMoal, M. (1985). Behavioral study after local injection of 6–hydroxy-dopamine into the nucleus accumbens in the rat. *Brain Research, 344*, 9–20.

Tobach, E. (1969). Developmental aspects of chemoreception in the wistar (DAB) rat: Tonic processes. *Annals of New York Academy of Science, 290,* 226–267.

Valzelli, L., (1969). Aggressive behavior induced by isolation. In S. Garattini & E. B. Sigg (Eds.), *Aggressive behavior,* pp. 70–76. Amsterdam: Excepta Medica Foundation.

Valzelli, L., & Bernasconi, S. (1979). Aggressiveness by isolation and brain serotonin turnover changes in different strains of mice. *Neuropsychobiology, 5,* 129–135.

Van Oortmerssen, G. A., & Bakker, Th. C. M. (1981). Artificial selection for short and long attack latencies in wild *Mus musculus domesticus. Behavior Genetics, 11,* 115–126.

Van Oortmerssen, G. A., & Busser, J. (1989). Studies in wild house mice 3: Disruptive selection on aggression as a possible force in evolution. In P. F. Brain, D. Mainardi, & S. Parmigiani (Eds.), *House mouse aggression: A model for understanding the evolution of social behaviour* (pp. 87–117). Chur (Switzerland): Harwood Academic Publishers.

Waddington, C. H. (1953). Genetic assimilation of an acquired character. *Evolution, 7,* 118–126.

Weerts, E. M., Miller, L. G., Hood, K. E., & Miczek, K. (1992). Increased $GABA_A$-dependent chloride uptake in mice genetically selected for low aggressive behavior. *Psychopharmacology, 108,* 196–204.

Werner, H. (1948). *Comparative psychology of mental development.* New York: International Universities Press.

Yamamoto, T., Matsuo, R., Kiyomitsu, Y., & Kitamura, R. (1989). Response properties of lateral hypothalamic neurons during ingestive behavior with special reference to licking of various taste solutions. *Brain Research, 481,* 286–297.

NOTES

1. Because this experiment may have introduced a possible confound between the developmental functions observed and the length of time spent in isolation, group-reared animals were also

observed at day 24. This control showed that 3 days in isolation were sufficient to create substantial and differential effects in the two lines.

2. Dr. Mark Lewis is currently at the Psychiatry Department of the Health and Science Center at the University of Florida, Gainesville.

3. A total of 16 animals per selected line was used for this purpose.

CHAPTER 10

Beyond Attachments
*Toward a General Theory
of the Development of Relationships
in Infancy*

Alison Nash

Objectives

As a developmental psychologist, I cannot help but appreciate the strides forward in the discipline as a direct result of John Bowlby's theory of attachment. Bowlby's ethological model of attachment inspired investigations of infant social signals and social capacities, which in turn led to the discovery of a myriad of social competencies in very young infants. William James' view of the blooming, buzzing, confusing world of the newborn has been replaced by the newer view of the socially competent newborn, who, within weeks and in some cases hours after birth recognizes his or her mother's voice (DeCasper & Fifer, 1980) and odor (MacFarlane, 1975), likes to look at faces (Fantz, 1963) and listen to language (Eisenberg, 1976), perceives and classifies phonemes (Eimas, Siqueland, Jusczyk, & Vigorito, 1971), imitates particular facial expressions (Meltzoff & Moore, 1977), and synchronizes his or her behavior with that of another person (Condon & Sanders, 1974). The infant's abilities to form close relationships, and the importance of these relationships, are now well documented (reviewed by Lewis, 1987).

Yet having been trained in comparative psychology in the tradition of T. C. Schneirla, I cannot help but be uncomfortable with some aspects of attachment theory. In his ethological theory of attachment, Bowlby proposed that innate predispositions, rather than associations with food and/or oral gratification, were responsible for the formation of relationships between infants and caregivers. Although it is now widely accepted that food is not necessary to mediate relationship formation, the alternative notion of innate predispositions has its shortcomings. Schneirla (1959, 1965), in his theory of approach/withdrawal, focused on the general problems with "innate" explanations of behavior. Rather than view particular behaviors as "innate," Schneirla believed that we need to examine how organismic and experiential variables work together in order to understand the development of adaptive behaviors. His approach/withdrawal paradigm provides the framework through which this fusion of nature and nurture can be investigated.

These ideas were developed in part in response to the ethological view of animal behavior. The ethologists suggested that behavior, like physical traits, could be inherited and thus subject to natural selection. Schneirla extended this notion by highlighting the importance of examining development as well as evolution in order to explain behavior. To do this, he proposed approach/withdrawal theory as a framework for understanding the phylogeny and ontogeny of early-appearing behaviors in all animal species. Schneirla suggested that biphasic processes underlie approach and withdrawal behavior in all young animals: that the approach system is elicited by low intensity stimuli, and the withdrawal system by high intensity stimuli. These responses are adaptive in that they bring animals in contact with what they need from their environment, while keeping them away from harmful or dangerous objects or animals. Thus, according to Schneirla, an understanding of behavior entails an examination of both evolutionary and developmental processes.

Schneirla's presentation of the approach/withdrawal paradigm included evidence of its utility in the study of social behavior in animals. He described studies which questioned the traditional ethological view that certain social behaviors are "innate," i.e., that stimuli resembling particular "innate schematas" simply "released" particular behavior patterns. For example, Schneirla described studies which revealed that bill-pecking behavior in young gulls is not simply "released" by the bright orange spot on the parent's bill; rather, experiments done using the approach/withdrawal paradigm revealed that the amount of retinal stimulation elicited by various characteristics of the parent's bill elicited approach or pecking.

Studies of other social behaviors using the approach/withdrawal framework yielded similar findings. A hawk silhouette was not a "releaser" of withdrawal behavior in young ducklings; rather the high intensity of retinal stimulation which occurs when a hawk-like figure flies overhead leads to the duckling withdrawal. The young curlew did not follow an innate image of mother away from the nest, but, rather, reacted to the decreasing retinal and acoustical stimulation which results from the mother's departure. Prehatching and early posthatching experience with various stimuli were also found to play a role in young bird's supposedly "innate" reactions. Studies such as these greatly enhanced our understanding of the development of various social phenomena. When these behaviors were not viewed as simply innate, the developmental processes became better understood. Schneirla's (1959, 1965) paradigm greatly improved our understanding of social behavior in animals. But his notion of the fusion of nature and nurture presents its greatest empirical challenge in the study of human social behavior. Many of the techniques for understanding approach and withdrawal in other animals are not available to investigators of human development. We cannot remove particular body parts, tamper with hormones, or raise humans in isolation. We can, however, use Schneirla's perspective to help sharpen and clarify our theories and conceptual frameworks. I attempt to do just this in this chapter. I would like to refine the ethological/evolutionary model of attachments by viewing it through the Schneirlian approach/withdrawal paradigm. This may be useful for expanding attachment theory to a conceptual framework with which to view the development of relationships in infancy.

I. Attachment Figures Versus Strangers

As with animal infants, social relationships involving human infants can also be viewed as consisting of approach and withdrawal behaviors. Infants may locomote toward or away from other individuals; they may smile or cry. They may cry when one person leaves and when another comes too close.

In classical attachment theory, infants' behavior with attachment figures is contrasted with their behavior toward strangers, creating a line of demarcation between the two. Approach is aligned with attachment figures, and withdrawal aligned with strangers. Studies of attachment focused on infants' use of "attachment" behaviors with familiar caregivers, behaviors which are by definition "approach" behaviors. That is, attachment behaviors are defined as behaviors which serve to promote proximity between an infant and caregiver. Studies of infants' responses to strangers focused on fear or wariness, forms of withdrawal.

Yet if we view development as the acquisition of familiarity, as Harriet Rheingold (1985) has proposed, the view that infants approach the familiar, and withdraw from the unfamiliar, becomes problematic. As Rheingold suggests, the novel must be approached in order to turn it into the familiar.

Rheingold's ideas about novelty and familiarity as fundamental aspects of experience around which elementary principles of behavior can be ordered, taken together with Schneirla's theory of approach and withdrawal, can provide a powerful conceptual framework for viewing human social relationships. Although Rheingold does not directly cite Schneirla, there are some striking similarities in their ideas. Like Schneirla, Rheingold has focused attention on very simple but salient variables, and argues that these simple dimensions are of fundamental importance for understanding development. In addition, she uses the comparative perspective in suggesting that novelty and familiarity are fundamental dimensions of experience for all animal species, and that they may be understood in terms of biological adaptation because they relate to how organisms learn about their environment and how they may survive in it. Consistent with the comparative approach, Rheingold views the acquisition of familiarity as the developmental task of all young, regardless of species, and, like Schneirla, views an understanding of both ontogeny and phylogeny as necessary for understanding behavior. Furthermore, Rheingold suggests that the concepts of arousal, varied stimulation, and optimal stimulation play a role in an individual's perception of and response to novelty and familiarity, reminiscent of the central role that stimulus intensity plays in Schneirla's approach/withdrawal theory. Finally, Rheingold questions the commonly held proposition that familiarity and novelty define the ends of a single dimension or variable. As she states, as familiarity increases the possibility of recognizing the novel also increases; the more we know, the more we recognize what we do not know. She suggests that rather than view novelty and familiarity as opposite ends of one dimension, that they be viewed as two variables; a variable of familiarity and a variable of novelty. Thus both dimensions may be invoked to various extents in a given situation, as for example when we see a familiar person in an unfamiliar setting. Novelty and familiarity can be viewed as separate dimensions, just as Schneirla views approach and withdrawal as separate systems (what he terms a "biphasic model") rather than opposite ends of the same system.

I am suggesting that Schneirla's biphasic theory of approach and withdrawal, in conjunction with Rheingold's ideas about novelty and familiarity, may enable us to understand aspects of the development of relationships in infancy which have been overlooked by attachment theory's single-dimensional view of approach and withdrawal, and of familiar people and strangers. Rather than assume that infants approach familiar individuals and withdraw from unfamiliar ones, we can examine their approach and withdrawal responses to strangers and familiar caregivers in an effort to identify the stimulus dimensions of these people which elicit approach or withdrawal behaviors. According to this perspective, both the novel and the familiar can elicit approach, and both the novel and the familiar can elicit withdrawal. This is a biphasic model—two separate systems, elicited by particular dimensions of stimuli.

There are ample observations in the social interaction literature to support this view. Many studies show that withdrawal responses are typical in infants' interactions with familiar people, including "attachment figures," just as approach processes are typical in their interaction with unfamiliar people. For example, Greenspan (1989) has described infants who withdraw from mothers' touch, or arch their bodies away when hugged or even held. He attributes this withdrawal to the intensity of stimulation, and suggests that these infants are particularly sensitive to touch. Several investigators (Brazelton, Koslowski, & Main, 1974; Cohn & Tronick, 1983; Stern, 1985; Stifter, Fox, & Porges, 1989) have described gaze aversion, a withdrawal response, as a basic component of infant-mother interaction. Ainsworth, Blehar, Waters, & Wall (1978, p. 93) reported that the majority of infants in their sample showed some avoidance of mothers. Similarly, approach behaviors have been described in many studies of infant-stranger interaction. Hay (1977) found that infants were as likely to follow an unfamiliar adult into a new room as they were to follow their mothers: following, a form of approach, is a classic attachment behavior. Rheingold and Eckerman (1973) reported that the majority of infants in their studies, who were at the peak age of "stranger anxiety," approached unfamiliar adults, physically contacted them, and allowed these strangers to pick up and to hold the infants.

The approach and withdrawal behaviors described in the above studies do not all necessarily fit neatly into Schneirla's paradigm. For example, as stated by Schneirla, seeking and avoidance are more complex, organized patterns of approach and withdrawal. Yet these studies do show that it may be misleading to assume that separate processes underlie infants' responses to attachment figures and strangers. It may be more useful to view infants' behaviors to both attachment figures and unfamiliar people as consisting of both approach and withdrawal behaviors.

Why, then, is there a dichotomy in the developmental psychology literature between attachment figures and strangers, with the assumption that approach behaviors occur to familiar caregivers, and withdrawal behaviors to strangers? The processes underlying the formation of attachments are assumed to be different from the processes underlying other relationships. This assumption springs directly from Bowlby's (1969, 1982) ethological theory of attachment. Bowlby proposed that infants are biologically prepared to form attachments with familiar caregivers. A corollary to this assumption is that other relationships are formed by different processes. These assumptions are discussed in the next section.

Bowlby's Ethological Theory of Attachment

The ethologists drew attention to evolutionary explanations of behavior: they introduced the notion that behaviors, like morphological structures, evolve through natural selection, and consequently can be better understood by examining their phylogeny. Thus began studies of the adaptive value of particular behaviors in animals. Meanwhile, John Bowlby, a psychiatrist trained in psychoanalytic theory, began to notice severe problems, such as failure to thrive, in institutionalized infants, despite their adequate physical and medical care. He took the then-radical position of viewing human attachments through ethological theory. In his 1969 treatise he presented his argument for the evolution of human attachments.

According to Bowlby, infants have an innate predisposition to maintain proximity with familiar caregivers. They are able to maintain this proximity at first through signals, such as crying and smiling, which bring and/or keep an adult nearby, and later through locomotion as well as signals. Although the behaviors used to effect proximity may change as the infant gets older, their goal remains the same. Infants are assumed to get a feeling of security through proximity. Attachment refers to the dimension of the infant-caregiver relationship that is concerned with the seeking of security by the infant and its provision by the caregiver. Bowlby suggested that the propensity to form attachments evolved through natural selection, as such attachments functioned to protect infants from predation in the human "environment of evolutionary adaptedness." Proximity to a caregiver is a human infant's best protection against predators and other dangers. Bowlby (1969, 1982) used the comparative method to argue that the process of attachment formation in humans is similar to the imprinting process through which other animals form intimate social bonds.

His ideas were not favorably received by members of his profession. Freud's view of the id-driven infant in search of gratification of primal needs was widely accepted at that time; there was much resistance to the notion that attachments themselves could be considered primary. Mary Ainsworth, who was very soon to become the leader of attachment research, initially claimed that no new theory was needed to explain babies' attachment to their mothers. "Some truths are self-evident: Babies become attached to their mothers because their mothers feed them . . . nursing is gratifying" (Ainsworth, in Levine, 1986, p. 211).

Yet Bowlby's theory provided an excellent framework for designing empirical studies of human relationships. A flurry of studies followed, helping to establish developmental psychology as a separate discipline, and leading to a much greater understanding of social development in infancy. By focusing on phylogeny, Bowlby paved the way for studying ontogeny. Studies of social development took two separate directions, which resulted in the emergence of two separate literatures.

One line of investigation offered a focus on infants' innate social signals, from which studies of a biological readiness for a variety of capacities for interaction emerged. These studies do not require the classification of unfamiliar and familiar people into separate categories. The social capacities revealed by these studies could be used with mothers and others alike. For example, capacities such as the categorization of phonemes (Eimas et al., 1971), preferences for looking at faces (Fantz, 1966; Dannemiller & Stephens, 1988), participation in interactive dialogues (Ross & Goldman, 1977; Bretherton, 1978) etc., are used with whomever interacts with an infant, parent and unfamiliar person alike.

The second line of investigation focused on the ontogeny of particular kinds of relationships, and the developmental outcome associated with each of these, i.e., individual differences in the security of attachment, its antecedents and consequences (reviewed by Lamb, Thompson, Gardner, & Charnov, 1985). The investigation of these correlates of attachment security fully accepts the proposition that relationships with primary caregivers are basically different from other relationships, i.e., the tenet of ethological-attachment theory that infants are biologically predisposed to form attachments to primarily one individual, the primary caregiver.

Monotropy

The notion of monotropy is central for testing certain predictions derived from the attachment model. Specifically, Bowlby states, "Because the bias of a child to attach himself especially to one figure seems to be well established and also to have far-reaching implications for psychopathology, I believe it merits a special term . . . 'monotropy'" (Bowlby, 1982, p. 309).

The influences of Bowlby's psychoanalytic training become apparent here, particularly in his adherence to the Freudian belief in the formative importance of the first relationship—that between infant and mother. According to Freud, the first relationship is "unique, without parallel, the prototype of all future love relationships" (Freud, 1940). This assumption is directly responsible for the separate bodies of research on attachments versus other relationships. If relationships with mothers are primary, then other relationships are derived from these. Thus, separate mechanisms are seen as responsible for the development of attachments to mothers and other relationships. Strangers are viewed as qualitatively different from mothers, and relations with them formed in different ways. Attachment theory reifies this notion by explaining relations with mothers as based on innate predispositions, i.e., a biological preparedness for forming attachments to primary caregivers (who are, as Bowlby suggests, typically mothers), whereas relations with new people are based on the quality of the infant-mother relationship. In other words, the infant-mother relationship is believed to be a precursor of later relationships. One way in which this hypothesis has been tested is through studies which examine the correlations between the security of early infant-mother attachment and later peer relations (reviewed by Lamb & Nash, 1989). The assumption then, is that social skills are honed and refined in relationships with mothers, and later applied to other people.

The precursor hypothesis highlights the central role of monotropy in attachment theory. Much of the research on attachment inspired by attachment theory focuses on correlates of attachment. However, although it is now widely accepted that infants form attachments to fathers, professional caregivers, etc. in much the same way as they do with mothers, correlates of these other attachments are seldom sought (cf. Howes, Rodning, Galluzo, & Myers, 1988; Oppenheim, Sagi, & Lamb, 1988). Embedded in the ethological-evolutionary theory of attachment is the Freudian assumption of the formative importance of the infant-*mother* relationship. Early difficulties in this relationship are said to be precursors of later pathology; a recent review of studies of the relationship between early attachment class-ification and later psychopathology included only studies of correlates of infant-mother attachment security and later pathology (Belsky & Nezworski, 1988).

It is the assumption of monotropy that has led traditional attachment theory to reach a blockade—the empirical research it has guided has outdistanced the theory. Bowlby's theory drew the scientific community's attention to the importance of emo-tionally close relationships in the lives of infants—to their psy-chological need for their mothers. A decade of research followed in support of this view. And then attachment research began to extend to other close emotional relationships—to fathers, later to siblings, childcare providers, and grandmothers. It is this extended view of attachments which has led to the realization of a deficiency in the model.

Multiple Relationships

The difficulty with the attachment model arises when the precursor hypothesis is applied to attachments to several people. Research on attachments to individuals other than mothers did not spring directly from attachment theory. Rather, it followed from developmental theorists who were becoming more inter-ested in the context of development (Bronfenbrenner, 1979; Rogoff, 1990), which led to the notion of a network of relation-ships during infancy (Lewis, 1982). Investigators began to study attachments to fathers (Lamb, 1977) because it was remembered that they were there; that they too, were important emotional figures in the lives of infants. Later, attachments to siblings (Teti & Lamb, 1986), grandparents (Myers, Jarvis, & Creasey, 1987) and childcare workers (Sagi, Lamb, Lewkowitz, Shoham, Dvir, & Estes, 1985; Howes, et al., 1988) were examined for similar reasons. Herein lies the problem. Attachment theory gives no framework for integrating the influences of several important relationships on later development. Most studies of the precursor hypothesis examined correlations between the quality of the infant-*mother* relationship and aspects of later functioning (reviewed by Lamb et al., 1985). There are a few studies which include other influences, but a clear model of how to put together these various influences is not provided (see Nash & Hay, 1993, for a review of these studies).

Comparative studies of relationships: Imprinting. Interestingly, imprinting research is somewhat in advance of developmental research in formulating models of multiple influences. There are two reasons for this: Those working with birds can perform deprivation experiments, cross-fostering experiments, etc., whereas those working with humans cannot. Secondly, imprinting researchers, trained in animal behavior or comparative psychology, are more likely to be influenced by Schneirla's perspective. By not accepting the notion of innate predisposition as explanation, Schneirla inspired experiments which were designed to isolate the particular stimuli which influence approach and/or withdrawal responses. For example, the relevant stimulus for eliciting the following response in newly hatched precocial birds was found to be one of low intensity, indicating that Lorenz' assumption of "innate perceptual patterns" (Schneirla, 1965, p. 364) as important for certain species was not correct. Schneirla's framework thus led to experiments which went beyond the prevailing explanations of development. We can thus turn, as Bowlby did, to contemporary imprinting literature to help construct a model of the impact of early relationships on later ones for humans.

The recent studies in the area of sexual imprinting are particularly relevant for the precursor hypothesis: In some species of birds the first relationships appeared to be the prototype, literally, of future love relationships. In many species, the figure to which a young bird imprints forms the basis of later recognition of suitable mating partners (Lorenz, 1935/1970); i.e., the first figure to which young birds imprinted appeared to form the prototype of what future mates should look like (e.g., zebra finches, as studied by Immelmann, 1972). However, more recent studies of zebra finches have indicated that young birds may imprint to several figures, and that each of these may contribute to the image of an appropriate mate (Ten Cate, Los, & Schilperoord, 1984). Recent studies of several different species have shown that companions typically found in the young bird's environment—siblings, neighbors, as well as parents—all contribute to later mate preferences: zebra finches (Kruijt, Ten Cate, & Meeuwissen, 1983); mallards (Lickliter & Gottlieb, 1985, 1988); Japanese quail (Bateson, 1982). Testable models of how these influences combine to influence later relationships have been proposed (Bateson, 1981; Ten Cate, 1987; Clayton, 1987).

Monotropy or Multiple Relationships?

Bowlby devotes very little attention—less than one page— to the notion of monotropy in both his original (1969) and revised (1982) treatises on attachment. Yet his assumption of monotropy is central for the precursor hypothesis. Very different models need to be constructed to test the influences of one primary relationship on later functioning than to test the influences of several relationships. The latter, of course, requires a much more complex model. Although the precursor hypothesis is a central component of attachment theory, and in fact the one most addressed by empirical research directly guided by this theory, it is vague about which relationships serve as precursors. One primary relationship is assumed, but no evidence is presented for this. And it is this assumption which is responsible for the assumption of separate processes underlying infant-mother relationships and other relationships, resulting in separate bodies of literature on primary attachments and other social relationships.

The vague areas in attachment theory can be clarified by applying Schneirla's perspective. The application of the approach/withdrawal view of development can help separate testable hypotheses from subjective assumptions. Rather than assume that attachments to primary caregivers are formed through different processes than other relationships, we can examine infants' reactions to people, and attempt to isolate the variables which lead to approach and to withdrawal responses. As stated earlier, there is no reason to assume that familiarity and novelty

are the relevant dimensions for eliciting approach and withdrawal respectively.

A central tenet of Schneirla's theory is that approach/
withdrawal systems are adaptive; organisms approach stimuli
which are useful or helpful, and withdraw from stimuli which
are harmful. He suggested that in order to understand the
development of specific approach and withdrawal responses,
one must understand both the phylogeny and ontogeny of these
responses (Schneirla, 1959). I will, therefore, first attempt to clarify ambiguities in Bowlby's evolutionary account of attachments,
and then show how the revised model may be helpful for
devising a theoretical framework for understanding the
ontogeny of relationships in general, rather than using separate
frameworks for primary attachments and for other relationships.

II. Parents, Peers, Relatives and Strangers: Forming Relationships in Infancy

Updating Ethological-Attachment Theory with Modern Evolutionary Concepts

Bowlby attempted to update concepts used to explain the
infant's social relations by applying then-current innovations in
bioevolutionary ways of thinking about social behavior. Since
Bowlby's explication, there have been new developments in evolutionary thinking. I will turn, as Bowlby did, to these recent
advances and attempt to bring attachment theory up to date with
contemporary evolutionary theory.

I would like to note at outset that although the concept of
adaptation was central to Schneirla's approach/withdrawal theory (1959), Schneirla cautioned against too-loose adaptionist
thinking and the nonempirical uses of ideas like innate and fitness. Bowlby's ethological/evolutionary theory of attachment
may somewhat fall into this category. I will nevertheless closely
examine these concepts in relation to attachment theory, in an
attempt to show that even Bowlby's argument, when re-
examined in terms of contemporary notions of fitness, supports

the notion of a biological readiness for relations in general, rather than for monotropic attachments.

Group Selection vs. Individual Selection

Interest in the evolution of social behavior was stimulated by Wynne-Edwards' (1962) theory of group selection as a mechanism of evolution. He proposed that certain social behaviors were selected for because they enhanced the survival of the species as a whole, even though in some cases they may not have enhanced the survival of a particular individual. In contrast, Hamilton's (1964) theory of "inclusive fitness" emphasizes individual reproductive success. According to Hamilton's theory, a behavior will be selected for only if it increases the reproductive success of those who have the gene for the behavior. Although the behavior may incur a cost (in terms of reproductive success, or the number of surviving offspring) to some individuals carrying the gene for it, it may benefit others carrying the same gene even more. As the concept of "inclusive fitness" is more consistent with Darwin's theory of evolution via natural selection, it subsequently replaced Wynne-Edwards' concept of "survival of the species" or group selection.

Explaining the evolution of various social behaviors in terms of individual reproductive success then became a primary concern for researchers in the field of evolutionary biology. Social behavior, by definition, involves more than one individual; for a behavior to be considered adaptive, in evolutionary terms, the benefits to all individuals involved must be elucidated. Theoreticians began to elucidate the costs and benefits to each individual involved in various kinds of social relationships thought to have evolved through natural selection (Orians, 1969; Trivers, 1972, 1974; Maynard-Smith, 1974; Emlen and Oring, 1977).

The shift toward the modern evolutionary perspective on social behavior based on inclusive fitness occurred after Bowlby advanced his evolutionary theory of attachment. He used the classical ethological perspective and thus emphasized the form and function of attachment behaviors. But, in order to explain the evolution of "attachment" in contemporary terms, the costs and benefits to each individual involved in the attachment relationship must be specified.

Does "Attachment" Refer to Individuals or Dyads?

Bowlby does not make explicit whether his evolutionary analysis pertains to particular infant behaviors, or to reciprocal behaviors between an infant and primary caregiver. At the time of his formulation (Bowlby, 1969), this distinction was not essential, as either could be explained in terms of "survival of the species." In other words, the primary caregiver in particular need not benefit from "attachment" behaviors, as long as the species as a whole benefitted. This distinction is essential, however, in examining attachment within the contemporary evolutionary framework. To do so, it must be made clear whether innate predispositions for attachment are genotypic characteristics of infants or are found within both infants and primary caregivers.

Such an explication is not found in either Bowlby's original treatise (1969) or the revised version (1982). However, an examination of his argument reveals that infant attachment behaviors may be considered adaptive only if they are responded to appropriately by the individual to whom they are directed. Infants who sought proximity to individuals who then failed to protect them from harm would be unlikely to survive. It thus appears that Bowlby's evolutionary account of attachment pertains to infant attachment behaviors in conjunction with adult caregiving behaviors.

Passages throughout the text support this reading. For example, he refers to the attachment behaviors on the part of the infant and caregiving behaviors on the part of the primary caregiver as a "shared dyadic program" (1982, p. 378). Furthermore, in discussing "the role of the child and mother," he informs us that "the role of the mother as partner must be considered" (p. 236). In discussing "attachment behavior and its place in nature" (p. 80), he lists two criteria which denote the presence of "attachments," i.e., the occurrence of proximity-seeking behaviors of parent and young to one another, and the specificity of these behaviors to one another. Finally, Bowlby posits "control systems," i.e., the mechanism by which attachment effects itself, in both the child and the parent. "The behavior of parents that is reciprocal to the attachment behaviors of juveniles is termed "caregiving behavior'" (p. 182). An entire section of the book is devoted to describing this caregiving behavior on the part of parents.

Thus, it appears that Bowlby's evolutionary model of attachment refers to an aspect of the infant-caregiver relationship. In other words, both infant care-soliciting behavior towards primary caregivers, and its complement in primary caregivers— caregiving behavior towards infants—are the outcome of natural selection. I have attempted to clarify whether Bowlby is referring to individuals or to dyads in his view of attachment as a biological adaptation, as this distinction is crucial in viewing attachment through contemporary evolutionary theory. Others (Cairns, 1972; Hinde, 1982; Lamb, et al., 1985) have also interpreted Bowlby's argument as referring to innate predispositions in both infants and primary caregivers to mutually respond to one another in particular ways.

If "attachments" have evolved through natural selection, the costs and benefits of "attachment" behaviors to the infant and their reciprocal behaviors in the caregivers need to be elucidated. To do so, the identity of "caregivers" must be clarified. Only then can we discuss the co-evolution of attachment-caregiving behaviors.

Identity of Caregivers

Bowlby does not specify precisely who falls into the category of caregivers. Although throughout his treatise he discusses the concept of "attachment" in terms of infants and mothers, early in his text he informs the reader, through a footnote, that when he uses the term "mother" he is in fact referring to a "mother-figure," or primary caregiver (Bowlby, 1982, p. 29). Bowlby recognized that parenthood is not necessary for attachments; attachments are formed between infants and primary caregivers, whether or not they are related.

The adaptive value of attachments to parents is obvious: survival of their offspring, and therefore of their genes. The contemporary evolutionary concept of inclusive fitness, however, must be invoked to explain the evolution of attachments between infants and nonparents. If the caregiver is a relative, caring for the young might increase his or her own inclusive fitness, as the caregiver and young would share some genes (Hamilton's, 1964, notion of "kin selection"). If the caregiver is not related, he or she may establish a relationship with the young or their parents, who in return, might then help that individual in some way which results in an increase in his or her own reproductive success (Trivers, 1971, notion of "reciprocal altruism").

Both kin selection and reciprocal altruism require that a relationship exist between the individuals involved. Indeed, once the concepts of kin selection and reciprocal altruism are invoked, as they must be to explain attachments with nonparents, they can be used not only to explain attachments, but close relationships in general. Reciprocal altruism and kin selection need not distinguish between attachments and close relationships. Thus a logical extension of Bowlby's theory, when viewed through contemporary evolutionary theory, is that infants and their conspecifics are predisposed toward the formation of relationships with one another.

If the predisposition for attachments is not between infant and one primary caregiver, but between infant and conspecifics, there is no reason to assume a tendency for monotropy. Although Bowlby proposed that there exists a biological predisposition towards monotropy, there is no logical support specifically for attachment or monotropy. Evolutionary theory can just as readily account for a predisposition for infants and their conspecifics to form close relationships with one another. In the next section, arguments for the adaptive value to infants and caregivers of multiple relationships versus monotropy are compared.

Adaptive Value of Monotropy Versus Multiple Relationships

Although Bowlby proposed that infants were predisposed to form attachments primarily to one individual, he did not describe what the adaptive value of monotropy in particular might be for the infant. Even if we accept Bowlby's proposal that the adaptive value of the infant-caregiver attachment to the infant is protection from predation (the validity of this proposal has been questioned by Hay, 1980), there is still no reason to assume that running or calling to one particular caregiver in times of danger provides better protection than running to any one of a number of individuals. Although incidents of predation of primates, and the primates' responses to it, are difficult to observe in the field (Washburn, Jay, & Lancaster, 1965), researchers have witnessed threats to infants by conspecifics. When threatened by other troop members, infants have been observed to run not specifically to their mothers, but to an individual who is close by (e.g. Japanese macaques: Kawamura, 1963; baboons: Hall & Devore, 1965). Hrdy (1980) had the opportunity to observe near fatal attacks on infant hanuman langurs. In this species, new males coming into a group may attack or kill the infants already in the group. Hrdy observed that several females, not just the infants' mothers, protected the infants and threatened the attacker. In fact, in one such attack, the "mother was the last of these four individuals (other troop members) to reach her infant" (Hrdy, 1980, p. 260).

Thus, at least under some circumstances, primate infants summon individuals other than their mothers to protect them, and individuals other than mothers protect infants from danger. There is some evidence that human infants, too, approach whomever is available when alarmed. Rosenthal (1967) found that when infant subjects were presented with a frightening stimulus, they tended to seek proximity to whomever was available in the test room, sometimes their mother, and sometimes an unfamiliar adult. Similarly, Ipsa (1981) found that infants' distress at being left alone in an unfamiliar room was decreased by the presence of a peer or unfamiliar adult.

It thus appears that multiple relationships provide as effective or better protection than monotropic attachments. Furthermore, in addition to offering no explanation of the adaptive value of monotropy for infants, Bowlby attempted no such explanation for the primary caregiver. Would it not be helpful to caregivers to receive assistance in caring for infants? Along these lines, Tronick, Winn, and Morelli (1985) speculated about the adaptive value of multiple relationships to both infant and caregiver in their discussion of multiple caregiving among the Efe of Zaire. First, the infant would have an increased chance of adoption if the mother dies, which, as Margaret Mead (in Schaffer, 1971) has pointed out, was probably a likely event among our human ancestors. Second, the overall quality of care received would increase, since fresh replacements are brought in, rather than one person doing all the caregiving. Third, the mother herself may be a better and healthier caregiver when given some relief from the infant and help with the chores. Finally, the infant is given wider and more varied social exposure. Mothers benefit by having free time to engage in work, and by getting some respite from the demands of caring for a young infant. The other caregivers may benefit by learning how to care for infants, or by incurring some reciprocal obligation to be redeemed from the mother in the future.

In summary, it appears that the notion of biological propensities for relationships is more consistent with contemporary evolutionary theory than is the notion of monotropy. Rather than assume that biological predispositions explain the infant's attachment to his or her mother in particular, we may better understand the proximal mechanisms involved in the formation of relationships if similar processes are assumed for infant-mother (or infant-primary caregiver) relations and infants' relationships with others.

Although Bowlby's evolutionary theory of attachments inspired research on infant social capacities, it did not lead to empirical studies of some of its tenets. In particular, there is no empirical evidence for monotropy; for the notion that separate processes underlie the development of attachments with primary caregivers compared to the development of other relationships. In the next section, I review empirical studies of infants' developing capacities to relate to others, in an effort to support the notion that if we assume biological propensities for attachments exist, similar processes may also underlie relationships in general.

Infants' Interactions with New People

Recent studies suggest that infants may use their emerging interactional capacities with whomever is available to them, including new people they meet, both adults and peers. These capacities were documented in studies guided by a diversity of conceptual frameworks. Unlike studies of attachments to parents, there is no unified theory of relationship formation in infancy. I have integrated findings from studies of perceptual abilities, cooperation, conflict, reactions to strangers, peer relations, social referencing, and guided participation to present the following overview of the development of relational capacities with a variety of individuals, peers as well as adults, during infancy.

Infants' very early preference for the perceptual and acoustical stimuli of the human face and voice (reviewed by Spelke and Cortelyou, 1981), and their early abilities to engage in behavioral and vocal dialogues (e.g. Brazelton, et al., 1974; Snow, 1977; Stern, 1985; Tronick, Cohn, & Shea, 1986) enable them to interact not only with parents or primary caregivers, but with others as well.

Infant-Peer Interaction

A belief in the unique nature of the infant-mother relationship implies that the mechanisms by which infants form relationships with mothers are different from those used to form relationships with others. However, no alternative framework has been proposed for viewing infants' developing relationships with such significant others as fathers, nonparent caregivers, or siblings.

In contrast, theoretical grounds for distinctions between infant-mother and infant-peer relations have been offered. Some theorists argue that, unlike attachments, infants are *not* biologically predisposed for peer relationships. Konner (1975) suggests that among the small bands of our human ancestors, the presence of same-aged infants was unlikely, and therefore propensities to interact with peers were unnecessary. Bronson (1981) reviewed contemporary studies of peer interaction and also concluded that infant peers have little capacity for "true interaction" or mutual communication. Like Konner, she believes that the "inherent predispositions" for infant-parent relations are not found for infant-peer relations. Likewise, Bowlby states that infants are predisposed towards forming attachments with individuals who are "older and wiser," thus precluding such predispositions among same-aged peers. Furthermore, attachment theorists (reviewed by Lamb & Nash, 1989) and learning theorists (Jacobson, Tianan, Wille, & Aytch, 1986), view peer relations as deriving from infant-mother relations, and cognitive theorists (Mueller, 1989) view infant-peer relations and infant-adult relations as separate systems.

In contrast, Hay's (1985) synthesis of the attachment and peer literatures revealed remarkable similarity in the emergence of relational abilities with peers. Perhaps, then, there is no reason to assume different underlying mechanisms in the infant's capacities to relate to parents and peers.

Those who see infant-peer and infant-mother relationships as developing along different pathways believe that interactional skills are honed and refined in the infant-mother relationship, and only later used with peers (reviewed by Lamb & Nash, 1989). This view predicts that infants' emerging capacities to interact with peers will lag behind their capacities to interact with their mothers. In contrast, the "parallel development" model views that infants' capacities for relationships with peers and with their mothers develop concurrently from the very beginning (Lewis & Rosenblum, 1975; Hay, 1985). In this section, I review studies of the infant's developing capacities for peer relations. The similarities in emerging capacities for interaction with mothers and peers appear more consistent with the "parallel development" model than the "maternal precursor" model of the development of peer relationships.

By 6 months of age, not only are infants readily initiating interactions by touching, vocalizing, and smiling at peers (Vandell, 1980; Vandell, Wilson, & Buchanan, 1980; Hay, Nash, & Pedersen, 1983), but the mutuality and reciprocity, both emotional and behavioral, found in interactions with their mothers are also found in interactions with peers. For example, 6-month-olds tend to continue an interaction when a peer is responsive, to stop when he or she is not, and to adjust their own rate of initiating interaction to that of their peer partner (Hay, et al., 1983). Additionally, as with their mothers (Tronick et al., 1986), their emotional state is influenced by the emotions expressed by a peer partner; 6-month-olds attend to a peer's distress, and if it continues, then they become distressed themselves (Hay, Nash, & Pedersen, 1981).

Between 6 and 12 months of age, infants increase the amount of behavior they direct toward peers, relying more on distal rather than proximal modes of interacting (Maudry & Nekula, 1939; Jacobson, 1981; Vandell, 1980). For example, during the second half of the first year infants begin to use conventional acts (gestures, such as pointing and offering objects, and words) to communicate with their peers (Bakeman & Adamson, 1986). The structural complexity of peer-directed acts also increases until by 9 months infants can synchronize several behaviors such as looking at and gesturing toward a peer at the same time (Becker, 1977: Vandell et al., 1980). In addition, they become better able to simultaneously direct attention to objects and their peers, thus engaging in joint play (Adamson & Bakeman, 1985). Infants express affect more during such periods of joint engagement with peers than when they are alone (Adamson & Bakeman, 1985). Also during this period, infants begin to distinguish between familiar and unfamiliar peers (Jacobson, 1981; Dontas, Maratos, FaFoutis, & Karangelis, 1985).

At the start of the second year of life, both cooperation and conflict can be identified in interactions between peers. Interactions which in general proceed harmoniously and may involve compliance, turn-taking, and/or games have been documented (Eckerman and Whatley, 1977; Goldman & Ross, 1978; Hay, Caplan, Castle, & Stimpson, 1991). The ability to engage in conflicts over toys and personal space, not present among 6-month-olds (Hay et al., 1983) is found at the start of the second year of life (Nash, 1986; Caplan, Vespo, Pedersen, & Hay, 1991). The social nature of such early conflicts was revealed by studies by Hay and her colleagues (Hay & Ross, 1982; Caplan et al., 1991), who found that 1- and 2-year-olds did not simply grab toys from one another, but used communicative acts such as gestures and vocalizations in order to resolve disputes. Additionally, when an infant yielded possession of an object to a peer, the winner would often then turn away from the object and turn their attention elsewhere, as though the interaction itself, and not a desire for the object, was important. Furthermore, duplicates of all toys were provided, so that many struggles occurred over objects of which duplicates were nearby. Thus the investigators concluded that infants do not simply view peers as obstacles to their attainment of toys. Rather, they appear interested in the dispute itself, i.e., the interaction is as or more salient than the object being fought over. Thus at an early age infants are interested in one of the basic problems of relationships—how to resolve disputes. Moreover, they are interested in the problem of resolving disputes with their agemates, indicating the potential for forming relationships with peers at this young age. It should also be mentioned that such conflicts did not predominate in their interactions with one another; Hay and Ross (1982) found that only 5 percent of infants' interactions with one another contained conflicts.

Thus infants appear to use their early capacities for interaction with one another. Their social competence with peers is highlighted by Nash's (1989) study of adult guidance of infant-peer interaction. The findings indicated that 15-month-old infants interacted more with one another without adult assistance than with adult assistance. Nash concluded that an infant may be more expert than an adult at interacting without the use of conventional forms of communication; i.e., with a nonverbal agemate.

Hay (1985) has suggested that studies directly comparing infants' relational capacities with mothers and peers were needed to evaluate the "maternal precursor" (attachment) versus "parallel development" model of relationships. Although this issue has not been directly examined (cf. Nash, 1986), such comparisons have been made in studies which explore other issues. These findings indicate that infants appear to use whatever social competencies they have in their interactions with their peers and mothers alike. For example, Vandell and her colleagues conducted longitudinal studies comparing infants' behavior with mothers and peers over the course of the first year of life. They examined the use of particular social behaviors, including looking, smiling, vocalizing, and touching (Vandell, 1980), and the frequency and structure of interactions (Vandell and Wilson, 1982, 1987), and reported that cross-lagged correlations indicated no evidence for social skills emerging first with mothers and later with peers.

Other studies of the emergence of particular social skills found no evidence for these skills first emerging with mothers and only later with peers. Bakeman and Adamson (Bakeman & Adamson, 1984, 1986; Adamson & Bakeman, 1985) examined the development of the ability to coordinate attention to both people and objects, the expression of affect and coordination of affect and attention to others, and the use of conventionalized acts (gestures and words). They observed the same infants with their mothers and with peers every 3 months when infants were from 6 to 18 months of age. For the majority of their subjects, skills first appeared with both mothers and peers at the same age. Additionally, Nash (1986) examined infants' use of social skills previously found to emerge at the start of the second year of life, and found that infants did not use the newly emerging abilities to take turns, protest, or comply more with mothers than with peers. Furthermore, significant correlations in the use of these skills with mother and peer indicated that as infants acquire new skills, they use them to the same extent with both partners.

Thus, it appears that as infants develop new interactional skills, they use them with mothers and peers alike. If the early appearance of these skills results from a biological readiness for learning the skills necessary for forming relationships, then this readiness would seem to apply to both types of social partners. Furthermore, infants' interest in forming relationships with individuals other than their mothers is also highlighted by studies comparing infants' interactions with mothers and peers. Several studies of infants of ages ranging from 10 to 19 months indicated that when given the choice between mother and peer, interactions were more frequent with peers than with their mothers when both were present (Eckerman, Whatley, and Kutz, 1975; Rubenstein & Howes, 1976; Rubenstein, Howes, & Pedersen, 1982; Nash, 1986).

In addition, Nash (1986) showed that infants' interest in peers was not simply due to mothers' minimal social participation, as she found that mothers of 13- to 15-month-olds initiated as many interactions as did peers, and initiated more interactions with their infants than vice-versa. Thus infants were not interested in their peer partner because the peer was active and the mother was not; when given the opportunity to interact with equally responsive mothers and peers, infants prefer the latter. The preference found for interacting with an unfamiliar peer over the mothers may reveal an interest in interacting with new people, as opposed to the familiar person with whom they interact daily. In this vein, Vandell, Wilson, and Hendersen (1985) found that twins engage in more interactions with unfamiliar peers (who were also twins, but not each subject's own twin) than with their own twin. This preference for interacting with new individuals may indicate a propensity for forming new relationships. This fits nicely with Rheingold's (1985) notion that interest in the novel allows the acquisition of familiarity.

Infants' Interactions with Unfamiliar Adults

This interest extends to new adults as well as peers. Although a wariness towards strangers has been described as emerging at about 8 months of age (Bronson, 1972; Emde, Gaensbauer, & Harmon, 1976), more recent studies have shown that in many situations infants do not show such wariness. The infant's response to a stranger appears to depend to a large extent on the behavior of the stranger. When an unfamiliar adult approaches an infant in a warm, friendly manner, the infant usually responds in kind (Bretherton, Stolberg, & Kreye, 1981; Clarke-Stewart, 1978; Rheingold & Eckerman, 1973). The parent's behavior, too, can affect the infant's response: infants whose mothers talked to them in a happy tone about a stranger were friendlier towards the stranger than infants whose mothers talked about her in a neutral tone (Feinman, Roberts, & Morissette, 1986). Thus when placed in a situation conducive to socializing (i.e., when those present act in a friendly manner), infants respond accordingly. Approach/withdrawal theory can help explain these reactions: infants may withdraw from the high intensity stimulation resulting from sudden approaches and/or intrusive physical contact, and approach the less intense stimulation resulting from a slower, more reserved but friendly approach. Mothers' reactions to the stranger may help modulate infant arousal.

A variety of studies have indicated that infants at the supposed peak age of "stranger anxiety" (8- to 18-month-olds) are quite interested in and able to interact with new people. Rheingold and Eckerman (1973) found that nearly all the 8- to 12-month-olds in their study looked and smiled at strangers and appeared comfortable in their presence. Many let the stranger pick them up while their mothers were out of the room. With both their mothers and a friendly, interactive stranger present, 12-month-old infants approached the stranger, and spent more time with her than with their mothers (Ross & Goldman, 1977). Furthermore, 9- to 12-month-old infants are as likely to follow an unfamiliar woman as their mothers into another room (Hay, 1977). Not only do infants approach and follow unfamiliar people, they also actively interact with them. Infants share objects with unfamiliar adults, both men and women (Hay & Murray, 1982; Rheingold, Hay, & West, 1976; Ross & Goldman, 1977) and engage in cooperative play (Bretherton, 1978) and games (Ross & Goldman, 1977). Eighteen-month-olds imitate an unfamiliar adult's actions towards another person to the same extent as they imitate actions modeled by their mothers (Hay, Murray, Cecire, & Nash, 1985), and help unfamiliar women and men with the household task of shelving groceries (Rheingold, 1982). In addition to offering to help unfamiliar adults, infants also request help from them by effectively communicating their desire for help in working a particular toy (Rogoff, Malkin, & Gilbride, 1984).

Not only are infants interested in new people, and able to interact with them; they are able to both understand emotional cues and to seek such cues in ambiguous situations, a phenomenon that has been termed social referencing (Klinnert, Campos, Sorce, Emde, & Svejda, 1983). As has been found in social referencing studies with mothers, 1-year-old infants approached an ambiguous stimulus—in this study a toy robot—more often or more quickly when the adult whom they have known for only 10 minutes smiled than when she expressed fear (Klinnert, Emde, Butterfield, & Campos, 1986).

Infants can thus respond emotionally to the emotional cues of people they have only known a short time. Does this emotional involvement enable a relatively unfamiliar person to provide emotional security for the infant? Using situations similar to that in which infants' attachment behaviors towards parents have been elicited, studies have shown that infants can show such attachment behavior towards people they have known for only a short while. Ten- to 14-month-olds who were cared for by an unfamiliar adult for $2\frac{1}{2}$ hours during each of 3 consecutive days formed attachments to this caregiver. They consistently approached her, and cried when she left them alone in a room with a person they had only seen for a few minutes (Fleener, 1973). One-year-olds who had interacted with a stranger for 8 minutes either did not cry when left alone with her, or were more effectively soothed by her than were infants who had interacted with a stranger for only 1 minute (Bretherton, 1978). Furthermore, infants cry when a stranger whom they have only just met departs, leaving them alone in an unfamiliar room (Ipsa, 1981).

Their interest, social competency, emotional involvement, and feelings of security with new people are precisely what is needed to form new close relationships. A variety of studies on infants' relationships with familiar caregivers other than parents indicates that infants form attachments with these people as well as with their parents. Infants were found to form attachments to caregivers both in daycare centers (Ainslie & Anderson, 1984; Ricciuti, 1974) and in Israeli kibbutzim (Fox, 1977; Sagi et al., 1985). Moreover, as with their parents, the type of attachments infants formed with caregivers were found to affect aspects of their personality several years later. Oppenheim et al. (1988) found that infants in an Israeli kibbutz who had been securely attached to their metaplot (group caregivers) at 1 year of age were more assertive and independent in the preschool setting at 5 years of age than infants who had been insecurely attached to their metaplot. This was the first study which looked at the influence of infants' relationships with individuals other than their parents on later development. These findings have been replicated in studies of American infants' attachments to professional caregivers. Like their Israeli counterparts, the quality of infants' attachments to their professional caregivers was found to influence later functioning (Howes et al., 1988). These findings indicate that like parents, relationships with others can have an impact on development. It appears, then, that there is no reason to assume that the process of attachment to parents is basically different from the process of relationship formation with other kinds of individuals. The way evolutionary-attachment theory has been used, and the separate literatures on attachment and other relationships, imply that separate processes are involved. What is now needed is a unified theory of relationship formation, rather than separate theories for different categories of individuals (parents, peers, strangers, etc.).

The Development of Relationships in Infancy

Although it is now widely accepted that biological processes influence the development of relational capacities in infancy, there exists no general framework for viewing these influences. Some investigations focus on the development of individual differences in the quality of attachment relationships; others focus on infants' early capabilities for social interaction. A unified theory of relationship-formation in infancy which integrates these two lines of investigation can promote understanding of the development of relationships (including the attachment component). In examining the limits of Bowlby's ethological view of attachment, I attempted to direct attention to the possibility that infants are biologically prepared for relationships in general, rather than for attachments specifically. We can then search for processes underlying infants' capacities for relating to others.

To do this, we need a framework to help us investigate the developmental processes involved in the oversimplified notion of "biological preparedness." Schneirla's approach/withdrawal theory precisely addresses the issue; it was in fact proposed in response to the limited explanatory value for concepts like innate schemata, releasers, and fitness. In Schneirla's words:

> As an alternative to instinctivist view, A/W theory envisages behavioral development as a program of progressive, changing relationships between organism and environment in which the contributions of growth are always inseparably related with those of the effects of energy changes in the environs. The formulation corresponds to the concept of modern embryology, according to which organism and developmental medium are inseparably related (Schneirla, 1959, p. 351–352).

Schneirla does not consider the labelling of something as "innate" as explanation. Rather, an understanding of development requires identification (through experimentation) of the relevant dimensions of the environment and the underlying physiological system in order to understand how environmental and organismic influences work together—the "fusion" of maturation and experience. Approach/withdrawal theory is thus particularly useful for investigation of behavior in young animals that had previously been described as instinctive, innate, or biologically prepared. The usefulness of this perspective is illustrated by DeCasper's (DeCasper & Fifer, 1980; Spence & DeCasper, 1987) approach to understanding the preference found in newborns for their mothers' voices. They showed that this preference is not simply "innate," but results from prenatal experience with their mothers' voices.

Several studies in this volume highlight the usefulness of the A/W approach in enhancing our understanding of close relationships in infancy. For example, Rosenblatt (this volume) has presented an elegant model of maternal behavior in rats based on biphasic A/W theory. In particular, he has located the relevant organismic stimuli (olfactory preferences; particular hormones) and external stimuli (particular pup behaviors) which activate and maintain the approach and the withdrawal systems. He very convincingly shows that both mothers and nonmothers show both approach and withdrawal reactions to pups based on the presence of various combinations of these stimuli. Similarly, Stifter (this volume) has examined organismic variables underlying approach and withdrawal to mothers and strangers alike in human infants. She focused on the approach and withdrawal aspects of adult-infant behavioral dialogues by examining the shift between infants' interest and expressivity toward their partners, and their withdrawal of attention by looking away from their partners. She is searching for the physiological mechanism underlying these shifts.

Stifter's findings directly support the view that similar processes underlie infants' relations with mothers and others. She found very little difference in infants' reactions to mothers and strangers; they showed similar amounts of approach and withdrawal behaviors to both. Furthermore, she found evidence for sympathetic nervous system arousal underlying infants' gaze aversion from both mothers and strangers, thus supporting Schneirla's (1959) hypothesized association between sympathetic nervous system arousal and withdrawal. These studies show clearly that viewing social relationships with mothers as developing from processes different from relationships with others is not parsimonious. Both Rosenblatt and Stifter found similar processes underlying infants' relations with mothers and others alike.

I want to make clear that I am not suggesting that "attachment figures" and strangers have the same meaning for infants, or are of equal importance in their lives. I am suggesting that there is no reason to assume that the processes by which infants form relationships with their mothers are different from those by which relationships with fathers, siblings, grandparents, childcare providers, and friends are formed. Infants may want to be held by parents, rather than by peers, because parents may have previously responded to their bids for contact comfort, whereas peers may have not. There is now ample evidence that from the time they are born, infants can adjust their own behavior and emotions to someone else's, the essence, in fact, of relating to others (e.g. newborns: Sagi & Hoffman, 1976; Condon & Sander, 1974; 3-month-olds: Cohn & Tronick, 1983; 6-month-olds: Hay et al., 1981, 1983; 1-year-olds: Klinnert et al., 1983). Such responsivity to the behavior and emotion of others can lead infants to relate differently to those who are emotionally involved in their lives, as their primary caretakers, and those who are not. Very different kinds of relationships, then, can result from this attunement to the behavior and emotions of others.

This view may help us better understand one of the postulates of attachment theory; that infants are biologically predisposed to form attachments with individuals who are *"older and wiser"* than themselves (Bowlby, 1969/1982). Rather than assume an innate preference for seeking comfort from adults, infants may learn that particular adults are more likely than peers and/or other adults to respond to their bids for comfort. Along these lines, Nash and Lamb (1987) found that when infants were left alone with an unfamiliar adult and peer, they did not initially make more bids for attention to the adult than to the peer. If the infant was upset, some adults, however, directed physical comfort to the infant. After repeated experience with this type of comfort from a particular adult, the infant might then seek such comfort *from that person*.

We do not yet understand the processes involved in forming relationships in infancy; rather, assumptions have been made about these processes. Using different conceptual frameworks to explore different aspects of relationships may have deterred a search for similar underlying processes. We need a better understanding of these processes, to know something more than that there exist "biological predispositions" for such capacities. Schneirla's perspective may be very useful in directing attention to the specific physiological processes and relevant environmental stimuli, and toward a better understanding of how the fusion of the two can lead to infants' remarkable abilities to relate to others.

REFERENCES

Adamson, L. B., & Bakeman, R. (1985). Affect and attention: Infants observed with mothers and peers. *Child Development, 56,* 582–593.

Ainslie, R., & Anderson, C. (1984). Daycare children's relationships to their mothers and caregivers. In R. C. Ainslie (Ed.), *Quality variations in daycare*. New York: Praeger.

Ainsworth, M. D. S., Blehar, M. C., Waters, E., & Wall, S. (1978). *Patterns of attachment: A psychological study of the strange situation.* Hillsdale, NJ: Erlbaum.

Bakeman, R., & Adamson, L. B. (1984). Coordinating attention to people and objects in mother-infant and peer-infant interaction. *Child Development, 55,* 1278–1289.

———. (1986). Infants' conventionalized acts: Gestures and words with mothers and peers. *Infant Behavior and Development, 9,* 215–230.

Bateson, P. (1981). Ontogeny of behavior. *British Medical Bulletin, 37,* 158–164.

———. (1982). Preferences for cousins in Japanese quail. *Nature, London,* *295*, 236–237.

Becker, J. M. T. (1977). A learning analysis of the development of peer-oriented behavior in 9-month-infants. *Developmental Psychology,* *13*, 481–491.

Belsky, J., & Nezworski, T. (1988). *Clinical implications of attachment.* Hillsdale, NJ: Erlbaum.

Bowlby, J. (1969). *Attachment and loss: Vol. 1. Attachment.* London: Hogarth Press.

———. (1982). *Attachment and loss: Vol. 1. Attachment.* Second Edition. New York: Basic.

Brazelton, T. B., Koslowski, B., & Main, M. (1974). The origins of reciprocity: The early mother-infant interaction. In M. Lewis & L. Rosenblum (Eds.), *The effect of the infant on its caregiver.* NY: Wiley.

Bretherton, I. (1978). Making friends with one-year-olds: An experimental study of infant-stranger interaction. *Merill-Palmer Quarterly*, *24*, 29–51.

Bretherton, I., Stolberg, U., & Kreye, M. (1981). Engaging strangers in proximal interaction: Infants' social initiative. *Developmental Psychology*, *17*, 746–755.

Bronfenbrenner, U. (1979). *The ecology of human development: Experiments by nature and design.* Cambridge: Harvard University Press.

Bronson, G. (1972). Infants' reactions to unfamiliar persons and novel objects. *Monographs of the Society for Research in Child Development,* *32* (4, Serial No. 112).

Bronson, W. (1981). Toddlers' behavior with agemates: Issues of interaction, cognition, and affect. L. Lipsitt (Ed.), *Monographs on infancy* (Vol 1). Norwood, NJ: Ablex.

Cairns, R. (1972). Attachment and dependency: A psychobiological and social learning synthesis. In J. L. Gewirtz (Ed.), *Attachment and dependency.* Washington, DC: Winston.

Caplan, M., Vespo, J., Pedersen, J., & Hay, D. F. (1991). Conflict and its resolution in small groups of one- and two-year-olds. *Child Development, 62,* 1513–1524.

Clarke-Stewart, K. A. (1978). Recasting the lone stranger. In J. Glick & K. A. Stewart (Eds.), *The development of social understanding* (pp. 109–176). New York: Gardner.

Clayton, N. (1987). Mate choice in male zebra finches: Some effects of cross-fostering. *Animal Behavior, 35,* 596–597.

Cohn, J. F., & Tronick, E. Z. (1983). Three-month-old infants' reaction to simulated maternal depression. *Child Development, 54,* 185–193.

Condon, W. S., & Sander, L. B. (1974). Neonate movement is synchronized with adult speech. *Science, 183,* 1174–1176.

Dannemiller, J. L., & Stephens, B. R. (1988). A critical test of infant pattern preference models. *Child Development, 59,* 210–216.

DeCasper, A. J., & Fifer, W. P. (1980). Of human bonding: Newborns prefer their mothers voices. *Science, 208,* 1174–1176.

Dontas, M., Maratos, O., Fafoutis, M., & Karangelis, A. (1985). Early social development in institutionally reared Greek infants: Attachment and peer interaction. In I. Bretherton & E. Waters (Eds.), Growing points in attachment theory and research. *Monograph of the Society for Research in Child Development, 50* (1–2, Serial No. 209), 136–146.

Eckerman, C. O., & Whatley, J. L. (1977). Toys and social interaction between infant peers. *Child Development, 48,* 1645–1656.

Eckerman, C. O., Whatley, J. L., & Kutz, S. L. (1975). The growth of social play with peers during the second year of life. *Developmental Psychology, 11,* 42–49.

Eimas, P. D., Siqueland, E. R., Jusczyk, P., & Vigorito, H. (1971). Speech perception in infants. *Science, 171,* 303–306.

Eisenberg, R. B. (1976). *Auditory competence in early life.* Baltimore: University Park Press.

Emde, R. N., Gaensbauer, T. J., & Harmon, R. J. (1976). Emotional expression in infancy: A biobehavioral study. *Psychological Issues,* Vol. 10 (No. 1).

Emlen, S. T., & Oring, L. W. (1977). Ecology, sexual selection, and the evolution of mating systems. *Science, 197,* 215–223.

Fantz, R. L. (1963). Pattern vision in newborn infants. *Science, 140,* 296–297.

Feinman, S., Roberts, D., & Morissette, L. (1986). *The effect of social referencing on 12-month-olds' responses to a stranger's attempts to "make friends."* Paper presented at the Fifth International Conference on Infant Studies, Los Angeles.

Fleener, D. E. (1973). *Experimental production of infant-maternal attachment behaviors.* Paper presented at the meeting of the American Psychological Association, Montreal.

Fox, N. (1977). Attachment of kibbutz infants to mother and metapelet. *Child Development, 48*, 1228–1239.

Freud, S. (1940). *An outline of psychoanalysis.* New York: Norton (translated and reprinted 1949).

Goldman, B. D., & Ross, H. S. (1978). Social skills in action: An analysis of early peer games. In J. Glick & K. A. Clarke-Stewart (Eds.), *The development of social understanding.* New York: Gardner Press.

Greenspan, S. I. (1989). The development of the ego: Insights from clinical work with infants and young children. In S. I. Greenspan & G. H. Pollack, *The course of life* (Vol. I, *Infancy*, pp. 85–164). Madison: International Universities Press.

Hall, K. R. L., & DeVore, I. (1965). Baboon social behavior. In I. De Vore (Ed.), *Primate Behavior* (pp. 53–110). New York: Holt, Rinehart, & Winston.

Hamilton, W. D. (1964). The genetical evolution of social behavior, I, II, *Journal of Theoretical Biology*, *7*, 1–16, 17–52.

Hay, D. F. (1977). Following their companions as a form of exploration for human infants. *Child Development, 48*, 1624–1632.

———. (1980). Multiple functions of proximity-seeking in infancy. *Child Development, 51*, 636–645.

———. (1985). Learning to form relationships in infancy: Parallel attainments with parents and peers. *Developmental Review*, *5*, 122–161.

Hay, D. F., Caplan, M., Castle, J., & Stimson, C. (1991). Does sharing become increasingly "rational" in the second year of life? *Developmental Psychology*, *27*, 987–999.

Hay, D. F., & Murray, P. (1982). Giving and requesting: Social facilitation of infants' offers to adults. *Infant Behavior and Development, 5*, 301–310.

Hay, D. F., Murray, P., Cecire, S., & Nash, A. (1985). Social learning of social behavior in early life. *Child Development, 56*, 43–57.

Hay, D. F., Nash, A., & Pedersen, J. (1981). Responses of six-month-olds to the distress of their peers. *Child Development*, *52*, 1071–1075.

———. (1983). Interaction between six- month-old peers. *Child Development, 54*, 557–562.

Hay, D. F., & Ross, H. S. (1982). The social nature of early conflict. *Child Development, 53*, 105–113.

Hinde, R. A. (1982). Attachment: Some conceptual and biological issues. In J. Stevenson-Hinde & C. M. Parkes (Eds.), *The place of attachment in human behavior* (pp. 60–76). New York: Basic Books.

Howes, C., Rodning, C., Galluzzo, D. C., & Myers, L. (1988). Attachment and child care: Relationships with mother and caregiver. *Early Childhood Research Quarterly, 3,* 403–416.

Hrdy, S. B. (1980). *The langurs of Abu.* Cambridge: Harvard University Press.

Immelmann, K. (1972). Sexual and other long-term aspects of imprinting in birds and other species. *Advances in the Study of Behavior, 4,* 147–174.

Ipsa, J. (1981). Peer support among Soviet day care toddlers. *International Journal of Behavioral Development, 4,* 255–269.

Jacobson, J. L. (1981). The role of inanimate objects in early peer relations. *Child Development, 52,* 618–626.

Jacobson, J. L., Tianan, R. L., Wille, D. E., & Atych, D. M. (1986). Infant-mother attachment and early peer relations: The assessment of behavior in an interactive context. In E. C. Mueller and C. R. Cooper, *Process and outcome in peer relationships* (pp. 57–85). Orlando: Academic Press.

Kawamura, S. (1963). The process of sub-culture propagation among Japanese macaques. In C. H. Southwick (Ed.), *Primate Social Behavior.* Princeton: Van Nostrand.

Klinnert, M. D., Campos, J. J., Sorce, J. F., Emde, R. N., & Svejda, M. (1983). Emotions as behavior regulators: Social referencing in infancy. In R. Plutchick & H. Kellerman (Eds.), Emotions in early development: Vol. 2. *The emotions* (pp. 57–86). New York: Academic Press.

Klinnert, M. D., Emde, R. N., Butterfield, P., & Campos, J. (1986). Social referencing: The infant's use of emotional signals from a friendly adult with mother present. *Developmental Psychology, 22,* 427–432.

Konner, M. (1975). Relations among infants and juveniles in comparative perspective. In M. Lewis & L. A. Rosenblum (Eds.), *Friendship and peer relations.* New York: Wiley.

Kruijt, J. P., Ten Cate, C. J., & Meeuwissen, G. B. (1983). The influence of siblings on the development of sexual preferences of male zebra finches. *Developmental Psychobiology, 16,* 233–239.

Lamb, M. E. (1977). The development of infant-mother and father-infant attachments in the second year of life. *Developmental Psychology, 13,* 237–244.

Lamb, M. E., & Nash, A. (1989). Infant-mother attachment, sociability, and peer competence. In T. J. Berndt & G. W. Ladd (Eds.), *Peer relationships in child development* (pp. 217–245). New York: Wiley.

Lamb, M. E., Thompson, R. A., Gardner, W., & Charnov, E. L. (1985). *Infant-mother attachment: The origins and developmental significance of individual differences in strange situation behavior.* Hillsdale, NJ: Lawrence Erlbaum.

Levine, A. (1986). Profile: Mary D. Ainsworth. In S. Scarr, R. A. Weinberg, & A. Levine (Eds.), *Understanding development* (pp. 210–213). San Diego: Harcourt Brace Jovanovich.

Lewis, M. (1982). The social network systems model: Toward a theory of social development. In T. Field (Ed.), *Review of human development* (Vol. 1). New York: Wiley.

——. (1987). Social development in infancy and early childhood. In J. D. Osofsky (Ed.), *Handbook of infant development* (pp. 419–493).

Lickliter, R., & Gottlieb, G. (1985). Social interactions with siblings is necessary for visual imprinting of species-specific maternal preferences in ducklings (*Anas platyrhynchos*). *Journal of Comparative Psychology, 99,* 371–379.

——. (1988). Social specificity: Interaction with own species is necessary to foster species-specific maternal preferences in ducklings. *Developmental Psychobiology, 21,* 311–321.

Lorenz, K. (1970/1935). Companions as factors in the bird's environment. In K. Lorenz (Ed.), *Studies on animal and human behavior.* Cambridge, MA: Harvard University Press.

MacFarlane, A. (1975). Olfaction in the development of social preferences in the human neonate. In *Parent-infant interaction* (CIBA Foundation Symposium No. 33). Amsterdam: Elsevier.

Maudry, M., & Nekula, M. (1939). Social relations between children of the same age during the first two years of life. *Journal of Genetic Psychology, 54,* 193–215.

Maynard-Smith, J. (1974). The theory of games and the evolution of animal conflicts. *Journal of Theoretical Biology, 47,* 209–221.

Meltzoff, A. N., & Moore, M. K. (1977). Imitation of facial and manual gestures by human neonates. *Science, 198,* 75–78.

Mueller, N. (1989). Toddlers' peer relations: Shared meaning and semantics. In W. Damon (Ed.), *Child development today and tomorrow* (pp. 312–331). San Francisco: Jossey-Bass.

Myers, B. J., Jarvis, P. A., & Creasey, G. L. (1987). Infants' behavior with their mothers and grandmothers. *Infant Behavior and Development, 10,* 245–259.

Nash, A. (1986, August). *A comparison of infants' social competence with mother and peer*. Paper presented to the American Psychological Association, Washington, DC.

———. (1989, April). *The role of adults in infant-peer interactions*. Paper presented to the Society for Research in Child Development, Kansas City, Missouri.

Nash, A., & Hay, D. F. (1993). Relationships in infancy as precursors and causes of later relationships and psychopathology. In D. F. Hay & A. Angold (Eds.), *Precursors, causes, and psychopathology* (pp.199–232). Chichester, England: Wiley.

Nash, A., & Lamb, M. E. (1987, April). *Becoming acquainted with unfamiliar adults and peers in infancy*. Paper presented to the Society for Research in Child Development, Baltimore, Maryland.

Oppenheim, D., Sagi, A., & Lamb, M. E. (1988). Infant-adult attachments on the kibbutz and their relation to socio-emotional development 4 years later. *Developmental Psychology, 24*, 427–433.

Orians, G. H. (1969). On the evolution of mating systems in birds and mammals. *American Naturalist, 103*, 589–603.

Rheingold, H. L. (1982). Little children's participation in the work of adults, a nascent prosocial behavior. *Child Development, 53*, 114–125.

———. (1985). Development as the acquisition of familiarity. *Annual Review of Psychology, 36*, 1–17.

Rheingold, H. L., & Eckerman, C. O. (1973). Fear of stranger: A critical examination. In H. W. Reese (Ed.), *Advances in Child Development and Behavior, Vol. 8* (pp. 185–222). New York: Academic Press.

Rheingold, H. L., Hay, D. F., & West, M. J. (1976). Sharing in the second year of life. *Child Development, 47*, 1148–1158.

Ricciuti, H. (1974). Fear and the development of social attachments in the first year of life. In M. Lewis & L. Rosenblum (Eds.), *The origins of human behavior: Fear*. New York: Wiley. 73–106.

Rogoff, B. (1990). *Apprenticeship in thinking*. New York: Oxford University Press.

Rogoff, B., Malkin, C. M., & Gilbride, K. (1984). Interaction with babies as guidance in development. *New Directions for Child Development, 23*, 31–43.

Rosenthal, M. K. (1967). The generalization of dependency behavior from mother to stranger. *Journal of Child Psychology and Psychiatry, 8*, 117–133.

Ross, H. S., & Goldman, B. D. (1977). Establishing new social relations in infancy. In T. Alloway, P. Pliner, & L. Krames (Eds.), *Attachment behavior: Advances in the Study of Communication and Affect*, Vol. 3. New York: Plenum.

Rubenstein, J., & Howes, C. (1976). The effects of peers on toddler interaction with mothers and toys. *Child Development, 47*, 597–605.

Rubenstein, J., Howes, C., & Pedersen, F.A. (1982). Second order effects of peers on mother-toddler interaction. *Infant Behavior and Development, 5*, 185–194.

Sagi, A., & Hoffman M. (1976). Empathetic distress in the newborn. *Developmental Psychology, 12*, 175–176.

Sagi, A., Lamb, M. E., Lewkowicz, K. S., Shoham, R., Dvir, R., & Estes, D. (1985). Security of infant-mother, -father, and -metapelet attachments among kibbutz-reared Israeli children. In I. Bretherton & E. Waters (Eds.), Growing points in attachment theory and research, *Monograph of the Society for Research in Child Development, 50* (1–2, Serial No. 209), pp. 257–275.

Schaffer, H. R. (1971). *The growth of sociability*. Middlesex, England: Penguin.

Schneirla, T. C. (1959). An evolutionary and developmental theory of biphasic process underlying approach and withdrawal. In M. R. Jones (Ed.), *Nebraska Symposium on Motivation*, Vol. 7 (pp. 1–42). Lincoln: University of Nebraska Press.

———. (1965). Aspects of stimulation and organization in approach-withdrawal processes underlying vertebrate behavioral development. In D. S. Lehrman, R. Hinde, & E. Shaw (Eds.), *Advances in the study of behavior*, Vol. 1 (pp. 1–71). New York: Academic Press.

Snow, C. E. (1977). The development of conversations between mothers and babies. *Journal of Child Language, 4*, 1–22.

Spelke, E. S., & Cortelyou, A. (1981). Perceptual aspects of social knowing: Looking and listening in infancy. In M. E. Lamb & L. R. Sherrod (Eds.), *Infant social cognition: Empirical and theoretical considerations* (pp. 61–84). Hillsdale, NJ: Erlbaum.

Spence, M. J., & DeCasper, A. J. (1987). Prenatal experience with low-frequency maternal voice sounds influences neonatal perception of maternal voice samples. *Infant Behavior and Development, 10*, 133–142.

Stern, D. (1985). *The interpersonal world of the infant*. New York: Basic.

Stifter, C. A., Fox, N. A, & Porges, S. W. (1989). Facial expressivity and vagal tone in 5- and 10-month-old infants. *Infant Behavior and Development*, *12*, 127–137.

Ten Cate, C. (1987). Sexual preferences in zebra finch males raised by two species: II. The internal representation resulting from double imprinting. *Animal Behavior*, *35*, 321–330.

Ten Cate, C., Los, L., & Schilperoord, L. (1984). The influence of differences in social experiences on the development of species recognition in zebra finch males. *Animal Behavior*, *32*, 852–860.

Teti, D. M., & Lamb, M. E. (1986, April). *Correlates of attachment and caregiving between infants and older siblings*. Paper presented at the International Conference on Infant Studies, Los Angeles.

Trivers, R. L. (1971). The evolution of reciprocal altruism. *Quarterly Review of Biology*, *46*, 35–57.

———. (1972). Parental investment and sexual selection. In B. Campbell (Ed.), *Sexual selection and the descent of man* (pp. 136–179). Chicago: Aldine.

———. (1974). Parent-offspring conflict. *American Zoologist*, *14*, 249–269.

Tronick, E. Z., Cohn, J. F., & Shea, E. (1986). The transfer of affect between mothers and infants. In T. B. Brazelton & M. Yogman (Eds.), *Affective development in infancy*. Norwood, NJ: Ablex.

Tronick, E. Z., Winn, S., & Morelli, G. (1985). Multiple caretaking in the context of human evolution. Why don't the Efe know the Western prescription for child care? In M. Reite & T. Field (Eds.), *The psychobiology of attachment and separation* (pp. 293–322). Orlando: Academic Press.

Vandell, D. L. (1980). Sociability of peer and mother during the first year. *Developmental Psychology*, *16*, 335–361.

Vandell, D. L., & Wilson, K. S. (1982). Social interaction in the first year: Infants' social skills with peers versus mother. In K. H. Rubin & H. S. Ross (Eds.), *Peer relationships and social skills in childhood* (pp. 187–208). New York: Springer-Verlag.

———. (1987). Infants' interactions with mother, sibling, and peer: Contrasts and relations between interaction systems. *Child Development*, *58*, 176–186.

Vandell, D. L., Wilson, K. S., & Buchanan, N. R. (1980). Peer interaction in the first year of life: An examination of its structure, content, and sensitivity to toys. *Child Development*, *51*, 481–488.

Vandell, D. L., Wilson, K. S., & Henderson, K. (1985, April). *Peer interaction in twin and singleton infants: Negative effects of peer familiarity and peer experience.* Paper presented to the Society for Research in Child Development, Toronto, Canada.

Washburn, S. L., Jay, P. C., & Lancaster, J. B. (1965). Field studies of Old World monkeys and apes. *Science, 150,* 1541–1547.

Williams, G. C. (1966). *Adaptation and natural selection.* Princeton: Princeton University Press.

Wynne-Edwards, V. C. (1962). *Animal dispersion in relation to social behavior.* Edinburgh: Oliver & Boyd.

SECTION IV

Approach/Withdrawal and Individual Differences

CHAPTER 11

The Approach/Withdrawal Concept
Associations with Salient Constructs in Contemporary Theories of Temperament and Personality Development

Michael Windle

Among the major contributions of T. C. Schneirla to current scientific thinking was his focus on approach and withdrawal processes, which were viewed as integrated behavioral patterns of evolutionary significance (e.g., Schneirla, 1939, 1959, 1965). Schneirla described approach and withdrawal as two distinct but interrelated processes influenced by the intensity of the stimulus. Approach processes involved movement toward stimulation, such as getting food or seeking warmth, with the associated activation of the parasympathetic branch of the autonomic nervous system (ANS)—heart rate deceleration, and more regular respiration and blood pressure. In contrast, withdrawal processes involved movement away from high intensity stimulation and were reflected in the activation of the sympathetic branch of the ANS and with heart rate acceleration and limb (e.g., arms, legs) muscular flexions. The biphasic approach and withdrawal processes were posited to act in opposition to one another, though both were viewed as significant in adaptive functioning in that they enabled the organism to respond flexibly to stimuli that were of variable intensity levels, and facilitated behaviors that were integral to the survival of species (e.g., obtaining food, avoiding danger, mating).

Schneirla (1959, 1965) proposed that biphasic approach and withdrawal processes existed in all animals and he studied these processes in comparative animal research. However, a central question posed by Schneirla was whether approach and withdrawal processes differed qualitatively across different phyletic levels. Tobach and Aronson (1970) succinctly describe Schneirla's comparative view and the need to identify distinct, multiple levels of the organism and the coordinated functioning of these levels to adequately understand a common process across phyletic levels. In reference to Schneirla, Tobach and Aronson state that:

> [H]e maintained that there is little scientific value in viewing the feeding behavior of all animals from protozoa to man as a common process, just because it results in the intake of food. There are major qualitative differences in morphology, physiology, neural, and psychological processes at various levels and these must be considered in the analysis of food consumption (Tobach and Aronson, 1970, p. xvi).

Thus, while emphasizing phylogenetic continuity in cross-species comparisons of biphasic approach and withdrawal processes, Schneirla (1959) recognized that ". . . through evolution, higher psychological levels have arisen in which through ontogeny such mechanisms can produce new and qualitatively advanced types of adjustments to environmental conditions" (p. 300). Schneirla (1959) also emphasized that ". . . ontogeny progressively frees processes of individual motivation from the basic formula of prepotent stimulative-intensity relationships" (p. 300). These features of Schneirla's thinking are important in this chapter, because the focus is on approach and withdrawal processes among humans and with regard to human development; it is generally recognized that humans differ qualitatively from other vertebrates with regard to learning (e.g., Macphail, 1982), and thus it is argued in this chapter that there is a need to view approach and withdrawal processes appropriate to the multiple levels of organismic functioning characteristic of humans.

For example, whereas approach and withdrawal processes may be more subject to (physical) stimulus-intensity characteristics in infancy, biological, cognitive, and social developmental processes in childhood, adolescence, and adulthood may attenuate the prepotent influences of strictly stimulus-intensity characteristics during these periods of development. As such, the prepotent stimulative-intensity relationships for humans tends to change across the lifespan as language and other cognitive-symbolic systems become more dominant in ontogeny. Further, initial biological differences, differential growth rates, and unique learning experiences produce marked individual variation in the stimuli that contribute to the intensity of responses. Note that this reasoning is not incompatible with Schneirla's (1959) basic principle that, "Intensity of stimulation basically determines the direction of reaction with respect to the source . . ." (p. 2), but does necessitate the consideration of the organism's prior experiences and cognitive and affective capacities in evaluating the effect of the stimulus (e.g., Lazarus & Folkman, 1984; LeDoux, 1989; Zajonc, 1984). In addition, distinctions must be made between stimulus intensity associated with physical systems (e.g., light, sound) and elementary sensory processes (e.g., seeing, hearing), the domains of much of the cross-species research of Schneirla, and stimulus intensity associated with social stimuli (e.g., meeting a new person, speaking in public) and higher-level cognitive appraisal processes in humans. LeDoux (1989) has emphasized the dynamic affective learning and memory capabilities of humans and primates that enable these organisms to change the valence of a stimulus; thus, a stimulus that initially may elicit fear and withdrawal may, with experience, become a stimulus that elicits approach behaviors.

Chapter Overview

In this chapter, I focus on the approach/withdrawal concept and its relationship to some prominent constructs in contemporary theories of temperament and personality development. I focus on research conducted with humans, though a considerable literature does exist with regard to the origins and functions of temperamental characteristics in other species (e.g., Diamond, 1957; Schneirla 1959, 1965). The chapter is divided into

four parts. After a brief historical review of the approach/
withdrawal concept, I discuss this concept in relation to other
temperament and personality theories and proposed cognate
constructs (e.g., shyness, behavioral inhibition). Next, I present
some research completed by myself and colleagues (e.g., J.
Lerner & R. Lerner, 1983; Windle et al., 1986) to illustrate one
empirical approach to the study of the approach/withdrawal
concept. Finally, some unresolved issues regarding the
approach/withdrawal concept are identified and some future
research directions are proposed.

Historical Sketch of Approach/Withdrawal Concept

The intellectual origins of concepts related to approach
and withdrawal processes, such as introversion-extraversion, can
be traced to the Hippocrates-Galen humoral theory of four temperaments (melancholic, choleric, phlegmatic, and sanguine) and
to subsequent elaborations and refinements by Kant (1912–1918)
and Wundt (1903). For instance, Wundt contributed to notions
regarding underlying temperament types that were later to become central to Eysenck's personality dimensions of introversion-extraversion and neuroticism-emotional stability (e.g.,
Eysenck, 1967, 1987). According to Wundt, the combination of
choleric and sanguine temperaments corresponded to extraverted types, and the combination of melancholic and phlegmatic temperaments corresponded to introverted types;
similarly, the combination of melancholic and choleric temperaments corresponded to high neurotic types, and the combination
of phlegmatic and sanguine temperaments corresponded to low
neurotic, emotionally stable types.

The Hippocrates-Galen humoral theory of temperament
and the two-dimensional representation of Wundt (1903) not
only influenced Eysenck (1967, 1987) and other personality theorists (e.g., Diamond, 1957), but also influenced some researchers
in motivational psychology. For example, Duffy (1949) proposed
that *all* behavior could be characterized by two dimensions, the
first along an intensity continuum ranging from inactivity to
high activity, and a second along a directional continuum rang-

ing from withdrawal to approach. Stagner (1948) also used a similar two-dimensional scheme of low-high activity and approach/withdrawal to characterize a more restrictive scope of behavior, namely affective features of behavior. Stagner theorized that emotional states of excitement and depression were at opposite ends of the activity dimension and that emotional states of pleasantness and unpleasantness were at opposite ends of the approach/withdrawal dimension. As such, pleasantness (approach) was a subjective emotional correlate associated with the satisfaction of basic needs such as the consumption of food (nutrients) and affiliative social behavior. Unpleasantness (withdrawal) was a subjective emotional correlate associated with the emergency, fight-or-flight, response or with other responses of withdrawal or rejection. Stagner further proposed that the four humoral temperaments of the Hippocrates-Galen theory could be represented using the two dimensions of activity and approach/withdrawal. For instance, a melancholic temperament type could be characterized as low on the activity dimension and high on the withdrawal dimension, thus manifesting a depressive, unpleasant affectional style. Similarly, a sanguine temperament type could be characterized as high on the activity dimension and high on the approach dimension, thus manifesting an excited, pleasant affectional style.

In addition to interest in and alternative proposals for dimensional (or structural) representations of temperament, in which approach/withdrawal was salient, much research has been conducted on the physiological basis of different temperament types. Whereas the Hippocrates-Galen theory proposed that variation in the quantity of different humors, such as black or yellow bile, was at the root of different temperament types, research in the twentieth century has focused principally on variation in biological structures of the autonomic and central nervous systems (e.g., Eysenck, 1967; Gray, 1982; Kagan, Reznick, & Snidman, 1987; Zuckerman, 1979). Unanimity among researchers regarding which specific biological structures most adequately account for individual variation in temperament has yet to be achieved, but most of these theoretical accounts use cortical and/or autonomic arousal as key constructs. That is, there is a general consensus that individual differences in sensitivity levels (e.g., differential thresholds), intensity and duration of response parameters, and general reactivity levels underlie major sources of individual variation in temperamental functioning. A somewhat more detailed description of a few of these theoretical accounts is provided below. However, prior to the presentation of these theoretical accounts, it is important to refer to another major historical figure, Ivan Pavlov, who contributed to pertinent issues associated with contemporary biological theories of temperament and personality.

Pavlovian Influence

Pavlov (e.g., 1927) was interested in individual differences in the speed and efficiency of conditioning and used a range of experimental learning procedures to study aspects of conditioning in dogs. Pavlov proposed that individual differences in CNS properties accounted for variation in the speed and efficiency of conditioning and furthermore suggested that temperament was the most general property of the CNS which modulates all activity of the organism (e.g., Valenstein, 1970). He proposed that the configuration of the three basic nervous system properties of strength of excitation, balance (or equilibrium), and mobility accounted for different temperament types. *Strength of excitation* referred to the capacity of the nervous system to endure high levels of prolonged stimulation. *Balance* referred to the CNS ratio of the strength of excitation to the strength of inhibition. *Mobility* referred to the ability of the CNS to "give way," or flexibly adjust, to external conditions and to give priority to the appropriate excitatory or inhibitory response.

Like many of his Western contemporaries, Pavlov was influenced by the Hippocrates-Galen temperament theory. Out of potentially numerous configurations of his three basic nervous system properties, Pavlov proposed four types that corresponded with those of the Hippocrates-Galen temperament theory. According to Pavlov, a sanguine temperament type was characterized by strong, balanced, and mobile CNS properties. A phlegmatic temperament type was characterized by strong, balanced, and slow (to adjust) CNS properties. A choleric temperament type was characterized by a predominance of excitation over inhibition. Finally, a melancholic temperament type was characterized by weakness of capacity to endure prolonged levels of stimulation. (For more detailed discussions of Pavlov's temperament types, see Gray, 1964; Strelau, 1983, 1989; Valenstein, 1970).

Pavlov's contributions to temperament were influential in the West (and the East) because they focused attention on individual differences in biological structures (i.e., CNS properties presumed to reflect the activity of nerve cells and the nervous system) as manifested by differential responsivity and learning (conditioning) to variable levels of stimulus intensity. Several researchers (e.g., Gray, 1964; Mangan, 1982; Strelau, 1983, 1989) have drawn parallels between Pavlov's concepts of excitatory and inhibitory nervous system properties and Western conceptions of arousal. In particular, Pavlov's research was quite influential in the development of Eysenck's personality theory (1967, 1987) which has, in turn, been influential in the stimulation of a burgeoning literature of biologically-based personality research studies and of alternative theoretical models (e.g., Cloninger, 1987a; Gray, 1982). Gray (1970), for example, has proposed that Pavlov's strong nervous system type is related to Eysenck's extraversion dimension and that the weak nervous system type is associated with introversion.

Summary

Many of the current prominent issues and guiding conceptual frameworks concerning approach/withdrawal and cognate concepts (introversion-extraversion) can be traced to historical influences such as the Hippocrates-Galen humoral theory of temperament and to subsequent elaborations and refinements by scholars such as Kant and Wundt. Consistent themes have included the conceptualization of temperament as an individual-difference variable domain with temperament attributes having a constitutional (biological) basis, with at least two dimensions (e.g., low-high activity and directional approach/withdrawal). Environmental, stimulus-intensity characteristics have been seen as influential in the dispositional expression of temperament attributes through mechanisms such as conditionability and learning. Schneirla's (1939, 1959, 1965) account of approach/withdrawal processes shares some similarities with these early contributions to the concept of temperament. However, for the comparative psychologist Schneirla, the analysis of *behavioral development across all organisms* was integral, and development as a method of organizing individual differences was secondary. In addition, Schneirla (1957) emphasized the concept of "circular functions" to account for the *development* of approach and withdrawal processes; development was not a central feature of many of the major historical influences in temperament. The concept of circular functions, which referred to feedback processes involved in the ongoing regulation of behavior, including approach and withdrawal processes, subsequently became a cornerstone of a major conceptual model of temperament development (e.g., J. Lerner & R. Lerner, 1983; Thomas & Chess, 1977). This conceptual model is discussed later in this chapter with regard to the "goodness of fit" model of temperament-context relations.

Approach/Withdrawal and Cognate Theoretical Constructs

There are a number of psychobiological temperament perspectives focused on cognate concepts of the approach/withdrawal concept, such as behavioral inhibition and behavioral activation. It is important to provide more detail for some of these perspectives because they represent approach/withdrawal-like conceptualizations within multilevel frameworks. For purposes of illustration, the research programs from several different laboratories are presented briefly. These illustrations are not intended to exhaust the research within any single research program, nor are they intended to imply that these programs are producing the "best" research. Rather, the intent here is to represent a sampling of a few well-developed research programs.

Kagan and Colleagues' Behavioral Inhibited/Uninhibited Types

Jerome Kagan and colleagues (e.g., Kagan, 1989a, 1989b; Kagan, Reznick, & Snidman, 1987; Kagan & Snidman, 1991) have been conducting longitudinal studies of two cohorts of children who had been selected between the ages of two to three on the basis of being either extremely cautious and shy (referred to as inhibited) or extremely fearless and outgoing (referred to as un-inhibited) in relation to unfamiliar peers, adults, and objects. Based on this conceptualization, uninhibited children would be expected to manifest a more approach-oriented behavioral style and inhibited children would be expected to manifest a more withdrawal-oriented behavioral style. Kagan (1989a) has used an extreme group approach (i.e., the lower and upper 10 percent of the score distribution) to identify qualitatively distinct inhibited and uninhibited temperament types. The studies by Kagan and colleagues have included: (1) the assignment of children to inhib-ited and uninhibited extreme groups on the basis of behavioral reactions to unfamiliar adults and objects with the first cohort, and on the basis of the child's reactions to an unfamiliar peer (matched on age and sex) with the second cohort; (2) the use of multiple methods of assessment, such as laboratory-based mea-sures of inhibited/uninhibited responses to unfamiliar persons and objects, heart rate and heart-rate variability, respiration rate, pupillary dilation, muscle tension, and norepinephrine and cor-tisol levels; and (3) longitudinal research designs that facilitate not only the assessment of stability and change of inhibited and uninhibited types, but also the inter-level relations among overt behavioral indexes and physiological parameters. Inter-level relations have been a prominent concern of Schneirla (1957) and those influenced by him (e.g., Aronson, 1984; R. Lerner, 1984).

Briefly, Kagan and colleagues (1987, 1991) have found some systematic interrelations between inhibited and uninhib-ited types and physiological indexes. For instance, inhibited children, relative to uninhibited children, had higher and more stable heart rates, significantly larger pupillary diameters under baseline and experimental task situations, higher cortisol levels across home and laboratory conditions, and somewhat higher levels of peripheral norepinephrine activity. Further, relatively high stability of individual differences was indicated for the extreme groups of inhibited and uninhibited children across two follow-up periods that occurred around ages four and five-and-a-half years. The stability coefficient (Pearson r) for the first cohort between measures of behavior at 21 months and five-and-a-half years was .52; for the second cohort, the stability coefficient between measures of behavior at 31 and 43 months was .59. Finally, the inter-level relations between inhibited and uninhibited types and some physiological indexes systematically covaried across time. For example, inhibited children who had higher, more stable heart rates at the first two occasions of measurement were more likely to remain classified as inhibited at the third occasion of measurement relative to inhibited children with lower, more variable heart rates at the first two occasions of measurement.

The research of Kagan and colleagues thus suggests that the response styles of inhibited and uninhibited (approach- and withdrawal-oriented) types are manifest in early childhood, are correlated significantly with several physiological indexes, and are relatively stable (for extreme groups) at least across early childhood. Kagan et al. (1987) propose that individual differences in inhibition ". . . are due, in part, to tonic differences in the threshold of reactivity of parts of the limbic lobe, especially the amygdala and hypothalamus, which result in enhanced activity of the pituitary-adrenal axis, reticular activating system, and sympathetic nervous system" (p. 1459).

Much research remains to be conducted to confirm Kagan et al.'s (Kagan, 1989a; Kagan et al., 1987) neurobiological account of the physiological structures underlying inhibited and uninhibited types. In addition, longer-term stability of the interrelations between inhibited and uninhibited behaviors and physiological indexes (e.g., into late childhood and adolescence) must be investigated in relation to variable environmental events. Perhaps a more acute issue raised by Kagan (1989a) for future conceptualizations and studies of inhibited and uninhibited types is his emphasis on extreme groups who are *qualitatively* distinct not only with regard to surface behaviors but also with regard to underlying biological correlates. This theoretical position would suggest that inhibition and disinhibition are not usefully envisioned along a single continuum, but rather as distinct types in which intermediate scores (e.g., mean scores) on inhibition measures are not necessarily useful for predicting inter-level relations (e.g., between surface behaviors and physiological indexes) or outcome variables (e.g., anxiety levels). The study of qualitatively distinct temperament types represents a radical departure from most contemporary perspectives of temperament and personality.

In summary, the research of Kagan and colleagues has provided some provocative findings regarding the inter-level relations between uninhibited (approach) and inhibited (withdrawal) types for extreme group members. Furthermore, the proposal of qualitatively distinct temperament types raises salient conceptual and measurement issues that have largely heretofore been ignored, despite the influential role of types via the Hippocrates-Galen theory.

Rothbart and Colleagues' Psychobiological Approach

Mary Rothbart and colleagues (e.g., Rothbart, 1988, 1989a; Rothbart & Derryberry, 1981; Rothbart & Posner, 1985) have used a psychobiological framework in conceptualizing temperament as reflecting individual differences in *reactivity* (i.e., the excitability, responsivity, or arousability of physiological and/or behavioral systems) and *self-regulation* (i.e., the neural and behavioral processes that modulate reactivity levels). Approach and withdrawal (or avoidance) behaviors are involved in the self-regulation of the quality and quantity of stimulation via activity that increases, decreases, maintains, or restructures stimuli. Rothbart reports that even in early infancy there are marked individual differences in both approach and avoidance responses (e.g., Rothbart, 1988). For example, at low levels of stimulation some infants immediately respond and try to avoid the stimulation, whereas others do not respond until the level of stimulation is much more intense. Similarly, some infants will readily reach for a toy that is within their grasp, whereas others may hesitate to grasp or never attempt to grasp the toy. Rothbart and colleagues have proposed that approach behaviors (e.g., leaning toward, reaching, and grasping) and avoidance behaviors (e.g., leaning away, turning away) among older infants enable them to begin to self-regulate levels of engagement with persons or objects. These researchers suggest that self-regulatory behaviors such as approach, withdrawal, and avoidance have increasingly important roles over the course of ontogeny in modulating reactivity levels of biological response systems (e.g., somatic reactions, ANS, neuroendocrine system) and in facilitating the coordinated functioning of the developing organism.

Similar to Schneirla (1957), Rothbart (1989b) views approach and withdrawal processes as oppositional, and distinguishes approach and withdrawal from two other oppositional aspects of behavior, that is, stimulus-seeking and avoidance. Stimulus-seeking and avoidance often arise somewhat later in development than do approach and withdrawal and are associated with the development of *effortful* (conscious) processes. Effortful processes become increasingly important in child, adolescent, and adult development because they are involved in self-regulatory activity that facilitates goal-directed activities. Effortful processes associated with goal-directed activities are important in many daily activities because approaching or withdrawing from some stimuli may be displeasurable. For example, withholding approach from a positive stimulus (e.g., a piece of chocolate cake) in order to avoid gaining weight requires effortful processes and a nonapproach response. Rothbart and Posner (1985) refer to these effortful processes as internal control and such internal control is associated with self-regulation through the selection of situations with varying levels of stimulation.

Rothbart's (1989b) broader conceptual framework attempts to integrate research findings from multiple disciplines (e.g., physiology, neuroendocrinology, psychology) and sub-specialties (e.g., psychobiological theories of personality, infant/child development). As noted previously, many of Rothbart's views on the development of approach and withdrawal processes are similar to Schneirla's (1957) and, furthermore, she distinguishes these two earlier processes from the later developing processes of seeking and avoidance. Central to Rothbart's framework for self-regulative behaviors are effortful (conscious) processes. Such processes, manifested in seeking and avoidant behaviors, are not inconsistent with Schneirla's view that these behaviors were of a higher evolutionary and developmental order and were, therefore, not necessarily germane across all phyletic levels.

Eysenck's Personality Theory

The research of Hans Eysenck (1967) and his introversion-extraversion concept have been influential in his own theory as well as several other current biological theories of personality (e.g., Cloninger, 1987a; Gray, 1982; Zuckerman, 1979). In his early theorizing, Eysenck believed that the biological source of individual variation in temperament was associated with visceral arousal; later his focus shifted to cortical arousal. Specifically, with regard to introversion-extraversion, Eysenck proposed that individuals were motivated to attain levels of arousal associated with positive and pleasurable emotional states (i.e., moderate levels of arousal) rather than levels associated with negative and unpleasurable emotional states (i.e., levels of arousal that were too high or too low). Individual differences in arousal were considered to result from differences in the ascending reticular activating system. Accordingly, extraverts were characterized as individuals with relatively low levels of cortical arousal who sought out high levels of environmental stimulation so as to increase and regulate optimal levels of arousal that would be moderate and therefore emotionally pleasurable. Introverts were characterized as individuals with relatively high levels of cortical arousal who regulated optimal levels of arousal through the selection of activities and environments with lower levels of stimulation. The active seeking of stimulation by extraverts was associated with a more sociable, moving-toward-people, interpersonal orientation.

A second major personality dimension proposed by Eysenck (1967) was neuroticism-emotional stability. It was proposed that this dimension was influenced by levels of reactivity in the ANS which, in turn, influenced and were influenced by limbic system functioning. Eysenck indicated that individuals scoring high on the neuroticism dimension were characterized by high intensity ANS activity and slow habituation. Eysenck further proposed that while introversion-extraversion and neuroticism-stability were statistically orthogonal dimensions, specific clinical subtypes could be identified within the two-dimensional space. For example, extraverted, anxious individuals were described as simultaneously having low levels of cortical arousal and high levels of ANS arousal. Thus, stereotypically, an extraverted, anxious individual may seek out stimulation to attain optimal cortical arousal and associated pleasurable emotional states, but simultaneously may have high levels of ANS arousal (manifested through heart palpitations, sweating, and visceral arousal) that are associated with thoughts about and actually engaging in these high-arousal activities (e.g., meeting new people, attending a party).

Gray's Rotated Two-Dimensional Personality Model

Jeffrey Gray found the two-dimensional model of Eysenck meritorious, but proposed that a more adequate representation of personality could be obtained by rotating the orthogonal axes of the two Eysenckian dimensions by $45°$ (e.g., Gray, 1982, 1987). The two new axes were referred to as anxiety and impulsivity. Anxiety and impulsivity were associated, respectively, with two major affective-motivational systems, the behavioral inhibition system (BIS) and the behavioral activation system (BAS). Trait scores on anxiety and impulsivity were postulated to reflect individual differences in the sensitivity or reactivity of these affective motivational systems.

The BAS, or approach system (e.g., Depue & Iacono, 1989; Gray, 1987), involves responses that facilitate the attainment of conditioned rewards and nonpunishment. That is, certain stimuli become learned through conditioning and subsequently elicit facilitating (approach) behaviors that maintain or increase exposure to these stimuli. Although relatively little is known about the neural basis of the BAS, Gray (1987) cites evidence to suggest that a dopaminergic pathway that ascends from nucleus A10 in the ventral tegmental area to innervate the nucleus accumbens and the ventral striatum may be one central neural pathway of significance to the BAS (more specifically with regard to incentive motivation). Depue and Iacono (1989) also reviewed neurobiological findings that indicate that the nucleus accumbens serves as an interface between limbic and motor systems and thus suggests that limbic forebrain structures, in interaction with hypothalamic nuclei, are integrative centers for the initiation of numerous goal-directed behaviors (e.g., sex, feeding, attack, socializing).

The second affective-motivational system, the BIS, involves response patterns associated with conditioned aversive stimuli. That is, exposure to stimuli that are associated with punishment or nonreward elicit a behaviorally inhibited response characterized by a cessation of overt activity, increased attention to the environment, and higher levels of arousal. Gray (1982) has conducted a number of animal studies indicating that the septal-hippocampal system is involved in the regulation of arousal in the BIS. For example, Gray has repeatedly found that anti-anxiety drugs reduce arousal when punishment is expected or when confronting novel environments. The administration of anti-anxiety drugs results in a decrease in arousal in the septal-hippocampal system, as well as overt behavioral inhibition. While most of Gray's research in this area has involved rats, he has speculated that the prefrontal cortex, in addition to the septal-hippocampal system, may influence the regulation of the BIS in humans.

Gray (1987) proposed that both the BAS and BIS were involved in the expression of behavior and in the regulation of arousal in human activity. Similar to Schneirla's (1957) views on the oppositional nature of approach and withdrawal processes, Gray views the BAS and BIS as oppositional. Introverts may be characterized as individuals whose BIS is dominant relative to their BAS; extraverts manifest the opposite pattern. Gray further proposed that individuals with a highly sensitive and reactive BIS are likely to manifest heightened behavioral inhibition and be characterized as clinically anxious.

Cloninger's Three-Dimensional Personality Model

Another biological model of personality influenced by Eysenck and Gray has been developed by Robert Cloninger (1987a, 1987b). Cloninger proposes a three-dimensional system of personality labeled *harm avoidance* (similar to Gray's behavioral inhibition dimension), *novelty seeking* (similar to Gray's behavioral activation system), and *reward dependence* (which refers to a tendency to respond intensely to reward and succorance). The three traits are assumed to be statistically independent, to manifest high heritability coefficients, and to be associated with different monoamine neuromodulators. Cloninger has suggested that the fundamental basis of these personality traits is genetic, but that environmental influences are significant with regard to the expression of these underlying biological dispositions. Serotonin is proposed as the principal neuromodulator of harm avoidance, dopamine as the principal neuromodulator of novelty seeking, and norepinephrine as the principal neuromodulator of reward dependence.

Similar to Gray's theory (1982), these three personality response systems are assumed to respond to specific stimulus conditions and conditioned stimuli, and to elicit specific behavioral responses. For instance, the novelty-seeking personality dimension is associated with responses to stimuli characterized as novel or potentially rewarding, with characteristic behavioral responses including exploration, approach, or active avoidance or escape. Cloninger suggests ways in which this tridimensional personality model might be used to provide a more adequate representation of personality disorders and other psychiatric disorders. He does so by offering combinations of low, moderate, and high levels of the three personality dimensions. For instance, individuals with antisocial personality disorders would be characterized as high on novelty seeking, low in harm avoidance, and low in reward dependence. Presumably, these individual differences in personality response systems would correspond with underlying differences in specific monoamine neuromodulators (e.g., serotonin).

Many portions of Cloninger's (1987a, 1987b) tridimensional personality model remain to be tested and criticisms have already been leveled at its potential adequacy (e.g., Van Praag et al., 1991; Zuckerman, 1988). For example, Zuckerman (1988) has suggested that our current knowledge regarding the functioning of monoamine neuromodulators is such that Cloninger's model is overly simplistic with regard to the proposed personality trait-single neuromodulator response system. Similarly, Van Praag et al. (1991) summarize findings indicating that serotonin is not likely to be associated narrowly with harm avoidance, but rather has a more general influence on mood states and is related to the expression both of anger and aggression as well as anxiety regulation. Nevertheless, Rothbart (1989b) indicated that of the limited number of relevant studies done with infants, findings have generally been consistent with Cloninger's model. Additional research is likely to result in some major revisions of Cloninger's tridimensional model, but his efforts have been directed toward a parsimonious, bilevel model of personality that includes key components of directional behaviors (e.g., harm avoidance and withdrawal responses).

Conceptual Distinctions and Cognate Attributes

My purpose in presenting this cursory description of Cloninger's theory, as well as the theories of others (i.e., Kagan, Rothbart, Eysenck, Gray), is not to provide a detailed critique of them. Rather, it is to suggest that the approach/withdrawal concept is integrally involved in these theoretical systems, though the exact nature of that involvement and the organismic bilevel or multilevel relations varies across the alternative systems. For example, the manner in which Gray (1982) and Cloninger (1987a) describe behavioral inhibition, or harm avoidance, differs substantially from the manner in which Kagan et al. (1987) use the concept of behavioral inhibition. For Gray, the major substantive dimension ranges from behavioral inhibition (anxiety) to behavioral approach (impulsivity). For Kagan et al. (1987), behavioral inhibition consists of the tendency to be extremely cautious and shy (inhibited) versus fearless and outgoing (uninhibited) to unfamiliar persons or events.

In order to further distinguish alternative conceptualizations of approach/withdrawal and cognate temperament and personality attributes, alternative definitions are provided in Table 1. I will use the approach/withdrawal definition of Thomas and Chess (1977) and Windle and Lerner (1986a) to make comparisons with other temperament concepts (e.g., shyness) for purposes of identifying common and unique

TABLE 1

Approach/Withdrawal and Cognate Attributes
Labels and Conceptual Definitions

Attribute label	*Definition*
1. Approach/withdrawal (Thomas & Chess, 1977; Windle & Lerner, 1986b)	Tendency to approach, that is, to move towards new persons, objects, situations, or events versus tendency to move away from these novel circumstances.
2. Sociability (Buss, 1988)	Tendency to prefer the presence of others to being alone.
3. Shyness (Briggs, 1988)	Involves discomfort and inhibition in the presence of others. The discomfort and inhibition are derived from the interpersonal nature of the situation rather than from other sources (e.g., threats of harm).
4. Introversion-Extraversion (Eysenck, 1967; Eysenck & Rachman, 1965)	Personality dimension along which individuals differ in habitual arousal levels, sensory thresholds, rates of conditioning and other physiological reactivity dimensions. Extraverts are typically highly sociable, have many friends, and are impulsive; introverts are typically less sociable and prefer activities such as reading and studying.
5. Behavioral Inhibition (Kagan et al., 1987)	Tendency to be extremely cautious and shy (inhibited) to unfamiliar events.

features. As a note of historical reference, Schneirla proposed the use of the term approach/withdrawal to Thomas and Chess when they were selecting appropriate labels for their measured constructs. The definition of approach/withdrawal by Thomas and Chess, and adopted by Windle and Lerner, describes approach as the tendency to move towards new persons, objects, situations, and events versus the tendency to move away from these novel circumstances. In contrast to approach/withdrawal, sociability (Buss, 1988) refers to a motive of preferring to be alone versus being in the presence of others. As such, sociability is referred to as a motive, versus approach/withdrawal, which is referred to as a behavioral style, and sociability focuses on the social context but does not include actions/reactions to new objects or events. The movement toward new people and the sociability motive would, nevertheless, suggest that the constructs would share some overlapping variance. Similarly, shyness involves discomfort and inhibition in the presence of others (e.g., Briggs, 1988). While restricted to the interpersonal sphere, this definition of shyness would be expected to share some overlapping variance with a withdrawal behavioral style. Introversion-extraversion would also be expected to manifest significant interrelations with approach/withdrawal in that an approach-oriented behavioral style would be expected to be more highly associated with extraversion (and number of friends, desire to attend and enjoy parties) and withdrawal behaviors would be expected to characterize the behavior pattern adopted by introverts (moving away from people toward lower levels of stimulation). Finally, the tendency to be behaviorally uninhibited (Kagan et al., 1987) would be expected to be related to an "approach" behavioral style and behavioral inhibition with a "withdrawal" behavioral style. Research designed to assess some of these empirical relations is presented subsequently.

In addition to cognate temperament and personality constructs related to approach/withdrawal, the post-Freudian psychoanalyst Karen Horney (1945) identified three modes of interpersonal functioning that reveal underlying neurosis. The three modes are *moving toward people*, *moving against people*, and *moving away from people*. Horney theorized that most healthy persons utilize all three modes of interpersonal functioning to flexibly interact with others. The mode used is contingent upon the relationship to the social other (e.g., spouse, boss, burglar), the objectives or purposes of a given exchange (e.g., initiate a conversation, request assistance, express dissatisfaction) and other situational cues. However, for some persons, one mode dominates their interpersonal style, reflecting a rigid, neurotic tendency motivated by a desire to compensate for a lack of love and affection not received in infancy and childhood. For example, the dominant tendency to move toward people is proposed as an attempt by the person to overcome anxiety and insecurity through excessive demands of love and affection by significant others. The dominant tendency to move against people is proposed as an attempt to cope with insecurity by establishing power, prestige, and dominance. The dominant tendency to move away from people is proposed as an attempt to avoid potential rejection and emotional hurt by not becoming involved with significant others.

It is evident from the literature discussed that the approach/withdrawal concept is salient in many contemporary perspectives of temperament, personality, and psychopathology. The specific meaning and functional role of approach/ withdrawal does of course vary to some degree across these perspectives and in relation to Schneirla's conceptualization. However, there does appear to be some general convergence in identifying approach/withdrawal as a directional tendency influenced by stimulus intensity dimensions, whether these are features of the physical environment or are social-cognitive constructions. Furthermore, most of the theoretical perspectives presented suggest that approach and withdrawal processes (or the associated cognate terms) are integrally involved in self-regulatory activity via approaching or withdrawing from various stimuli (or physical and social settings).

Very little of Schneirla's research and theorizing about ap-proach and withdrawal processes focused on humans beyond the infancy stage of development, and much of the emphasis by Schneirla and his followers was on approach and withdrawal responses in relation to sensory processes (e.g., Pfaffman, 1961; Schneirla, 1959; Tobach, 1969) rather than higher cortical functions (e.g., executive functions). Nevertheless, Schneirla contributed to contemporary theories of temperament and per-sonality development in several ways. First, Schneirla's (1957) perspective provided a major alternative conceptual model for animal behaviorists who had been strongly influenced by the deterministic, genetically controlled instinct theory of Konrad Lorenz (1965). Schneirla's conceptualization focused on the "fusion" of maturation (nature) and experience (nurture), and thus implied that the independent study of instincts (or learning) was not a useful enterprise. Second, Schneirla (1957) proposed that development was a dynamic, ongoing, reciprocal process characterized by circular functions. That is, an organism's behaviors may alter features of the environment which, in turn, provide feedback that may alter the behaviors of the organism. Thomas and Chess (1977) were influenced by Schneirla's conceptualization and incorporated the circular functions notion in their goodness of fit model of person-environment relations. The goodness of fit model is discussed in more detail subsequently, but the point here is that Schneirla influenced the thinking of Thomas and Chess who, in turn, have been major figures in stimulating renewed interest in temperament research in the 1980s and 90s (e.g., Kagan, 1989b; J. Lerner & R. Lerner, 1983).

Measurement of the Approach/Withdrawal Construct

Much of what has been presented thus far in this chapter on the approach/withdrawal concept has been more conceptual, descriptive, and focused on inter-level relations. There have been a number of empirical studies that have assessed the interrelations between the measured construct of approach/withdrawal and other temperament and personality attributes, as well as studies focused on the concurrent and predictive validity of approach/withdrawal. These empirical studies illustrate the research application of the approach/withdrawal construct and facilitate an evaluation of the observed similarity/dissimilarity of the construct with cognate temperament and personality constructs. Further, these studies enable the assessment of hypothesized predictive relations with other features of adaptive/maladaptive functioning such as depression and general mental health, psychological adjustment and self-esteem, and intellectual functioning. The empirical literature reviewed is selective and is based on research conducted with a specific measure, the Revised Dimensions of Temperament Survey (DOTS-R) (Windle & Lerner, 1986b). This temperament measure includes the assessment of approach/withdrawal and while the measure is of recent origin, it has had relatively widespread use, especially with childhood, adolescent, and young adult samples.

The DOTS-R (Windle & Lerner, 1986b) is a 54-item, multifactorial questionnaire designed to measure salient dimensions of temperament, or behavioral style, consistent with those identified by Thomas and Chess (1977) in the New York Longitudinal Study. Three different age groups were used in the scale construction of the DOTS-R—preschoolers, elementary school children, and college students. Mother's ratings of temperament were used for the preschoolers and the self-report method was used for the two other samples. A series of data analytic procedures, including content analysis, item-total statistics, and factor analyses were used to identify homogeneous dimensions across all three samples. Items pertaining to approach/withdrawal were homogeneous across all three samples, with internal consistency estimates ranging from .77 to .85. Approach/withdrawal is defined in the DOTS-R as the tendency to approach, or move towards new persons, objects, situations, or events versus the tendency to withdraw, or move away from these novel circumstances. The ten-factor representation of the DOTS-R and the integrity of the approach/withdrawal construct have been replicated in an independent adolescent sample (Windle, 1992), and cross-cultural invariant relations were found for Japanese samples of preschoolers, early and late adolescents (e.g., Windle, Iwawaki, & Lerner, 1987, 1988).

Four studies have included data relevant to the interrelations between approach/withdrawal, as measured by the DOTS-R, and constructs measured by other temperament and personality measures. With a college sample, Windle (1989a) correlated approach/withdrawal with constructs measured by the Emotionality, Activity, Sociability, Impulsivity (EASI-II) measure of Buss and Plomin (1984) and by Eysenck's Personality Inventory (EPI) (Eysenck & Eysenck, 1968). The correlations are summarized in Table 2. (High scores on the withdrawal-approach scale are indicative of a more approach-oriented behavioral style.) The correlations indicate that an approaching behavioral style is associated with higher levels of sociability, extraversion, and activity, and with lower levels of neuroticism. A separate study by Ruch (1991) using similar measures with a sample of German late adolescents/young adults produced highly similar findings regarding interscale correlations among the DOTS-R, EASI-III, and EPI.

TABLE 2

Pearson Correlations between DOTS-R Approach/Withdrawal
Dimension and Attributes from Other Temperament
and Personality Inventories

Temperament and Personality Attributes	Withdrawal-Approach
EASI-II (Buss & Plomin, 1984)[a]	
Emotionality	.05
Activity Level	.26[**]
Sociability	.42[**]
Impulsivity	.03
EPI (Eysenck & Eysenck, 1968)[a]	
Extraversion	.44[**]
Neuroticism	-.23[**]
Lie Scale	.11
16 PF (Cattell, Eber, & Tatsuoka, 1970)[b]	
Scale A (Reserved, detached vs. Outgoing, warmhearted)	.27[**]
Scale E (Humble, accommodating vs. Assertive, independent)	.39[**]
Scale F (Sober, serious vs. Happy-go-lucky, lively)	.32[**]
Scale H (Shy, restrained vs. Venturesome, socially bold)	.35[**]
MMPI (University of Minnesota)[b]	
Scale 2. Depression	-.25[**]
Scale 9. Hypomania	.17[*]
Scale 0. Social Introversion	-.33[***]

[a] Data reported in Windle, 1989a

[b] Data reported in Chuguy, Kolpakov, Chepkasov, 1989

[*] $p < .05$ [**] $p < .01$ [***] $p < .001$

A third study investigated the interrelations between several different self-report questionnaires for a sample of
157 German college students (mean age = 24.1 yrs.) to examine

the robustness of the Five-Factor model of personality (e.g., McCrae & Costa, 1987) with the inclusion of prominent measures of personality and temperament (Angleitner & Ostendorf, 1991). The short form of the NEO Five-Factor Inventory, developed by Costa and McCrae (1989), was one of the measures used to assess marker variables for the Big Five factors. Factor analyses were conducted on the correlation matrix of subscale scores of the self-report questionnaires. Consistent with the findings presented in the two previous studies (Ruch, 1991; Windle, 1989a), approach, as measured by the DOTS-R, loaded significantly on extraversion (factor loading = .42) and inversely on neuroticism (factor loading = -.22). In addition, approach loaded significantly (factor loading = .58) on the dimension of openness to experience, along with subscales measuring sensation seeking and the markers of openness to experience. There is considerable controversy over the most appropriate conceptualization and label for the openness to experience factor (e.g., Costa & McCrae, 1992), but it has often been characterized as a manifestation of intellectual curiosity, aesthetic sensitivity, a high need for variety, and a liberal value system. I will return to this association between approach and openness to experience subsequently when discussing temperament-intelligence relations.

The fourth study was conducted with late adolescents and adults in the former Soviet Union (Chuguy, Kolpakov, & Chepkasov, 1989) and the DOTS-R attributes were correlated with the 16 PF (Cattell, Eber, & Tatsuoka, 1970) and the MMPI (University of Minnesota). An approach behavioral style was associated with a 16 PF personality profile characterized by outgoingness, assertiveness, independence, liveliness, and venturesomeness. A withdrawal behavioral style was associated with a MMPI profile characterized by depression, social introversion, and low hypomania.

The results of these four studies provide initial evidence that the approach/withdrawal construct, as measured by the DOTS-R, is significantly related to constructs similarly labeled in several major temperament and personality inventories. Further, the findings were relatively consistent cross-culturally. There was both convergent validity for the approach/withdrawal construct in these studies, as there were significant correlations with similarly labeled constructs, and discriminant validity as approach/withdrawal was not significantly correlated with constructs dissimilarly labeled. The pattern and magnitude of significant correlations does suggest, however, that approach/withdrawal is not an alternative measure of introversion-extraversion or of sociability, but rather is a distinct attribute.

Approach/withdrawal was significantly correlated with the two orthogonally measured EPI (Eysenck & Eysenck, 1968) dimensions of introversion-extraversion and neuroticism-stability of the EPI. Thus, similar to proposals by Gray (1982, 1987) and Briggs (1988) regarding the respective constructs of behavioral inhibition and shyness, it appears that approach/withdrawal diagonally intersects the orthogonal extraversion and neuroticism dimensions of the EPI, as it shares overlapping variance with both dimensions. Figure 1 provides a Venn diagram of proposed relations among the four constructs of approach/withdrawal, extroversion, neuroticism, and shyness.

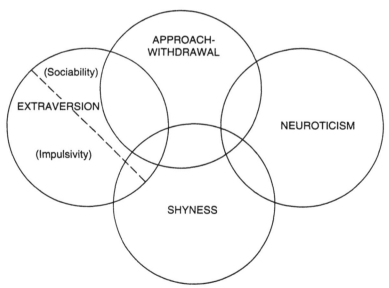

Figure 1. Venn diagram of interrelations between Approach-Withdrawal, Extraversion, Neuroticism, and Shyness

The interrelations between approach/withdrawal and extra-version are portrayed as larger than those between approach/ withdrawal and neuroticism, and the overlap is hypothesized to be attributable to the sociability aspects of extraversion. Evident from Figure 1 is that approach/withdrawal is related to but not identical with the other three personality constructs.

In addition to studies conducted with respect to inter-inventory relations of similarly labeled constructs, several studies have been completed regarding associations between approach/withdrawal and adjustment indexes and cognitive factors (e.g., Carson, Council, & Volk, 1989; Matheny, 1989; Windle, 1989b,c; Windle et al., 1986). The results of these studies are summarized in Table 3. Overall, the studies concerning adjustment indexes consistently indicate that an approaching behavioral style is associated with lower levels of depression, distress, anxiety, and alienation, and with higher levels of self-esteem, positive well-being, and general mental health. Two findings are significant with regard to studies regarding cognitive factors. First, an approaching behavioral style was significantly associated with higher IQ levels on the WISC for a sample of 12-year-old children (Matheny, 1989). Second, an approaching behavioral style was associated with perceived self-competence in the cognitive and self-worth domains for early and late adolescents, as well as in the social and physical domains for late adolescents (Windle et al., 1986). As exemplars, these findings regarding interrelations between approach/ withdrawal and IQ and perceived self-competence identify a research agenda encouraging more systematic study of temper-ament and cognition. Matheny (1989) has noted that "Formal theoretical statements permit temperament and cognition to be defined so that investigators within each domain have been isolationists by practice. In the traffic of the ongoing behaviors of the child, however, relations between the two domains are such that developmental commerce between the two domains is inevitable" (p. 277). R. Lerner and J. Lerner (1981) have also emphasized evolving temperament-intelligence reciprocities across the lifespan.

TABLE 3

Pearson Correlations Between DOTS-R Approach/Withdrawal Dimension, Adjustment Indexes, and Cognitive Factors

Adjustment Indexes (Sample)	Withdrawal-Approach
Depression/Mental Health	
Depressive symptoms (late adolescents)[a]	-.26[***]
Positive well-being (late adolescents)[b]	.29[***]
Low Distress (late adolescents)[b]	.13[*]
General Mental Health (late adolescents)[b]	.21[**]
Depressive symptoms (midadolescents)[c]	-.21[***]
Psychological Adjustment/Self-esteem	
Social nonconformity (adult women incest victims)[d]	-.07
Emotional expression[d]	.67[***]
Discomfort and anxiety[d]	-.48[***]
Alienation[d]	-.45[***]
Defensiveness[d]	.16
Self-esteem[d]	.34[**]
Cognitive Factors	
WISC Verbal IQ (12 year olds)[e]	.41[**]
WISC Performance IQ[e]	.32[*]
Perceived Competence (early adolescents)[a]—	
Cognitive	.33[***]
Social	.17
Physical	.09
General self-worth	.25[**]
Perceived Competence (late adolescents)[a]—	
Cognitive	.28[***]
Social	.46[***]
Physical	.18[*]
General self-worth	.31[***]

[a] Data reported in Windle et al., 1986   [d] Data reported in Carson et al., 1989
[b] Data reported in Windle, 1989b   [e] Data reported in Matheny, 1989
[c] Data reported in Windle, 1989c   [*] $p < .05$ [**] $p < .01$ [***] $p < .001$

Linkage Between Approach and Openness to Experience

Linkages between temperament functioning and cognition, in general, and approach/withdrawal and cognition specifically, are important because they may facilitate the interpretation of findings reported by Angleitner and Ostendorf (1991) regarding the high association between approach, as measured by the DOTS-R, and openness to experience. The logical argument for this relationship follows. Openness to experience has been described as an individual difference variable related to intellectual curiosity, aesthetic sensitivity, and a high need for variable stimulation (Costa & McCrae, 1992). In addition to the high factor loading of approach/withdrawal on the Openness to Experience factor, a second DOTS-R dimension of rigidity-flexibility also had a high factor loading (factor loading = .55). Rigidity-flexibility refers to the tendency to respond flexibly to changes in the environment. A recent second-order confirmatory factor analysis of the DOTS-R with a large sample of adolescents indicated that approach/withdrawal, rigidity-flexibility, and positive mood quality all loaded significantly on a single, second-order factor (Windle, 1992).

The substantive significance of this second-order factor, referred to as Adaptability/Positive Affect, and its association with openness to experience, may be related to a positive social reward system (McDonald, 1988). McDonald has proposed that the reward system, a central feature of several of the psychobiological theories discussed earlier in this chapter (e.g., Cloninger, 1987a; Gray, 1987), is multi- rather than uni-dimensional (also see Zuckerman, 1991). He describes one dimension of the positive social reward system as similar to that underlying Zuckerman's (1979) sensation-seeking trait, characterized by thrill-seeking and risk-taking behaviors and a second dimension that is characterized by prosocial behaviors such as warmth, nurturance, and love. McDonald further provides a developmental account of the positive social reward system that is analogous to the elaboration and differentiation of nerve fibers in the brain associated with maze learning in rats. Specifically, the analogy suggests that ". . . affectively positive stimulation would result in the progressive elaboration of the neural basis of the positive social reward system, making individuals more sensitive to the rewarding behaviors of others" (p. 54). As such, there is a developmental correspondence between socialization experiences fostering prosocial (versus antisocial) behaviors and neural connections that recognize and evaluate such experiences as rewarding.

This description by McDonald (1988) of the positive social reward system and its development is consistent with a perspective that emphasizes dynamic reciprocities between the Adaptability/Positive Mood factor and the Openness to Experience factor. More specifically, those individuals who, early on, manifest characteristics highly valued by their culture, such as friendliness, positive mood, and prosocial behaviors, are more likely to receive positive feedback that contributes to growth in multiple biological, psychological, and social domains (e.g., R. Lerner, 1982; R. Lerner & Busch-Rossnagel, 1981; Thomas & Chess, 1977). Conversely, those individuals who, early on, manifest characteristics (e.g., aggression) not highly valued by their culture, are more likely to receive aversive feedback that may retard development in key domains associated with socioemotional and cognitive development (e.g., Coie, 1990; Patterson, DeBaryshe, & Ramsey, 1989). R. Lerner (1982) has suggested that it is through the establishment of such regulatory feedback loops, or "circular functions," in ontogeny (Schneirla, 1957) that children and adults may be viewed as major contributors to their own development. Thus children who manifest a temperamental style characterized by approach, flexibility, and positive mood are more likely to receive positive feedback from others which, in turn, is likely to increase prosocial attitudes and behaviors and perpetuate successful encounters in academic/achievement settings and other aspects of personal growth that may be reflected in openness to experience. While such a developmental progression may plausibly account for the associations between the Adaptability/Positive Mood and Openness to Experience factors, subsequent research is required to confirm these linkages and to relate them to the underlying neural functioning and brain structures.

Much of what has been presented thus far in this chapter has focused on conceptual definitions of approach/withdrawal and cognate constructs and the proposed biological bases. These are important foci in understanding some commonalities and unique features associated with diverse conceptualizations and methodological procedures relating to approach/withdrawal. They also highlight the significance of examining approach/withdrawal within a bi- or multi-level framework (Schneirla, 1957). Now I am going to expand on some developmental features of approach/withdrawal from a "goodness of fit" theoretical formulation (e.g., J. Lerner & R. Lerner, 1983; Thomas & Chess, 1977). Specific reference is given to the functional significance of approach/withdrawal in relation to cognitive factors as well as adjustment indexes.

Goodness of Fit Model

The basic tenet underlying the goodness of fit model of temperament-context relations is that optimal conditions for behavioral development occur when temperament attributes are consonant with the prevailing environmental presses and conversely, that sub-optimal conditions for behavioral development occur when temperament attributes are dissonant with prevailing environmental presses (e.g., J. Lerner & R. Lerner, 1983; Thomas & Chess, 1977). The key processes involved in the "goodness" or "poorness" of fit are the circular functions (Schneirla, 1957), or reciprocal feedback loops, that contribute to the regulation of functional or dysfunctional transactional processes atemporally across different contexts, and temporally across the lifespan. Thus, if an infant's or a child's temperamental style conforms with the expectations of significant others (e.g., parents, teachers, peers), then development and adjustment will be facilitated through more positive behavioral exchanges, more assistance-providing behaviors, and more self-esteem boosting interactions (e.g., Werner, 1986). However, if an infant's or a child's temperamental style is dissonant with the expectations of significant others, then development and adjustment may be hampered. For example, Quinton and Rutter (1985) reported that within the family context, paternal hostility tended to be directed toward those children who manifested a temperamental style described as difficult and dissonant with prevailing parental expectations.

It is important to emphasize that the goodness of fit model relies on the *relation* between personal attributes and contextual conditions rather than suggesting that the adaptiveness of temperament can be determined without attending to contextual features. For example, DeVries (1984) reported that during famine conditions in Africa a "difficult" temperament was protective in leading to survival. Presumably, infants who were more irritable and cried more often demanded and received more attention and food.

It is proposed that the consistent relationships between an approaching behavioral style and positive mental health, high IQ, and high perceived competence reflect adaptive functioning within the familial and cultural regulatory rules and social contingencies associated with the accomplishment of salient developmental life tasks (e.g., Erikson, 1968; Havighurst, 1972). For example, salient life tasks in adolescence include developing interpersonal relations with significant others toward the selection of a lifelong marital partner, and decision-making with regard to a career path. Caspi, Elder, and Bem (1988) used archival data from the Berkeley Guidance Study to investigate the adult sequelae of children who were characterized as shy during childhood. As noted previously, shyness and a withdrawal behavioral style are viewed as related, but not identical, constructs in that shyness refers to discomfort and inhibition in the presence of others, whereas a withdrawn behavioral style refers to a behavioral tendency to move away from new persons, objects, situations, or events. Caspi et al. reported that shy boys were more likely than their nonshy peers to be off-time for transitions through major life tasks of late adolescence/early adulthood. Specifically, shy boys were delayed in their entry into marriage, parenthood, and stable careers, and manifested a pattern of lower occupational stability and achievement as well as more marital instability.

Caspi et al. (1988) interpreted the longitudinal findings between childhood shyness and adult off-time functioning as attributable to two kinds of developmental continuities. The first, referred to as *cumulative continuity*, refers to behaviors that are sustained across time by the progressive accumulation of their own consequences. Thus shy boys tend to select environments and engage in activities that will minimize social contact with others. The second kind of continuity is referred to as *interactional continuity*, and refers to the dynamic transactions between persons and environments that can perpetuate continuity via behavioral and cognitive processes. Thus a shy person who is "forced" into a social situation and commits a blunder may maintain and perpetuate visceral arousal states and subjective feelings of anxiety in subsequent social situations. These findings by Caspi et al. help to demonstrate how a personal attribute (i.e., shyness) "fits" (or "misfits") with contextual presses (i.e., cultural expectations regarding the establishment of a family and a career), thus influencing aspects (e.g., the timing) of salient developmental life tasks (i.e., late entry into marriage, parenthood, a career).

Caspi et al.'s (1988) concepts of cumulative continuity and interactional continuity are analogous to processes that Scarr and McCartney (1983) have termed niche-picking (cumulative continuity) and evocative (interactional continuity) in characterizing genotype-environment relations across the lifespan. Windle and Lerner (1986a) were influenced by the conceptualization of Scarr and McCartney (1983) and combined it with the circular functions concept of Schneirla (1957) to discuss the goodness of fit model of temperament-context relations. Specifically, Scarr and McCartney conceptualized three types of genotype-environment correlations. The first type is referred to as *passive* genotype-environment correlations that arise from the interrelations between, for example, features of individuality which infants are born with and environments that foster these features. Therefore, an infant born to parents who have high intelligence is not only likely to inherit genotypes such that higher intelligence is probable, but is also likely to be raised in an environment that is rich and varied in educational material with potent role models, and with an achievement-oriented family value system. The second type is referred to as *evocative* genotype-environment correlations, and refers to features of individuality (e.g., temperament, physical attractiveness) that evoke differential reactions in socializing with others. Thomas and Chess (1977) described the "difficult" temperament profile as one that evoked negative behavioral interactions with significant others (e.g., parents, teachers, peers) and thus contributed to disordered behavioral development. The third type is referred to as *active* genotype-environment correlations, or niche-picking. This relationship occurs when individuals with specific characteristics select or shape environments in a manner that is consonant with features of individuality such as temperament.

Whereas Scarr and McCartney (1983) have proposed using the three types of genotype-environment correlations for behavior genetic studies, Windle and Lerner (1986a) have proposed the analogous use of these types for *person-environment*, rather than *genotype-environment correlations*; therefore, Windle and Lerner have substituted "person" for "genotype" for each of the three person-environment relationships. With regard to niche-picking for example, Windle and Lerner are concerned with the role of temperamental characteristics such as approach/withdrawal on the cross-temporal selection and shaping of features of an individual's environment, including features such as peer quantity and quality, leisure-time pursuits, career choices, and level of engagement with parents, teachers, and significant others. The adoption of this conceptualization of *person-environment correlaions* does not preclude behavior genetic studies, but rather focuses on the phenotypic behavior per se, rather than decomposing the variability of the phenotype into genetic and nongenetic sources and their interrelations across time. This conceptualization of person-environment relations is consistent with Schneirla's (1957) notion that behavior represents the "fusion" of genetic, biological, and experiential factors.

Most of the research on the goodness of fit model has implicitly investigated temperamental attributes within an evocative type of temperament-environment relation (e.g., J. Lerner & R. Lerner, 1983; Windle et al., 1986). That is, cross-sectional research designs were used to assess temperament, environmental "presses," and their statistical interaction to investigate whether evocative temperamental attributes that were dissonant with environmental presses would predict outcome variables such as academic performance, perceived competence, and depression. To investigate niche-picking temperament-environment correlations it is necessary to use longitudinal designs with subjects old enough and resourceful enough to select and influence the environments that they inhabit. That is, infants and children typically are either not at liberty or have limited power to select their family members, choose their diet or leisure activities, remove themselves from sexually or physically abusive family members, etc. As individuals become older, for example in adolescence and adulthood, they are at more liberty to select activities and contexts that may conform more with their personal (temperamental) styles and preferences.

At least two ongoing longitudinal research studies are currently being conducted that more adequately address temperament-environment correlations. The first, referred to as the PEATS (Pennsylvania Early Adolescent Transitions Study) (e.g., R. Lerner, J. Lerner, & Tubman, 1989) involves a two-year, four-occasions-of-measurement study of 150 sixth graders across the transition to junior high school. The second, referred to as the MAVS (Middle Adolescent Vulnerability Study) (e.g., Windle, 1989c), involves a two-year, four-occasions-of-measurement study of over 1,000 high school sophomores and juniors. Both studies include the repeated assessment of temperament (including approach/withdrawal), salient features of psychosocial functioning (e.g., parent and peer relations), and indexes of adjustment (e.g., behavior problems, anxiety). With these studies it will be possible, for instance, to trace the developmental trajectories of children/adolescents low and high on approach/withdrawal and to examine if the social environments that they construct are predicted from their approach/withdrawal scores. For example, will withdrawal-oriented children manifest a trajectory characterized by a limited number of acquaintances, few or no close friends, emotional distancing from family members, and few, if any, significant relations with teachers or other adults (e.g., grandparents, clergymen)? What kinds of occupations will children with a withdrawal-oriented behavioral style pursue? Are children with a withdrawal-oriented behavioral style at higher risk for low self-esteem, depression, or substance abuse?

Summary and Future Directions

This chapter has selectively reviewed alternative theoretical models and empirical research in temperament and personality psychology to identify the integral role that the approach/withdrawal concept has had and continues to exhibit. Schneirla (1939, 1959, 1965) made several contributions to the approach/withdrawal literature, including a focus on the stimulus intensity dimensions associated with approach and withdrawal processes, and a concern with the phylogenetic continuity/discontinuity of these processes and their evolutionary significance. Much research remains to be completed with regard to the approach/withdrawal concept and its role in different theoretical systems. Nevertheless, many of the research directions are geared toward a multilevel, integrated organismic functioning perspective (Schneirla, 1957). That is, much research is focused on the inter-level relations between biological systems (e.g., cortical arousal, heart-rate variability, monoamine neuromodulators) and coherent behavioral styles (e.g., inhibited/uninhibited), and between behavioral style attributes and demands in various social groups such as parents, teachers, and peers (e.g., J. Lerner & R. Lerner, 1983). Finally, there is much more emphasis on developmental, cross-temporal process models of approach and withdrawal behavior response systems and on circular functions that contribute to their development and maintenance (e.g., J. Lerner & R. Lerner, 1983; Rothbart & Derryberry, 1981; Windle & R. Lerner, 1986a). A focus on the origins, underlying biological structures, and cross-temporal developmental continuities and discontinuities will further clarify our understanding of the functional and evolutionary significance of approach/withdrawal.

REFERENCES

Angleitner, A., & Ostendorf, F. (1991). *Temperament and the big five factors of personality*. Paper presented at the Conference on the Developing Structure of Temperament and Personality in Childhood, Wassenar, The Netherlands, June 17–20.

Aronson, L. R. (1984). Levels of integration and organization: A reevaluation of the evolutionary scale. In G. Greenberg & E. Tobach (Eds.), *Behavioral evolution and integrative levels* (pp. 57–81). Hillsdale, NJ: Erlbaum.

Briggs, S. R. (1988). Shyness: Introversion or neuroticism? *Journal of Research in Personality*, *22*, 290–307.

Buss, A. H. (1988). *Personality: Evolutionary heritage and human distinctiveness*. Hillsdale, NJ: Erlbaum.

Buss, A. H., & Plomin, R. (1984). *Temperament: Early developing personality traits*. Hillsdale, NJ: Erlbaum.

Carson, D. K., Council, J. R., & Volk, M. A. (1989). Temperament as a predictor of psychological adjustment in female adult incest victims. *Journal of Clinical Psychology*, *45*, 330–335.

Caspi, A., Elder, G. H., Jr., & Bem, D. J. (1988). Moving away from the world: Life-course patterns of shy children. *Developmental Psychology*, *24*, 824–831.

Cattell, R. B., Eber, H. W., & Tatsuoka, M. M. (1970). *Handbook for the sixteen personality factor questionnaire*. Champaign, IL: Institute for Personality and Ability Testing.

Chuguy, V. F., Kolpakov, V. G., & Chepkasov, I. L. (1989). *Correlations between temperament and personality traits in adolescence*. Unpublished manuscript, Institute of Cytology and Genetics, Novosibirsk, USSR.

Cloninger, C. R. (1987a). A systematic method for clinical description and classification of personality variants. *Archives of General Psychiatry*, *44*, 573–588.

———. (1987b). Neurogenetic adaptive mechanisms in alcoholism. *Science*, *236*, 410–416.

Coie, J. D. (1990). Toward a theory of peer rejection. In S. R. Asher & J. D. Coie (Eds.), *Peer rejection in childhood* (pp. 365–401). New York: Cambridge University Press.

Costa, P. T., Jr., & McCrae, R. R. (1989). *NEO PI/FFI manual supplement*. Odessa, FL: Psychological Assessment Resources.

———. (1992). Four ways five factors are basic. *Personality and Individual Differences*, *13*, 653–665.

Depue, R. A., & Iacono, W. G. (1989). Neurobehavioral aspects of affective disorders. *Annual Review of Psychology*, *40*, 457–492.

DeVries, M. W. (1984). Temperament and infant mortality among the Masai of East Africa. *American Journal of Psychiatry*, *141*, 1189–1194.

Diamond, S. (1957). *Personality and temperament*. New York: Harper & Brothers.

Duffy, E. (1949). A systematic framework for the description of personality. *Journal of Abnormal Social Psychology*, *44*, 175–190.

Erikson, E. H. (1968). *Identity, youth and crisis*. New York: Norton.

Eysenck, H. J. (1967). *The biological basis of personality*. Springfield, IL: C. C. Thomas.

———. (1987). Arousal and personality. In J. Strelau & H. J. Eysenck (Eds.), *Personality dimensions and arousal* (pp. 1–13). New York: Plenum Press.

Eysenck, H. J., & Eysenck, S. B. (1968). *Manual: Eysenck Personality Inventory*. San Diego, CA: Educational and Industrial Testing Service.

Eysenck, H. J., & Rachman, S. (1965). *The causes and cures of neuroses*. San Diego, CA: Knapp.

Gray, J. A. (1964). *Pavlov's typology*. Oxford: Pergamon Press.

———. (1970). The physiological basis of introversion-extraversion. *Behavior Research and Therapy*, *8*, 249–266.

———. (1982). *The neuropsychology of anxiety*. Oxford: Clarendon.

———. (1987). The neuropsychology of emotion and personality. In S. M. Stahl, S. D. Iverson, & E. C. Goodman (Eds.), *Cognitive neurochemistry* (pp. 171–190). Oxford: Oxford University Press.

Havighurst, R. J. (1972). *Developmental tasks and education* (3rd ed.). New York: McKay (Original work published in 1948).

Horney, K. (1945). *Our inner conflicts*. New York: W.W. Norton.

Kagan, J. (1989a). Temperamental contributions to social behavior. *American Psychologist*, *44*, 668–674.

————. (1989b). The concept of behavioral inhibition to the unfamiliar. In J. S. Reznick (Ed.), *Perspectives on behavioral inhibition* (pp. 1–23). Chicago: University of Chicago Press.

Kagan, J., Reznick, J. S., & Snidman, N. (1987). The physiology and psychology of behavioral inhibition in children. *Child Development, 58,* 1459–1473.

Kagan, J., & Snidman, N. (1991). Temperamental factors in human development. *American Psychologist, 46,* 856–862.

Kant, I. (1912–1918). *Anthropologie in pragmatischere hinsicht* (Vol. 4). Berlin: Bruno Cassiner.

Lazarus, R. S., & Folkman, S. (1984). *Stress, appraisal, and coping.* New York: Springer.

LeDoux, J. E. (1989). Cognitive-emotional interactions in the brain. *Cognition and Emotion, 3,* 267–289.

Lerner, J. V., & Lerner, R. M. (1983). Temperament and adaptation across life: Theoretical and empirical issues. In P. B. Baltes & O. G. Brim, Jr. (Eds.), *Life-span development and behavior* (Vol. 5) (pp. 197–231). New York: Academic Press.

Lerner, R. M. (1982). Children and adolescents as producers of their own development. *Developmental Review, 2,* 342–370.

————. (1984). *On the nature of human plasticity.* New York: Cambridge University Press.

Lerner, R. M., & Busch-Rossnagel, N. A. (Eds.) (1981). *Individuals as producers of their development: A lifespan perspective.* New York: Academic Press.

Lerner, R. M., & Lerner, J. V. (1981). Temperament-intelligence reciprocities in early childhood: A contextual model. In. R. M. Lerner & N. A. Busch-Rossnagel (Eds.), *Individuals as producers of their development: A lifespan perspective* (pp. 399–421). New York: Academic Press.

Lerner, R. M., Lerner, J. V., & Tubman, J. (1989). Organismic and contextual bases of development in adolescence: A developmental contextual view. In G. R. Adams, R. Montemayor, & T. P. Gullota (Eds.), *Biology of adolescent behavior and development* (pp. 11–37). Newbury Park, CA: Sage.

Lorenz, K. (1965). *Evolution and modification of behavior.* Chicago: University of Chicago Press.

Macphail, E. M. (1982). *Brain and intelligence in vertebrates.* Oxford: Clarendon Press.

Mangan, G. (1982). *The biology of human conduct: East-West models of temperament and personality*. Oxford: Pergamon.

Matheny, A. P. (1989). Temperament and cognition: Relations between temperament and mental test scores. In G. A. Kohnstamm, J. E. Bates, & M. K. Rothbart (Eds.), *Temperament in childhood* (pp. 263–282). Chichester: Wiley & Sons.

McCrae, R. R., & Costa, P. T., Jr. (1987). Validation of the five-factor model of personality across instruments and observers. *Journal of Personality and Social Psychology*, 52, 81–90.

McDonald, K. B. (1988). *Social and personality development: An evolutionary synthesis*. New York: Plenum Press.

Patterson, G. R., DeBaryshe, B. D., & Ramsey, E. (1989). A developmental perspective on antisocial behavior. *American Psychologist*, 44, 329–335.

Pavlov, I. (1927). *Conditioned reflexes*. London: Oxford University Press.

Pfaffman, C. (1961). The sensory and motivating properties of the sense of taste. In M. R. Jones (Ed.), *Nebraska Symposium on Motivation* (Vol. IX) (pp. 71–108). Lincoln, NE: University of Nebraska Press.

Quinton, D., & Rutter, M. (1985). Family pathology and child psychiatric disorder: A four-year prospective study. In A. R. Nicol (Ed.), *Longitudinal studies in child psychology and psychiatry* (pp. 91–134). New York and London: John Wiley and Sons.

Rothbart, M. K. (1988). Temperament and the development of inhibited approach. *Child Development*, 59, 1241–1250.

———. (1989a). Biological processes in temperament. In G. A. Kohnstamm, J. E. Bates, & M. K. Rothbart (Eds.), *Temperament in childhood* (pp. 77–110). Chichester: Wiley & Sons.

———. (1989b). Temperament in childhood: A framework. In G. A. Kohnstamm, J. E. Bates, & M. K. Rothbart (Eds.), *Temperament in childhood* (pp. 59–73). Chichester: Wiley & Sons.

Rothbart, M. K., & Derryberry, D. (1981). Development of individual differences in temperament. In M. Lamb & A. Brown (Eds.), *Advances in developmental psychiatry*. Boston, MA: Erlbaum.

Rothbart, M. K., & Posner, M. I. (1985). Temperament and the development of self-regulation. In L. C. Hartlage & C. F. Telzrow (Eds.), *The neuropsychology of individual differences: A developmental perspective* (pp. 93–123). New York: Plenum Press.

Ruch, W. (1991). *The superfactors P, E, and N and temperament: An analysis of selected scales*. Paper presented at the first workshop of the

European Association of Personality Psychology on Cross-Cultural Research on Temperament, Nieborow, Poland, September 7–12.

Scarr, S., & McCartney, K. (1983). How people make their own environments: A theory of genotype-environment effects. *Child Development, 54*, 424–435.

Schneirla, T. C. (1939). A theoretical consideration of the basis for approach/withdrawal adjustments in behavior. *Psychological Bulletin, 37*, 501–502.

———. (1957). The concept of development in comparative psychology. In D. B. Harris (Ed.), *The concept of development* (p. 78–108). Minneapolis, MN: University of Minnesota Press.

———. (1959). An evolutionary and developmental theory of biphasic process underlying approach and withdrawal. In M. R. Jones (Ed.), *Nebraska symposium on motivation* (pp. 297–339). Lincoln, NE: University of Nebraska Press.

———. (1965). Aspects of stimulation and organization in approach/withdrawal processes underlying vertebrate behavioral development. In D. S. Lehrman, R. Hinde, & E. Shaw (Eds.), *Advances in the study of behavior* (Vol. 1) (pp. 344–412). New York: Academic Press.

Stagner, R. (1948). *Psychology of personality* (2nd Ed.). New York: McGraw-Hill.

Strelau, J. (1983). *Temperament-personality-activity*. New York: Academic Press.

———. (1989). The regulative theory of temperament as a result of East-West influences. In G. A. Kohnstamm, J. E. Bates, & M. K. Rothbart (Eds.), *Temperament in childhood* (pp. 35–48). Chichester: Wiley & Sons.

Thomas, A., & Chess, S. (1977). *Temperament and development*. New York: Brunner/Mazel.

Tobach, E. (1969). Developmental aspects of chemoception in the Winston (DAB) rat: Tonic processes. *Annals of the New York Academy of Sciences, 290*, 226–268.

Tobach, E., & Aronson, L. R. (1970). T. C. Schneirla: A biographical note. In L. R. Aronson, E. Tobach, D. S. Lehrman, & J. S. Rosenblatt (Eds.), *Development and evolution of behavior: Essays in memory of T. C. Schneirla* (pp. xi–xviii). San Francisco, CA: W. H. Freeman & Co.

Valenstein, E. S. (1970). Pavlovian typology: Comparative comments on the development of a scientific theme. In L. R. Aronson, E. Tobach, D. S. Lehrman, & J. S. Rosenblatt (Eds.), *Development and evolution of behavior: Essays in memory of T. C. Schneirla* (pp. 254–280). San Francisco, CA: W. H. Freeman & Co.

Van Praag, H. M., Brown, S. L., Asnis, G. M., Kahn, R. S., Korn, M. L., Harkavy-Friedman, J. M., & Wetzler, S. (1991). Beyond serotonin: A multiaminergic perspective on abnormal behavior. In S. L. Brown & H. M. Van Praag (Eds.), *The role of serotonin in psychiatric disorders* (pp. 302–332). New York: Brunner/Mazel.

Werner, E. E. (1986). Resilient offspring of alcoholics: A longitudinal study from birth to age 18. *Journal of Studies on Alcohol, 47*, 34–40.

Windle, M. (1989a). Temperament and personality: An exploratory interinventory study of the DOTS-R, EASI-II, and EPI. *Journal of Personality Assessment, 53*, 487–501.

――――. (1989b). Predicting temperament-mental health relationships: A covariance structure latent variable analysis. *Journal of Research in Personality, 23*, 118–144.

――――. (1989c). Adolescent temperament: Childhood problem precursors and problem behavior correlates. Paper presented at the annual meeting of the American Academy of Child and Adolescent Psychiatry, New York, NY.

――――. (1992). The revised dimensions of temperament survey (DOTS-R): Simultaneous group confirmatory factor analysis for adolescent gender groups. *Psychological Assessment: A Journal of Consulting and Clinical Psychology, 4*, 228–234.

Windle, M., Hooker, K., Lenerz, K., East, P. L., Lerner, J. V., & Lerner, R. M. (1986). Temperament, perceived competence, and depression in early- and late-adolescents. *Developmental Psychology, 22*, 384–392.

Windle, M., Iwawaki, S., & Lerner, R. M. (1987). Cross-cultural comparability of temperament among Japanese and American early- and late-adolescents. *Journal of Adolescent Research, 2*, 423–446.

――――. (1988). Cross-cultural comparability of temperament among Japanese and American preschool children. *International Journal of Psychology, 23*, 547–567.

Windle, M., & Lerner, R. M. (1986a). The "goodness of fit" model of temperament-context relations: Interaction or correlation? In J. V. Lerner, & R. M. Lerner (Eds.), *Temperament and social interaction in infants and children* (pp. 109–119). San Francisco, CA: Jossey-Bass.

——. (1986b). Reassessing the dimensions of temperamental individuality across the life span: The Revised Dimensions of Temperament Survey (DOTS-R). *Journal of Adolescent Research, 1,* 213–230.

Wundt, W. (1903). *Grundzuge der physiologischen psychologie* (5th ed., Vol. 3). Leipzig: W. Engelmann.

Zajonc, R. B. (1984). On the primacy of affect. *American Psychologist, 39,* 117–123.

Zuckerman, M. (1979). *Sensation-seeking: Beyond the optimal level of arousal.* Hillsdale, NJ: Erlbaum.

——. (1988). Sensation-seeking and behavior disorders. *Archives of General Psychiatry, 45,* 502–503.

——. (1991). *Psychobiology of personality.* New York: Cambridge University Press.

CHAPTER 12

Approach/Withdrawal Processes in Infancy
The Relationship between Parasympathetic Tone and Infant Temperament

Cynthia A. Stifter

T. C. Schneirla has been a largely unacknowledged influence on human development research (cf., Turkewitz, 1987). His Approach/Withdrawal (A/W) theory (Schneirla, 1957) has particular relevance to newborn and early infant behavior. The basic principle underlying Schneirla's A/W theory is that stimuli of low intensity tend to elicit approach responses while stimuli of high intensity evoke withdrawal reactions. Such a pattern of responses, according to Schneirla, is basic to all adaptive behavior in animals. For example, the swooping of a hawk produces withdrawal reactions among hatchlings due to a sudden increase in retinal stimulation while the low-intensity licking of the newborn lamb produces head-turning and orienting toward mother. Overwhelming empirical support for this principle can also be found in studies of human infants. Differential responding to different tastes (Fox & Davidson, 1984; Lipsitt, 1978) and visual stimuli varying in novelty (Maisel & Karmel, 1978; Turkewitz, Gardner, & Lewkowicz, 1984) have been demonstrated. In an excellent review of infant visual approach behavior, Turkewitz and colleagues (1984) concluded that "for young infants, the source of input is relatively unimportant, and it is the overall amount of stimulation to which infants respond."

Schneirla (1957, 1959, 1965) adds an additional level to the quantitative principle of approach/withdrawal behavior and it is this additional level that is of interest to our discussion. Schneirla proposed that adjustments in approach/withdrawal behavior will occur at higher psychological levels involving learning and memory, and that these changes are the result of maturation and experience. Thus, while approach/withdrawal behaviors may be elicited by varying levels of stimulus intensity in the earliest stages of infancy, learning during development may modify or reverse the expression of these behaviors. This principle provides the foundation for more current approaches to human development such as the life-span development perspective (Baltes, Reese, & Lipsitt, 1980; Lerner & Busch-Rossnagel, 1981); the temperament approach (Thomas, Chess, Birch, Hertzig, & Korn, 1963; and the organizational view of development (Sroufe, 1979). Recent studies on the development of infant behavior provide strong empirical support for Schneirla's concept of behavioral organization.

Much of newborn behavior is in direct response to stimulus intensity (Turkewitz et al., 1984). Moreover, recent evidence suggests that this relationship exists in 37- to 40-week-old fetuses (Lecanuet, Granier-Deferre, Cohen, Houegec, & Busnel, 1986). During the newborn period, for example, smiling, an approach behavior, was reliably elicited through tactile and auditory stimuli of low intensity (Wolff, 1987). But by two to three months of age maturation and interactions with the environment combine to alter the meaning of the stimulus for the infant. Consequently, an increase in the infant's smiling behavior to social stimuli can be observed (Emde et al., 1976). Concurrent with this developmental change in smiling patterns is a more organized sleep/wake cycle, a decrease in fussiness, and increasing control of the visual system. The result is an infant who actively seeks both familiar and unfamiliar stimuli. Moreover, when the stimulation becomes too intense the infant has the capability to either use attentional strategies such as looking away or gaze aversion to regulate input or the infant may elicit through facial and vocal expression appropriate interventions from the caretaking environment.

As the infant approaches the second half of the first year of life, further advances in several areas of development converge (Emde et al., 1976). Dramatic differences in approach/withdrawal behaviors to novel persons and objects are observed during the 7–9 month age period. The research literature is unequivocal about the developmental change in approach to novel objects and persons. While younger infants show non-discriminatory approach behaviors toward the familiar and unfamiliar, older infants display less approach behaviors and more withdrawal behaviors when confronted with novel objects or persons. A more complex interaction may exist, however, between the two processes of approach and withdrawal at this time. Several infant researchers maintain that at approximately 7 to 9 months of age infants respond to novel situations and persons with both affiliative/approach behaviors and withdrawing/avoidance behaviors (see Rheingold & Eckerman, 1973). The infant's affiliative tendencies are clearly demonstrated by his or her interest and smiling toward the stranger and willingness to interact with the stranger. Negative reactions to novelty are also evident in both subtle (gaze aversions) and extreme forms (frank distress). Sroufe and others (Skarin, 1977; Sroufe, Waters, & Matas, 1974; Waters, Matas, & Sroufe, 1975) speculate that the timing and quality of both approach and withdrawal behaviors directed toward the stranger may be influenced by the context and the infant's appraisal of that context. In a series of studies using behavioral and physiological indicators of emotional response, they found that setting (home vs. laboratory), familiarization time, and sequencing mediate how an infant responds to a stimulus.

Taken together, these studies show that with maturation and experience infants develop more complex integrated expressions of approach/withdrawal by the end of the first year of life. Later in this chapter, we will discuss our findings from a study of approach (smiling) and withdrawal (gaze aversion) behaviors exhibited during a positive interaction (Stifter & Moyer, 1991) which suggest that these integrated responses emerge before the sixth month of life.

A second principle of A/W theory postulated by Schneirla (Schneirla, 1957) is that the two branches of the autonomic nervous system may underlie approach and withdrawal behaviors.

> Theoretically, the ontogeny of mammalian withdrawal adjustments is primarily centered in high-threshold mechanisms in afferent, neural, flexor-abductor muscles and in the sympathetic autonomic and related visceral systems; that of approach adjustments is centered in low-threshold, afferent, neural, extensor-abductor muscles and the parasympathetic and related visceral systems (p. 99).

Support for this principle can be found in psychophysiological studies of infant emotion. For example, infants exhibit heart rate deceleration, a parasympathetically-mediated response, during sustained attention and smiling (Berg & Berg, 1979; Provost & Gouin-DeCarie, 1979), two behaviors Schneirla defined as approach. Heart rate accelerations indicative of sympathetic activation have been found to accompany negative emotions and states such as behavioral avoidance and fear (Campos, 1976; Kagan, Reznick, & Snidman, 1987). Currently, we are investigating the relationship between the parasympathetic nervous system and approach/withdrawal behaviors. Our interest in this relationship draws upon previous work on the autonomic nervous system and attention.

The relationship between infant attention and the autonomic nervous system has been of significant interest to psychophysiologists because of the physiological responses that attention requires. This relationship was articulated by Lacey and Lacey (1970) who proposed a feedback loop between the cardiovascular and central nervous systems. They speculated that heart rate deceleration observed during attention operates afferently sending messages to central mechanisms. Attention is then prolonged or maintained through the inhibition of centrally mediated physiological responses such as heart rate and respiration, and behavioral responses such as motor activity. Studies of attention and heart rate activity have consistently revealed that during periods of attention the infant's heart rate decreases significantly (see Berg & Berg, 1979). Thinking has changed in recent years, however, about these phasic changes in heart rate activity (Porges, 1973). Changes in heart rate are multiply-determined. Increases in heart rate, for example, may be the result of sympathetic activation or parasympathetic inhibition or both. Research has now undertaken the task of exploring which mechanisms underlie these phasic changes (Porges, 1974; Richards, 1987).

There is evidence that the degree of change in beat-to-beat intervals, or what is commonly referred to as heart rate variability (HRV), is related to heart rate response (Lacey & Lacey, 1958; Porges, 1972, 1974). For example, infants who exhibit high baseline HRV will show greater heart rate deceleration to a visual stimulus than infants with low HRV (Porges, 1974). HRV, however, is influenced by extraneural factors such as temperature and movement. Interest, therefore, has moved toward decomposing HRV into components which reflect centrally-mediated parasympathetic and sympathetic activity (Grossman & Weinthes, 1986; Porges, 1986).

The vagus is the major nerve of the parasympathetic nervous system extending from the medulla to various organs such as the heart, lungs, stomach, larynx and liver. Neural modulation of the heart is through the vagus via its relationship with respiration. Respiration acts as a gating mechanism for these vagal afferents such that inspiration which inhibits vagal input will result in heart rate acceleration while expiration which produces maximal vagal output will result in heart rate deceleration. Further studies have demonstrated that the amplitude of the changes in periodic heart rate due to respiration, called respiratory sinus arrythmia, reflects the degree of parasympathetic control on the heart (Grossman, 1983; Katona & Jih, 1975). Through the use of digital filtering and time series statistics, Porges (1985) has developed a measure, $\hat{V}$, that can be thought of as an estimate of vagal tone, or the degree of parasympathetic control.

We have employed this measure in a number of studies with the purpose of identifying the biological substrates of temperament (Fox & Stifter, 1989; Stifter & Fox, 1990; Stifter, Fox, & Porges, 1989). Specifically, we have been examining the relationship between vagal tone and behaviors which reflect approach/withdrawal.

These studies were conducted from a temperamental perspective which has been influenced by A/W theory. A comprehensive review of the historical background of this perspective can be found in the chapter by Windle (Ch. 11). Specifically, our studies were guided by the theoretical perspective of Rothbart and colleagues (Rothbart & Derryberry, 1981) and those who influenced her work such as Pavlov and Strelau (see Strelau, 1989 for a synopsis of this work). Temperament, according to these scientists, is defined as constitutionally-based differences in reactivity and regulation. Reactivity is "the individual's reaction to changes in the environment as reflected in somatic, endocrine, and autonomic nervous system" (Rothbart & Derryberry, 1981), while regulation refers to the processes that modulate this reactivity such as attentional strategies or approach/withdrawal behaviors. Differences in reactivity are measured by the temporal and intensive characteristics of an individual's response and are proposed to be related to regulatory ability. Thus an infant who is highly reactive to novelty but has the motoric ability to move away from the stimulus differs dramatically from the infant who is as reactive but does not have the means to regulate the level of response. Behaviors which reflect these constructs, e.g., emotional responsivity, gaze aversion activity, were the focus of the following studies.

A Study of Approach/Withdrawal Behaviors during Positive Interactions

Previous research on infant approach/withdrawal responses have often been discussed within the context of a negatively arousing event. For example, Cohn & Tronick (1983) examined infant responses to maternal depressed affect and found infants to cycle between wariness, protest, and looking away. Other research (Brazelton, Koswolski, & Main, 1974; Stern, 1974) has shown that infants momentarily avert their gaze throughout playful interactions. These withdrawal behaviors are believed to be used by the infant to regulate the arousal produced by this interaction. This proposal is supported by studies using heart rate activity (Field, 1981a; Waters et al., 1975). In these studies increases in infant heart rate were observed prior to gaze aversion while decreases in heart rate were observed subsequent to averting gaze away from a positive stimulus (their mothers). Our goal was to extend this research to the study of infant approach /withdrawal behaviors exhibited during a pleasurable interaction. However, in an effort to test the A/W stimulus intensity principle, we proposed to produce some variation in the intensity of the stimulus by having infants interact with a familiar person, their mother, and an unfamiliar person.

Recent advances in behavioral coding systems which derive emotion categories from facial muscle configurations (i.e., FACS, MAX) now make it possible to confidently identify periods of emotion, including expressions of joy (Ekman & Friesen, 1983; Izard, 1979). Because of the microanalytic nature of these systems it is also possible to use the parameters of duration and intensity coded from these systems as indirect measures of arousal. Studies using adult subjects have confirmed the relationship between these parameters and self-reported, felt arousal (Ekman, Friesen, & Ancoli, 1980; Winton, Putnam, & Kraus, 1984). Using a microanalytic facial coding system, we investigated the levels of positive arousal produced by interactions with mother and with a stranger. We hypothesized that high levels of arousal would require some method of emotion regulation, in this case, by gaze aversion. Further, we hypothesized that high positive arousal as represented by smiles of high intensity and long duration would be followed by more frequent gaze aversions of longer duration. We also predicted that the novelty of an unfamiliar person would be more arousing to infants and thus would result in fewer smiles and more frequent gaze aversions. Finally, we were interested in whether the level of activity exhibited by mothers during mother-infant interaction would produce more withdrawal behavior.

To test these hypotheses, 60 healthy, full-term 5-month-olds participated in a peek-a-boo game with mother and an unfamiliar female person for 90 seconds each (Stifter & Moyer, 1991). The only instruction to the mother was to play peek-a-boo as she normally would using her hands. Infants sat in an infant seat at eye level across from the mother/stranger. The stranger was the same person for all infants.

Smiling was coded using Ekman and Friesen's (1983) EMFACS coding system. EMFACS is an anatomically-based coding system which identifies those facial muscles which in combination represent certain emotions and has been adapted for use with infants (Oster & Rosenstein, 1982). One of the features of this system is that some of the facial components, including those associated with joy, are coded with a 5–point intensity rating based on the degree of change in the facial muscles that produce smiling. Durations were coded from the onset of the expression through its apex to the time any facial configuration changed or returned to a neutral state. Two types of gaze aversions were coded, gaze aversions occurring in response to positive arousal as indicated by a smile and gaze aversions occurring at random or in response to negative arousal. The duration of gaze aversion was also coded. Lastly, the activity level of the mothers during peek-a-boo was coded on a 7-point scale ranging from infrequent verbal, facial and body activity to nearly constant verbalizations, body movements and smiling behavior.

Our first question was whether infants responded with more smiling to their mothers than to the stranger. While we found that young infants did indeed exhibit more smiles to mother, this was only a trend. It may be that differential smiling toward familiar persons and unfamiliar persons is just beginning to emerge at 5 months of age and that individual differences in the rate of development accounts for the near-significant finding. Alternatively, it may be that 5-month-old infants are responding to the stimulus property of intensity of interaction rather than to the familiarity of the stimulus. Our results on maternal interactive style (see below) suggest that infants respond differently to variation in activity. Since the same stranger was used for all stranger-infant interactions but the mothers varied, differences in the mother's style may account for our results. In light of A/W theory, however, we are more inclined to believe that infants tend to smile more to their mothers because of the familiarity of her face, voice, and behavior which does not produce as much perceptual "tension" as the novelty of the stranger (Sroufe, 1979). Consequently, the infants are able to participate and respond to the peek-a-boo game with the mother more readily and positively than with the stranger.

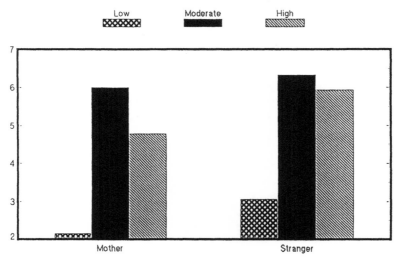

Figure 1. Comparison of the intensities of smiles exhibited prior to gaze aversions exhibited during mother and stranger peek-a-boo. From Stifter and Moyer 1991. Reprinted by permission from Ablex Publishing Corp.

We confirmed our hypothesis that positive arousal would result in more gaze aversion activity. Using the parameters of smile intensity and duration as measures of arousal we found that infants who exhibited high intensity smiles averted their gaze more often than infants who exhibited low intensity smiles. As can be seen in Figure 1 this result was true for both mother and stranger. It is important to note that both moderately intense and highly intense smiles produced more gaze aversions but the difference between these intensity levels was not significant. Interestingly, we also found that the smiles after which an infant exhibited gaze aversion as compared to the smiles after which no gaze aversions were displayed were more intense during both mother and stranger interactions. The relationship between smile duration and the number and duration of gaze aversions was also tested and found to be significant for both mother and the stranger peek-a-boo interactions. Infants who displayed longer smiles also displayed more frequent and longer gaze aversions.

Finally, we were interested in whether the intensity of the stimulus influenced the number of withdrawal behaviors. We used the activity level of the mother and used gaze aversions as our measure of withdrawal. As can be seen in Figure 2 our findings suggest that infants interacting with moderately active mothers displayed more gaze aversions than infants interacting with mothers rated as being low active or high active.

Maternal Activity Level
during Peek-a-boo

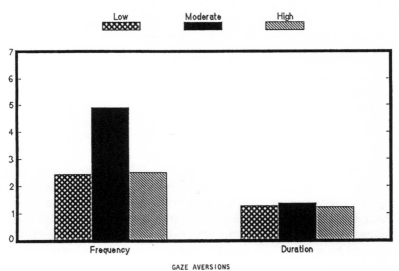

GAZE AVERSIONS

Figure 2. The frequency and duration of gaze aversions exhibited during varying levels of maternal activity. From Stifter and Moyer 1991. Reprinted by permission from Ablex Publishing Corp.

Taken together, our results suggest that during peek-a-boo interactions infants are positively aroused by both a familiar and unfamiliar person and that gaze aversions are related to the number and duration of smiles the infant exhibits (Stifter & Moyer, 1991). The frequency with which gaze aversions accompany increases in positive arousal is in keeping with the research literature that infants use these periods of withdrawal to regulate their internal state (Brazelton et al., 1974; Field, 1981b; Stern, 1974). Whether arousal is deemed positive or negative depends on several factors such as stimulus intensity, arousal threshold, and familiarity with the stimulus. The role of gaze aversion in reducing or modulating arousal has been primarily discussed in relation to aversive conditions and as such gaze aversions are believed to function to remove the infant from the stimulus. The use of gaze aversions within the context of a positive interaction, however, may function in a different manner than that for conditions eliciting negative responses. In the present study gaze aversions were observed in conjunction with a positive expression of emotion. Gaze aversions in this context were quite short, generally lasting a second or two. This brief, oft-times subtle interruption allows the infant to maintain both a postural and social approach toward the positive stimulus. In other words, gaze aversions act as momentary breaks from the interaction that allow the infant to keep their bodies oriented toward the interactant as well as to reduce arousal so that interaction with the pleasurable stimulus may resume. Moreover, these behaviors— smiling, approach orientation, and short periods of gaze aversion, clearly convey the message that the infant is enjoying the interaction and wants it to continue.

In his 1965 paper Schneirla outlines the development of A/W processes and how they interact to produce changes in behavior. He suggests that if W-processes lack support for their continuation in arousing withdrawal behavior then their role may be one of "indirectly facilitating A-arousal—with the possibility of a continuity in individuals of abnormally high tension" (Schneirla, 1965). In the case of our 5-month-olds we find that positive interactions with mother are arousing and consequently produce gaze aversions. If the condition were more aversive and negatively arousing then the continuation of withdrawal behaviors such as looking away would be supported. However, since the interaction is pleasurable, then gaze aversions may function to continue the approach behaviors. Borrowing McGuire & Turkowitz's (1978) diagram which illustrates the relationship between approach and withdrawal responses and stimulus intensity, we believe that the infants in our study who exhibited high and moderate intensity smiles were most likely alternating between the approach and withdrawal thresholds. That is, when the intensity reached a particular level (withdrawal threshold), the infant used withdrawal behaviors to reduce the level of arousal to the point at which he/she could resume approach. This dynamic is represented by the bi-directional arrow in Figure 3. (For more on threshold models, also see Hood, this volume, and Rosenblatt, this volume.)

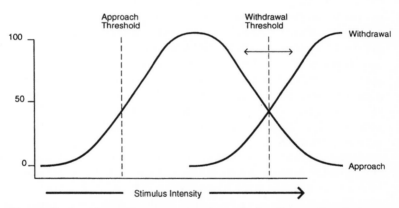

Figure 3. A schematic representation of the fluctuation between approach and withdrawal behaviors for five-month-olds during peek-a-boo. From McGuire and Turchewitz 1978. Reprinted by permission from the Society for Research in Child Development, Inc.

Our result that moderately active mothers produced more gaze aversions than low or high active mothers is intriguing. Given Schneirla's position that high intensity stimuli should lead to withdrawal behaviors and the findings of other infant researchers that low and high active partners lead to *more*, rather than less, gaze aversions (Field, 1981a), we took a closer look at these differing levels of activity. What we found with this post hoc analysis was a difference in both smiling and nonpositive gaze aversions (gaze aversions exhibited during negative or neutral expressive states). Smiles in response to low and high active mothers were less frequent and of lower intensity than smiles in response to moderately active mothers. Hence, the moderately active mother elicited more smiles of higher intensity than the other two types, suggesting that this activity level is optimal for creating high levels of positive arousal. Perhaps more significant is the finding that infants who played peek-a-boo with a low or high active mother showed more nonpositive gaze aversions, that is they displayed gaze aversions that were unrelated to smiling behavior. It appears that infants interacting with a low or high active mother are neither positively aroused nor interested in the peek-a-boo game. This may be easily attributed to the low active mother since her level of play may not be stimulating enough to evoke overt approach responses, but how might the response to the high active mother be explained?

One explanation might be that the high active mothers' behavior is an effect of the infants' lack of interest or joy rather than its cause. These mothers may have increased their "peek-a-boo" pace because they were sensitive to their infants' state. Alternatively, these mothers may have been more concerned with performing the required task than responding contingently to their infants. We are currently attempting to determine this relationship by examining the sequencing of both mother and infant behavior during peek-a-boo.

It is important to note that when comparing the number of gaze aversions exhibited in response to the varying levels of maternal activity we concentrated only on those gaze aversions occurring during or subsequent to a smile rather than gaze aversions in general. Other studies did not make this distinction. For example, still-faced, imitative, and attention-getting interactions were used by Field (1981) to represent the varying levels of stimulation and the results showed a curvilinear effect but in the opposite direction from what we found—infants interacting with low active and high active mothers exhibited more gaze aversions than infants with moderately active mothers. While the affective responses of the infants in response to these situations was not reported it is well-documented that a still-faced mother produces increasing levels of negative arousal and frequent gaze aversion activity (Cohn & Tronick, 1983; Field, 1984; Tronick, Als, Adamson, Wise, & Brazelton, 1978). The attention-getting interaction did produce increases in arousal as indicated by an increase in heart rate but, again, whether the infant was positively or negatively aroused is not known. Though the results of the 1981 Field study may not be comparable to the present study, together these studies suggest that the content of the stimulus and the affective response of the infant are important to assessing the relationship between the amount of stimulation and the frequency of gaze aversion.

Parasympathetic Nervous System and Approach/Withdrawal Behaviors

Schneirla (1965) has suggested that the predominant behavior during early infancy is approach behavior. Attention, smiling and reaching are three such representative behaviors. The elicitation of these behaviors is by stimulus intensity but sometime within the first 6 months, Schneirla argues, infant experiences ("anticipative motivated adjustments"), perceptual development and these early biphasic excitory states overlap to reorganize the infant's response to stimulus intensity so that approach behaviors become more selective "seeking" behaviors and withdrawal develops into "avoidance." For example, in early infancy low intensity stimuli readily elicits smiling, but with development of the visual system and experience with caretakers, social smiling at familiar persons emerges.

Concurrent to the emerging adaptive behavior exhibited by infants is the functional development of the autonomic nervous system and its parasympathetic and sympathetic branches. Schneirla believed the sympathetic branch to arouse withdrawal-type functions and the parasympathetic branch to arouse approach-type functions. In our research we have investigated this relationship by examining a measure of parasympathetic tone and emotional behavior in young infants.

Emotional Expressivity and Parasympathetic Tone

Facial expression is an important mode of communicating state or mood, particularly in the first year of life. We know that infants are capable of expressing a range of emotions and that these expressions are read by the caregiver as meaningful (Izard, Huebner, Risser, McGinnes, & Doughterty, 1981). Expressions of interest and joy (smiling), for example, may be viewed as having multiple effects: They represent manifestations of the infant's response to novel events and may act as regulators during social interactions. An infant who shows interest and smiling behavior to mother enhances his or her chances that mother will continue the interaction. On the other hand, if the infant turns away from mother and does not exhibit much smiling behavior the mother might adjust the pace and intensity of her behavior in an attempt to re-engage her infant. We investigated the relationship between parasympathetic (vagal) tone and facial expressivity in a cross-sectional study of 5- and 10-month-old infants (Stifter, Fox, & Porges, 1989). Infants participated in a standardized stranger/mother approach paradigm during which the mother/stranger gradually approaches the infant in a neutral or positive manner. EKG was recorded for five minutes before the start of the procedure. Expressions of emotion were coded using the AFFEX facial coding system (Izard, 1979), a macroanalytic system developed specifically for infants and children. The duration of look-away behaviors which included both gaze aversions and behavioral avoidance was also coded.

Behaviorally, the difference in expressions for the 2 age groups were as expected. Ten-month-olds exhibited more interest expressions than 5-month-olds. The 5-month-olds, however, showed longer durations of interest to both mother and stranger than 10-month-olds. This finding is not surprising when the significant age effect for look-away behaviors is considered. While 10-month-olds did not show interest for as long as the younger infants, they looked away more often and for longer periods of time. This pattern of high-frequency interest and high-frequency look-away behaviors is similar to that of wariness (Sroufe, Waters, & Matas, 1976).

The relationship between vagal tone ($V\hat{\ }$) and facial expressivity revealed some significant effects for the 5-month-olds but not for 10-month-olds. Infants with greater $V\hat{\ }$ displayed more joy and interest expressions. Interestingly, this relationship was found only for those expressions exhibited to the stranger. A relationship also emerged between $V\hat{\ }$ and look-away behaviors. Five-month-old infants with higher vagal tone exhibited more look-away behaviors during the stranger approach than infants with low vagal tone. The only relationship to emerge for mother approach was a negative one between $V\hat{\ }$ and duration of look-away behavior—infants with greater vagal tone looked away from mother for shorter periods than infants with low vagal tone.

The results of this study suggest that high parasympathetic tone in early infancy may be related to approach behaviors. An unexpected result was the significant relationship between vagal tone and behaviors believed to reflect withdrawal. Infants with high vagal tone were interested and reacted positively with smiling behavior toward the stranger as well as looked away more. It may be that withdrawal behaviors, in this case looking away, which may function to maintain approach, are also related to the parasympathetic nervous system. Moreover, the negative relation between vagal tone and the duration of looking away during mother's approach suggests this behavior may have been used to regulate arousal created by mother's approach. That is, high $V\hat{\ }$ infants may have been aroused by their mother but the level of arousal created by this stimuli only required short periods of withdrawal for the purposes of modulating arousal and maintaining social contact with their mothers. As was discussed previously, interactions with mother and stranger are very powerful stimuli that the 5-month-old infant enjoys. At the same time, however, the arousal created by that interaction is such that they required a short period of withdrawal (Stifter & Moyer, 1991). The present findings suggest that those infants with high vagal tone need only a short period to recover from an arousing event, as seen by the 5-month-old's frequent and short-duration look-away behaviors.

Izard (1979; Langsdorf, Izard, Rayias, & Hembree, 1983) has conceptualized interest as an expression seen during active attention and has found a positive association between heart rate deceleration and interest expressions. The fact that infants displayed more interest and look-away behaviors to the stranger than the mother indicates that they may be actively attending and processing the approach of an unfamiliar person. Our findings indicate that the expression of interest and look-away behaviors during stranger approach may function to regulate the child's emotional response to novel events and that this process may be mediated by the infant's level of parasympathetic tone.

The observed disassociation between vagal tone and expressivity in the 10-month-old group indirectly supports Schneirla's argument that development is a process whereby behaviors are reorganized to serve adaptive functions. As the infant matures and develops more selective modes of communication, expressive behavior may not parallel development of neural mechanisms. Rather, with development, the selective expression of emotions may be a complex product of perceptual maturation, increased mobility and affective input from the environment.

Parasympathetic Tone and Temperament

The next set of studies looked at the predictability and stability of infant reactivity and regulation and its relationship with vagal tone. In this longitudinal study infants were seen at 3 ages—newborn, 5 months, and 14 months (Stifter & Fox, 1990; Fox & Stifter, 1989). Neonatal reactivity (cry/no cry) and regulation (latency to soothe) was obtained through a pacifier withdrawal task. Five-month reactivity was elicited in two ways—positive reactivity (facial expressions of joy) was elicited through a peek-a-boo interaction and negative reactivity (facial expressions of distress/anger) was elicited through an arm restraint procedure (see Stifter & Fox, 1990, for a detailed description of these procedures). At 14 months of age infants participated in a free play session during which an unfamiliar adult was introduced, a novel toy was presented, and the infant was separated briefly from mother. Latencies to approach the stranger and novel toy and latency to cry to maternal separation were coded from videotapes of these procedures. Baseline EKG was recorded during all visits.

No significant relationships were found for the newborn data either concurrently or predictive to 5-month or 14-month vagal tone or behavior. Five month $\hat{V}$, however, was significantly related to emotional reactivity at 5 months. Infants with high vagal tone reacted more quickly and intensely to having their arm restrained with expressions of negative emotion than infants with low vagal tone. At 14 months 2 extreme groups of infants were formed based on their measures of vagal tone. Both 5 month $\hat{V}$ and behavior were different for these groups. Infants with high $\hat{V}$ at 14 months showed more negative affect at 5 months during the arm restraint procedure. That is, infants who exhibited high levels of baseline $\hat{V}$ at 14 months were those infants who displayed greater negative reactivity at 5 months. In addition, 14-month $\hat{V}$ was positively related to $\hat{V}$ measured at 5 months of age. Finally, 14-month $\hat{V}$ was also associated with 14-month behavior. Infants who exhibited high vagal tone were quicker to approach a stranger and a novel object (robot). There was also a tendency for 14-month-olds with high $\hat{V}$ to show a shorter latency to cry to mother's departure.

The pattern of results from this longitudinal study illustrate two important points. First, there is a concurrent relationship between the level of vagal tone and approach behavior at 14 months. Infants with high vagal tone were more sociable and outgoing and less inhibited in their interactions. These results confirm the association between other forms of vagal tone and social behavior found by Kagan (Kagan et al., 1987). Second, the data indicate that highly reactive infants also exhibit greater vagal tone and that these behaviors may be precursors of sociability. The 14-month-olds who readily approached the unfamiliar adult and novel object were the ones who were most likely to cry when restrained. At first glance this unexpected relationship appears difficult to explain unless one considers the effect high reactivity has on caretaking responses. It may be that higher levels of vagal tone facilitate affective responses to emotion-eliciting stimuli. In the present study infants with high vagal tone responded more quickly and more intensely to an aversive stimulus. The predictive relationship between negative reactivity and later sociability might result from the regulatory functions of negative reactivity for the infant and caregiver. Because the arm restraint procedure is a moderately aversive stimulus, the negatively reactive infant's response is considered an appropriate one. Facial and vocal expressiveness is the major communication mode for young infants. The infant who responds appropriately to a situation can effectively signal his/her caregiver. The caregiver then infers the emotional state of the infant and acts to remedy discomfort or maintain pleasure. Negative reactivity, when appropriately expressed in response to aversive events, functions to elicit caretaking responses thereby contributing toward the infant's social opportunities and affiliative tendencies.

Summary and Conclusions

The rapidly changing nature of the biphasic pattern of approach/withdrawal is most dramatically demonstrated in the development of the human infant. While Schneirla hypothesized the human infant's behavioral responses to progress from intensity-determined to more complexly determined responses he did not specify when these transitions occurred. Since his time, however, much has been discovered about the organization of infant behavior. In this chapter we have presented several studies which suggest that by 5 months of age the infant is responding in sophisticated ways to high intensity events and that these behaviors are related to underlying physiological mechanisms. Our results showed that at 5 months of age more subtle withdrawal behaviors such as gaze aversions and looking-away behavior can help to facilitate and maintain approach. We also found that during positive interactions, infants aroused to levels of moderate to high intensity will display gaze aversion activity. These short breaks from a moderately active interaction were interpreted as reducing the infant's arousal to acceptable levels so that pleasing interchanges may continue. Our findings were limited to 5-month-old infants during interaction with mother and a stranger. Others have shown that for older infants a change in the meaning of the stimulus will influence the use of withdrawal behaviors. Gaze aversions may be longer, more frequent or substituted with more intense withdrawal behaviors (Sroufe, 1979).

These and other data indicate, however, that by 10 months of age, the relationship between physiology and behavior may be obscured by the increasing behavioral complexity of the developing infant. While we did find a relationship between vagal tone and infant approach behavior at 14 months these were of infants who exhibited extremes in vagal tone. Similar findings have been reported by Kagan (Kagan et al., 1987), who looked at extremes in behavioral inhibition and sociability. It may be that extremes in behavior and physiology maintain their monotonic relationship because they are less malleable and more resistant to changes that come with development.

A final note—while Schneirla proposed that approach behavior was related to the parasympathetic branch of the autonomic nervous system and withdrawal behavior to the sympathetic branch, he was not specific about the nature of their involvement. Recent advances in technological recording and statistical analysis now make it possible to consider the underlying mechanisms of behavior. We used in our studies a baseline measure of parasympathetic tone as a measure of individual differences. Several past studies of infant cardiac reactivity and behavior have found that these baseline measures of vagal tone are important to understanding the degree of heart rate response to stimuli (Porges, 1974; Porter, Proges, & Marshall, 1988; Richards, 1987). For example, Porges (1974) found that high levels of vagal tone were related to quicker heart rate decelerations in response to visual and auditory stimuli. Ideally, the next research step would be to examine both baseline measures of vagal tone and changes in heart rate during approach behaviors to fully understand the underlying physiological mechanisms associated with approach.

REFERENCES

Berg, W. K., & Berg, K. M. (1979). Psychophysiological development in infancy: State, sensory function and attention. In J. Osofsky (Ed.), *Handbook of infant development* (pp. 283–343). New York: Wiley.

Campos, J. J. (1976). Heart rate: A sensitive tool for the study of emotional development in the infant. In L. Lipsitt (Ed.) *Developmental psychobiology: The significance of infancy*. Hillsdale, NJ: Erlbaum.

Brazelton, T. B., Koslowski, B., & Main, M. (1974). The origins of reciprocity. In M. Lewis & L. Rosenblum (Eds.), *The effect of the infant on its caregiver* (pp. 49–76). New York: Wiley.

Cohn, J. F., & Tronick, E. Z. (1983). Three-month-old infants' reaction to simulated maternal depression. *Child Development, 54,* 185–193.

Ekman, P., & Friesen, W. V. (1983). *EMFACS Facial Coding Manual*. San Francisco, CA.

Ekman, P., Friesen, W. V., & Ancoli, A. (1980). Facial signs of emotional experience. *Journal of Personality and Social Psychology, 39,* 1125–1134.

Emde, R. N., Campos, J., Reich, J., & Gaensbauer, T. J. (1978). Infant smiling at five and nine months: Analysis of heartrate and movement. *Infant Behavior and Development, 1,* 26–35.

Emde, R. N., Gaensbauer, T. J., & Harmon, R. J. (1976). *Emotional expression in infancy: A biobehavioral study*. New York: International Universities Press.

Field, T. (1979). Visual and cardiac responses to animate and inanimate faces by young term and preterm infants. *Child Development, 10,* 41–48.

———. (1981a) Infant gaze aversion and heart rate during face-to-face interactions. *Infant Behavior and Development, 4,* 307–315.

———. (1981b). Infant arousal attention and affect during early interactions. In L. Lipsitt (Ed.), *Advances in infancy*, Vol. 1 (pp. 57–100). New York: Ablex.

———. (1984). Early interactions between infants and their postpartum depressed mothers. *Infant Behavior and Development, 7,* 527–532.

Fogel, A., Diamond, G., Langhorst, B., & Demos, V. (1981). Affective and cognitive aspects of the 2-month-olds' participation in face-to-face interaction with its mother. In E. Tronick (Ed.), *Joint regulation of behavior*. Baltimore: University Park Press.

Fox, N. A., & Davidson, R. J. (1984). Hemispheric substrates of affect: A developmental model. In N. Fox & R. Davidson (Eds.), *The psychobiology of affective development* (pp. 353–381). Hillsdale, NJ: Erlbaum.

Fox, N. A., & Stifter, C. A. (1989). Biological and behavioral differences in infant reactivity and regulation. In G. Kohnstamm, J. Bates, & M. Rothbart (Eds.), *Temperament in Childhood* (pp. 169–183). Sussex, England: Wiley.

Grossman, P. (1983). Respiration, stress, and cardiovascular function. *Psychophysiology*, 20, 284–300.

Grossman, P., & Wienthes, K. (1986). Respiratory sinus arrhythmia and parasympathetic control: Some basic issues concerning quantification, application and implications. In P. Grossman, K. Janssen, & D. Vaitl (Eds.), *Cardiorespiratory and cardiosomatic psychophysiology* (pp. 117–138). New York: Plenum.

Izard, C. E. (1979). *The maximally discriminative facial movement coding system (MAX)*. Newark, DE: Instructional Resources Center.

Izard, C. E., Huebner, R. R., Risser, D., McGinnes, G. C., & Dougherty, L. M. (1981). The young infant's ability to produce discrete emotion expressions. *Developmental Psychology*, 16, 132–140.

Kagan, J. (1971). *Change and continuity in infancy*. New York: Wiley.

Kagan, J., Reznick, J. S., & Snidman, N. (1987). The physiology and psychology of behavioral inhibition in children. *Child Development*, 55, 1459–1473.

Katona, P. G., & Jih, F. (1975). Respiratory sinus arrhythmia: Noninvasive measure of parasympathetic cardiac control. *Journal of Applied Physiology*, 39, 801–805.

Lacey, J. I., & Lacey, B. C. (1958). The relationship of resting autonomic activity to motor impulsivity. *Research Publications Association for Research in Nervous and Mental Disease, 36*, 144–209.

———. (1970). Some autonomic-central nervous system interrelationships. In P. Black (Ed.), *Psychophysiological correlates of emotion* (pp. 205–227). New York: Academic.

Langsdorf, P., Izard, C. E., Rayias, M., & Hembree, E. (1983). Interest expression, visual fixation, and heart rate change in 2-to-8-month-old infants. *Developmental Psychology*, 19, 375–386.

Lancanuet, J. P., Granier-Deferre, C., Cohen, H., Le Houezec, R., & Busnel, M. C. (1986). Fetal responses to acoustic stimulation depend on heart rate variability pattern, stimulus intensity and repetition. *Early Human Development*, 13, 269–283.

Lipsitt, L. P. (1979). The pleasures and annoyances of infants: Approach and avoidance behavior. In E. Thoman (Ed.), *Origins of infants' social responsiveness* (pp. 125–153). Hillsdale, NJ: Erlbaum.

Maisel, E. B., & Karmel, B. Z. (1976). Contour density and pattern configuation in visual preferences of infants. *Infant Behavior and Development, 1,* 127–140.

McGuire, I., & Turkewitz, G. (1978). Visually-elicited finger movements in infants. *Child Development, 49,* 362–370.

Nelson, N. M. (1976). Respiration and circulation before birth. In C. Smith & N. Nelson (Eds.), *The physiology of the newborn infant.* Springfield, IL: Thomas.

Oster, H., & Rosenstein, D. (1988). *Analyzing facial movement in infants.* Unpublished manuscript.

Porges, S. W. (1972). Heart rate variability and deceleration as indexes of reaction time. *Journal of Experimental Psychology, 92,* 103–110.

———. (1974). Heart rate indices of newborn attentional responsivity. *Merrill-Palmer Quarterly, 20,* 131–154.

———. (1985). *Method and apparatus for evaluating rhythmic oscillations in aperiodic physiological response systems.* Patent No. 4,510,944.

———. (1986). Respiratory sinus arrhythmia: Physiological basis, quantitative methods, and clinical implications. In P. Grossman, K. Janssen, & D. Vaitl (Eds.), *Cardiac-respiratory and cardiac-somatic psychophysiology* (pp. 206–211). New York: Guilford.

Porges, S. W., McCabe, P. M., & Yongue, B. G. (1982). Respiratory-heart rate interactions: Physiological implications for pathophysiology and behavior. In J. Cacioppo & R. Petty (Eds.), *Perspectives in cardiovascular psychophysiology* (pp. 223–264). New York: Guilford.

Porter, F. L., Porges, S. W., & Marshall, R. E. (1988). Newborn cries and vagal tone: Parallel changes in response to circumcision. *Child Development, 59,* 495–505.

Provost, M. A., & Gouin-Decarie, T. (1979). Heart rate reactivity of 9- and 12-month-old infants showing specific emotions in a natural setting. *International Journal of Behavioral Development, 2,* 109–120.

Rheingold, H., & Eckerman, C. (1973). Fear of the stranger: A critical examination. In H. Reese (Ed.), *Advances in Child Development and Behavior.* Vol. 8 (pp. 186–222). New York: Academic Press.

Richards, J. E. (1987). Infant visual sustained attention and respiratory sinus arrhythmia. *Child Development, 58,* 488–496.

Rothbart, M. K. (1973). Laughter in young children. *Psychological Bulletin*, *80*, 247–256.

Schneirla, T. C. (1957). The concept of development in comparative psychology. In D. Harris (Ed.), *The concept of development* (pp. 78–108). Minneapolis: University of Minnesota Press.

———. (1959). An evolutionary and developmental theory of biphasic processes underlying approach and withdrawal. In M. R. Jones (Ed.), *Nebraska symposium on motivation*. Vol. 7 (pp. 297–339). Lincoln: University of Nebraska Press.

———. (1965). Aspects of stimulation and organization in approach-withdrawal processes underlying vertebrate behavioral development. In D. S. Lehrman, R. Hinde, & E. Shaw (Eds.), *Advances in the study of behavior*. Vol. 1 (pp. 344–412). New York: Academic Press.

Skarin, K. (1977). Cognitive and contextual determinants of stranger fear in six- and eleven-month-old infants. *Child Development*, *48*, 537–544.

Spitz, R. (1965). *The first year of life*. New York: International Universities Press.

Sroufe, L. A. (1977). Wariness of strangers and the study of infant development. *Child Development*, *48*, 731–746.

———. (1979). Socioemotional development. In J. Osofsky (Ed.), *Handbook of infant development* (pp. 462–516). New York: Wiley.

Sroufe, L. A., Waters, E., & Matas, L. (1974). Contextual determinants of infant affective response. In M. Lewis & L. Rosenblum (Eds.), *The origins of fear* (pp. 49–72). New York: Wiley.

Stern, D. (1974). Mother and infant at play: The dyadic interaction involving facial, vocal, and gaze behaviors. In M. Lewis & L. Rosenblum (Eds.), *The origins of fear* (pp. 187–213). New York: Wiley.

Stifter, C. A., & Moyer, D. (1991). The regulation of positive affect: Gaze aversion activity during mother-infant interaction. *Infant Behavior and Development*, *14*, 111–123.

Stifter, C. A., & Fox, N. A. (1990). Infant reactivity: Physiological correlates of newborn and five month temperament. *Developmental Psychology*, *26*, 582–588.

Stifter, C. A., Fox, N. A., & Porges, S. W. (1989). Facial expressivity and vagal tone in 5- and 10-month-old infants. *Infant Behavior and Development*, *12*, 127–137.

Tronick, E., Als, H., Adamson, L., Wise, S., & Brazelton, T. B. (1978). The infant's response to entrapment between contradictory messages in face-to-face interaction. *Journal of American Academy of Child Psychiatry, 17,* 1–13.

Turkewitz, G. (1987). Psychobiology and developmental psychology: The influence of T. C. Schneirla on human developmental psychology. *Developmental Psychobiology, 20,*

Turkewitz, G., Gardner, J. M., & Lewkowicz, D. J. (1984). Sensory/perceptual functioning during early infancy: The implications of a quantitative basis for responding. In G. Greenberg & E. Tobach (Eds.), *Behavioral evolution and integrative levels* (pp. 167–195). Hillsdale, NJ: Erlbaum.

Waters, E., Matas, L., & Sroufe, L. A. (1975). Infants' reactions to an approaching stranger: Description, validation, and functional significance of wariness. *Child Development, 46,* 348–356.

SECTION V

The Concept of Levels in Approach/Withdrawal Theory

CHAPTER 13

One View of the Concept
of Integrative Levels

Ethel Tobach

Although there are clear, cogent statements of the concept of integrative levels (Novikoff, 1945; Aronson, 1984, 1987), the way in which the concept of integrative levels is used (how it is "defined") continues to become part of the discussions of many issues in the study of the development and evolution of behavior. This is especially so when explanations of behavioral processes are considered to be anthropomorphic, that is, attribution of human behavioral characteristics to other animals; zoomorphic, that is, attribution of behavioral characteristics of other animals to humans; or reductionist, that is, invoking explanatory reductionism in Mayr's sense. In this sense explanatory reductionism is "The view that the mere knowledge of its ultimate components would be sufficient to explain a complex system. . ." (Mayr, 1992). The concept of integrative levels can be seen as an alternative to all three formulations described above.

In general, those who defend the use of anthropomorphic, zoomorphic and reductionist explanations point out that anthropomorphic formulations suggest questions for research; for example, observing behavior in nonhuman animals that looks like human parental caregiving might lead one to investigate what it is about that particular animal that leads to such a relationship between parent and offspring (Tolman, 1938). Zoomorphism is offered as a useful expression of the fact that all organisms are in some sense related through evolutionary processes.

The successful method of analysis, which may be termed "constitutive reductionism," is equally recognized by all as a necessary step in finding answers to questions. As Mayr writes, "No scientist objects to . . . 'constitutive reductionism' because it consists of the reduction of the studied object into its most basic constituents" (Mayr, 1988). The definition of "the basic constituents" I believe is furthered by the use of the concept of integrative levels as developed below. And the synthesis of the information found by such an analysis is also furthered by the use of the concept of integrative levels.

Thus anthropomorphism, zoomorphism and reductionism are all limited as explanations. These approaches are less likely than the concept of integrative levels to generate explanations that encompass the variations of behavior as it changes in time and context (for example, in the development of the social behavior of parents towards young and in sex-related behavior). The concept of levels integrates the similarities and differences between and among apparently related behavior patterns. For example, it helps clarify whether the teaching of humans by humans is the same as the apparently purposeful modification of the behavior of young apes or birds by the behavior of adults; or whether apparent collective problem-solving as in "mobbing behavior" of a predator by a flock of birds is the same as group problem-solving by humans.

An integrative levels approach starts with questions about the level of neural, social and communicative integration in the various species being compared. This leads to the formulation of alternative hypotheses such as processes of social facilitation and communication to define the primary continuities in these behavioral patterns in nonhuman animals. Social facilitation and communication may be seen as continuous processes on many phyletic levels, and at various stages of development in a variety of species, including humans. But at the human level, the dominance of socializing processes produces a discontinuity in "social facilitation," in which the planning of activities and the definition of goals become part of the interactive process between two or more individuals. The production of language at the human level defines the discontinuity in communication. The two categories, socialization and language, rather than social facilitation and communication, become integrated so that one can reasonably speak about "teaching" and "cultural problem-solving" as uniquely human activities, different from, and not attributable to nonhuman organisms. The integration of social facilitation and communication is also seen in a variety of nonhuman organisms, but the level of planning and goal formation is significantly and sufficiently different from that of human societal processes involved in teaching and cultural problem-solving to obviate mistaken equating of the human and nonhuman behavior. The concept of integrative levels may be seen as a tool devised by humans to reconcile the diversity of and continuous change in natural phenomena, with the commonality and stability of these same phenomena.

It is, however, when nature/nurture, heredity/environment and other dichotomous explanations of behavior are at issue that the concept of integrative levels is most frequently brought into the discussion. Schneirla (Aronson, Tobach, Lehrman, & Rosenblatt, 1972) and his students have been most productive in applying the concept of integrative levels to the resolution of these widely accepted explanatory dichotomies. It should be noted that it was Schneirla's emphasis on developmental processes that provided the strongest theoretical resolution of these apparent dichotomies. However, it was his integration of the concept of integrative levels with the concept of historical categories, such as evolution and development, that offered an approach that has led to some of the most fruitful research in comparative psychology (Aronson, 1963; Lehrman, 1970, 1971; Rosenblatt, 1991; Topoff, 1990; Turkewitz, 1987).

In the following brief discussion of the concept of integrative levels, some of the history of the concept will be considered, as well as some of the issues related to the conceptualization being offered here.

History of Formulations of the Concept and Its Usage

In the published symposium (Redfield, 1942) that was the occasion for Alex B. Novikoff's clear and extremely useful statement of the concept of levels of integration (1945), the various

authors used the term "levels" predominantly in regard to organization of units, whether of cells and unicellular animals as by
Hyman (1942) or of individuals that were organized into social
groups as by Emerson (1942). Jennings (1942) discussed functional aspects of organization that result in new levels of social
formation, but, in general, levels were formulated primarily as
structural and *hierarchical,* although the subject of the symposium
was *levels* of integration.

The notion that the organization of matter is relational has
been accepted since written history throughout all cultures
(Needham, 1936, 1937; Morgan, 1933; see also Foskett, 1977). This
view of matter as relationally organized, and continuous, rather
than random, pervades the scientific literature (Kennedy, 1992).
The terms "hierarchy," "levels of organization," "levels of integration," and "stages," have all been used to indicate this view of
matter. These terms have different histories and adumbrations
that lead to different conceptualizations of the organization of
matter. Most of these conceptualizations vary significantly from
the concept of "integrative levels" that can be derived not only
from Schneirla's own writing on the subject, but from his research and application of the concept to issues in comparative
psychology and other behavioral sciences (Aronson, Tobach,
Lehrman, & Rosenblatt, 1972).

The term "levels" is used variously (Brothers, 1983; Feibleman, 1954; Grobstein, 1976; Petterson, 1978; Ugolev, 1989; Zhirmunsky & Kuzmin, 1988). Kolka and Pickett (1989) substitute the
word "entities" for levels; they distinguish their concept from
"hierarchy" and see biological organization as inclusive of
integration and hierarchy. The term "levels" has been used interchangeably with hierarchy by many (Allen & Starr, 1982;
Goertzel, 1972; May, 1988; Salthe, 1985) to mean some kind of
orderly series arrangement in which entities, phenomena, structures or functions are related to each other in terms of smaller to
larger, lower to higher, or simple to complex. Novikoff's concept
of levels is even questionably included in the definition of hierarchy in the Third Edition of Webster's International dictionary.

Another term, "stage," used to describe an orderly progression, frequently in relation to time and development, also

has been used interchangeably with level. However, it is not usually used interchangeably with hierarchy.

Issues in Defining the Concept of Integrative Levels

Two terms in the concept of integrative levels require definition or elaboration: levels and integrative.

Levels

The term "level" as used in the concept of integrative levels is not a scalar unit as in measurement, nor does it mean evenness, or equivalence. The common meanings of stage, platform or substrate come closest to the way it is used by some writers.

It is also different from the term "hierarchy." In Webster's Unabridged Dictionary (3rd Edition), although given as a synonym of level, the definition of hierarchy shows it is not derived from a concept of change. The relationship among the orders in a hierarchy is derived from their increasing size, number or other quantitative characteristics, or from authoritarian or didactic prescription of the relationship among ascending sequential units. Zylstra (1992) develops his concept of "hierarchy" to include "levels" and distinguishes between the "authoritarian" or "controlling" aspects of hierarchy, and a hierarchy based largely on the enkapsis theory of Dooyeweerd (cited in Zylstra, 1992). In this theory, as Zylstra uses it, a prior level is not affected by being encapsulated or enclosed in the enclosing level, giving as an example the physico-chemical functioning of molecules in a cell. However, to understand how new levels are produced, I suggest that it is helpful to see the relationship between and among levels as one in which preceding or earlier levels are subsumed in consequent or later levels through processes of change inherent in the characteristics of each level. In other words, the physico-chemical functions of any molecule also change, as they are interdependent, interconnected and interrelated with the physico-chemical functions of other molecules. The types of molecules present in the cell vary and thus characteristics of the physico-chemical functions should vary as well. On submolecular levels these same relationships of change pertain, and should be affected by their interrelationship with other submolecular entities with which they are encapsulated.

It has been suggested that these changes in the subsumption and succession of levels can be described in terms of complexity. The term "complexity" has been used as variously as "levels" (Bronowski, 1970; Heingardner & Engleberg, 1983; Kaufmann, 1991; Newman, 1970; Packel & Traub, 1987; Simon, 1962; Stern, 1964; van der Leeuw, 1981; Wimsatt, 1964; Wolfram, 1984).

If one synthesizes the meanings of "complex" as given in standard dictionaries, that is, that "complex" means composed of related parts; intricate; perplexing; tangled; not simple; it becomes clear that each level is complex. The component parts of each level, their relationship, the questions they pose (perplex), and their entanglement are indeed "complex," but these are the characteristics of the level itself. It would be redundant to define levels in terms of complexity; the changes and differences in complexity are the changes and differences in the levels.

Every organization of matter is complex, in that the relationships of its component parts are continuously changing and entering new relationships. Thus matter on the subatomic level is complex, as is matter on the cosmological level. The level of the neurone is a complex integration of structure/function in a spatial/temporal process of change. The complexity of the human brain, derived in part from the complexity of the neurone, is different from the complexity of the neurone. To arrange these levels in terms of complexity does not define the processural relationships among them. It is not useful as a discriminandum of levels, because the analytic question asked defines the level of investigation, its methods, instrumentation and its complexity. Studying the membrane characteristics of a neurone reflects complexity of the processes of change at the membrane (one level of integration). Studying the biochemical productions of a neurone (another level of integration) reflects complex processes. The function of a particular neurone in the integrative level of a functional structural cortical nucleus or entity reflects another complexity. The analyses of each level, and the relationship among them, are not aided by a descriptor of complexity. The qualitative differences in complexity result from the characteristics of each level and its relationships with other levels (Bohr, 1958; Stern, 1964).

Integrative (Integration)

The term "integration" or "integrative" rather than "organization" is used here to indicate that the relationship between and among levels is not only one of structure, but of function as well. A level is the result of labile integration, fusion, and resolution of internal and external contradictions in the Hegelian sense (Tobach, 1987), rather than the addition, combination, or mechanistic, cybernetic interaction of its components (Makarov, 1987; Tobach, 1972). It is through this integration that the whole becomes more than the sum of its parts (Schneirla, 1965). The relationship between and among levels within a category is one of integration. Each of the levels within the organism is temporally and successively subsumed, as, for example, the biochemical, physiological and behavioral levels that are integrated in the individual organism.

The temporal aspect of the integrating processes producing levels, expressed as earlier or preceding, is inherent in the conceptualization of levels, and is an expression of the historical (i.e., the evolutionary and developmental) integration of levels. An example of the application of these formulations, and of the value of differentiating between stages and levels, each with their continuities and discontinuities in evolution and development, is the concept of approach/withdrawal processes (A/W) proposed by Schneirla (1965) as fundamental to the behavioral category traditionally referred to as motivation.

Two aspects of the A/W concept should be considered. First, the concept refers to organisms; that is, it is based in the developmental processes of an organism. Second, its evolutionary aspect is reflected in the level of integration of the particular organism. The A/W process is continuous throughout the evolution of different phyla; that is, organisms—plant and animal—move, either in part, as in the case of plants and some animals, or as a whole, which is more likely to be true of animals, toward or away from an adequate, focused source of change (a stimulus). The valence of the specific intensity of the adequate stimulus to bring about approach or withdrawal is, in part, a function of the phyletic level of the organism. The A/W processes of the plant, of the acellular animal organism and of the human demonstrate both the continuities and discontinuities produced by the integration of adequate stimulation from their environment (external changes) and the characteristics of their intraorganismic processes (internal changes). For the plant, the integration of the biotic aspects of its environment is differently brought about, primarily produced by contemporaneously acting mechanical and chemical stimuli each with different degrees of intensity, e.g., pressure brought about by the tropistic and taxic responses of living organisms in its environment to gravity, light, etc. (Holland, Parton, Detling, & Coppock, 1992; Janzen, 1988). In the human, the functional intensity of pressure and chemical stimuli (external changes) is an integration of the history of social experience of the individual (as integrated internal changes) with the physical characteristics of the stimuli. The integration of these external and internal changes is different in the plant and in the human, leading to differences in the significance of stimulus intensity.

To analyze the A/W aspects of behavioral activities, the category of the behavior needs to be explicated. For example, if one were to analyze the psychomotor activity of a human, as Schneirla did (1965), "psychomotor" would be the designated category. In addition, the evolutionary aspect (species, human) and the stage of development (infancy) would be defined. The A/W concept places the intensity of stimulation as the primary process, or the major external contradiction, in the Hegelian sense, and the state of the organism as the secondary process, as the minor internal contradiction. The resolution of these two contradictions produces the behavioral pattern of approach or withdrawal (for a philosophical discussion of contradiction, see Marquit, 1980; Marquit, in press).

Both the external and internal contradictions have their own inherent major and minor contradictions. For example, the internal contradictions of the organism derive from the integration of major and minor contradictions in structure/function. A major internal contradiction would be the status of the organism; that is, the contemporary experiential state, as for example, state of adaptation of sensory systems to prevailing levels of external stimulation, such as dark or light adaptation, or state of motor systems (muscular tone) as a function of preceding activity, such as increased motor activity in a state of hunger. A minor contradiction would be changes brought about by the physiological changes in the organism as a function of the intensity of stimulation (Lawson, Turkewitz, Platt & McCarton, 1988). Thus intensity of stimulation, defined physically (e.g., Hz) functions more or less adequately, to result in A- or W- processes, depending upon the state of the organism.

The above analysis of A/W processes is an example of the application of the concept of integrative levels.

One View of the Concept of Integrative Levels

A level is a temporal/spatial relationship of structures functioning synthetically and synchronously in relative stability so that it is definable as an entity. The synthesis and synchrony are labile; that is, the level has antithetical, asynchronous and disparate characteristics that produce new spatial/temporal relationships of structure/function. Each level is the product of internal contradictions that integrate with external contradictions. External and internal contradictions (antithetical, asynchronous and disparate changes) act in relation to the contradictions brought about by other levels. The contradictions within, between and among levels are responsible for the relative stability as well as for the development of change that ultimately produces the qualitative differences among levels.

At the moment of definition, the level is the contemporary result of the changes that have taken place previously, that is, of its history. Levels are definable within categories, which may be specified prior to the definition of the levels of the category, but the validity of the category may be tested by the definition of the characteristics of its levels, and the relationships among the levels. That is, if changes in the levels and the relationships among levels, within the category maintain the integrity of the category through the resolution of the contradictions within and among the levels, beginning with the earliest level in the history of the category and continuing through succeeding levels, as they sub- sume preceding levels, the category may be seen as valid. The category acts in relation to other categories that may furnish the external contradictions that fuse with the internal contradictions of the levels within the category (Tobach, 1987).

Overview

As can be seen in the discussions in this volume by Richard Lerner, Georgine Vroman, and Leo Vroman, as well as others in this volume, there are many different views of and aspects of the concept of integrative levels to be elaborated and tested. It has also been suggested that the concept needs to be applied systematically to levels of human thought and knowl- edge (mathematics, logic, theories, etc.) in order to develop its usefulness. Much remains to be done also in regard to the newly defined "cognitive behavior" in nonhuman animals, as for example, social deception, numerosity concept, hypothesis formation, etc. Schneirla was interested in the comparison of the mental activity of different species, but this was represented in a small part of his research (1942 with N. R. F. Maier; 1946, 1949).

The concept of integrative levels has been criticized vari- ously (Foskett, 1978), including a characterization as being vague—that is, so inclusive as to be useless; that as a theoretical basis for research it would require too many researchers using many different kinds of techniques and instruments. Given the proper leadership and capabilities, however, it is possible to carry out research on more than one level in one laboratory (Giordano, Siegel, & Rosenblatt, 1989 inter alia; Rosenblatt, 1965; Siegel, & Rosenblatt, 1978). Advances in instrumentation now provide data at a number of levels; the integration of these levels can yield meaningful, explanatory descriptions and definitions of processes at any one level, as well as among levels. The data for all levels need not be gathered in one laboratory; the concept of integrative levels can be used productively to elucidate the relationships and processes involved.

The concept of integrative levels is indeed inclusive; to integrate is to include. Using this concept, Schneirla was able to include biochemical, physiological and behavioral processes in his analysis of the complex cyclicity in doryline ant colonies (1957). The so-called vagueness of the concept is actually its general applicability to such varied phenomena as social behavior (Schneirla, 1949, 1951, 1953, 1961 with J. S. Rosenblatt; 1968 with E. Tobach); intraorganismic integrity (Schneirla, 1965); and cognitive function (Maier & Schneirla, 1935).

The value of the concept of integrative levels as a tool for the study of the development and evolution of behavior can only be demonstrated in the crucible of activity designed to change existing reality and existing knowledge. The questions that are formulated for research cannot be independent of previous knowledge, experience and methods. Research is carried out within a societal context that sets its own rules for such activities, and the individual scientist must take these rules into consideration if the research is to be realized. Yet there is no value in attempting to restrict the curiosity and idiosyncracies of the human mind. The application of the concept of integrative levels to the formulation and carrying out of research, and thus the possibility of its usefulness being tested, are matters of probability defined by factors other than the intrinsic merits of the concept.

ACKNOWLEDGMENTS

I wish to thank all those who read various versions of this paper and gave me the benefit of their criticisms, that is; Lester R. Aronson, Kathryn Hood, Erwin Marquit, Christopher Robinson, J. S. Rosenblatt and G. S. Vroman. Of course, they are not responsible for any misreading of their ideas that may have become incorporated into the paper. I also thank Nancy K. Innis for the Tolman reference.

REFERENCES

Allen, T. F. H., & Starr, T. B. (1982). *Hierarchy*. Chicago: University of Chicago Press.

Aronson. L. R. (1963). The central nervous system of sharks and bony fishes with special reference to sensory and integrative mechanisms. In P. W. Gilbert (Ed.), *Sharks and survival* (chapter 6). Boston: D. C. Heath.

———. (1984). Levels of integration and organization: A re-evaluation of the evolutionary scale. In G. Greenberg & E. Tobach (Eds.) *Behavioral evolution and integrative levels* (pp. 57–81). Hillsdale, NJ: LEA.

———. (1987). Some remarks on integrative levels. In G. Greenberg & E. Tobach (Eds.), *Cognition, language and consciousness: integrative levels.* (pp. 269–286). Hillsdale, NJ: LEA.

Aronson, L. R., Tobach, E., Lehrman, D. S., & J. S. Rosenblatt (Eds.) (1971). *Selected writings of T. C. Schneirla*. San Francisco: W. H. Freeman Press.

Bohr, N. (1958). *Atomic physics and human knowledge.* New York: John Wiley & Sons.

Bronowski, J. (1970). New concepts in the evolution of complexity: stratified stability and unbound planes. *Zygon*, pp. 18–40.

Brothers, D. J. (1983). Nomenclature at the ordinal and higher levels. *Systematic Zoology, 32*, 34–42.

Emerson, A. E. (1942). Basic comparisons of human and insect societies. In R. Redfield (Ed.), *Levels of integration in biological and social systems* (pp. 163–176). PA: The Jacques Cattell Press.

Feibelman, J. K. (1954). Theory of integrative levels. *British Journal of Philosophy and Science, 5*, 59–66.

Foskett, D. J. (1978). The theory of integrative levels and its relevance to the design of information systems. *Aslib Proceedings, 30*, 202–208.

Giordano, A. L., Siegel, H. I., & Rosenblatt, J. S. (1989). Nuclear estrogen receptor binding in the preoptic area and hypothalamus of pregnancy-terminated rats: correlation with the onset of maternal behavior. *Neuroendocrinology, 50*, 248–258.

Goertzel, B. (1972). What is hierarchical selection? *Biology and Philosophy, 7*, 27–33.

Grobstein, C. (1976). Organizational levels and explanation. In M. Grene & E. Mendelsohn (Eds.), *Topics in the philosophy of biology* (pp. 145–152). Dordrecht-Holland: D. Reidel Publishing Co.

Heingardner, R., & Engelberg, H. (1983). Biological complexity. *Journal of theoretical Biology, 104*, 7–20.

Holland, E. A., Parton, W. J., Detling, J. K., & Coppock, D. L. (1992). Physiological responses of plant populations to herbivory and their consequences for the ecosystem nutrient flow. *The American Naturalist, 140*, 685–706.

Hyman, L. H. (1942). The transition from the unicellular to the multi-cellular individual. In R. Redfield (Ed.), *Levels of integration in biological and social systems* (pp. 27–42). PA: The Jacques Cattell Press.

Janzen, D. H. (1988). Costa Rican anachronisms: Where did the Guana-casta tree come from? In Abelardo Brenes (Ed.), *The comparative psychology of natural resource management:* Costa Rica (pp. 13–26). Advances in Comparative Psychology, Volume 1, Naples: The International Society for Comparative Psychology and the University of Calabria.

Jennings, H. S. (1942). The transition from the individual to the social. In R. Redfield (Ed.), *Levels of integration in biological and social systems* (pp. 105–119). PA: The Jacques Cattell Press.

Kauffman, S. A. (1991). Antichaos and adaptation. *Scientific American, 265*, 78–84.

Kennedy, J. S. (1992). *The new anthropomorphism.* Cambridge, MA: Cambridge University Press.

Kolka, J., & Parker, S. T. A. (1989). Ecological systems and the concept of biological organization. *Proceedings of the National Academy of Science, USA, 86*, 8837–8841.

Lawson, K. R., Turkewitz, G., Platt, P., & McCarton, C. (1985). Infant state in relation to its environmental context. *Infant Behavior and Development, 8*, 261–281.

Lehrman, D. S. (1970). Semantic and conceptual issues in the nature-nurture problem. In L. R. Aronson, E. Tobach, D. S. Lehrman, & J. S. Rosenblatt (Eds.), *Development and evolution of behavior* (pp. 17–52). San Francisco: W. H. Freeman & Co.

———. (1971). Experiential background for the induction of reproductive behavior patterns by hormones. In E. Tobach, L. R. Aronson, & E. Shaw (Eds.), *The biopsychology of development* (pp. 297–302). New York: Academic Press.

Maier, N. R. F., & Schneirla, T. C. (1935). *Animal psychology*. New York: McGraw-Hill.

———. (1942). Mechanisms in conditioning. In L. R. Aronson, E. Tobach, J. S. Rosenblatt, & D. S. Lehrman (Eds.), (1971). *Selected writings of T. C. Schneirla* (pp. 541–555). San Francisco: W. H. Freeman & Co.

Makarov, I. M. (Ed.) (1987). *Cybernetics of living matter: nature, man, information*. Moscow: MIR Publishers.

Marquit, E. (1980). Physical systems, structures and properties. *Science and Society, 44*, 155–176.

———. (In press). *Contradiction as source of structure and development in nature and society*. Bulgarian Academy of Science.

May, R. M. (1988). Levels of organization in ecology. In J. M. Cherrett (Ed.), *Ecological concepts* (pp. 364–375). Oxford: Blackwell Scientific Publications.

Mayr, E. (1988). The limits of reductionism. *Nature, 331*, 475.

Morgan, C. L. (1933). *The emergence of novelty*. London: Williams & Norgate, Ltd.

Needham, J. (1936). *Order and Life*. MA: The M.I.T. Press.

———. (1937). *Integrative levels: A revaluation of the idea of progress*. Oxford: Clarendon Press.

Newman, S. A. (1970). Note on complex systems. *Journal of Theoretical Biology, 28*, 411–413.

Novikoff, A. B. (1945). The concept of integrative levels and biology. *Science, 101*, 209–215.

Packel, E. W., & Traub, J. F. (1987). Information-based complexity. *Nature, 327*, 29–33.

Pettersson, M. (1978). Major integrative levels and the fo-so series. *Aslib Proceedings, 30*, 215–237.

Redfield, R. (Ed.) (1942). *Levels of integration in biological and social systems*. PA: The Jacques Cattell Press.

Rosenblatt, J. S. (1965). The basis of synchrony in the behavioral interaction of mother and young in the rat. In B. F. Foss (Ed.), *Determinants of infant behavior*. III (pp. 3–45). London: Methuen.

———. (1991). A psychobiological approach to maternal behavior among the primates. In P. Bateson (Ed.), *The development and evolution of behavior* (pp. 191–222). Cambridge: Cambridge University Press.

Rosenblatt, J. S., & Schneirla, T. C. (1961). Behavioral organization and genesis of the social bond in insects and mammals. *American Journal of Orthopsychiatry, 31*, 223–253.

Salthe, S. N. (1985). *Evolving hierarchical systems.* New York: Columbia University Press.

Schneirla, T. C. (1946). Ant learning as a problem in comparative psychology. In L. R. Aronson, E. Tobach, D. S. Lehrman, & J. S. Rosenblatt (Eds.) (1971). *Selected writings of T. C. Schneirla* (pp. 556–579). San Francisco: W. H. Freeman & Co.

———. (1949). Levels in the psychological capacities of animals. In L. R. Aronson, E. Tobach, D. S. Lehrman, & J. S. Rosenblatt (Eds.) (1971). *Selected writings of T. C. Schneirla* (pp. 199–237). San Francisco: W. H. Freeman & Co.

———. (1951). The "levels" concept in the study of social organization in animals. In L. R. Aronson, E. Tobach, D. S. Lehrman, & J. S. Rosenblatt (Eds.) (1971). *Selected writings of T. C. Schneirla* (pp. 440–472). San Francisco: W. H. Freeman & Co.

———. (1953). The concept of levels in the study of social phenomena. In L. R. Aronson, E. Tobach, D. S. Lehrman, & J. S. Rosenblatt (Eds.) (1971). *Selected writings of T. C. Schneirla* (pp. 238–253). San Francisco: W. H. Freeman & Co.

———. (1957). Theoretical consideration of cyclic processes in doryline ants. In L. R. Aronson, E. Tobach, D. S. Lehrman, & J. S. Rosenblatt (Eds.) (1971). *Selected writings of T. C. Schneirla* (pp. 806–852). San Francisco: W. H. Freeman & Co.

———. (1965). Aspects of stimulation and organization in approach-withdrawal processes underlying vertebrate behavioral development. In L. R. Aronson, E. Tobach, D. S. Lehrman, & J. S. Rosenblatt (Eds.) (1971). *Selected writings of T. C. Schneirla* (pp. 344–412). San Francisco: W. H. Freeman & Co.

Siegel, H. I., & Rosenblatt, J. S. (1978). Duration of estrogen stimulation and progesterone inhibition of maternal behavior in pregnancy-terminated rats. *Physiology and Behavior, 21*, 99–103.

Simon, H. A. (1962). The architecture of complexity. *Proceedings of the American Philosophical Society, 106*, 467–482.

Stern, A. W. (1964). Quantum physics and biological systems. *Journal of Theoretical Biology, 7*, 318–328.

Tobach, E. (1972). The meaning of the cryptanthroparion. In L. Ehrman, G. Omenn, & E. Caspari (Eds.), *Genetics, environment and behavior* (pp. 219–239). New York: Academic Press.

Tobach, E. (1987). Integrative levels in the comparative psychology of cognition, language and consciousness. In G. Greenberg & E. Tobach (Eds.), *Cognition, languge and consciousness: Integrative levels*. Hillsdale, NJ: LEA.

Tobach, E., and Schneirla, T. C. (1968). The biopsychology of social behavior in animals. In R. E. Cooke (Ed.), *The biological basis of pediatric practice* (pp. 68–82). New York: McGraw-Hill.

Tolman, E. C. (1938). The determiners of behavior at a choice point. *Psychological Review, 45,* 1–41.

Topoff, H. R. (1990). The evolution of slave-making behavior in the parasitic ant genus *Polyergus. Ethology, Ecology, and Evolution, 2,* 284–287.

Turkewitz, G. (1987). Psychobiology and developmental psychology: The influence of T. C. Schneirla on human developmental psychology. *Developmental Psychobiology, 20,* 369–575.

Ugolev, A. M. (1989). Principles of organization and evolution of biological systems. *Journal of Evolutionary Biochemisty and Physiology, 25,* 136–150.

van der Leeuw, S. W. (1981). *Archaeological approaches to the study of complexity*. Amsterdam: A. E. van Griffen Institut, University of Amsterdam.

Wimsatt, W. C. (1972). Complexity and organization. In K. F. Schaffner & R. S. Cohen (Eds.), *Book studies in the philosophy of science* (pp. 67–86). Dordrecht-Holland: D. Reidel Publishing Co.

Wolfram, S. (1984). Cellular automata as models of complexity. *Nature, 311,* 419–424.

Zhirmunsky, A. V., & Kuzmin, V. I. (1988). *Critical levels in the development of natural systems*. Berlin: SpringerVerlag.

Zylstra, U. (1992). Living things as hierarchically organized structures. *Synthese, 91,* 111–133.

CHAPTER 14

The Concept of Levels of Integration

Georgine Vroman

Without commenting specifically on the definitions by Lerner and Tobach, instead a general observation: Any discussion should acknowledge the fact that the concept of levels of integration has a wider usefulness than that of the present context. It should ideally include, but also go beyond, the framework of the Schneirla conferences. As Tobach's historical introduction makes clear, the concept has had a considerable historical development, which the definition should reflect. It has, for instance, contributed significantly to the description of different levels of social organization and the place of the individual within this framework. I consider it essential not to try to be too specific (and therefore limiting) in formulating the definition in order not to lose this wider usefulness.

There is a tendency to make the definition "complete." This leads to the inclusion of specifics and clarifications that do serve a necessary function but make it too unwieldy to be practical. It seems to me that it would be more useful to keep the definition simple and add a commentary or discussion if that is considered necessary.

Maybe we must learn to live with the idea that the concept of integrative levels is likely to have a somewhat different meaning for its different users (i.e., both as individuals and as representatives of different disciplines) and abandon the hope of formulating the one detailed definition, acceptable to all who work with the concept, that coincides with our own, possibly overly specific, requirements. Still, these different interpretations can be formulated and debated and some kind of concensus could evolve. It may be possible to agree on a simple, concise definition of the concept. The participants in the debate can still give as specific and detailed an interpretation of their own use of the concept as they deem necessary. The ongoing interactive process of shaping the concept and exploring its usefulness in applying it to, and thus explaining, observed phenomena should be an important research topic. It is, or should be, a deliberate interdisciplinary endeavor.

My Concept of Levels of Integration

Definition: Natural or social events can be conceived of as existing at (or consisting of) several levels, each comprised of interacting entities that share certain characteristics that determine the nature of the specific level. Each level is also part of one or several more encompassing levels that together make up a series of sets which ranges, essentially, from the subatomic to the social. Each entity belonging to one level may also belong to other levels that can be different for each of these entities. Integration is the characteristic process that provides cohesion within each level and between levels. The concept of levels of integration is a model that helps explain observable phenomena.

Discussion

The concept of levels of integration can have many applications. One example is to see it as the organizing principle for the relationships of the organism with its internal and external environment. Another is that of a model for evolutionary processes. In each example the stress may be on different aspects of the entities that make up each level, and on the relationships that occur between these entities within each level as well as those that occur across levels. I see the concept of levels of integration as shifting continuously depending on the focus of our investigation. It is particularly well suited to making sense of the different dynamic processes that we observe.

CHAPTER 15

Definitions of Levels of Integration

Leo Vroman

A *level* is an observable interruption of a continuity. A level of integration is a level where several entities (e.g., objects that can be defined and named) jointly have reached integration to such a degree that they are forming a new entity.

An entity is a complex of subunits perceived as so markedly different from each and all of its subunits that it requires a new definition and a new name for itself or for its category. It will be found integrated to a degree that it has become indivisible—as indivisible as its subunits still may be at their own level. Each subunit may be a more or a less essential member of more than one "superunit." One person may simultaneously be a very essential member of a national government and a less essential patient in a mental ward. One cell may simultaneously be a less essential member of a group that forms an organ and at the same time be an essential disseminating member of a malignant tumor.

Hierarchy may be seen as an unrealistically linear description of *essentiality*. Essentiality of a subunit is often expressed and therefore measured as a magnitude of change caused by its removal or introduction. The appendix proves less essential than the brain. A molecule of cyanide is more essential than a molecule of carbon dioxide. One gene is more essential than another one. All of these evaluations are made in relation to the host organism and with the assumption that the organism itself is most essential—independent of its relative essentiality in the social group to which it belongs.

A name, if not a "proper name" for one individual entity, indicates a *category* and fails to convey much information that should express the essentiality and uniqueness of that specific entity within its category (or group). Human, female, nine-year-old, caucasian, cannot approach the description given by the name Kassie Hopkins. Carbohydrate, glucose molecule, or even glucose molecule in my brain, are categories that cannot approach the description of the one glucose molecule consumed by writing this. The aim of language is to penetrate the unavoidably categorical property of words by integrating them into an entity that is unique, and where each word becomes more like a "proper" than a categorical description.

Observation and measurement of change appears to require tools that fit the size and rate of change of the entity E to be observed. As E is more than the sum of all n of its subentities SE_1 to SE_n, any change observed in E cannot be regarded as the mere sum of changes in relations among its SE's. Yet, as a general rule, we tend to observe E less closely (meaning both less carefully and at a greater distance) than any of its own SE's, and merely because of this greater distance we tend to become less aware of the changes in any SE.

Since changes in the relatively small SE's tend to appear more rapid than those in their encompassing host, E, our poor perception of details at a distance will—again as a rule—make us believe events slow down at "higher" (larger and more complex) levels. There are obvious exceptions. The arm of a tennis player who fills our mental screen moves faster than do the pseudopods of any one of his leukocytes when it fills our mental screen, but may well move relatively no faster than the tail of one of his sperm cells. Perhaps these general rules of perspective, limiting our scale of observation, have led to the concept of levels to begin with. Long ago, when single cells began to be observed, there were speculations on links between activities of cells and of their entire host; and with the discovery of hormones—molecules formed in one organ and acting on another organ—such links became sharper. Only quite recently we have learned to follow a single molecule's adventures through an entire organism that can be a billion times larger, even if the molecule is not an essential one and is carrying out some function shared by thousands of other "identical" ones. However, because of its infinitely complex and unique past, no molecule can be regarded as identical to any other molecule; even if it is chemically the same, it will be in a different place. Only the recent mathematical approach of "deterministic chaos" will give a strict model of a few chains of events that any molecule always undergoes; and such a model will reveal the fundamental unpredictability of an SE. By pure and very rare coincidence then, the molecule we selected may turn out to be indeed essential—meaning that it happens to be a single molecule that can jump the levels of cell and organ and affect its entire host. Such a jump, be it physical or perceived, may transmit the unpredictability of the chosen SE to that of the entire E.

In this discussion what is most essential is perhaps the jump itself, such as from molecular to organismic level—a kind of jump that modern instrumentation, techniques, and communication allow.

Jumps over one or more levels may, in other words, be made by nature as well as by technology. Those made by nature are often detected by consequences of failing jumps: a genetic defect causing a wrong amino acid to be inserted in a coagulation protein and thus causing a patient to bleed, for example. It is detected only because a large number of identical jumps fail simultaneously: All the millions of molecules of this protein will be defective and their failure will then be large enough to be observed in a test tube. Many of our experiments in vitro cause similar very numerous and simultaneous "errors." When some blood is placed into a test tube, the mere magnitude of the tube, needed to make events visible, causes synchronization of a series of changes undergone by millions of "identical" protein molecules—so many that their multitude lifts the sample from a molecular level to a level that is defined by the size of the test tube.

This kind of synchronization of course stereotypes the synchronized molecules to such a degree that we identify them by a single name, even though we now know that molecules of one protein species can display a nearly infinite variety of shapes. The closer we look into a society, a tissue or a drop of blood, the more individually different every subentity will prove to be, but the farther we will drift away from any ability to describe the large entity it is a part of. With each ten-fold reduction of our scale of observation, we must observe a thousand times more areas to rebuild the original object. Obviously, we cannot have it all.

Beauty. We may define beauty as an awareness of structure without awareness of the laws on which it is based. This awareness creates the feeling that what we observe is indivisible and unique. Efforts to analyze the movements of a tree in the wind, or the beauty of a painting, drown in the overwhelming details that created their beauty as an entity and are only rewarding for drawing us into the beauty of every subentity within and around us.

CHAPTER 16

The Integration of Levels and Human Development
A Developmental Contextual View of the Synthesis of Science and Outreach in the Enhancement of Human Lives

Richard M. Lerner

In developmental psychology dualities have played, and continue to play, an all too prominent role. Examples of such dualities are nature versus nurture, continuity versus discontinuity, stability versus instability, male versus female, agency versus communion, and secure versus insecure attachment. Another duality, associated not only with developmental psychology but with all of psychology—and indeed with science in general—is basic research versus applied research. An example of the unfortunate, and often pernicious, societal implications of this tendency in developmental psychology—in behavioral science and in society in general—to impose contrived dichotomies on the reality of social life may be found in the writing of John Edgar Wideman (1992). Commenting on the 1992 Los Angeles riots that followed the acquittal of the police officers charged in the beating of Rodney King, Wideman noted that:

The work on this chapter was supported in part by grants from the W. K. Kellogg Foundation, the C. S. Mott Foundation, and NICHD Grant HD23229. I thank Valora Washington and Marvin McKinney for their comments about this chapter.

The peculiar and perhaps fatal American violence is the refusal to connect. We simplify the world with categorical divisions—black/white, male/female, old/young—and then cling to these in spite of the evidence of our intellects, our senses. A violence so disruptive and irrational it blinds us to our self-interests. A violence epitomized by a juror who sympathizes with the fear of a dozen armed police-men as they beat a black man to his knees but can't acknowledge Rodney King's pain as the blows were inflicted. . . . Were the outraged voices condemning the violence of rioters reading from the double-columned, white-reality-here, black-reality-over-there book, forget-ting the violence that permits whole cities to fester? Were those voices promising to stop violence with violence attempting to close the racial divide or preparing us to plunge deeper into the chasm? (Wideman, 1992, pp. 153–154)

At least in some areas of social or behavioral science, dichotomies may be useful at an initial stage of inquiry. For instance, they may designate marker variables indexing the pres-ence of an important behavioral phenomenon (Gollin, 1981). But, when the categorical thinking which may accompany such dichotomous conceptualization leads one to ignore the investi-gation of the change processes involved within and across the categories, important issues pertinent to the dynamic and devel-opmental nature of organismic functioning are lost. In addition, when such dichotomous thinking creates a false division be-tween the scientist seeking to understand human behavior and the people he or she *should be serving* through this understanding (and here I acknowledge that I am making an explicit statement of values), societal havoc may be produced (cf. Schneirla, 1966; Wideman, 1992).

From the perspective of a developmental psychologist ad-hering to a developmental contextual perspective, it would be unfortunate if the concept of approach/withdrawal were dealt with in this categorical way. At least since Schneirla's paper in Harris' (1957) *The concept of development* volume, developmental psychologists have had available to them the conceptual tools for avoiding such a risk, not only for the approach/withdrawal concept but for the superordinate notions of nature and nurture and organism and environment within which the approach/ withdrawal concept may best be understood.

Today, due in no small part to Schneirla's (1956, 1957, 1959) contributions, developmental psychologists understand the need to search for integrative processes—that is, the processes spanning biological, psychological, and social- and physical-contextual levels of organization, and linking nature and nurture, organism and environment (Ford & Lerner, 1992; Gottlieb, 1991, 1992; Lerner, 1991; Tobach, 1981). Within the study of human development, consideration of the "fused" (Tobach & Greenberg, 1984), dynamically interactive (Lerner, 1978, 1986), or reciprocally influential relations among variables from these multiple, integrated levels, means that one will *not* view approach and/or withdrawal phenomena as necessarily distinct characteristics of different organisms, or as characteristics of an organism's functioning which are associated with independent (or, in other words, with nonintegrated) processes. Rather, the fusion of variables from distinct levels of organization—a fusion which comprises the basic nature of the developmental process across ontogeny—indicates that approach and withdrawal are best conceived of as but points along a behavioral continuum which may mark an organism's functioning under different conditions or at different points in its ontogeny. In turn, the potential for differential location across ontogeny along this approach/withdrawal continuum means that developmental analyses should be directed to understanding the conditions under which continuity or discontinuity could arise in organism environment relations—a point made compellingly by Cairns and Hood (1983) in their seminal chapter on processes of continuity and discontinuity in the *Life-span development and behavior* series.

Furthermore, a developmental psychologist may take from this literature the need to identity processes differentiating the *psychological levels* of species, to use Schneirla's (1957) term, *and* processes differentiating points in ontogeny, within a given species, that is distinct points in the species *functional order* of a species, to again use Schneirla's (1957) term. A key distinction to keep in mind when making such phyletic or ontogenetic comparisons is between biosocial and psychosocial processes. The former, biosocial processes pertain, in the main, to organisms closer to the stereotypy end of a plasticity-stereotypy continuum (Hebb, 1949; Lerner, 1976; Schneirla, 1957). Such organisms, it is important to note, are at a psychological level which attains its highest order of functioning relatively early in its ontogeny. To a developmental psychologist interested in approach/withdrawal within such a species, processes of prime interest would be ones melding biochemical variables—genetic, neural, or hormonal in nature—with social functioning (Gottlieb, 1991, 1992). The early portions of the organism's life span would be the period within which it would be appropriate to focus most scientific attention.

However, early life is not the whole story for the study of approach/withdrawal processes within all organisms. Among organisms that are capable of functioning psychosocially, that is organisms closer to the plasticity end of the above-noted contin-uum (and here humans are of course the exemplar) a high psy-chological level means that the highest order of functioning is reached very late in ontogeny. Indeed humans, as perhaps the most neotenous of all species (Gould, 1977), are as well the most paedomorphic one (Gould, 1977). All of the life span becomes, then, the appropriate ground for studying approach/withdrawal processes, and our concerns should be more with the transitions and transformations of these processes—for example, with conditions for and timing of the emergence in ontogeny of a particular psychosocial characteristic—than it should be in attempting to find a general description which holds across all of human ontogenetic time.

I believe that such an agenda would bring us back full cir-cle to a discussion of dichotomous thinking, but here with the ability to suggest a fluidity of thought which may be capitalized on to go beyond simplistic or erroneous categorization. The emergence in human life of representational ability—of language and other symbolic systems—may represent the key point of emergence of true, or potentially maximally plastic, psychosocial functioning. Here, physical stimulus intensity can become trans-formed cognitively by a "switch" (e.g., through a relabeling) in the meaning attached to a stimulus. Indeed, although the appro-priate developmental research has to my knowledge not been conducted I am certain it would be fairly easy to demonstrate the increasing ability with age to—with more and more rapid facility—embed the same stimulus in a nomological net involving approach versus a net involving withdrawal.

Several examples may be given. For instance, in adolescence, love relationships change valence despite physical characteristics (e.g., attractiveness) staying the same. One can love another person one day and hate him or her the next. A second example involves the parents and peers of adolescents. With parents, relationships may fluctuate from affection or commitment on one day to, on another day, abhorrence and distancing. This change may be coupled with a turning to the peer group which, in turn, may suffer the same fluctuant fate in a matter of days, if not hours. Dieting and food stimuli provide another example. Symbolic behavior in adolescence may enable the person to overcome desires for specific foods or eating in general; as such, through relabeling or reinterpretation, an intensely appetitive food stimulus may become a moderate or an irrelevant one, and may attain this status with rapidity and facility. At an extreme, such cognitive revalencing of an appetitive food stimulus to an aversive one may be involved in eating disorders prevalent in adolescence, for example, anorexia and bulimia.

In essence, then, among humans who are functioning at or near the maximum of their plasticity, the functional world is not one of physical stimuli but one wherein cognitive and affective interpretations are paramount. Stimulus intensity is no longer a term analyzable along physical dimensions. Instead, ethnographic, hermeneutic, or other qualitative methods may be needed to understand the behavioral valence a given stimulus, situation, or event has for a person.

Given that the person's meaning system functions to link him or her to the context, such analyses can best be understood in the context of the superordinate integration involved in human life, that is, changing person-context relationships or, in the terms of Tobach and Greenberg (1984), changing person-context "fusions." The study of such fusions is the focus of an approach to understanding human development across the life span termed developmental contextualism (Lerner, 1986, 1991, 1992). The analysis of these changing person-context relations may allow one to understand the conditions in ontogeny when person and context combine in such a way as to be associated with interpretations promoting approach to a stimulus, withdrawal from it, or anything in between. Moreover, the same sort of analysis may allow us to understand the person and social context conditions that lead to, or perhaps diminish as well, unfruitful dichotomous thinking—both in science and in society more generally.

As Schneirla (1966) explained in his review of Konrad Lorenz's (1966) *On aggression*, the interpretative system that leads to viewing the sources of development as lying either in nature or nurture can wreck havoc not only for science but for social policy and human welfare as well. Accordingly, perhaps the key dualities to be transcended by the use of Schneirla's (1956, 1957, 1959) ideas about integrative levels and approach/withdrawal, at least insofar as these ideas are used within developmental contextualism, is the dichotomy of science versus service or "outreach" (i.e., the extension, application, or utilization of knowledge within the community in order to address the problems of human life that are identified through a collaboration between scholars and members of the community). Often this dichotomy is also cast as one between basic research and applied research.

In short, an analysis of the human developmental transitions involved in the transformation of approach/withdrawal processes into primarily symbolic systems may lead to an understanding of the conditions associated with our personal tastes and aversions and our social preferences and hatreds. I submit then that embedding Schneirla's (1959) concept of approach/withdrawal in a developmental contextual frame demonstrates not only the richness of the concept but, as well, how—as with much of the work associated with Schneirla's career—he has helped empower us to improve our science and perhaps at the same time enhance our world.

Accordingly, I turn to a brief overview of the developmental contextual perspective. This presentation will be followed by a discussion of the use of this perspective for understanding the way in which the process of changing person-context relations may be studied in a manner that enhances human life through the integration of heretofore usually dichotomized activities: research and outreach.

The Developmental Contextual Perspective

Developmental contextualism is a perspective about human development that takes an integrative approach to the multiple levels of organization presumed to comprise the nature of human life; that is, "fused" (Tobach & Greenberg, 1984) relations among biological, psychological, and social contextual levels comprise the process of developmental change in human life. In other words, rather than approach variables from these levels of analysis in either a reductionistic or in a parallel-processing approach, the developmental contextual view of development rests on the idea that variables from these levels of analysis are dynamically interactive—they are reciprocally influential over the course of human ontogeny.

Within developmental contextualism levels are conceived of as integrative organizations. That is:

> The concept of integrative levels recognizes as equally essential for the purpose of scientific analysis both the isolation of parts of a whole and their integration into the structure of the whole. It neither reduces phenomena of a higher level to those of a lower one, as in mechanism, or describes the higher level in vague nonmaterial terms which are but substitutes for understanding, as in vitalism. Unlike other "holistic" theories, it never leaves the firm ground of material reality. . . . The concept points to the need to study the organizational interrelationships of parts and whole (Novikoff, 1945a, p. 209).

Moreover, Tobach and Greenberg (1984, p. 2) have stressed that:

> The interdependence among levels is of great significance. The dialectic nature of the relationship among levels is one in which lower levels are subsumed in higher levels so that any particular level is an integration of proceeding levels. . . . In the process of integration, or fusion, *new* levels with their own characteristics result.

If the course of human development is the product of the processes involved in the "fusions" (or "dynamic interactions"; Lerner, 1978, 1979, 1984) among integrative levels, then the processes of development are more plastic than often previously believed (cf. Brim & Kagan, 1980). Within this perspective, then, the context for development is not seen merely as a simple stimulus environment, but rather as an "ecological environment . . . conceived topologically as a nested arrangement of concentric structures, each contained with the next" (Bronfenbrenner, 1979, p. 22) and including variables from biological, psychological, physical, and sociocultural levels, all changing interdependently across history (Riegel, 1975, 1976a, 1976b).

The central idea in developmental contextualism, then, is that reciprocal relations (i.e., dynamic interactions; Lerner, 1978, 1979) between individuals and the multiple contexts within which they live comprise the essential process of human development (Lerner, 1986; Lerner & Kauffman, 1985). Thus all the issues raised by this perspective derive from a common appreciation of the basic role of the changing context in developmental change. It is the functional significance of this changing context that requires adoption of a probabilistic epigenetic (Gottlieb, 1983) view of the components of an organism's development; in this probabilistic view of the course of development the role of the *timing* of dynamic interactions are central in shaping the specific features of the course of a human life.

The Role of the Concept of "Interaction" in Developmental Contextualism

A developmental contextual perspective captures the complexity of a multilevel context: (1) Without ignoring the active role of the organism in shaping, as well as being shaped by, that context; and (2) without sacrificing commitment to useful, universal principles of developmental change. These two foci are integrated within the contextual orientation at the level of the presumed *relation* between organismic and contextual processes. The developmental contextual conceptualization of this relation differs substantially from those of the organismic and mechanistic perspectives (Lerner, 1986). That is, a *strong* concept of organism-environment interaction (Lerner & Spanier, 1978, 1980; Overton, 1973), transaction (Sameroff, 1975), or dynamic interaction (Lerner, 1978, 1979) is associated with developmental contextualism. This version of interaction stresses that organism and context are always embedded each in the other (Lerner, Hultsch, & Dixon, 1983), that the context is composed of multiple levels changing interdependently (integratively) across time (i.e., historically), and that because organisms influence the context that influences them, they are efficacious in playing an active role in their own development (Lerner & Busch- Rossnagel, 1981; Tobach, 1981).

Moreover, because of the mutual embeddedness of organism and context, a given organismic attribute will have different implications for developmental outcomes in the milieu of different contextual conditions; this is the case because the organism attribute is only given its functional meaning by virtue of its relation to a specific context. If the context changes, as it may over time, then the same organism attribute will have a different import for development. In turn, the same contextual condition will lead to alternative developments in that different organisms interact with it.

To state this position in somewhat stronger terms, *a given organismic attribute only has meaning for psychological development by virtue of its timing of interaction; that is, its relation to a particular set of timebound, contextual conditions*. In turn, the import of any set of contextual conditions for psychosocial behavior and development can only be understood by specifying the context's relations to the specific, developmental features of the organisms within it.

This dynamic interaction between organismic processes (e.g., those linked to biological functioning, such as genetic action or maturation) and contextual influences and changes (e.g., arising from the effects of social institutions and normative or non-normative ecological events; Baltes, Reese, & Lipsitt, 1980) are assuredly quite complex. One means for considering this complexity is presented below.

Biology and the Contexts of Human Life

The core idea in developmental contextualism is that organism (organismic attributes or, most generally, biology) and context cannot be separated (Gottlieb, 1991, 1992; Lerner, 1984; Tobach, 1981). Both are fused across life. One way to begin to illustrate just what is involved in this relation, even for one person, is to consider the diagram presented in Figure 1 (cf. Lerner, 1984, 1986). In the figure I use the circle on the center-left to represent an individual child. Within the child are represented (as slices of a "pie") several of the dimensions of the child's individuality: his or her health, physical, and biological status; personality and temperament; behaviors; and demands placed on others (parents in this figure). All of these dimensions, as well as others (included in the figure by inserting the pie slice "etc."), are represented as existing in a manner contingent on the child's development level, which is a final pie slice within the child figure. In short, what I have represented by this portion of Figure 1 is that a child is a complex, differentiated, and integrated biological, psychological, and behavioral organism, and that this differentiation is not static; rather it develops across time.

However, just as biological (e.g., genetic) processes are reciprocally embedded within a differentiated, multilevel environment, so too are children. Accordingly, I have used a circle on the center-right of Figure 1 to represent a parent of the child. As is the case for the child, the parent also is a complex and differentiated biological, psychological, and behavioral organism and is, as well, a person who is developing across his or her life.

The mutual influence between child and parent, their fusion with each other, is represented in the figure by the bidirectional arrows between them. It is important to point out that we may speak of dynamic interactions between parent and child which pertain to either *social* or *physical* (for instance, biological or physiological) relationships. For example, in regard to social relationships, the parent "demands" attention from the child who does not show it; this "lights" the parent's "short fuse" of tolerance; he or she scolds the child, who then cries; this creates remorse in the parent, and elicits soothing behaviors from him or her; the child is calmed, snuggles up to the parent, and now both

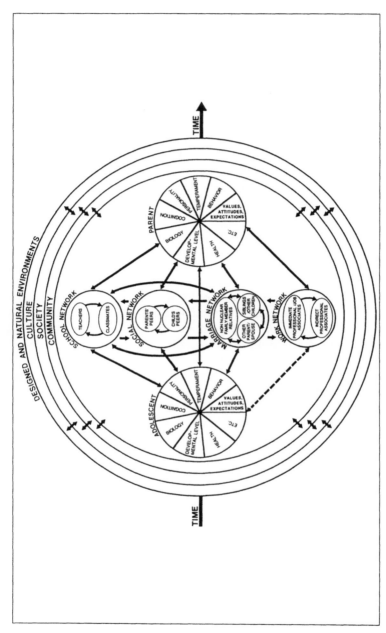

Figure 1. A developmental contextual model of human development. People are "fused" with their contexts across life.

parties in the relationship show positive emotions and are happy (for example, see Tubman & Lerner, (1994), for data pertinent to such parent-child relationships).

In turn, I may illustrate also dynamic interactions which involve not only the exchange of "external" social behaviors but involve also biological or physiological processes. For example, parental religious practices, rearing practices, or financial status may influence the child's diet and nutritional status, health, and medical care. In turn, the contraction of an infectious disease by either parent or child can lead to the other member of the rela- tionship contracting the disease. Moreover, the health and physi- cal status of the child influences the parent's own feelings of well-being and his or her hopes and aspirations regarding the child (Finkelstein, 1993).

Thus the child's internal, physiological status and devel- opment are not disconnected from his or her outer, behavioral and social context (in this example, parental) functioning and development (e.g., see Finkelstein, 1993; Ford & Lerner, 1992; Howard, 1978). The inner and outer worlds of the child are, then, fused and dynamically interactive. In addition, of course, the same may be said of the parent and, in fact, of the parent-child relationship. Each of these foci—child, parent, or relationship—is part of a larger, enmeshed *system* of fused relationships among the multiple levels which compose the ecology of human life (Bronfenbrenner, 1979).

For instance, illustrated in Figure 1 is the idea that both parent and child are embedded in a broader social network, and each person has reciprocal reactions with this network too. This set of relationships occurs because both the child and the parent are much more than just people playing only one role in life. The child may also be a sibling, a peer, and a student; the parent may also be a spouse, a worker, a peer, and an adult child. All of these networks of relations are embedded also within a particu- lar community, society, and culture. And, finally, all of these relations are continually changing across time, across history. Simply, for all portions of the system of person-context, or biol- ogy-environment, relationships envisioned in developmental contextualism change across time is an integral, indeed inescap- able, feature of human life.

The Integration of Research and Outreach within Developmental Contextualism

From the perspective of developmental contextualism, the focus of inquiry in the study of human life is on the changing, bidirectional connections between the specific individual and the particular and actual (i.e., "ecologically valid") settings within which he or she lives. This focus has brought to the fore of concern in the social and behavioral sciences an emphasis on *diversity* (individual differences) and *context* (of people's specific array of sociocultural institutions). In turn, the developmental contextual stress on the changing relation between the individual and his or her context has also resulted in the recognition that a synthesis of perspectives from multiple disciplines is needed to understand the multilevel (e.g., person, family, and community) integrations involved in human development (Lerner & Miller, 1993). In addition, there has been a recognition that to understand the basic process of human development—the process involved in the changing relations between individuals and contexts—both descriptive and explanatory research must be conducted within the actual ecology of people's lives. It is this embeddedness within real world settings that results in the synthesis of the dichotomies of basic research versus applied research, and of science versus outreach more generally.

Consider the case of explanatory studies, that is, of studies of how development happens within the actual setting wherein it happens. From a developmental contextual perspective, such investigations by their very nature constitute intervention research.

The role of the developmental researcher conducting explanatory research is to understand the ways in which variations in person-context relations account for the character of human developmental trajectories, life paths that are enacted in the "natural laboratory" of the "real world." Therefore, to gain understanding of how theoretically relevant variations in person-context relations may influence developmental trajectories, the researcher may introduce policies and/or programs as, if you will, "experimental manipulations" of the proximal and/or distal natural ecology; evaluations of the outcomes of such interventions become, then, a means to bring data to bear on theoretical issues pertinent to person-context relations and, more specifically, on the plasticity in human development that may exist, or that may be capitalized on, to enhance human life (Lerner, 1984). In other words, a key theoretical issue for explanatory research in human development is the extent to which changes—in the multiple, fused levels of organization comprising human life—can alter the structure and/or function of behavior and development.

The accumulation of the specific roles and events a person experiences across life—involving normative age-graded events, normative history-graded events, and non-normative events (Baltes, Reese, & Lipsitt, 1980)—alters each person's developmental trajectory in a manner that would not have occurred had another set of roles and events been experienced. The interindividual differences in intraindividual change that exist as a consequence of these naturally occurring interventions attest to the magnitude of the systematic changes in structure and function—the plasticity—that characterizes human life.

Explanatory research is necessary, however, to understand which variables, from which levels of organization, are involved in particular instances of plasticity that have been seen to exist. In addition, such research is necessary to determine which instances of plasticity may be created by science or society. In other words, explanatory research is needed to ascertain the extent of human plasticity or, in turn, the limits of plasticity (Baltes, 1987; Lerner, 1984).

From a developmental contextual perspective, the conduct of such research requires the scientist to alter the natural ecology of the person or group he or she is studying. Such research may involve either proximal and/or distal variations in the context of human development (Lerner & Ryff, 1978); but, in any case, these manipulations constitute theoretically-guided alterations of the roles and events a person or group experiences at, or over, a portion of the life span.

These alterations are indeed, then, interventions: They are planned attempts to alter the system of person-context relations that constitute the basic process of change; they are conducted in order to ascertain the specific bases of, or to test the limits of, particular instances of human plasticity (Baltes & Baltes, 1980; Baltes, 1987). These interventions are a researcher's attempt to substitute designed person-context relations for naturally occurring ones in an attempt to understand the process of changing person-context relations that provides the basis of human development. In short, then, from a developmental contextual perspective basic research in human development *is* intervention research. As such, within developmental contextualism the dichotomy between basic research and applied research disappears.

Accordingly, the cutting-edge of theory and research in human development lies in the application of the conceptual and methodological expertise of human development scientists to the natural ontogenetic laboratory of the real world. Multilevel, and hence, multivariate and longitudinal research methods must be used by scholars from multiple disciplines to derive, from theoretical models of person-context relations, programs of what has in the past been typically termed "applied" research; these endeavors must involve the design, delivery, and evaluation of interventions aimed at enhancing—through scientist-introduced variation—the course of human development (Birkel, Lerner, & Smyer, 1989).

This relationism and contextualization has brought to the fore of scientific, intervention, and policy concerns issues pertinent to the functional import of diverse instances of person-context interactions. Examples are studies of the effects of maternal employment on infant, child, and young adolescent development; the importance of quality day care for the immediate and long-term development in children of healthy physical, psychological, and social characteristics; and the effects of marital role strain and marital disruption on the healthy development of children and youth.

Accordingly, as greater study has been made of the actual contexts within which children and parents live, behavioral and social scientists have shown increasing appreciation of the *diversity* of patterns of individual and family development that exist, and that comprise the range of human structural and functional characteristics. Such diversity—involving racial, ethnic, gender, national, and cultural variation—has, to the detriment of the knowledge base in human development—not been a prime concern of empirical analysis (Fisher & Brennan, 1992; Hagen, Paul, Gibb, & Wolters, 1990).

Yet there are several reasons why this diversity must become a key focus of concern in the study of the development of children, adolescents, and their families (Lerner, 1991). Diversity of people and their settings means that one cannot assume that general rules of development either exist for, or apply in the same way to, all children and families. Accordingly, a new research agenda is necessary. This agenda should focus on diversity and context while at the same time attending to commonalities of individual development, family changes, and the mutual influences between the two. In other words, diversity should be placed at the fore of our research agenda. Then, with a knowledge of individuality, we can determine empirically parameters of commonality, of interindividual generalizability. Thus, we should no longer make a priori assumptions about the existence of generic developmental laws or of the primacy of such laws, even if they are found to exist, in providing the key information about the life of a given person or group.

Simply, integrated multidisciplinary and developmental research devoted to the study of diversity and context must be moved to the fore of scholarly concern. In addition, however, scholars involved in such research must have at least two other concerns, ones deriving from the view that basic, explanatory research in human development is, in its essence, intervention research.

Implications for Policies and Programs

The integrative research promoted by a developmental contextual view of human development must be synthesized with two other foci. Research in human development that is concerned with one or even a few instances of individual and contextual diversity cannot be assumed to be useful for understanding the life course of all people. Similarly, policies and programs derived from such research, or associated with it in the context of a researcher's tests of ideas pertinent to human plasticity, cannot hope to be applicable, or equally appropriate and useful, in all contexts or for all individuals. Accordingly, developmental and individual differences-oriented policy development and program (intervention) design and delivery must be integrated fully with the approach to research for which I am calling.

As emphasized in developmental contextualism, the variation in settings within which people live means that studying development in a standard (for example, a "controlled") environment does not provide information pertinent to the actual (ecologically valid) developing relations between individually distinct people and their specific contexts (for example, their particular families, schools, or communities). This point underscores the need to conduct research in real-world settings, and highlights the ideas that: (1) Policies and programs constitute natural experiments, i.e., planned interventions for people and institutions; and (2) the evaluation of such activities becomes a central focus in the developmental contextual research agenda I have described (Lerner & Miller, 1993).

In this view, then, policy and program endeavors do *not* constitute secondary work, or derivative applications, conducted after research evidence has been compiled. Quite to the contrary, policy development and implementation, and program design and delivery, become integral components of the present vision for research; the evaluation component of such policy and intervention work provides critical feedback about the adequacy of the conceptual frame from which this research agenda should derive. This conception of the integration of multidisciplinary research, endeavors centrally aimed at diversity and context, with policies, programs (interventions), and evaluations is illustrated in Figure 2.

To be successful, this developmental, individual-differences, and contextual view of research, policy, and programs for children and youth requires not only collaboration across disciplines. In addition, multiprofessional collaboration is essential. Colleagues in the research, policy, and intervention communities must plan and implement their activities in a synthesized manner in order to successfully develop and extend this vision. All components of this collaboration must be understood as equally valuable, indeed, as equally essential. The collaborative activities

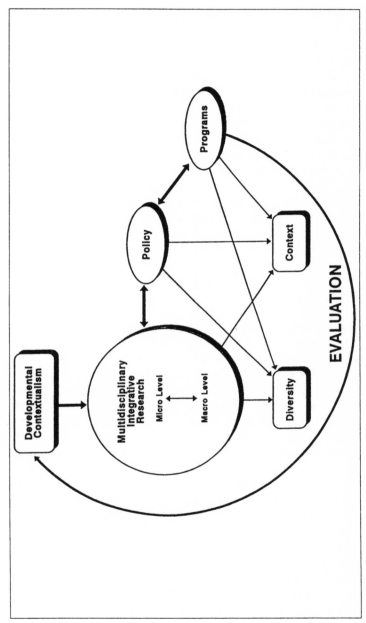

Figure 2. A developmental contextual model of the integration of multilevel, multidisciplinary research, aimed at diversity and context, with policies, programs, and evaluations.

of colleagues in university extension, in service design and delivery, in policy development and analysis, and in academic research are vital to the success of this new agenda for science and service for children, youth, and their contexts, for example, their families, schools, and communities. Moreover, such collaborative activities must involve the communities within which such work is undertaken. In other words, to enhance its ecological validity, and to provide empowerment and increased capacity among the people we are trying to both understand and serve with our synthetic research and intervention activities, we must work with the community to co-define the nature of our research and program design, delivery and evaluation endeavors. This viewpoint leads to some observations about directive themes that might organize the future activities of scholars studying children, youth, families, schools, and communities.

Potential Scholarly and Service Themes

Together the above-noted facets of developmental contextual-oriented scholarship in the study of children, youth, and contexts suggest several important themes for research, training, and service. First, a developmental, individual differences perspective is required to understand *both* children and families; this perspective must focus on the relations within the family between parents and children and, as well, on the relations between each family member and the other settings within which he or she functions (e.g., children and day care settings and parents and the work place). In addition, the relations among settings must become a focus of developmental analysis as well (Bronfenbrenner, 1979). The compilation of such information will afford a profile of the individual people and relations that comprise a specific family.

Second, the study of children and parents must become broadly contextualized. Variables from multiple levels of organization—ranging from biology and health through social institutions involving education, politics, and the economy—affect people across their lives. It is the array of these variables as they extend across life that can make each person increasingly individually distinct from others in his or her family, social group, cohort, or society (Tobach, 1981).

Moreover, as noted above, the contextual and developmental approach to the study of children and their parents must emphasize diversity. There is no one developmental path that is ideal for all people. As such, a key scientific concern of scholars of children, youth, and families must be the understanding of the richness of human life reflected in racial, ethnic, gender, national, and cultural variation. Education, intervention, outreach, and policy endeavors similarly should emphasize the specific patterns of contextual variation associated with the diverse peoples of concern to scholars.

Third, then, because no one discipline or professional area has an experiential or a knowledge base (or a repertoire of methodologies) sufficient to understand this diversity, or the interrelated influences of multiple levels of analysis on children and families, a multidisciplinary and multiprofessional approach to training, research, and service is required. In other words, to study the phenomena and problems of children, youth, and families, as they function and develop in their real-life settings, and to provide effective health, family, and human policies and services, we need interdisciplinary conceptualizations and multiprofessional collaborations.

This integration should be a key facet of the mission of any academic fields aimed at advancing science and service for children, youth, and families. The knowledge base which may be generated in activities associated with such a mission may be extended into programs and services for the children and families of the state, of the nation, and—given the proper collaborative arrangements—the world.

Conclusions

Developmental contextualism is a theoretical approach to the science of, and outreach for, human development. Building on the integrative ideas found in Schneirla's (1956, 1957, 1959; Tobach, 1981) thinking, developmental contextualism represents a model of human life that transcends the dichotomies found so often in developmental psychology, social and behavioral science, and society, e.g., nature-nurture, organism-environment, person-context, and research-outreach. This chapter has focused on the implications of using developmental contextual thinking to transcend the latter dichotomy.

From a developmental contextual perspective, research must be conducted with an appreciation of the individual differences in human development, differences that arise as a consequence of diverse people's development in distinct families, communities, and sociocultural settings. In turn, policies and programs must be similarly attuned to the diversity of people and context in order to maximize the chances of meeting the specific needs of particular groups of people. Such programs and policies must be derived appropriately from research predicated on an integrative multidisciplinary view of human development. The evaluation of such applications should provide both societally important information about the success of endeavors aimed at the enhancement of individuals, *and* theoretically invaluable data about the validity of the synthetic, multilevel processes posited in developmental contextualism to characterize human development.

Meeting the challenge represented by the need to merge research with policy, and with intervention design, delivery, and evaluation, will bring the study of people and their contexts to the threshold of a new intellectual era. The linkage between research, policy, and intervention I have envisioned will demonstrate to scientists that the basic processes of human behavior are ones involving the development of relations between individually distinct people and the specific social institutions they encounter in their particular ecological setting.

This demonstration will be a matter, then, of bringing data to bear on the validity of the developmental contextual conception of basic process and of basic research (Lerner, 1991). Simply, studying changing relations between diverse peoples and contexts alters the core analytic frame in investigations of human development from a personological one to a person-context relational one (Lerner, 1991); this alteration makes the evaluation of the programs and policies aimed at changing developmental patterns of individuals a theoretically vital activity, one providing critical empirical feedback about the conceptual usefulness of the ideas of multilevel integration, ideas from which the policies and programs should have been derived.

It is for these reasons, then, that I have argued that policy and program design, delivery, and evaluation are not "second-class citizens" to basic research. Within the frame of the fused levels of organization that comprise human behavior and development, they constitute necessary *and basic* empirical tests of the core, relational process of life. Accordingly, if we wish to meet the challenge of human development, the activities of colleagues whose expertise lies in policy and program design, delivery, and evaluation are not to be set apart from "basic" scientific activity. The expertise of policy and program professionals must be integrated with that of the researcher, in a fully collaborative enterprise, if we are to make continued progress in the understanding and enhancement of people across their entire life spans.

In other words, the knowledge generation-application avenue is not a one-way street. Indeed, just as the practicing physician is often a source of issues that medical scientists then address, colleagues in the policy and program delivery arenas—whose roles emphasize the interface with the individual, family, and community—can provide invaluable feedback both about how the fruits of scholarship are being received and used *and* about new concerns that might be addressed with this scholarship.

In essence, then, the burgeoning high quality scientific activity in the developmental contextual study of human development has involved: First, the recognition of the importance of theory and research aimed at elucidating the relations between individually different, developing people and their diverse and changing contexts; *and*, second, the growing appreciation of the necessary linkage among research, policy, and intervention which must exist for the nature of human development—and, more specifically, its individuality and plasticity—to be understood and for the challenges of all periods of life to be best met.

In sum, the developmental contextual view of what constitutes the basic process of human development brings to the fore the cutting-edge importance of a continued empirical focus on individual differences, on contextual variations, and on changing person-context relations. These foci afford a transcendence of the dichotomy between science and outreach. That is, nothing short of the above emphases can be regarded as involving a scientifically adequate developmental analysis of human life. And nothing short of data involving these emphases should be seen as useful for formulating policies and programs suitable for individually different people developing in relation to their specific contexts.

REFERENCES

Baltes, P. B., Reese, H. W., & Lipsitt, L. P. (1980). Life-span developmental psychology. *Annual Review of Psychology*, *31*, 65–110.

Brim, O. G., Jr., & Kagan, J. (Eds.) (1980). *Constancy and change in human development*. Cambridge: Harvard University Press.

Bronfenbrenner, U. (1979). *The ecology of human development*. Cambridge, MA: Harvard University Press.

Cairns, R. B., & Hood, K. E. (1983). Continuity in social development: A comparative perspective on individual difference prediction. In P. B. Baltes & O. G. Brim, Jr. (Eds.), *Life-span development and behavior* (Vol. 5). New York: Academic Press.

Finkelstein, J. W. (1993). Familial influences on adolescent health. In R. M. Lerner (Ed.), *Early adolescence: Perspectives on research, policy and intervention* (pp. 111–126) Hillsdale, NJ: Erlbaum.

Ford, D. H., & Lerner, R. M. (1992). *Developmental systems theory: An integrative approach*. Newbury Park, CA: Sage.

Gollin, E. S. (1981). Development and plasticity. In E. S. Gollin (Ed.), *Developmental plasticity: Behavioral and biological aspects of variations in development*. New York: Academic Press.

Gould, S. J. (1977). *Ontogeny and phylogeny*. Cambridge: Belknap Press of Harvard University.

Harris, D. B. (1957). *The concept of development*. Minneapolis: University of Minnesota Press.

Hebb, D. O. (1949). *The organization of behavior*. New York: Wiley.

Howard, J. (1978). The influence of children's developmental dysfunction on marital quality and family interaction. In R. M. Lerner & G. B. Spanier (Eds.), *Child influences on marital and family interaction: A life-span perspective* (pp. 275–298). New York: Academic Press.

Lerner, R. M. (1976). *Concepts and theories of human development*. Reading, MA: Addison-Wesley.

———. (1978). Nature, nurture and dynamic interactionism. *Human Development, 21,* 1–20.

———. (1979). A dynamic interactional concept of individual and social relationship development. In R. Burgess & T. Huston (Eds.), *Social exchange in developing relationships* (pp. 271–305). New York: Academic Press.

———. (1984). *On the nature of human plasticity*. New York: Cambridge University Press.

———. (1986). *Concepts and theories of human development* (2nd ed.). New York: Random House.

Lerner, R. M., & Busch-Rossnagel, N. (1981). Individuals as producers of their development: Conceptual and empirical bases. In R. M. Lerner & N. A. Busch-Rossnagel (Eds.), *Individuals as producers of their development: A life-span perspective* (pp. 1–36). New York: Academic Press.

Lerner, R. M., Hultsch, D. F., & Dixon, R. A. (1983). Contextualism and the character of developmental psychology in the 1970s. *Annals of the New York Academy of Sciences, 412,* 101–128.

Lerner, R. M., & Kauffman, M. B. (1985). The concept of development in contextualism. *Developmental Review, 5,* 309–333.

Lerner, R. M., & Miller, J. R. (1993). Integrating human development research and intervention for America's children: The Michigan State University model. *Journal of Applied Developmental Psychology.*

Lerner, R. M., & Spanier, G. B. (1978). A dynamic interactional view of child and family development. In R. M. Lerner & G. B. Spanier (Eds.), *Child influences on marital and family interaction: A life-span perspective* (pp. 1–22). New York: Academic Press.

———. (1980). *Adolescent development: A life-span perspective*. New York: McGraw-Hill.

Lorenz, K. (1966). *On aggression*. New York: Harcourt, Brace & World.

Novikoff, A. B. (1945). The concept of integrative levels of biology. *Science*, 62, 209–215.

Overton, W. F. (1973). On the assumptive base of the nature-nurture controversy: Additive versus interaction conceptions. *Human Development*, 16, 74–89.

Riegel, K. F. (1975). Toward a dialectical theory of development. *Human Development*, 18, 50–64.

——. (1976a). The dialectics of human development. *American Psychologist*, 31, 689–700.

——. (1976b). From traits and equilibrium toward developmental dialectics. In W. J. Arnold & J. K. Cole (Eds.), *Nebraska symposium on motivation* (pp. 349–408). Lincoln: University of Nebraska Press.

Sameroff, A. (1975). Transactional models in early social relations. *Human Development*, 18, 65–79.

Schneirla, T. C. (1956). Interrelationships of the innate and the acquired in instinctive behavior. In P. P. Grasse (Ed.), *L'instinct dans le comportement des animaux et de l'homme* (pp. 387–452). Paris: Mason et Cie.

——. (1957). The concept of development in comparative psychology. In D. B. Harris (Ed.), *The concept of development* (pp. 78–108). Minneapolis: University of Minnesota Press.

——. (1959). An evolutionary and developmental theory of biphasic processes underlying approach and withdrawal. In M. R. Jones (Ed.), *Nebraska Symposium on Motivation, 1959*. Lincoln: University of Nebraska Press.

——. (1966). Instinct and aggression. *Natural History*, 75, 16ff.

Tobach, E. (1981). Evolutionary aspects of the activity of the organism and its development. In R. M. Lerner & N. A. Busch-Rossnagel (Eds.), *Individuals as producers of their development: A life-span perspective* (pp. 37–68). New York: Academic Press.

Tobach, E., & Greenberg, G. (1984). The significance of T. C. Schneirla's contribution to the concept of levels of integration. In G. Greenberg & E. Tobach (Eds.), *Behavioral evolution and integrative levels* (pp. 1–7). Hillsdale, NJ: Erlbaum.

Tubman, J. G., & Lerner, R. M. (1994). Affective experiences of parents and their children from adolescence to young adulthood: Stability of affective experiences. *Journal of Adolescence*, 17, 81–98.

Wideman, J. E. (1992). Dead Black men and other fallout from the American dream. *Esquire, 118* (3, September), 149–156.

How Does A/W Operate over Levels?

Discussion among the authors of this volume centered on several recurrent issues, which are summarized here. The asymmetry of A and W implies that A responses may readily become integrated into complex forms, while W responses may be difficult to integrate or elaborate, due to their interruptive nature. The W-system habituates, while the A-system may habituate only when it contacts the stimulus. If the stimulus is reinforcing, as is likely in the A system, then A responses will be strengthened. The asymmetry of A and W systems may be reflected in the asymmetry of the sympathetic and parasympathetic systems.

How does A/W operate in the developing organism? Schneirla's "organic set," perhaps consisting of sensory filters and selective attention produced by the history of the organism, will show developmental heterochrony as sensory systems develop at different rates, and as cross-modal transfer of intensity perception develops, for example, in the olfactory system. Qualitative features of the environment (edges, movement, direction of movement, olfaction) may be related to quantitative features (intensity) through neural systems in which intensity codes and quality codes operate in parallel arrays: the developmental course of these arrays may also show developmental heterochrony. It is through these processes, and their developmental integration, that features of the environment may have stage-characteristic functions that are linked to developmental heterochronies in the organism.

Levels of temporal scaling distinguish the approaches to A/W processes: from instantaneous changes that occur in microseconds to interactional changes over minutes or days to ontogenetic changes over months or years. The integrated account of events over multiple levels of scaling may include the transformation of instantaneous events (here conceived as vibration or fluctuation around a threshold) into threshold shifts over days that alter the balance of opposed A/W systems. Long-term changes may become consolidated into individually stable biases toward A or W processes. These varieties of A/W bias may be of advantage in particular environments: understanding these combinations will usefully inform attempts to improve environmental conditions for specific individuals and groups.

The A/W analysis of complex social behaviors was furthered by the proposal that considering the functional effects of dyadic interactions on the social partner may clarify the analysis. For example, attacks involve an initial approach to the partner, but the effect of attacks is to cause the partner to disperse, thereby reducing stimulation; by the dyadic analysis, attack would then be classified as withdrawal behavior. Infant cries, which are powerful aversive stimuli, may function to elicit approach behavior, because adult responses may reduce the too-intense stimulation causing the infant to cry, and reduce the aversive stimulus of crying, producing negative reinforcement of the adult's behavior. By extending the analytical framework to include *both* social partners, the A/W parameters of complex social behaviors such as lactation, weaning, and courtship and mating (behaviors which occur for the first time *after* the period of infancy) may become part of a fundamental developmental account. The process of natural selection for dyadic outcomes can then be formulated in relation to coupled A/W synchronies over predictable developmental transitions.

Extending A/W concepts to include social processes that occur after infancy opens the possibility of applying an A/W analysis to complex human meaning systems as they appear in development, with the eventual emergence of control, self-regulation, and social responsibility. The test of these exploratory proposals may follow from successive applications of dialectical logic, continually questioning the analysis in relation to multiple levels (including all systems involved in the functioning of each level) to ask: "What was it?" "What did it become?" "What is its historical character?" "What does it contain in the way of levels?"

Kathryn E. Hood

Contributors

Dr. Enrico Alleva
Laboratory of Pathophysiology
Istituto Superiore di Sanita
Viale Regina Elena 299
1–00161 Rome, ITALY

Gemma Calamandrei
Laboratory of Pathophysiology
Istituto Superiore di Sanita
Viale Regina Elena 299
1-00161 Rome, ITALY

Andrea L. Clatworthy
Department of Physiology and Cell Biology
University of Texas
Health Sciences Center, Houston
P.O. Box 20708
Houston, TX 77225

Dr. Jean-Louis Gariépy
Department of Psychology, CB 3270
University of North Carolina, Chapel Hill
Chapel Hill, NC 27599–3270

Dr. Gary Greenberg
Department of Psychology
Wichita State University
Wichita, KS 67208

451

Dr. Kathryn E. Hood
Department of Human Development and Family Studies
110 Henderson Building South
The Pennsylvania State University
University Park, PA 16802

Dr. Richard M. Lerner
Institute for Children, Youth, & Families
Paolucci Building, 2
Michigan State University
East Lansing, MI 48824

Anne D. Mayer
Institute of Animal Behavior
Rutgers University
101 Warren Street
Newark, NJ 07102

Dr. Alison Nash
Department of Psychology
State University of New York
New Platz, NY 12561

Dr. Steven Rose
Biology Department
The Open University
Milton Keynes MK7 6AA
U.K.

Dr. Jay S. Rosenblatt
Institute of Animal Behavior
Rutgers University
101 Warren Street
Newark, NJ 07102

Dr. Cynthia Stifter
Department of Human Development and Family Studies
110 Henderson Building South
The Pennsylvania State University
University Park, PA 16802

Dr. Ethel Tobach
American Museum of Natural History
Central Park West at 79th Street
New York, NY 10024–5192

Dr. Howard Topoff
Department of Psychology
Hunter College of CUNY
695 Park Avenue
New York, NY 10021

Leo Vroman
Columbia University
Department of Chemical Engineering
New York, NY 10027

Dr. Georgine M. Vroman
Bellevue Hospital Center
Geriatric Clinic
New York, NY 10016

Dr. Edgar T. Walters
Department of Physiology and Cell Biology
University of Texas
Health Sciences Center, Houston
P.O. Box 20708
Houston, TX 77225

Dr. Michael Windle
Research Institute on Addictions
1021 Main Street
Buffalo, NY 14203

Index